THE VERNEY FAMILY DURING
THE CIVIL WAR

VOL. II.

PRINTED BY
SPOTTISWOODE AND CO., NEW-STREET SQUARE
LONDON

Sir Edmund Verney, Kt.
Knight-Marshal & Standard Bearer
from a picture by Vandyck at Claydon House.

MEMOIRS OF THE VERNEY FAMILY
DURING THE CIVIL WAR

COMPILED FROM THE LETTERS AND ILLUSTRATED BY
THE PORTRAITS AT CLAYDON HOUSE

BY

FRANCES PARTHENOPE VERNEY

'Let us sit upon the ground
And tell sad stories of the death of kings'

IN TWO VOLUMES—VOL. II.

The Naval & Military Press Ltd

in association with

The National Army Museum, London

Published jointly by

The Naval & Military Press Ltd
Unit 10 Ridgewood Industrial Park,
Uckfield, East Sussex,
TN22 5QE England

Tel: +44 (0) 1825 749494
Fax: +44 (0) 1825 765701

www.naval-military-press.com
www.military-genealogy.com
www.militarymaproom.com

and

The National Army Museum, London
www.national-army-museum.ac.uk

In reprinting in facsimile from the original, any imperfections are inevitably reproduced and the quality may fall short of modern type and cartographic standards.

PREFACE
TO
THE SECOND VOLUME

AFTER laying aside the work for some years, Lady Verney made great efforts latterly to complete the first volume of these memoirs. The MS. was left tied up and labelled, 'A Birthday Gift for my dear Harry, December 8, 1889.' Of the materials she had prepared for continuing the work she wrote : ' I think the second volume will run more easily ; the agony is piled up both for the family and the nation, and that seems to melt down the infinity of small details, which worry one so much, into a coherent whole, and makes it more easy to write. I shall end with the year '49, which will simplify it.' Eventually Lady Verney decided to include 1650, to complete the life of Dame Mary Verney, who, after Sir Edmund's death, is the most interesting character in the memoirs.

Ample materials exist at Claydon for carrying on the life of Sir Ralph Verney through the period of the Commonwealth and the Restoration to his death in 1696—if those who have followed the story of his career in these two volumes have so much sympathy with him as to wish to know the rest.

If it is permissible to apply to a chapter in the domestic history of England what was written about a great fragment of the 'History of the World,' I should like to quote Raleigh's words : 'I forbear to style my readers, *gentle, courteous*, and *friendly*, thereby to beg their good opinions, or to promise a 3rd volume, which I also intend, if these receive grace and good acceptance ; for t' is certain let us claw the reader with never so many courteous phrases— yet shall we evermore be thought fools that write foolishly.'

MARGARET M. VERNEY.

CLAYDON HOUSE : *March* 31, 1892.

CONTENTS

OF

THE SECOND VOLUME

	PAGE
PREFACE	v
NOTES ON THE ILLUSTRATIONS	xiii

CHAPTER I.

DAME MARGARET VERNEY.

Dame Margaret's death in 1641—Lady Sussex's condolences—Review of Margaret's early life at Hillesden and her married life at Claydon—Her mother-in-law and her mother—Infant mortality—Epitaphs on infants—The grandchildren—Margaret's father, Sir Thomas Denton—Her household management—The Plague in 1636—The Verney ladies avoid the Court—Ralph's grief at his mother's death—Expenses of mourning—Her will 1

CHAPTER II.

SIR RALPH'S NOTES—THE GRAND REMONSTRANCE AND THE ATTEMPT ON THE FIVE MEMBERS.

Sir Ralph's notes of the Debates—On the advancement of learning—On Church music—On Eliot's imprisonment—On the Queen's health and her journey to Holland—Toleration denounced—The Grand Remonstrance—Excitement in the House—Palmer imprisoned—Mobs at Westminster—The king's reception by the City on his return from Scotland—The king's attempt to arrest the five members—List of men chosen by the Commons to command the militia . . . 20

CHAPTER III.

THE RISING IN MUNSTER, 1641-42.

Consternation in England—Strafford's successors—Sir John Leeke's letters from Munster—Terror of the Loyalists—Destruction of property—Sir John deplores the loss of 'Queen Elizabeth's rodd'—Youghal holds out—Dungarvan lost and regained—Lord Barrymore killed—Irish homes broken up . 41

CHAPTER IV.

CARY VERNEY'S MARRIAGE.

Sir Edmund marries his daughter to Captain Gardiner—Sir Thomas Gardiner, Recorder of London—His violent behaviour—His committal to the Tower—The bride's linen and lace—The wedding in 1642—The young couple at Cuddesdon—Captain Gardiner joins the king's army in the North—The Gardiners object to Sir Ralph's politics—Cary hears of her father's death and her husband being taken prisoner—Cary a widow—Birth of her daughter—Unkindness of the Gardiners—Second marriage to Mr. Stewkeley—Prosperous days . 58

CHAPTER V.

THE RAISING OF THE STANDARD, 1642.

War imminent—Lady Sussex's apprehensions—Her brother Sir Francis Wortley in trouble with the Parliament—Mrs. Eure's account of distress in Yorkshire—Painful position of Sir Edmund—Strained relations between him and Sir Ralph—Sir Edmund joins the king at York—The Standard raised at Nottingham—The Standard and the Standard-Bearer—Letters from the king's army in the North—Family divisions . . 80

CHAPTER VI.

SIR EDMUND STRIKES HIS LAST BLOW FOR THE KING.

Arms used in the Civil War—Battle of Edgehill—The struggle round the Standard—Sir Edmund's death—Ghost stories—The Standard retaken—Sir Ralph's grief—Sir Edward Sydenham made Knight-marshal—Character of Sir Edmund Verney. 109

CONTENTS OF THE SECOND VOLUME ix

CHAPTER VII.

CONCERNING EDMUND, THE YOUNG CAVALIER.

PAGE

The army disbanded in 1641—Edmund at Claydon—His pay in arrears—Sent to Ireland—The soldiers without food or pay—Edmund in command of Dathcoffy Castle—Remonstrates with Ralph on his taking the Parliament side—Wounded at Rathconnel—Serves under Ormonde—Edmund's distress at his father's death—Money troubles—The Alnage—The Verney girls petition Parliament—The law's delays 128

CHAPTER VIII.

SIR RALPH'S CHOICE, THE COVENANT OR EXILE.

Tom's complaints from the Fleet—Troubles at Gorhambury—'Sogers' and plunderers—Heavy taxes—Tom's marriage and release from prison—Current news from Lady Sussex—Doll Leeke's advice to Ralph—Sir R. Burgoyne's letters—The Covenant taken by the House—Ralph refuses to sign, and resolves to go abroad—His uncomplaining heroism—Henry's imprisonment—The influenza—Ralph's preparations for departure—Transport of luggage—His sisters and children—Household difficulties at Claydon—The Covenant pressed upon Members—Final arrangements, will, and farewells—The voyage to Rotterdam—Despatch of goods to Rouen . 148

CHAPTER IX.

THE BURNING OF HILLESDEN HOUSE.

Sir Ralph's letters home—Hillesden and the Dentons—Aunt Isham's grievance—Hillesden House fortified, besieged, taken and burnt—Sir Alexander Denton's letters from the Tower—Tom imprisoned at Cambridge—Two love-stories—Captain Abercrombie's death—Colonel John Denton's death—Sir Ralph's condolences—Sir Alexander's death—Mrs. Isham's troubles 186

CHAPTER X.

IN EXILE.

Sir Ralph offends both sides—Gossip in the 'Diurnals'—Sir Ralph voted out of the House of Commons—His distress at the news—The life in exile—Sir Ralph's books—Lady

CHAPTER X.—*continued.*   PAGE

Verney's housekeeping—An Englishman and his French lacquey—Waiting-maids and waiting-gentlewomen—Luce and Besse—French schools—Christmas stores lost—Wigs, pomatums, fans and fashions—Lord Devonshire goes home—'Mischiefe' to the rescue—A sad parting 210

CHAPTER XI.

MARY LADY VERNEY 'SOLICITING.'

Mary in England—Cipher names—Expense of London lodgings—Friends estranged—Mary sick with a fever—The Committee of Sequestration—Interviews with Lady Warwick—Puritan services—Henry's 'horrid tricks'—Birth of Mary's third son—Ralph's christening and journey to Claydon—Tom's abuse—Mary goes to Claydon and Misterton—'The wayes, the soldiers, and the sicknesse'—Troublesome creditors. . . 243

CHAPTER XII.

MARY LOSES HER CHILDREN AND WINS HER SUIT.

Household cares—Rats, moths and rust—Soldiers quartered at Claydon—The Rector and the Agent quarrel—The 'ritch fatt' lawyer—Mrs. Allcock's wedding—Jack and Ralph—Peg's illness and death at Blois—Ralph's death at Claydon—Bitter sorrow—Sir Ralph's counsels of despair—Mary's petition granted—The sequestration of Claydon taken off—Dr. Denton has a wedding feast—Mary's journey—Husband and wife reunited 283

CHAPTER XIII.

'SIR MUN' IS TREACHEROUSLY SLAIN.

Sir Edmund, the young cavalier, Governor of Chester—Siege and surrender of Chester—Edmund with Ormonde in Ireland—Money troubles—Edmund at Paris—Siege of Colchester—Sir George Lucas shot—Edmund in Ireland again—False report of his death at Dublin—Siege of Drogheda—Edmund killed in cold blood—Cromwell's letters 320

CONTENTS OF THE SECOND VOLUME   xi

CHAPTER XIV.

THE 'MACHES' OF THE FIVE GIRLS.

PAGE

Marriage treaties, portions and bargainings—Penelope and her cousin—Susan and her widower—Money troubles—Susan in need of a trousseau—Margaret marries Sir Thomas Elmes—Their domestic quarrels—Susan's marriage—Mr. Alport in the Fleet—Penelope marries John Denton—Lady Verney's opinion of her sisters-in-law—Troubles with Mary and Elizabeth—Elizabeth at school—The Alports at Overton Manor—Susan's death—Her funeral at Malpas Church—Margaret Elmes' death—Mary marries Robert Lloyd, of Chester . . 349

CHAPTER XV.

THE END OF MANY THINGS AND PEOPLE.

Sir Ralph and Mary at Blois—Sir Puckering Newton, the gay butterfly of society—Cromwell in power—Execution of King Charles—Loyalty of Westminster School—The King's funeral—'Eikon Basilike'—Mary fails in health—Drinks the Bourt on waters—Tom in trouble again—Henry lives 'like the wandering Jew'—Mary's merry messages—News of Edmund's death—Mary's death—Sir Ralph's despair and self-reproaches—Dr. Denton's counsels—Mary's funeral at Claydon—Her husband's tribute to her memory—Review of the characters of Sir Edmund and Sir Ralph Verney 391

APPENDIX.

Documents concerning Sir Edmund Verney's claims on the Alnage. From Nalson's Collection of MSS., Vol. XV., in the possession of the Duke of Portland, printed by his kind permission :—

Petition of the Verney Girls to the Honble. Committee of the King's Revenue 431

The Committee refer the Petition to the Solicitor-General for his Report 433

Report of Oliver St. John, Solicitor-General . . . 433

Order of the Committee that St. John's Report be reported to the House of Commons 437

INDEX 439

NOTES ON THE ILLUSTRATIONS
TO VOLUME II.

SIR EDMUND VERNEY, KT., KNIGHT-MARSHALL AND STANDARD-
BEARER . . . . *Frontispiece*
    From a picture by Vandyck at Claydon House. Vandyck painted this picture by order of Charles I., who gave it to Sir Edmund. It is mentioned in all the lists. It was exhibited at the old British Institution Exhibition of Old Masters, and pronounced by the Curator of the Louvre 'diablement beau'; it was also in the Vandyck Exhibition. Sir Edmund has a ruddy complexion and fair hair; he is in armour with a red sash, with his Marshall's staff, the original of which hangs below the picture at Claydon; the helmet was delayed by the armourer during the Scotch war (Vol. i. 315), and arrived after peace was declared; he said he should keep it henceforth to boil his porridge in.

MARY BLAKENEY, WIFE OF THE 1ST SIR EDMUND VERNEY   *to face p.* 3
    From a picture at Claydon House. Two pictures of 'ould Lady Verney' appear in the old lists; one, now lost, is called 'large, with a book & a crutch'—this seems to be the one mysteriously described as 'Grandmother Verney without any Strainer!' it was labelled at the back 'a Turville,' the name of her first husband.

DAME SUSAN DENTON . . . . *to face p.* 6
    From a picture at Claydon House on panel, in a black embroidered dress and beautiful pearls. This is the old lady who threatened to dress in sackcloth lined with ashes (Vol. i. 284) when her daughter married a Papist, and who was so kind to her great-grandson, Mun Verney.

DAME MARGARET VERNEY . . . . . . *to face p.* 20
    From a bust in Middle Claydon Church, from the monument Sir Ralph put up to his father and mother, his wife and himself; he had the busts done in Rome, and, excepting his own, they were all taken from pictures. Dame Margaret's, with a veil on her head, is sweet, grave, and tender in expression.

FACSIMILE OF SIR RALPH'S PENCIL NOTES TAKEN IN THE HOUSE
OF COMMONS DURING THE ATTEMPTED ARREST OF THE FIVE
MEMBERS . . . . *to face p.* 37

CHARLES I. . . . . *to face p.* 80
> From a picture by Vandyck at Claydon House, given to Sir Edmund Verney by the king. Charles was much pleased with this portrait, and had several replicas made; one was burnt in the fire at Whitehall, another is in the Dresden Gallery. The ring figured below was also a present from the king to Sir Edmund, and is now at Claydon. The miniature is exquisitely finished, but it is a careworn face painted in the plain daylight of ordinary prose, and, in contrast with the Vandyck, shows how much the memory of Charles has owed to the magic of that great painter's art.

SIR EDMUND VERNEY, KT. MARSHALL, STANDARD-BEARER TO
CHARLES I. . . . . *to face p.* 126
> From a bust in Middle Claydon Church. A fine soldierly-looking head in armour, done at Rome.

INTERIOR OF HILLESDEN CHURCH . . . . . *p.* 188
> From a pencil drawing by Lady Verney, showing the large Denton tomb inside the altar-rails, removed when the church was restored; the small monument catching the light in the S.E. corner is that of Dr. William Denton.

SIR THOMAS DENTON, KT., OF HILLESDEN . . . *to face p.* 189
> From a picture at Claydon House. A stiff old portrait in the dress of James I.'s reign, with large eyes like his daughter Margaret Verney's.

SIR ALEXANDER DENTON, KT., OF HILLESDEN . . *to face p.* 200
> From a picture at Claydon; in armour, with a richly embroidered scarf over his shoulder; a good face, but too sensitive for the evil days in which his lot was cast.

DAME MARY VERNEY, DAU. OF JOHN BLACKNALL, ESQ. . *to face p.* 243
> From a picture by Vandyck at Claydon House. This graceful picture, painted in 1636, of the daughter-in-law Sir Edmund loved so tenderly, has suffered much from cleaning and scraping by a wicked restorer; the dress is pale blue satin over white, with pearls; the lively expression which earned her the name of 'Mischiefe' defied the painter's art. Dr. Denton writes to her that all her portraits 'are guiltie of one fault, which is a simperinge about the corners of the mouth, which, though tolerable in your worship because it appears but sometimes, yett is not gracefull in a picture, because its always there, and looks like affectation.'

DR. WILLIAM DENTON, PHYSICIAN TO CHARLES I. . *to face p.* 295
> From a picture at Claydon; in a red velvet coat and buff mantle. Shrewd, kindly, caustic, clever, he had a sharp word for his friends' little failings, and untiring aid and sympathy for them in real troubles.

Sir Edmund Verney, Kt. . . . . . . *to face p.* 320

 From a picture at Claydon House, described in one of the old lists, with a passionate vehemence very unlike their dry-as-dust style, as 'killed in cold blood by the Arch Usurper Cromwell after the siege of Drogheda.' In armour, a charming face, intelligent and brave like his father's, but gentler, and with the same reddish-brown hair.

Sir George Lisle, Kt. . . . . . . *to face p.* 341

 From a picture at Claydon House; in armour, an unfinished picture, probably the copy of a Vandyck.

Dame Mary Verney . . . . . . *to face p.* 414

 From a bust in Middle Claydon Church. The light in the church is unfavourable for photographing this bust; it is therefore difficult to render the gentle gravity, good-sense, and sweetness of the expression in the original. Her curls and her pearl necklace are managed by the sculptor with great skill; the busts give a high idea of the art at Rome in the year 1652.

MEMOIRS OF THE VERNEY FAMILY

DURING

THE CIVIL WAR

CHAPTER I.

DAME MARGARET VERNEY.

> The clouds that gather round the setting sun
> Do take a sober colouring from an eye
> That hath kept watch o'er man's mortality!
> Another race hath been, and other palms are won.
> WORDSWORTH.

IN the beginning of April 1641 Margaret Lady Verney died somewhat suddenly. She is mentioned as having been ailing for some time past, but no one seems to have apprehended any danger. Even Lady Sussex, who was in weekly communication with Sir Edmund and his son, had not the least expectation of such a failure in her strength, and writes to Ralph, April 9: 'The unexpectede sade neuse [news] gave me a harty soro, most for your lose of such a mother and for myselfe of soe deare a friend. This world is full of changes. God fit us for his pleasure. As you are truly good, so in this show your religon by a discrete soro, that you fall not ill this sickly time. Belive non wishes more happinesse both to yourself and family.' She adds that she would have written also to his wife, but 'I am out of tune with physicke, belive me i truly cuffer [suffer].'

Again on April 26 she writes : 'S^r I shoulde not say anythinge to renue your soro, but a better woman livede not then your good mother, who sartinly inioyes the fruite of her goodnes with the blesede sants, i am glade you have parlyment bisynes to take you off your sade thoughts. . . . I shall ever believe I have so great an interest in your favour that I may take the same fridom with you I have formerly don uppon my occasyons. I entendede a cote [coat] to my godsone this Easter, and now I know he is in mourninge therefore have sent him a porringer to ete his breakfast in.'

The 'cote' that Lady Sussex had planned for little Mun was of a lovely sky-blue figured, satin. She had written to Ralph to get her the stuff in town, and the pattern she sent still exists, pinned to the scrap of paper on which he wrote down her many commissions ; the colour is as brilliant as ever, and seems a mute reminder amongst the old brown letters, of the many bright things that were changed to mourning when the mother of the family died.

Margaret Verney was all her life what the French happily call *très entourée* ; whenever we see her she is claimed by a chorus of little voices, and surrounded by a troop of little pattering feet. In her old home she was the eldest daughter in a family of eleven, and she kept up her intimacy with

Mary Blakeney.
wife of the 1st. Sir Ed: Verney.
from a picture at Claydon House.

Mary Varney

her brothers and sisters, and the ever-increasing number of her nephews and nieces. Married at eighteen, she returned to her mother's roof for her many confinements ; her elder children were the contemporaries of her younger brothers and sisters ; and her granddaughter Anna Maria was a year old when her youngest child Betty was born.

Something has already been told of the large circle of friends constantly entertained at Claydon in the happy years before the Civil War, and of her motherly care of her eldest son's wife Mary, with whom she lived on terms of such intimate affection. It was a remarkable household of capable women, and besides her own six daughters, her daughter-in-law, and her grandchildren, Margaret had the older generation to consider, her mother and her mother-in-law. Sir Edmund's mother shared their house in London, and expected to be consulted when plans were made or changed. James Dillon writes to Mary after a visit to Claydon in July 1633, when the dowager's feelings had been unfortunately ruffled : 'Be pleased I pray you to lett my Ladie Verney [Margaret] knowe, that I noe sooner came to towne than presently I gave your grandmother heare an account of her messuage by me, which for ought I could say (or see) seemed not sufficient unto my ould Lady Verney to prevent exception on her parte against your mother,' and he then gives his advice as to how a letter may be sent by coach to pacify her.

In 1638 'Lady Verney the Elder' desired her grandson Edmund to go over to Albury and see the condition of the vault in which her husband, Sir Edmund Verney, had been laid in 1599. He writes to Ralph, that he could not go there himself, 'but according to her direction I acquainted old Roades with it, who sent a messenger thither on purpose with a noate to the parson (one Gilpin, a Maudlen Hall man in my time, and I think in yours too), who came over to Claydon himself and brought the answer, that it was as handsome and in as good repair as it was when my grandfather was buryed there, he proffered one complement, which I durst not acquaint my grandmother with, that upon a weeke's warning he would be provided of an excellent funerall sermon for her!'

There was ample time for the Reverend Mr. Gilpin to polish his complimentary periods, as the old lady, according to a note of Lord Fermanagh, lived to the age of 95, having survived her third husband for 43 years. Sir Ralph, writing in '47, mentions a legacy which grandmother left to Moll, 'in that will my father was left sole executor, but hee died before grandmother (14 or 15 daies), soe I tooke out the administration and payd all legacies,' etc. This fixes the date of old Lady Verney's death as November 7 or 8, 1642; a fortnight after the battle of Edgehill.[1]

---

[1] It is an amusing instance of the inaccuracy of an otherwise valuable work that Lipscomb in his history of Bucks states that 'a

Margaret also spent a part of the year with her mother, Dame Susan Denton, who survived her by a few months.[1] Both these vigorous old ladies lived to superintend the bringing up of their great-grandchildren.

Indeed, Lady Denton, who was so stern to her own daughters, pleaded for a gentler régime than was the fashion of the day for the little ones of the fourth generation. Edmund, Ralph's eldest boy, had been left entirely in her charge at Hillesden, till in October 1639 he was sent for to London. His father and grandfather complained that he was shy and rustic. 'i heare,' wrote Lady Denton, 'he is disliked, he is so strange. Sonn, you did see he was not soe, nor is not soe, to any where he is a quanted, and he must be woone with fair menes. Let me begge of you and his mothar that nobody whip him but Mr. Parrye; yf you doe goe a violent waye with him, you will be the furst that will rue it, for i veryly beleve he will reseve ingery by it.' She goes on to remind these unreasonable men that she can remember when they, too, were shy and awkward children. 'Indede, Raphe, he is to younge to be strudgeled in any forsing waye. i had intelygence your father was trobled to see him soe strange. i pray tel him frome me, I thought he had had more witt then to thinck a childe of his adge woulde be a quanted presently. He knowes the popular and uncontradicted tradition has always represented that Sir Ed. Verney's mother died at his birth.'

[1] Lady Denton's mother, Lady Temple, the most prolific of her race, lived to see 370 of her descendants.

childe was feloe good a nofe in my house. i praye shewe him what I have written abought him, and be shore that he be not frited by no menes : he is of a gentel swet nature, sone corrected.' It gives one an idea of the awful severity of nursery rule in those days, that the great-grandmother should have to plead that *only* ' Mr. Parrye ' should whip a child not yet three years old, whose face and ways when at his ease were so engaging, that his soldier uncle, Edmund, wrote of him, ' that sweete promising countenance of your pretty sonn is able to inspire even the ignorant with such a prophesying spirit ; there's not that lineament either in his face or body, but prognosticates more for itself than we cann doe for it.'

' I have carryed his nurse the Rhubarb, and shee promiseth he shall constantly drinke it,' says another letter about this much-tried infant.

But in spite of the ' whippinges,' the vomitings, the ' sweating pills,' the purgings and the bloodlettings which appear in the family records with painful reiteration and detail, Dame Margaret's government of her nursery was eminently successful and judicious. Her children were devoted to her, and ten out of the twelve lived to grow up in health and vigour of body and mind—a most unusual proportion in those days.

In a family life so happy and so like our own, it is quite startling to find what good sensible women allowed their daughters to be married as mere children. ' Sweet seventeen ' is often a matron inured

Dame Susan Denton.
from a picture at Claydon House.

Susanna Denton

to family cares, and either the mother of a family, or mourning the loss of two, and sometimes three babies. The deaths in childbed, the premature births, and the large proportion of children who died before they were ten years old, passionately loved and tenderly cared for, is most pathetic; the poetry of the day is full of epitaphs upon infants; two such are found in the Verney manuscripts, copied out more than once by loving hands.[1]

Mary had her full share of these troubles. She was only sixteen when a little daughter was born to her at Claydon on July 21, 1632, baptized the same day in her mother's name, and buried the next.

> The cup of life just to her lips she press'd,
> Found the taste bitter, and refused the rest,
> Then gently turning from the light of day,
> She softly sighed her little soul away.

How tenderly little Mary's memory was cherished appears in an allusion to her name, in a letter of Ralph's to his wife, fifteen years afterwards. We have a shadowy glimpse of another baby, who apparently came and went in the following year, for there is a

---

[1] *On an Infant.*

Heere lies a blossum of the worlds greate tree
W^{ch} was as faire as Buds of Roses bee.
She died an Infant : Heaven was made for suche.
Live thou as Infants doe shalt have as muche.

On an Infant.

Tred softly passenger for heere doethe lie
A tender parsell of sweet Infancie,
A Harmeless Babe that only came and criede
Through Baptisme to be washte from sinn. So died.

letter of condolence from Ralph's old tutor Crowther, in the autumn of 1633, full of well-turned phrases and pious platitudes. In August 1634 Crowther writes to him again : 'I shall wish and pray for your happinesse in the safe delivery of your wife and the glad newes of a lusty heyre.'

The child proved to be a girl, and was welcomed with rapturous affection. She was named Anna Maria; James Dillon was her godfather, and she was christened on September 16, in Middle Claydon church. There had been another happy family gathering at Claydon a fortnight before for the christening of George, son of Sir Alexander Denton and Mary Hampden his wife. How much Sir Edmund and Dame Margaret loved their grandchildren is shown in the pathetic letter written at one o'clock in the morning by Sir Edmund on May 19, 1638, when little Anna Maria was taken ill in her father's absence.

'Raphe, your sweete child is going apace to a better woarld; shee has but a short time to staye with uss. I hope you have such a sence of God's blessings to you as you will not repine at his decrees; make all convenient haste to your good wife who wants your comfort, yet come not too faste for that maye heate your bludd; and that maye give an end to all our comforts; as ever I shall intreat anything from you take care of yourselfe, for this is a dangerous yeare for Heats and colds. The God of Heaven Bless you, your loving father. Ed. Verney.'

As the little one was buried three days later,

Ralph can hardly have been in time to see his child again. She was not quite four years old, but Ralph's letter in the following January to the usually unsympathetic Henry, then serving in the Netherlands, shows what a favourite she had been in the family :

'You shall herewithal receive a ringe filled with my deare gerle's haire ; shee was fond of you, and you loved her therefore I now send you this to keepe for her sake.'

But the empty cradle was filled again, and before Margaret died she had the happiness of seeing Ralph and Mary with three healthy children : Edmund, Lady Sussex's godson, and old Lady Denton's protégé, born on Christmas Day, 1636 ; Margaret, born in January 1638 ; and John, born November 5, 1640.

We hear less of Margaret's father, Sir Thomas Denton, in the family annals than of her mother, but Ralph was much attached to him, and on his death in September 1633 he wrote a passionate letter of regrets to Dillon : 'The greate God in whose hand is the soull of every livinge thinge hath by death taken my grandfather into an endlesse life.' James replies affectionately, grieving for the loss of ' that Living comfort which he was unto you'; but he goes on to remind him that although it is 'noe small crosse to loose a grandfather,' yet the event could not have been wholly unexpected—' he was long a diseased man, and unlikely to live.' He therefore advises him to divert his thoughts with 'Breerwood's Logicke,' and 'the

Figures and Tropes Rhetoricall' which he sends him ; whether they proved a more effectual medicine for a sad heart than Crowther's divinity we are not told.

The letter is directed outside, 'To my dearest freinde Raphe Verney Esqre at Claydon,' and he concludes with greetings to the three generations of Verney ladies : 'I will end my Letter, but without end continue yours faythfully, Ja : Dillon. My service I beseech to Sir Edmund, both the Ladies, M$^{rs.}$ Verney, and my sweet brother.'

There are incidental notices of her servants that seem to show that Margaret was a good mistress, and that she was well served. The maids whom she mentions in her will continued in faithful attendance upon her daughters, when the altered fortunes of the family, and the great reduction of the household, must have made their situations at Claydon far less desirable than they had been under their old mistress.

Until her eldest son was old enough to help her, the affairs of the family were all managed by Lady Verney ; her busy husband seems to have relied implicitly upon her judgment and business capacity, whether in making arrangements for Tom's voyage to Virginia, in the management of the estate at Claydon, or in respect to those powders, 'excellent to prevent the gowte,' which she keeps for him, and sends after him to Scotland, when he is tormented by 'crewell twinges.'

In April 1636 Sir Edmund wrote to her from

London: 'Good Puss, The plaage is likely to encrease. If eyther you or my daughter [i.e. Ralph's wife] can thinke of what you shall necessarily want, as gloves & such things, lett me know it in time & I will provide them. I would faine have the carrier bring up a cart about this daye fortnight, if it maye be no prejudice to him, & then if the sicknesse encrease I will send down some more wyne, & what els you think fit; for if it encrease this next tow weekes it is much to be feared that it will be a dangerous time here.' Sir Nat. Hobart writes during the summer from Highgate to thank Ralph 'for the frendly care you have taken to provide us a place of refuge during this contagion . . . The K^t Marshall Sir Edmund Verney graced us lately with his company some two houres, not reckoning one spent in knocking at the gate, for the house was soe drownde in sylence that there wanted nothing but a red cross to make him believe the plague was there.'

The number of deaths from the plague at this time was very serious; but such was the unsanitary state of London that threatenings of infectious diseases akin to the plague, if not the scourge itself, were continually rife until the fire of London had purified the town in its own uncompromising but very effectual manner. There had been a bad outbreak in the year of the king's accession, and again in 1630.

Margaret was arranging to send up some poor people to be touched by the king, and her husband writes again, 'Good Puss, for those people you wright about to have cure for the King's Evil, I will have all the charge of them I can, but till good Fryday he will heal none. I believe he will heal that day and in Easter hollidayes.' About the cure itself there seems to be no doubt !

It is a proof of the kind of estimation in which Henrietta Maria's Court was held by the graver and more religious of the English ladies that there is no sign that either of the Lady Verneys, Lady Sussex, although a Peer's wife, or Mrs. Eure, ever attended it. They were all women well-born, well-connected, of fortune and position, but the only notices of the queen in any of the letters consist in a scornful phrase of Lady Sussex 'that the Quene will be quite happy now with so many favorites about her' (Harry Jermyn being mentioned just before, whom it was supposed that she married after Charles's death when living as a widow at St. Germain), and Sir Ralph's laughing excuse that he cannot go to some place as a friend requests him, for that, 'according to the example of our gratious sovereign, I must obey my wife and she comands my presence on the 26th.'

It was the more remarkable in the case of Sir Edmund's wife, as he was himself in attendance on the king during so large a part of the year, that her absence from Court must have been somewhat marked. Margaret Verney was, however, a gentle, retiring woman, much occupied with her duties at home, and whose ideas of life more resembled those of Mrs. Hutchinson and Rachel Lady Russell than of the ladies whom Henrietta Maria gathered about her in the years of her splendour.

Such a woman Habington describes in his 'Castara,' the second edition of which appeared in 1635 :—

> She sailes by that rocke, the Court,
> Where oft honour splits her mast,
> And retir'dnesse thinks the port
> Where her fame may anchor cast.
> Vertue safely cannot sit
> Where vice is enthron'd for wit.

The converts to Roman Catholicism, whom the queen patronised so ostentatiously, would not recommend the society of the Court to women of such strong Protestant feeling as the Verneys.

The fatigues, anxieties, and conflicting duties of her later years, the necessity of leaving her young children at Claydon very much to their own guidance, or of giving up the comfort of the husband who required a home in London for a large part of the year, and to whom she was so warmly attached, had evidently all told upon her health. There were also perpetual money difficulties, the most wearing of all cares to the mistress of a family. Her ten children, each and all, were becoming more and more expensive; none of them, excepting Ralph, independent of home help, while Sir Edmund's resources diminished. In addition to these causes for disquietude there was the growing antagonism between the two parties in the State. Her son Ralph had very decidedly taken the Parliament side, while her husband was in a most painful position; attached to the king by all his prepossessions and inherited feelings of loyalty, but torn in sunder by his political and religious sympathies, which drew him the other way. The fear of an estrangement between the two who loved each other so well, signs of which sometimes now began to appear, must have been peculiarly distressing to so tender a wife and mother as Margaret. It was hardly to be wondered at if a little more illness than usual under such circumstances should prove fatal.

She kept up to the last, and seems to have been alarmingly ill only for a few days in Covent Garden. Her husband and son were both with her and accompanied her body down to Claydon, where she was buried in the chancel close to the house. The absorbing duties of Parliament admitted of no long absence; they were in the very midst of Strafford's trial, and as soon as the funeral was over Sir Edmund and Sir Ralph seem both to have returned to Westminster. Young Edmund did not hear till July of his mother's death, and then wrote to Lady Verney: 'My dearest Sister, I wondered not at all at your silence, because the conveyance of letters is soe uncertaine, but now I know why you did not write I am very sorry not for your silence, tho' nothing could be more wellcome to me than your letters but for having so sadd a cause for it. Tis most true the lose of our Mother was infinite, but I'll not torture you by expressing it more largely.'

Ralph, dearly as he loved his mother and truly as he lamented her loss, could not resist the temptation of making his grief curvet and prance in the most approved forms and fashions of the day. On June 7 he wrote to Lady Barrymore in Ireland : 'that I writ no sooner I wonder not, for I have been soe much a troubled, soe much a perplexed man, that I confesse I could neither write nor speak nor thinke anything but one, and that a thinge alas too sorrowful to write or speake or thinke. My deare Mother is dead, nor sighs, nor groans, nor prayers could withhold her from the jaws of death, nor the desiers and petitions of all who knew her. By death shee is gone into an endless life. I have lost a deare and careful Mother, and you a faithfull servant.' He then goes off into politics, which at that moment could hardly be set aside.

The expenses of mourning must have been very great, as it was the custom to send it to all intimate friends as well as to near relations. Lady Sussex thanks Ralph for the offer of it, but says that as she is seeing no one at Gorhambury, where her husband is seriously ill, she will not accept of any. Everything belonging to a widow or widower was to be black. On April 6, Ralph mentions the black bed and hangings 'that my father borrowed of my aunt Eure' which she had caused Ralph to buy for her at the death of her own husband three years before, when her whole room was hung with black and the furniture covered with it. A list of thirteen 'pieces' is mentioned, 'blacke clothe hanginges three yardes deepe and foure and a halfe yardes longe,' two others 'three yardes deepe and three yardes longe.' The effect must have been most depressing upon those whom custom thus compelled, at the very moment when they wanted cheering, to inhabit a room where they could not for a moment forget their loss. An excuse is made in one of the letters for having even a white coverlet thrown over the bed of a young Verney widow forty years after this time, because she is sick and cannot bear black cloth.

On August 3 Sir Edmund writes to Roades to 'gett the oulde saddles at home covered with blacke, against I use them, which I thinke will be about the beginning of the next weeke. You may do them at Buckingham either with cloath or baize, and if you have no blacke bridels, sende me worde and I will buy some here.' Even the use of a 'blacke coche,' for some time after a death was considered correct, and Sir Ralph sends to borrow one for his own use after the death of his son John's wife about thirty years later.

Lady Barrymore, writing in July from Castle Lyon in answer to Ralph's letter, says: 'Noble Enemey, I shall begge your belief that there is no one so unfortunate as to have so littel acquaintance with my lady that was more truly sorrowfull for her loss than myself. Butt schach grete blessinges are not given us from God with a fixte time when wee should parte with them or how long wee shall keepe them, because we should always pray to him for the continuance of the happiness; and my prayers shall be that we may all tread in those paths she did, that we may enjoy the felicity shee now doth and ever shall possess. As in the fruition of her unspeakable content I beseech you to comfort yourself.'

Lady Verney's will, which was made in the year 1639 and was addressed to Ralph, is very touching. She had a good fortune, indeed a large one for the time, but this seems to have been merged in the Claydon estate, as she mentions 'All such of my goods wch y^r father hathe given me leave to dispose of. . . . A hundred pounds in my Red Box give your father toe by what hee pleases toe keepe for me.' (She seems to have kept a good deal of money in the house.) She is very particular about the disposal of her linen and the fine holland sheets of four breadths, &c., 'which were never yet washed.' 'Give your wiffe, my diamonde clapses, sheepe heade and the reste of my odd diamonds and my sable muffe and six of my new greate smockes.' His eldest son, then four years old, was to have the sheets and a diamond ring and 100*l*. 'put out until he is a neare toe bee married, then, bestow it in good plate as ffarr as it will in that wh^{ch} is moste yousefull for him. . . . Give Allcocke[1] 40*l*., the poore at Middle Cleadon five pounds, Mr. Aris[2] 5*l*.; . . . Betty Coleman 10*l*. toe plase [place] her and pray take som care toe see her plased with it. . . . If cooke is with me give her sum 3*l*. and sum of my worser gowns, and give my

---

[1] The housekeeper. [2] The rector.

man accordinge as he is. . . . Give your father my guilte tankard and the case of silver-hafted knives, and dessier him to leave them to your elldist sonn. . . . Bestow sum 1*l*. apeece of toyes or blake ringes for my mother, my brothers and sisters and their husbands and wives. . . . There are 4 verry fine smokes [smocks] in your father's little linnen tronke and one of my four breadthe Hollande sheets for your owne Gerle Pegge . . . there is monie enough in the Red Box which with the firste halfe years intrust will pay your father and the 1 pound toys presently. . . . Pay the undermaids, and poore, and Mr. Aris next before the bigger sums. . . .'

The items are sadly mixed, but she returns touchingly to her husband again and again. 'Take your father's tablett Picktuer yourselfe and give him Prince Henneris. They boathe lye in the Red Box, and I dessier your father that hee will nott lett anie of my Housolde Linnen bee soulde, but that it may goe toe you and your elldiste sonn and I hope to his sonn toe, only sum of my brodeste of my owne makinge give toe your sisters. . . . Now pray lett non of my papers bee seene; but doe you burne them yrselfe. All but my noats and account and medsinable and coockery Boockes, such keep. . . . Let me be buried in leade att Claydon next where y^r ffather porposes to ly himselfe, and lett noe strandger winde me, nor doe nott lett me bee striptte, but put me a cleane smoke over me . . . and lett my fase be hid and doe you stay in the roome and see me wounde and layed in the firste coffin, which must be woode if I doe nott dye of anie infectious disease, ellse I am so far from dessieringe it that I forbid you to com neare me. So the God of Heaven bless you all.'

Probably the marks of the great burns made the poor woman unwilling that any 'strandger should winde her,' and to ask her beloved Ralph to see that all such tender offices were reverently done, though with the pathetic proviso that he was not to come near her to his own hurt. Thus died Margaret Verney, aged 47 ; taken away from the evil to come, before the death of her husband in battle, the burning down of her old home at Hillesden and the death of her brother ; before the sequestration of Claydon and the long weary years of her beloved Ralph's exile ; before the murder in cold blood of her gallant son Edmund and the downfall of that monarchy which her own and her husband's family had made so many sacrifices to uphold.

CHAPTER II.

SIR RALPH'S NOTES, THE GRAND REMONSTRANCE, AND THE ATTEMPT ON THE FIVE MEMBERS.

> *Pym.*   A goodly thing
> We all say, friends, it is a goodly thing
> To right that England. Heaven grows dark above :
> Let's snatch one moment ere the thunder fall,
> To say how well the English spirit comes out
> Beneath it ! All have done their best, indeed,
> From lion Eliot, that grand Englishman,
> To the least here : and who the least one here,
> When she is saved (for her redemption dawns
> Dimly, most dimly, but it dawns—it dawns)
> Who'd give at any price his hope away
> Of being named along with the Great Men ?
> We would not—no, we would not give that up.
>   BROWNING's *Strafford.*

ON Wednesday, April 7, 1641, Ralph had buried his mother in the little church at Middle Claydon, where her grave, gentle face, in white marble, has looked down upon so many successive generations, working, rejoicing, sorrowing, in the place where she too loved to worship. On the Monday following, her son had perforce laid aside his grief, and was taking notes again in his place in the House of Commons. All through that eventful year the men who were making the history of England were debating all possible subjects, human

*Dame Margaret Verney.
from a bust in Middle Claydon Church.*

and divine, and in the intervals of Strafford's trial Sir Ralph makes notes of discussions on the privilege of Parliament, on the payment of the Navy and Army, on restraining persons in holy orders from intermeddling in secular affairs, on the abolishing of episcopacy, and a scheme for the 'advancement of lerninge.

'1. A grammer schole to be maintayned by every Cathedral church, and they are to appoint scholmasters and send out best schollers.

'2. Encouragement of students. This is the prize they aim at. Noe schollards admitted; noe bookes sould'—a free education for the poor being apparently aimed at. They are anxious to utilise cathedrals, 'the first monuments of Christianity.' While in these points we have hardly yet attained to the ideal of the Long Parliament, a degenerate generation no longer desires as they did to revive ' Local statutes to appoint sermons *almost every day*. Desier a spur in this'; they even discuss with more interest than we should expect from our present House of Commons, the question of church music. ' 'Tis not edifiing,' said the learned Dr. Hackett, ' being soe full of art, but leave a solome musick.' Here their zeal was, however, sadly misplaced. It was the golden age of English Church music. The anthems and chants of Tallis, Farrant, and Orlando Gibbons, were at once deeply learned, dignified, and beautiful. These discussions were the first mutterings of the storm which swept away the

Cathedral and Collegiate Choirs, the organs and the music books throughout the kingdom.[1] Music in its turn is succeeded by the grievances of the vintners, the abuses of the farmers of the customs, the intense excitement about the Army Plot, and the stirring debate upon the prosecution of Sir John Eliot, Selden, and others, for their conduct in the Parliament of 1629. 'Sir Ralph Verney's note of this case,' says Mr. Bruce, 'is a good specimen of his ability as a reporter. He tells the tale briefly but clearly, with legal precision and completeness, and not without one or two glances at the pathetic incidents which distinguished it. For eight months, we learn, these patriotic men were kept "without use of pen, inke or paper," and such was the rigour of their confinement that Eliot's casement being open, the lieutenant of the Tower was chidden.'

In July, 1641, Sir Ralph sat on a committee with Pym, Hampden, Sir Henry Vane, Sir John Hotham, Sir Nathaniel Fiennes, and others, to settle a most curious and delicate piece of business. The queen desired to take the Spa waters for the recovery of her health, 'which her Majesty alledged was much impaired by some discontents of mind and false rumours and libels spread concerning her.' She also stated that she wished to take to Holland her daughter Mary, who had been betrothed in person at ten years old to the Prince of Orange, aged fourteen, in the midst of all the excitement of Strafford's trial. Her

[1] See Rockstro's *History of Music*, p. 160, &c.

enemies contended that there was nothing the matter with her, 'that greate quantities of treasure are prepaired to be transported' to raise troops for the king in France and Holland, and to intrigue in general with those diabolical enemies to God and man—the Papists.

Could an odder task be undertaken by some half-dozen English gentlemen than to determine, when the first lady in the land said that she was sick, whether her symptoms were feigned or genuine, and to settle for her the proprieties and decorums of her daughter's marriage?

The committee, nothing daunted, commanded the 'phisition to bee sworne'; it was not Dr. Denton this time, but Sir Theodore Mayerne, who had attended Prince Henry in his last illness. He would have been a miserable Court physician if he could not have proved that the queen was seriously ill, when she desired to be so, and when the committee submitted to him that 'the water may as well come hither as to Utrik,' he was equal to the occasion; it was not a question of whether the water could be brought to London, he said, 'Spaw water is not fit for her at present, her body not being prepared,' . . . 'any change of aire would doe her good, bee it what it will.' When told that the queen specially desired to drink the waters, he admits that 'Shee hath a greate oppinion of the Spaw water,' that 'Waters have twice donn her good and Spaw water is better then the best waters in England.' But 'to cure her body, her mind must be quieted, the Queen is sick in body and in minde, and *thinks* shee cannot recover'; she must be 'out of reach of imployments that may disturbe her.' '*Shee believes* she is very ill,' he is careful to lay some of the responsibility on the patient; 'Unlesse remedies bee used she cannot live,' there should be no delay, this was the 14th of July, 'and the waters must be taken between this and the midle of August.'

Beaten on the question of health, the committee decided that, 'As it will bee a dishonour not to have the queen attended as she should bee, so it will bee unsupportable to afford her so much cost as will support the jorney.' As to the Princess Mary, Sir Ralph (honest man, whose own wife was betrothed to him as a child, and then brought up under his mother's roof) and his colleagues, are horrified at the gross impropriety of the princess going under her mother's care to visit her future husband's family. They protest against 'the dishonour that may happen to this nation in respect the princess is not of years, and soe the match may breake, and she sent back with dishonour,' and 'the disadvantage it will bee to have her kept with her husband untell the marriage is accomplished.' A contemporary portrait represents the child-bride as a rather prim little girl, in a red frock and white cap and apron, with a gold coin of her father's attached to a ribbon hung over her shoulder.

The queen bowed to the storm, and Sir Ralph reports her answer to the committee of both Houses which came with 'reasons to disswade her.' She thanks them with ironical courtesy for 'there greate care of my health and for there affection to me'; she is ready 'at the hazard of my life' to forego the 'Spaw' water and the change of air to 'serve the Kinge and this kingdom,' and she apologises 'for the imperfectnesse of my English, I had rather have spoke in any other language, but I thought this would bee most acceptable.' When Henrietta Maria next determined to go abroad, in February 1642, she did not wait to consult her affectionate friends the Commons, she certainly did her best to justify all their previous objections to her leaving the country, but she took good care of her little daughter whose education she superintended during the year she remained in Holland, and whom she left under the personal care of the Princess of Orange.

In November the House was absorbed in the preparation of the Grand Remonstrance, the greatest step yet taken towards a breach with the king; it was, in fact, an appeal to the nation, not an address to the crown.

The Remonstrance declared that 'the malignant and pernicious design of subverting the fundamental laws and principles of government, upon which the religion and justice of the kingdom rested, was entertained by the papists, bishops, and evil counsellors, who had suppressed the purity of religion, favoured Arminians,'[1] countenanced opinions and ceremonies

[1] 'What do the Arminians hold?' was asked of Morley, afterwards Bishop of Winchester and one of Sir Ralph's correspondents. 'All the best Bishoprics and Deaneries in England,' answered he.

fitted for Popery, and had depressed the Puritans. They expressly declare that there must be conformity in religion; each party thinks 'that Heaven is the lock to its own key.'

Toleration was indeed part of the creed of the Independents, but public opinion was not ripe for it, and intolerance was equally bitter amongst High Churchmen and Presbyterians. A Presbyterian tract, written certainly two years after this time, seeking to blacken the Sectaries, says : ' Under these fair colours and handsome pretexts do Sectaries infuse their poison, I mean their pernicious God-provoking, truth-defacing, church-ruinating and state-shaking Toleration.' Edwards, in the 'Gangrene,' says: 'A Toleration is the grand designe of the Devil, his Masterpeece, and cheif Engine he works by at this time . . . most compendious, ready, sure way to destroy all Religion, lay all waste, and bring in all evil. It is a most Transcendent, Catholike, and Fundamental evil, for this Kingdom of any than can be imagined.' (That the adjectives should run in threes was evidently held to have a most convincing effect in such documents.) 'A Toleration hath all Errors in it and all Evils.'

In 1648 the Presbyterians passed an ordinance in Parliament 'for the suppression of blasphemies and heresies, enacting, that if the party doth not abjure his error, or having abjured should relapse, he should suffer death without benefit of clergy'; while 'the Church of Manchester' drew up a protest against the evil thing, which said: 'We have searched the Scriptures and cannot find that ever such a thing was practised with approbation from God, from the time that Adam was created on the earth.'

When Presbyterianism had become nominally the established religion in England, Sir Ralph's opinion is as strong as was that of Milton, that 'new Presbyter is but old Priest writ large.'

Sir Ralph's notes of the debate on the Remonstrance of November 22, 1641, furnish, as Mr. Bruce says, 'a brief but most valuable report' of it; but, brief and authentic as they are, the notes are tiresome reading, and only an abridged account of them is given here.

The discussion had begun on Saturday, November 20, but it was so late in the day that it was delayed till the Monday following. 'Why would you have it put off?' said Cromwell to Falkland. 'There would not have been time enough, for sure it will take some debate,' answered the other. 'A very sorry one,' Cromwell replied contemptuously.

Sir Ralph first reports 'Mr. Hide's' speech, in which he declared that 'the end of this remonstrance is peace,' and that 'wee stand upon our liberties for the king's sake, least hee should bee king of meane subjects, or wee subjects of a meane king.' Lord Falkland, who spoke next, complained both of the attack on the Arminians and the bishops. 'Bellum episcopale,' he observed, had only been said by one bishop, yet it had been laid upon all; it was the same also with the 'bringing in of idolatry,' and in spite of the bishops and Popish lords sitting in Parliament it was confessed that many good laws were made there.

Sir Edward Dering supported Falkland: he had on a former occasion brought up the 'Root and Branch Bill' for the abolition of episcopacy, with the consent of Pym and Hampden, not that he desired it to pass, but that he had thought thus to force the peers to consent to the exclusion of the bishops from the Upper House. He now argued that the advancement of learning would suffer if the bishoprics were abolished; as he expressed it, 'take the greate bason and euer out of the lottery and very few will venture to throw.'

Sir John Culpepper declared that 'the declaration going but from this house goes but on on legg'—that the Lords should have been invited to join in it, and that all remonstrances should be addressed to the king, as he only could redress grievances. To send a 'declaration' like this to the people at large was 'daingerous for the publique peace.' To this Pym replied that the honour of the king lay in the safety of the people, and that the plots had all been traced to the Court and the Popish party. 'Wee have suffered soe much by councellours of the king's chusing that wee desier him to advise with us about it.' Hampden and Holles spoke in the same strain, and the debate rolled on till midnight, when the Remonstrance itself was carried by yeas 159, noes

148, which Sir Benjamin Rudyard compared to the verdict of a starved jury. Hampden then proposed that it should be forthwith printed and published, and this produced a scene of the wildest uproar, which lasted three or four hours.

In the midst of the confusion Hyde rose, vehemently opposing Hampden's motion; if it were carried he desired that he 'might have liberty to protest.' A friend of his, one Jeffrey Palmer, then started to his feet, and shouted, 'I do protest,' speaking for himself, he said, 'and all the rest.' The noise became uproarious; some members waved their hats in their excitement, others 'took their swords in their scabbards out of their belts and held them by their pommels in their hands, setting the lower part on the ground,' according to D'Ewes's account. The House not being prepared or intended for night sittings, the chamber was so dimly lighted, Warwick says, 'that it was like the valley of the shadow of death.' In the darkness the tumult increased. There are two red lines in the matting of the floor of the House, a few feet before the front benches, beyond which it is not etiquette that any member should step when speaking. It is curious to look on these and to remember that at the time when they were originally laid down, the danger of an encounter with swords by excited members (as may be seen in this instance) was only too real, and one requiring to be vigilantly guarded against. The uproar continued until Hampden spoke, and turned the attention of the excited members into another channel by asking Palmer 'how he could know other men's minds?' The confusion then ceased, and further discussion was postponed until another day. Warwick, whose sympathies were on the other side, and who is therefore an unprejudiced witness in Hampden's favour, declares that 'we had catcht at each other's locks, and sheathed our swords in each other's bowels, had not the sagacity and great calmness of Mr. Hambden by a short speech prevented it.'[1]

As the members went out in the early morning, Falkland asked Cromwell whether 'there had not indeed been a debate?' 'I will take your word for it another time,' said the other, adding, 'If the Remonstrance had been rejected, I would have sold all I had the next morning, and never have seen England any more; and I know there are many other honest men of this same resolution.' 'So near,' says Clarendon, 'was the poor kingdom at that time to its deliverance.'

When the House met again on the 24th, Sir John Hotham, according to Sir Ralph's notes, 'charged Mr. Palmer with protesting on Mounday night, in the name of himselfe and others, and that in a way to move us to mutinie, and made himselfe the head of a party.' Hyde declared that the charge was against the orders, 'being he was only charged with words, and not with any ill carrage,' and that

[1] Pym, as quoted by Clarendon, also said 'that it might probably have engaged the House in blood.'

his words were not excepted against at the time. If a man might be questioned for words, spoken a month or a year previously, they might be forged, ' then how can a man answere for himselfe, and this takes away the greate priviledge of freedom of speech.'

' Mr. Hollis, after three houers debate, sayd hee would charg him with a new charg, in making a pernicious motion.' It was in vain that Palmer attempted to excuse himself for his conduct, also declaring that he did not remember using the words ' in the name of himself or others.' The House would not let him off, and at the next day's sitting he was sentenced to go to the Tower by a majority of 41. Clarendon says that he himself had been selected for punishment, but that Palmer was taken instead. His imprisonment only lasted twelve days, but the excited debates on the subject added to the uneasiness of the Puritan party without.

On the 29th a crowd, armed with swords and staves, assembled outside the House, with a view of supporting the popular party, and very nearly came to a collision with the trained bands whom the king had lately caused to take the place of the guard hitherto stationed there by command of Essex. Sir Ralph gives an account of the examination into the occurrence at the next day's sitting. The crowd was apparently largely composed of apprentices.

' One sayd, hee was newly come from Westminster armed, and that 1000 men were redy there.

Hee sayd the parliment men sent for them. The reason of his going was, because the well affected party [i.e. of Pym and Hampden] were likely to bee over-voted by the worser, but, being they agreed well together, hee and his fellows cam all away in peace.' 'There had been an uprore in the parliment house,' said another witness, ' and swords drawne.' One apprentice declared ' that his master gave him a sourd, and bid him goe, and hee beeleaves the masters of the other apprentices did the like.'

Such supporters as these were hardly likely to do good to any cause, and the interference of the great assemblages which now often surrounded the Houses of Parliament and the Palace was ominous of mischief.

The king meantime had returned from Scotland, and on signifying his intention of passing through the City, had been received there with a grand procession and a splendid banquet. To secure the support of the rich citizens was of great moment to him, and he made the most of this auspicious occasion by setting forth his good intentions with regard to the redress of their grievances and the re-establishment of their trade, promising to maintain the Protestant religion 'if need be to the hazard of my life, and all that is dear to me.' He then retired to Hampton Court, where the queen and her adherents were urging him to take strong measures against the Puritan leaders, whom they now regarded as absolute traitors.

His first step was to dismiss the guard which

had been placed round the two Houses, declaring that it was not wanted, and that there was no danger to be apprehended.

Lady Sussex, writing to Ralph on November 29, says :

'Your glorious show we have in printe; my thinkes the kainge should love his pepell of inglande best; for suer ther bonty and obedynce is most to him; i pray God sende your parlyment agree will; i am sory the kainge is gon to hamton court for ther will bee much time for ther pouerfull par-swasyons; my thinkes ther was littill show of love to your hose to desier your garde should be dismist thes trublesom times; i becech the god of heaven to bles and keepe you all safe from any filinus parties; ther will bee much bisynes in your hose suer, now the kainge is com; god power is above all; and i hope he will derect you to do for the best, every way. Thow i am ever most glade at your lettirs i forbide them but when you have lesuer, for i know you can not but bee tyerde out ever day with bisynes.'

A few days later a deputation from the Commons carried the Remonstrance to the king at Hampton Court, and he was warned by a petition accompanying it, against the 'ill affected party,' and asked to 'join the Parliament in taking away the votes from the bishops, and in removing oppressions and unnecessary ceremonies.' Charles's answer was scornful and unsatisfactory, and the next day when he went to the House of Lords he made a speech, as quoted by Ralph, to the effect that he had been 'absent longer then hee expected . . . but with good successe for he hath left Scotland a happy nation. But his expectation is deceived here, for heere was many destractions, but hee found the affections of his people reall by the entry into London . . .' and then 'that his greatest thought was in the good affections of the people.'

The Grand Remonstrance had but widened the breach between him and the Parliament, and mutual distrust increased daily. On December 15 the Commons resolved to print it, and thus appeal from the king to the nation.

With the opening of the year 1642 came an attempt on the part of the king, perhaps the most ill-advised of any that he made, to strike a blow at the leaders of the popular party. Pym, Hampden, Holles, Hazlerigg, and Strode, were the men marked out for attack.

Sir Ralph's notes of the attempted arrest of the five members begin on Monday, January 3 :

'The king sent Mr. Francis, a serjeant at armes, to Mr. speaker with a message, and hee was cald in to the house, and deliverd it at the barr, but hee was not sufferd to bring in his mace.

'The message was thus, "Mr. speaker, the king comanded mee, uppon my aleageance, to repaire to you where you are now sittinge, and to demaund five gentlemen, members of this house, Mr. Hollis, Sir Arthur Hazlerigg, Mr. Pim, Mr. Hampden, and Mr.

William Strood, and, when they are deliverd, hee comanded me in his name to arrest them for high treason."

'Uppon this hee was comanded to withdraw, and the house resolved to send four members to the king, to let him know they had received the message, and would take it into consideration, but, being there was noe charge deliverd in against those five gentlemen, they have not deliverd them, but have taken care to have them in a readinesse to answere any legall charge. And then the house commanded Mr. speaker to call upp these five gentlemen by name, and injoyned them to attend de die in diem, till the house took farther order. The serjeant of the house was sent to tell sergeant Francis, that wee had sent to the king about these five gentlemen.

'Mr. Pim and Mr. Hollis had there papers and studdies sealed upp, by warrant under the king's hand, and the house sent a serjeant at armes to arrest those that did it, and breake of the seales, and had a conference with the lords, and they likewise sent to breake oppen the seales, and it was donn accordingly. Wee sent to them [the lords] to joine with us, because they had protested with us to defend the privileges of parliament.'

We have four independent accounts given by eye-witnesses of the next day's scene. Of these the most detailed is that of Rushworth, a young clerk-assistant lately taken into the service of the House, who, in the midst of the intense excitement, went on steadily writing at the table, as Sir Ralph, in much less comfort, wrote on his knee. His account completes our knowledge of the details of that memorable day.

'Tuesday, January 4, 1641.—The five gentlemen which were to bee accused cam into the house, and there was information that they should bee taken away by force. Uppon this, the house sent to the lord maior, aldermen, and common councell to let them know how there priviledges were like to bee broken, and the citty put into dainger, and advised them to looke to there security.

'Likwise some members were sent to the four inns of court, to let them know, how they heard they were tampred withall to assist the king against them, and therfore they desierd them not to come to Westminster.

'Then the house adjorned till on of the clock.

'As soone as the house mett againe, 'twas moved, considering there was an intention to take these five men away by force, to avoyd all tumult, let them bee commanded to absent themselves. Uppon this, the house gave them leave to absent themselves, but entred noe order for it, and then the five gentlemen went out of the house.

'A little after, the kinge came, with all his guard, and all his pentioners, and two or three hundred soldiers and gentlemen. The king comanded the soldiers to stay in the hall, and sent us word hee was at the dore. The speaker was commanded to sit still, with the mace lying before him, and then the

FAC-SIMILE OF A PAGE OF SIR RALPH VERNEY'S NOTES.
(*Written when the King tried to arrest the five members.*)

king came to the dore, and tooke the palsgrave [his nephew] in with him, and comand all that cam with him, uppon their lives not to come in. So the dores were kept oppen, and the earle of Roxborough stood within the dore, leaninge uppon it. [This is a touch we have from Sir Ralph alone.] Then the kinge cam uppwards, towards the chaire, with his hat off, and the speaker steped out to meet him. Then the kinge steped upp to his place, and stood uppon the stepp, but sate not down in the chaire. And, after hee had looked a greate while, hee told us, hee would not breake our priviledges, but treason had noe priviledge; hee cam for those five gentlemen, for hee expected obedience yeasterday, and not an answere. Then hee calld Mr. Pim, and Mr. Hollis, by name, but noe answere was made. Then hee asked the speaker if they were heere, or where they were. Uppon that the speaker fell on his knees and desierd his excuse, for hee was a servant to the house, and had neither eyes, nor tongue, to see or say anything but what they comanded him. Then the king told him, hee thought his owne eyes were as good as his, and then said, his birds were flowen, but hee did expect the house would send them to him, and if they did not hee would seeke them himselfe, for there treason was foule, and such an on as they would all thanke him to discover. Then hee assured us they should have a faire triall, and soe went out, putting off his hat till hee came to the dore.

'Uppon this the house did instantly resolve to

adjorne till toomorrow at on of the clock, and in the intrim they might consider what to doe.'

'The Commons at once adjourned,' says Mr. Gardiner, 'with the sense that they had but just escaped a massacre. The orderly D'Ewes testified his opinion of the danger by stepping to his lodgings and immediately making his will.' That this opinion was shared by the country is shown by Lady Sussex's letter to Sir Ralph, written as soon as the news reached Gorhambury.

'Thes distractede times put us all in great disorder, but i hope wee shall not bee kaillede; yet i think you are in greater danger then wee are in the contry; i pray god bles you with safety; your parlyment flyes hye; truly itt is a happy thinge, i thinke, the haue so much corige to stand to mentane ther right; the good tone of london it semes will do so to; truly the are to bee commendede; surely the kainges party will bee to weke; that he must yelde to the parlyment; i pray god derect all your harts to do for the bes for the good of us all; if wee now be ouer cam wee are undon for euer; i hope thos gentillmen the kainge woulde haue from your hose shall bee safe; the stand so much for the generall good that it was a miserable thinge the shoulde cuffer; thes lettir will com safe, or else i shoulde not haue adfentiure to have sade so much. It was a blesede thinge thos gentilmen was from the parlyment when the kinge cam, he had ill counsill surly to com in such a way. I pray god all may conclude will, and that you may be as happy as you are wishede by your true frinde,' &c.

On February 1 Sir Ralph notes the Commons' Petition for the command of the Tower and of the militia, 'a decided move in the headlong march to confusion,' as Mr. Bruce calls it; on the 10th he records the names of those persons chosen by the Commons as fit to command the militia of their respective counties, and to be sent to the king. The list seems of sufficient interest to be given here.

Berks	Holland		Middlesex . .	Holland
Bedford . . .	Bullingbroke		Northampton	. Spencer
Bucks	Paget		Nottingham .	. Clare
Cambridg . .	North		Northumberland, Newcastle, and Berwick . . .	. Northumberland
Cheshire . . .	Strainge			
Cornwall . . .	Roberts			
Cumberland . .	Grey of Werk			
Darby	Rutland			
Devonshire . .	Bedford		Norfolke . . .	. Warwick
Dorset . . .	Salisbury		Oxford . . .	. Say et Seale
Isle of Purbeck .	Sir John Banks		Rutland . . .	. Exeter
Durham . . .	Sir Henry Vaine, senior		Shropshire . .	. Littleton
			Somersetshire .	Mar. Hartford
Essex	Warwick		and Bristol	. Mr. Hollis
Glocester . . .	Shandois		Stafford and Litchfield .	. Essex
Hampshire and Isle of Wight .	Pembroke		Suffolke . . .	. Suffolke
Hartford . . .	Salisbery		Surrey . . .	. Nottingham
Hereford . . .	Dacres		Sussex . . .	. Northumberland
Huntington . .	Mandivill			
Kent	Leicester		Warwick . . .	. Brooke
Lancashere . .	Wharton		Westmerland .	Cumberland
Leicester . . .	Stamford		Wilts	. Pembroke
Lincolne ; Kesteven, Lincolne, and Holland . . Linsey . . .	Lincolne Willoby of Parum		Worcester . .	. Edward Howard, Escreek
			Yorke, and Kingston uppon Hull, and the citty Yorke	. Essex

London . . .	Six aldermen or 3 of them, 12 common councell or 6 of them, and serjeant major Skippon	Carnarvan .	. Pembroke
		Denbeigh. .	. Feildinge
		Flint . . .	. Feildinge
		Glamorgan .	. Phillip Herbert
		Moungomery	. Essex
		Marioneck .	. Pembroke
		Pembroke .	. Northumberland
Monmouth .	. Phillip Herbert		
Cardigan . .	. Kerberic	Radner . .	. Littleton
Carmarthen .	. Kerbery		

CHAPTER III.

THE RISING IN MUNSTER, 1641-42.

> When History's Muse the memorial was keeping
> Of all that the dark hand of Destiny weaves,
> Beside her the Genius of Erin stood weeping,
> For hers was the story that blotted the leaves.—MOORE.

ON November 1, 1641, news reached London of the rebellion in Ulster, which had broken out on October 23. No one who knows what was the state of Ireland in the preceding year, can wonder at some such outbreak occurring, but horror and indignation naturally filled all minds in England on hearing the news, and of the atrocities committed by the rebels. The Parliament at once voted that 50,000*l*. should be borrowed, and an army of 8,000 men be raised to assist their countrymen in their extremity. In the meantime every post brought news of fresh horrors.

For eight years Strafford had ruled Ireland with a stern but successful sway. Now the strong man was removed. His insignificant successor, Wandesford, had died in 1640. Leicester, who was next appointed, never went to Ireland at all, and neither order nor prosperity could be maintained by the inefficient Borlase and the unprincipled Parsons, the two

Lords Justices, in whom his authority was vested. Sir John Borlase was a worn-out old soldier, and Sir William Parsons a land-jobber, who was suspected of encouraging land confiscation for his own purposes.

The general feeling of discontent increased from the beginning of 1641. There were growing rumours that the Catholic population was to be rooted out. Charles, with his ill-advised intrigues with the Irish Catholic lords, rather helped than hindered the inevitable outbreak. The movement began in Ulster and spread to the south, and the letters from the Verneys' Irish friends, living chiefly in Munster, give a terrible picture of the state of the country.

Sir John Leeke writes to Sir Edmund at the end of the year 1641, in the extremity of distress:

'The frights and terrors wee heere live in, cannot welbe expressed but by such as suffer and feele the distraction, whereof many are com for England that cann relate itt as eie witnesses, which you will hear of befor this letter cann come to yor hands, as the noble Incyquin and Mr. Jepson. I before sent letters by Mistress Jepson, whos passadg we much sorrow for, the next day being extream tempestuous. With her went the Lady St. Leger, and the good Lady of Incyquin and many children. God of his mercy bless them all and land them all safe. You may perceive by thes greate personages going away, our danger. Lady Kilnalmechy hath enough I believe of Ireland, she is a most noble and sweetly disposed lady. I beseech you assone as she comes to Court, see her and give thanks for her kindness.' He asks Sir Edmund ' by gaining the king or some great man's letters to procure for me a Company of foote, I shall prevayle to have them garrisoned at Youghal when we leave the field.' Lady Barrymore cannot pay the money sent through her, ' and we perish meantime for want.' ' Lady ffenton and many of my good friends take houses at Tanton and entend to recyde there or at Minhead.' ' I protest I am most miserable, for though I have friends, yet noe friend to lend me tenn pounds. No man will part with a peny of money, and by all that is good in heaven and earth, I nor my wife have in purse 40s.—We have 20 good cowes, wee may have none tomorrow, such is the case of many men. I have barreled beefe and porke and some littell wheat and mault for a moneth, God healp us and send the English forces to us, o^r hearts wowld be light and our corrages stronge, for thes English wee have here have gott good things abowght them, and themselves and ther goods gott into stronge townes. The country is abandoned and in my Lords country is nothing left but ther cattell and a servant or tow in ther house. I howld yett in the parke, but one Munday or Tewsday I must to Yoghall, my wife is in that extremitie of feares (as cause she hath poore sowle) that I must not delay longer but leav the Lodg, nether will I mayntayne the Lodg with my life and what I have, and my lord allow me nothinge to itt. . . . P.S.—Barrymore taks the field tomorrow with 60 dragowns and 70 lancers. Browghall goeth to the rendevous as stronge if not stronger.' He asks that a case of pistols may be sent him, 'for I will not stay in Yoghall, but will into the field with Barrymore, and see something that may inable my knowledge. I lack a sword wth a garded hilte, I want other armes, but have noe way to have them—bee we as patient as we can.'

Ralph, in alarm for the safety of his friend Lady Barrymore, writes to her: 'Your stay [in Ireland] afflicts mee extreamly least you should bee suddainly surprised by those Barbarous Rebells who (if Fame belye them not) delight in cruelty, and take pleasure in insolency, above and beyond ye worst of infidells. truly maddame though I have never been much in love with Papists, yet I beeleeved them to bee christians, but if they offer violence to you, or yours, I shall change my opinion. . . . now you see it utterly impossible to infuse any humanity into those pagan Irish, bee pleased to come over and make us happy heere.'

Sir John writes again in January 1642 from Youghal: 'I have not long since writ to you by Mr. Booth and again by Mistress Jepson, they all tend to one tune—a relation of our distractions and miseries.' 'Clomell, the key of Munster is taken on Saturday last; Dungarvan and the castle is taken both by the treachery of the townsmen; Kilkenny ten days since was taken by the Lord Mont Garratt and his four sons and sons-in-law. My Lady of Ormund and her children are in the castle and there imprisoned, Mountgarratt is in the castle with a face to secure the Lady, but a false heart. I am now come to Yoghall with my company, where we are as secure as in any Irish town; God knows there is no security but where a good English garrison doth secure. The virtuous Lady Kilnalmechy hath commanded this letter, which she will deliver to you with her own hands; she can give our miseries to the life. My Lord of Broghall went before the town of Dungarvan, the next day it was surprised, with 60 horse and 50 foot, and took the praye of the town, which consisted of 120 cows and horse, and near 400 sheep, and carried them to Lismore, which was 8 miles. The present Monday, the 10th, my Lord Dungarvan intended to have met his brother at Dungarvan with 80 brave armed horse and 100 foot, but when 25 of his horse were ferried over, an express came to my Lord Dungarvan from my Lord President to command him into the field to join with him and Barrymore, which army will be near 400 brave horse, besides 1,200 foot, and some pieces of ordinances; Barrymore hath 60 Dragoons which hath done good service and execution; this army carryeth a brave resolution though but small in number, yet courageous and discreetly commanded; they fight for honour and their lands, all is at stake; there is not a country we can hear of but the county of Corke but are in action; Oh! we sigh and grieve for the English forces, we believe they will come, but the kingdom will be so near losing, or at least destroying, that the regaining will cost more blood and charge than the first conquest did or all the wars in Queen Elizabeth's time. We hear this night that Dungarvan is fortified with 2 or 3,000 men, and as is noised, under command of my Lord of Ormund's only brother; the rebels are so strong between Dublin and us that the Earl of Ormund cannot come from Dublin where he is, either to succour his wife, his country, or chastise his brain-sick brother; his country is more infested than any of our parts. Three Lords of the Butlers are in action. God of his mercy send us succors and fight for us and with us to the distruction of thes ungratious rebells that fullness of bread and to to gratious favors of our Royall Kinge have given them (since Queene Eliz roodd was taken from them) and have bine blessed with the sweet of peace and w^{h}out disturbance inioyd ther conciences But beasts that have bine used to the yooke, growe more crooked and perverse when they are putt to fatt pasture. . . . I do believe that whosoever shall live to this day twelvemonth shall see such a dearth and famine as hath seldom or hardly been known in Ireland; what cattle the rebels cannot come at, we are inforced to barrell up, for if the rebels take our cattle (which they have done in infinite number, both of fair sheep and goodly cattle as most in England), what they eate they kill with their skeens and let them lie and stink. The first work they did was to rob all the

English of their cattle, to starve them which cannot subsist of roots and oats as they do. To conclude, our state is lamentable, if we but look to what was, to what now is, and to what of certain must be. For my particular I know not what to do in the turmoils; cattle I have in the park, but how long I am not certain, yet we are in a safe place as long as Yoghall continues good, which God grant. Monies are not to be had for any thing unless arms, swords, and muskets, which are gold and silver, and friends too; friends for money are not; plate, household stuff are not merchantable . . . There are not any women of quality but are come to England, nor any that have wealth. . . . The old Earl of Cork is full of distractions, not like the man he was; his sons are most noble, and you should hear brave things of their undertakings and performances. . . . I should be loath to leave Ireland until the fire burns my heels. I beseech you send me a case of pistols and a close hilt sword. I have a desire (tho' I am old) not to be an idler; a word from a friend or yourself might gain me a company to be garrisoned in Yoghall. I believe it not very difficult, considering my Lord of Leicester is my noble friend, and this virtuous Lady Kilnelmechy my anchor to trust to, for so hath she offered and promised. . . . P.S. this Wednesday morning the 12 wee have the ill newes the Rebells are within 4 myles of Lismore. my lord Dungarvan sent out xxiiii horse under the command of his cornett Honest Jack Travers who was by an ambush betrayd and himselfe slaine and 2 footmen. 500 were of the Rebells well appoynted.'

It is not surprising that the English soldiers, on their arrival in Ireland, were filled with rage at the sights they saw and the relations they heard, and were not inclined to be very merciful to the doers of such outrages. Compared, however, with the manner in which war was carried on at that time in the Low Countries and in Germany, and with Cromwell's deeds in Ireland a few years later, the conduct of the English officers and soldiers can hardly be complained of.

In March Sir John writes: 'Sir Charles Vavesor a noble gentillman who doth assure me he left you well and took his leave of you the day before he sett one his jorney for Irelande hath brought over 1,000 as brave carcases of men, as ever I beheld wth my eies and would fayne be in the feild and fightinge. they had well hooped that they should have fallen to pillaging the Irish of the towne of Yoghall and meetinge wth some Irish wemen that hadd mantells and crucefixes abowght ther neckes, wch the soldiers teore from them, but by ther commander were quieted, the preests are all stole out of the towne and noe masse sayd yesterday, beinge Sunday . . . wee expect this day or tomorrow to see my Lord of Incyquine, if the wind hould fayre as itt is. The very noyse of the landinge the troops have blowne away rebells, that lay neere Yoghall, but abowght Lismore, where Browhall hath killed and hanged many, some loss he hath receved as a brave gentillmann his Cornell. The Rebells did use much cruelty before ther departure by dragginge a gentillman out of his howse, and bindinge his hands, layinge him on a banke, and shott him to death; 4 poore English that were ther, they hanged, drawinge them up to a hovell post, and held them until they were dead, and this was done within Lismore precincts; the rebells were 71 colours in one place and 8 or 9 in another, but they vanished in a moment to the mountaynes. Ther Gennerall the Lord Mount-Garratt is fallen from the Lord Roch and gone into his one contry with 6,000 men. . . . . They marched to Mallo, wher were tow castels, Mr. Jepson's house is very stronge and well appoynted, the other not bigger than an ordinnary steeple, but 25 good men at Least, and a stowt commander; the Rebells summoned the castell but they were answered wth muskett Bulletts, in short they killed neere 200 Rebells and hurt many, att last powder faylinge, they accepted quarter and went to Mr. Jepsons castell; the English lost very few. The next day the Rebells parted ther army. Killnalmechy keeps his towne of Bandon Bridge . . . this last week he fell most bravely on the enimy; 400 of the Rebells came neer Bandon with some p^{r}vision and necessaries of usqubach, wine, bread, some munition and ther apparrell, 3 cartloads. Killnalmechy drew out 200 musketteeres and himselfe and 70 horse, putt them to rout, and running killed 104, tooke prisoners and hanged them, many prime gentillmen were slayne. . . .

VOL. II.   E

Our lands are all wasted, and we shall have no p-fitt this many yeares.' He entreats Sir Edmund to get him a company or to lend him some money. 'I have gott four soldiers to keepe the house. . . . Here no man hath anythinge, nor shall not this many yeares; the stocke of English sheep and cattel are almost destroyed, the Rebells stole English sheepe from a frende of mine, but some dayes after the English troops tooke some of the sheepe and other cows from the Rebells; the troopers sell the sheepe for 12d. 8d., and 6d. when ther skinne were well worth 16d, and so sould thus all turnes as mischeefe to the poore English; littell or noe restitution unless the proprietor be in pursuite and recover . . . God healp us. . . . Tom Badnedg [his son-in-law] is . . . now Capt. of the gard of our Yoghall, it is creditt but not a pownde proffittable. his dilligence and care is a great security to the towne. Wee have many Irish and few trew harted as wee feare but o^r English are a bridell in ther nose: yett the townsmen pfesse and ptest much loyalty . . . While I am writing a messenger is come in from the army that assures us my Lord President hath regayned Dungarvan wth the slaughter of many, the castell howlds out, but cannot Longe; in itt are men of qualitie, as Sr Nycholas Welsh and some of the Bullers . . . ther are 5 or 600 cooped in betwixt the sea and the blackwater wch must falle. My Lord Barrymore is in the field wth the President and hath most bravly and loyally behaved himselfe, to the great terror of his countrymen; itt wilbe a most bloody warre, for none can be spared; the Irish women[1] are most cruell in execution; I pray God bless you in England and knitt your harts in unitie. trust no Papist for here they betray ther dearest frendes. . . . I Intreat yor cowncell and comfort to yor poore brother John Leeke.'

He writes again a few days later:

'My Lord President with his one and the regiment of Sir Charles Vavisor have rescued Dungarvan with the castel from the rebells, killed 300 att least, and gave quarter to 80 that were in the castel, the reason that favour being the suddayne risinge of the Lord of Muscary, who contrary to all menns expectation and his own vowes and protestations is now with 7,000 men within 5 myles of Corke, the President is not withstanding got into Corke, but hath not power sufficient to keep the field, but doth strengthen all our townes until new supplies come and then he will not be pent up. . . . I am most miserable, money I have none, rent none to be paid, the rebells within a mile of the towne, the river only between, our towne supposed not to be sownd at heart, I mayntayned a gard of 4 men and a boy and a mayd to dress theire

[1] The mother of Adamnan, living in Ireland, Abbot of Iona in 704, was so shocked at seeing a battle where women were engaged on both sides, and especially by the sight of one woman running a reaping-hook through the breast of her enemy, that she persuaded her son to obtain a decree from an assembly of chiefs and abbots against such practices, for 'men and women went equally to battle at that time,' says the Celtic book of Irean.

meate until 3 weekes since from 9ber, which was hard for me to keep tow houses, . . . my long service to his father and himself are forgotten. . . . If I may not get a company I cannot here live, no man can see to the end of this rebellion, nether will (if we had peace) 7 yeares reduce us into order and that time is more than I can expect to live. I wish I had some pretty farm that might keepe my 20 cowes in any cuntry about you.'

On March 8, 1642, Magdalen Faulkner writes from 'Castel Lyones,' to Sir Ralph : 'I receved your leter and in that the sadest nues that ever I louck to hear [Lady Verney's death], that I have just cauese to say that mesfourtune stel folloes me in the lose of soe many of my derest frindes. Wee are here in a most pettyful and lamemuntabel case as ever pore pepul ware in. God help ous, we have and here of nothing but fier and the sword and pettyful sites of pouer pepel strept nacked as ever they ware borne and we can expect nothing but famen for thay destroye al—they which at mickelmust last wore worth thre or fore thousen poundes nowe beges at ouer dore. My Lord behaves himselfe gallantly in this besnes for we have fefty famely in ouer houses for safty, and fouer times as many in ouer other castel, and none of my lords one cuntre is yet in rebelone, but we fere them ever daye and louck to be beseged and our towne fiered, for the enemy tackes our cows and catel to ouer very dore God helph ous we knoe not what to do.' She begs pardon for the faults in the letter, 'I am so friten with suden alarmes that I knoe not [what] to do.'

Lady Barrymore also writes :

'I live every hour at the mercy of our increasing enemies and dare not as yet stir because the safety of so many depends upon my stay here, and we have daily the objects of the Papist's cruelty, which doth some what terrify mee.' She will not give particulars of their suffering, 'for I desier you may onely heare of it by the bye and never have a full relation of the many misereyes this poore kingdome is redust to, and much like to be worse, without you grave parlament men doe speedily send us more aide, which I begge you to doe that you may presarve in Ierland your unconstant enemy but faithfull freind to sarve you.

'H. BARRYMORE.'

Their fears proved but too well founded, for in her next letter Magdalen Faulkner says :

'We are fled from our one house, for the enemy came with soe greate a number aganst ous, that my Lord durst not let my lady and the cheldren stay. I thinke the next remove will be into England, for the enemy persues ous ever wher and voues oure deth, becase we wil not goe to mase which god almite kepe ous from.'

Sir Ralph replies in June to Lady Barrymore :

'You are so hardened by this winter's sufferings, that neither fire nor sword can fright you into England ; 'tis truth there's little left that may invite you hither, the unhappy distractions of this kingdom have not only reduced ourselves into a sad condition, but made Ireland far more miserable. Till these are settled here, I shall not expect to see the rebels quiet there, especially considering these distempers have wrought so many doubtings in the minds of men, that I fear 'twill be very hard to raise a considerable sum of money, unless there do appear greater hopes of peace than yet are evident.'

The case of the poor English in Ireland was indeed deplorable unless their countrymen at home were agreed in supporting them. The Parliament had sent reinforcement of troops to their aid early in the year, as many as their funds could provide, but now, with Civil War imminent in England, little assistance could be looked for. The king's proposal of going himself to Ireland to quell the rebellion was absolutely opposed by the Puritan party, who feared his gaining strength there for further oppression at home. No better plan for improving the state of poor Ireland was thought of than fresh confiscations and plantations.

Magdalen Faulkner writes in June '42 to Sir Ralph: ' Here is noe newes but what you knoe alredy—but onley this last weeke Caredealahand castel is taken and the Lord Roches castel and cuntre burnt within to miles of ous. it was taken by my lord and the to regementes we have here, the lord presedent is past al hopes of life and he is genaral of munster but he wose not in the feld this quater of a yere. my lord is very good and doth take great panes and care for the helph of the englesh.'

A few months later Lord Barrymore was killed, to the great loss of the loyalists of the neighbourhood. According to one account, ' All the English that were robbed and stripped in Roche's and Condon's countries, many of whom his lady clothed, were carried by him safe to Youghall with his troop of horse, which together with two companies of foot, he maintained at his own charge. He headed them at the battle of Liscarrol and died of his wounds there on Michaelmas day, aged only thirty-eight. The Irish threatened to destroy his house, but he sent them word that he would defend it while one stone remained upon another.' 'He left a distressed lady,' says another writer, 'and four children, with an encumbered and disjointed estate, and all his country wasted.' His eldest son was only nineteen, and Magdalen writes to beg Ralph to help him; she was now married to Mr. Bruce, but apparently stayed on with Lady Barrymore. She writes in November 1642:

'... I ret to you sence the deth of my Lord to doue the best you can for the young lord, for he hath nothing left him; I hope you wil al conseder of it, for his father hath dun very good sarves as any man hath dun in this kingdum, but that mesenger wose unfortunately tacken by the pyrets; the rebels com every daye to our towne [village]; they towke a praye from my lady fore nites ago, 24 fat oxen, three score and ten melch cowes, besides our working oxen, thaye vowe to fier our towne and house and we have letel resestance for them. God help ous out of this mesry for we are in gret disstres, for in the lose of my lord we lost the prop and stay of our contrey.' A month later: 'I fere we shale be forst to leve this kingdom very suddenly for want of meet, men and menishone, for al that is out of the enemyes hand will not sarve the English three month God helph ous; the paralement hath made a fresh presedent and he is our general of this provence; he hath soe many of his frindes and kindred in rebellyone and soe many of his frindes and kindred whiche gives proteckone and are protected by him that thay and dooe [undo] al ous pore pepel; if you give not a remove to him I fere you and ous wil have cose to repint of it; sence my lord died thaye fere nobody for when he lived he kept al his one contrey in order, thaye durst not aman stur and thaye be as bad as the worst: thay are protected by the president within a mile of ouer castel; god almite loucke one ous for these are miserable times; . . . my lady presentes hir sarves to you and soe doth meˢ Freck; she is strept out of al that she hath.'

After this date there is little more correspondence between the Verneys and their unfortunate Irish friends. Sir John Leeke, ruined and hopeless, took refuge in England, and was followed by Lady Barrymore and her family.

The want of cohesion among the Irish made the rebellion hopeless from the outset. The peasants were often joined by men of more education and position as may be seen in the letters, and by uniting with any one of the three parties, the Scotch, the parliament, or the king, into which the English warfare was cut up, the Irish might probably have brought about a success and have made pretty much their own terms; but the great mass of the people were ignorant savages, and though their complaints of the English rule were well-founded, the Irish were incapable of united action, or of constructing a government, and the hatred aroused against them in England had terrible and far-reaching consequences. Mr. Gardiner thus sums up the memories left by this bitter struggle:

'If, in the darkness, Englishman could not discern the face of Englishman, how could it be hoped that he would discern the face of the Irish Celt? His rebellion and cruelty had left no room, if there had been room before, for any remembrance of the wrongs he had suffered.'[1]

[1] Gardiner's *Fall of the Monarchy of Charles I.*, vol. ii. p. 340.

CHAPTER IV.

CARY VERNEY'S MARRIAGE.

'Tell me not, sweet, I am unkind,
  That from the nunnery
Of thy chaste breast and quiet mind
  To arms and war I fly.

'True, a new mistress now I chase,
  The first foe in the field,
And with a stronger faith embrace
  A sword, a horse, a shield.

'Yet this inconstancy is such
  As you too shall adore;
I could not love you, dear, so much
  Loved I not honour more.'

LOVELACE.

IN the midst of the anxieties and troubles of the beginning of 1642, the excitement of the attempt on the five members by the king, the painful struggles of the best men of both parties to find out the right course, amidst the jarring conflict of opinion on all points, political and religious, young men and maids were still marrying and giving in marriage.

Sir Edmund had promised his fourth daughter, Cary,[1] his 'shee darling' as Dr. Denton calls her,

---

[1] Cary does not seem to have been an abbreviation of Caroline, as in Sir Edmund Verney's will, where Sue and Pen and Betty are given their Christian names in full, Cary's name is unaltered, and she transmitted it to a Denton godchild; she was probably called after Sir Edmund's friend, Mrs. Cary, afterwards Mrs. Herbert.

aged fifteen, to a young captain of dragoons in the king's service, the eldest son of Sir Thomas Gardiner, Recorder of London, and who afterwards succeeded St. John as Solicitor-General. He had an estate at Cuddesden, near Oxford, about twenty miles from Claydon. The two had made acquaintance at the end of 1641, for when young Edmund was staying with his sisters at Claydon at that time, he writes to Ralph concerning Cary who was ill: 'My sister Cary desiers you will excuse her not writing to you; she hath been extreame ill this day and much by fitts. Believe me, brother, shee is of ass sweet a disposition ass any creature I know living, and her affection to you is such that I thinke it expresseth what affection is or can be. In the extremitie of her fitte she will wish to me privately besides your lady for three men, my father and you are two, I thinke you may soone guesse the third, yet truely she nam'd him not. This is the first day but I thinke she hath had twenty fitts in it. I pray god they may soone cease with her. I am now in haste to goe to her therefore, . . .' etc.

In the Long Parliament, Sir Thomas Gardiner, the king's candidate for the Speakership, a hot-headed, violent man, was complained of to the House with the Lord Mayor, in December 1641, for 'putting obstructions in the way of persons signing a petition' for the removal of bishops and Catholic lords from Parliament and in support of the policy of Pym. Sir Ralph gives the answer of witnesses examined before Committee as to what Sir Thomas had said: that 'the petition tended to sedition and set men togeather by the eares'; and being told that it was intended for peace, he said: 'Is this your way of peace? Noe, it is for blood and cutting of throates, and if it cam to cutting of throates, thanke yourselves, and your blood bee on your owne heades'; 'I hate a papist, and I hate the petition worse.' On March 9 he was committed to the Tower by the House of Lords for his conduct as one of the counsel of Sir Edward Herbert, the Attorney-General, in his impeachment; and on the 22nd Gardiner was impeached himself for opposing the proceedings of Parliament on the militia in the Common Council, and getting petitions signed against the Ordinance. 'The recorder, a chiefe actor in a seditious petition. . . . The contriving was malignant in him. Hee endeavored to hinder the caling this parliament and now to destroy it. He was an abettor of Ship-money, . . . and beeing told it was against law, hee said, "Wee shall find a law for it ere long." . . . He said every man was bound by his alegence to serve the king, and noe charter could excuse them; they had already felt the waite of his little finger in Londonderry and it was a daingerous thing to anger the king.' These are some of Sir Ralph's notes of the accusations against him.

Lady Sussex writes: 'Your father I finde is full of sade thoughts. I am very sorry for Mr. Gardiner, for I fear swete Cary will cuffer for it.' And again, a few weeks later: 'Swete Cary, i hear, is now a marrede wife; i pray god it may bee happy every way to her. Your father i presume wase far ingagede or otherways i belive he woulde not have don it att this time.' The marriage had gone forward in spite of the very untoward circumstances connected with the bridegroom's father: Sir Edmund was not one to turn away from a man because he was in disgrace either with king or Parliament.

There is a pathetic list in his own hand, written amidst all the perplexing business during this, the last year of his life, of some of the linen and lace left by his wife, which he wished to give to his child on her marriage, and which he seems to have felt to be almost too sacred to be left even to Ralph's loving charge; the 'fine-lased day coyfe,' and 'fine-lased day cornet,' 'the seven handkerchers lased for pockets,' 'the twelve paires of plaine bottome cuffs,' and the 'on sette lased Lawn roled up in paper,' &c. Cary was married from her father's house in Covent Garden, and some four or five weeks after, in June 1642, the pair went on their honeymoon trip to the bridegroom's sister Palmer, living at Hill in Bedfordshire. They were of course on horseback and slept at the halfway house at Welwyn, about twenty miles from London, whence young Sir Thomas Gardiner writes to his sister-in-law, Lady Verney, whom he had just left with the rest of the family: 'After an indifferent pleasant journey, we came to our Inn at Wellen, neither came there any sorrow uppon us untill some object or other gave us an occasion to thinke on Common Garden, and truly we might well be greeved to leave such company and converse onely with hedges and ditches and durty wayes.' But he hopes for 'better entertainment tomorrow at Hill,' and sends messages to all his friends, 'which done you shall understand likewise that I am neither Puritan nor Roundhead, but am faithfully and sincerely and with all my heart, Deare madam, your truly affectionate brother.'

In another month or so, the young captain and his child-wife reach Sir Thomas Gardiner's house at Cuddesdon; he seems to be already released from prison by Parliament, and Cary writes to Ralph with great pleasure of her reception by her husband's family.

July 28.—' I must let you know how wel I lik this place. I am confident you do wiss mee so wel ass to be glad of my contentment. Except the lose of all your good companie i have more than i did look for. Whin I came my granmother bid me very wellcom and made what entertanement shee cod, more a gret dele then I expeckted, and Sir tomas and my laydy bid mee very wellcom to Coddisdon and sade they wisht it might bee my one [own] and truly uesis mee very civilly. . . . All my sistars [in law] with a grit dele of complimentes did bid mee very wellcom and truly for the contarry pleshar wee have it, for we ar abrod every day tordis evening in the coche. . . . I hope i shall give no cos to bar myself of so grit a plesshur as contentment. Deare brother lit mee now have bot contentment more that is as to let mee heare how my father and yourselfe dus. Pray when that you wright to my father present my ombel duty to him, and let him kno I am will.'

Sir Edmund was with the king at York. Ralph replies from Gorhambury : ' your letter brought mee the welcomest newes I have had a greate while [his father had been angry at his conduct in parliament]; for as I must bee a sharer in all your sufferings, soe you must give mee leave to joy in all your contentments. Those good people with whom you are now setled will still continew there love and kindnesse unlesse you faile in your due respects to them, which I am confident you will never doe. . . . I longe to meete you, . . . if the times prove quiet I purpose to visite Cudsden this sumer; however it will bee a greate contentment to mee to heare from you often.' Shortly after his marriage Captain Gardiner had joined the king's army in the north, and the young bride, writing to Ralph's wife about linen which she had been buying for her use, says : 'i never grougd my husband of any hapyness in my life more thin i did his seein of you and my missin of so mouch ioy. i cannot say anything of him for i have not sene him almost this fore months. hee is 2 hondard mils distance from mee. think what a trobill it is to mee which has so good a husband. i du pray for a hapy meeting of us all.'

It did not appear that her desire would be granted.

The Civil War began in earnest, and the decided part taken by Ralph in favour of the Parliament was very ill-looked on by the Gardiners. In September 1642 he received a taunting letter in his sister's name, but the English, handwriting, and spelling utterly unlike poor Cary's confused, ill-written scrawls. It was evidently from one of the Gardiners, probably from Sir Thomas himself.

Cary had apparently offended the fiery old royalist by wishing well to both sides 'for her owne endes,' as she wished to go to London later to stay with her brother Ralph who, as being on what was at that moment the winning side, was credited with all the evils coming on the kingdom. The wish was, no doubt, not a wise one, but certainly no unpardonable offence in the young bride of fifteen, with her father and husband fighting for the king, and her much-loved brother for the Parliament. The letter, dated September 5, Cuddesdon, was addressed 'For my Deare sister The Lady Verney, in the Peatch in Coven Garden.' It begins with contradicting some news which 'on my worde is a lye' . . 'I heare newes here wch I hope is as false . wch is that your husband is become a Traytor, but I cannot beleive that he will live and dye with the Earle of Essex to beare armes against his father, but I hope that is but his mind when he is amongst the crowd, but when he comes to take councell with his Pillow he is more wisely minded. But indeed the world now accounts it pollicy for the father to be on one side and the son on th' other, but I will resolve to wish well to both sides or at least to say nothing of either, but it shalbe for my owne ends that I may be welcome to some of my freindes at London this winter, where I would willingly be if quietnese soe soone follow this troublesome summer, so wth my best love I rest y^r most affec^{ate} sister and servant.'

The letter was some time reaching Lady Verney, but she is fully equal to the occasion and answers as soon as she receives it, with proud confidence in her husband's disinterested integrity.

September 23.— ' This day I receaved a letter with your name to itt to make me beleeve it came from you, butt truly I cannot, because itt has neyther your hand nor stile. If I knew whose itt was I would tell you [*sic*] whatt I think of itt. Butt if itt be yours I must desire you to keepe to your old opinion and believe your brother is honester then those thatt told you he was a trayter ; for a crowde he ever hated itt and I know he is soe good y^t he will nott suffer his concience to be guyded by pollecy or any hope of possible gain [scratched out]. You may if you pleas beleeve this truth butt however lett me intreat you nott to conceale your opinion for those pryvate ends you speke of in your lett, for if I were you I would nott purchase my wellcome to any place at so dere a rate ; and now sweet sister, since you cannot right yourself, I guess it will be troublesom to you to read long epistles, therfore Ile conclude myself yours to sarve you, M. V.'

Cary's husband had evidently no hand in the false letter; the handwriting is not his, and he writes to Lady Verney the same day from Cuddesdon beginning with apologies for not having written oftener, at the same time laying the blame on her own party. 'Give me leave to tell you that were not your Parliamentary officers so buisy in stopping and opening Letters, I would presume to write oftener to you. But I hate to have my secrets laid open to everybodie's view, not that I am conscious to my selfe of any ill in them, for in that respect I would not care to have them published to all the world, but me thinkes t'is neither fitt nor just that those thinges which in their owne natures were meant for a private conference betwixte one freind and another, should be read openly in Westminster Hall, and those things which were intended for the closett, to be proclaimed at the Crosse.' He thanks her for her letter, ' wherein every line was pleasant to me save onely one, and that was, you say you never had more cause to be sadd than now ; Thinke you (Madam) that God hath outlawed you and putt you out of his protection. I am confident your goodnesse will not lett you thinke soe, or doe you suppose there is an Army of wilde Beastes, such as Lyons or Tygers are come to invade the land, for if you are to deale with men endued with rationall soules, your vertues will be a sufficient sanctuary from any violence. Besides I beleeve that neither King nor Parliament have any quarrell against women, who never did either hurt save only with their tounges; and, which is most of all, if in earnest we have any warrs in the Kingdome (which I hope God will prevent) yet I dare proclaime you safe and immoveable in despight of fortune. . . . You have a father to defend you on the one side, and a husband that will doe the like on the other. These things considered, your saddnesse is to be envied, not to be pittied, and you should rather blesse God that hath so well provided for your safety in these troublesome times, than be sadd and drooping. For my owne part, come what will, I shall make sorrow a stranger to me as often as I call to mind that I hold some part in your account and love. This honour is an Antidote unto me against any affliction, &c. &c., and I shall never esteem myself miserable so long as you conceive a good opinion of me,' &c.

A week later Cary writes to Ralph himself, this time unmistakably in her own person: ' Deare brother I only writ these fu lines tu you as an expresion of the love and affection as i ow you, or els i shud a bin sillent for i am in a gr^t dill of vexsation for pore Oxford, for this day ther is 12 hondored solgars com ther, and I am afrad that thay will macke a grit masacar of all the books. They du threten them exstremly. What cannot be billeted in the toune at Oxford is sent tu all the tounes about. Wee look for thim sodenly in hopp thay willbee betar thin ther promyses, for if thay ar not, the gentell men of the contary will have litell left. Truly i spack this with a soro for we are lick tu tast it if threts prove tru, i am in a myty fright ; . . my comfort is that i think i have a louing brothar of you . . I have sente you a somethings of min which i desiar hous rome for ; i thot it wos the safest ; i hop they willbee no trobell tu you ; i thot it best to direckt tu you, becos it might not be opened. My lady and Sir tomos remembars ther sarvices to you and Mrs. Gardinar,'—Mary, afterwards maid-of-honour to the queen.

Ralph wrote to his brother-in-law in a kindly manner about 'the trunke' full of valuables. Each side accused the other of carrying off goods, 'plondaring' and confiscating, both probably with reason, as the conduct of the scattered bodies of troops going to and fro to join their respective armies was often very lawless. Sir Thomas replies rather majestically that he has not written 'because you beeing buisied about serious and difficult affaires, such indeed as the whole kingdome stands to gaze at, it might be well accounted uncivilitie (pardon me if I mistake) to write without some certainety of your acceptance beforehand. S^r my meaning is this, you have been pleased to doe me a favour and you may well expect thanks. You have given a protection to my Trunke, which my wife sent you, and you cannot desire lesse than an acknowledgment. The truth is we could trust it here no longer, for other counties are ignorant of the miseries of ours. One extravagant word, spoken but by one man, is enough to confiscate the goods of a whole family to the Parliament souldiers ; what their cause is I judge not, but methinks t'is a strange kind of justice to doe that by force which cannott be done by reason, and I am persuaded that Conscience hath much to doe on both sides, which though it may chance to be Erroneous yett ought to be respected. But these considerations enter not into vulgar hearts. The Gentry (say they) have been our Masters a long time and now we may chance to master them, and now they know their strength it shall goe hard but they will use it. I will make no Invectives, it shall suffice me to rest secure under your favour and countenance, and as your care of me hath been in some respect fatherly, so my relation must be dutifull.'

Ralph with his forgiving nature answers amicably from London : ' Swete brother I thanke you for your letter . . . . for your trunke we cannot give it protection, but if you will venture it heare, it shall run the same fortune that my owne must doe. How full of hasard that may bee, I leave to your better judgment, for they say the King is cominge hither with all his forces, I beleave he is on the march already. You say it is strang justice that the parliament soulddiers should doe that by force which cannot be done by reason. Tis true tis very unfitt for them to make themselves judges of what is reasonable, but on the other side you know when reason will not prevaile, force must be used ; the Law were nothing without a coersive power, but enough of this.

'I shall not need to tell you of the sad occasion

that keeps me thus long silent [the small-pox at Claydon amongst his children and sisters]. I am sure you know it already, and are so sensible of it that in compassion you will pardon your most affectionate brother.'

Cary replies from Hill in Bedfordshire, whither she had gone when she was first married. 'Your letter wos very willcom for last weeke wos the forst nues as i harde of the misfortin you hav had amonst you so latly. all the hous at Coddisdone and heare at Hill knuit, bot thay ware all my frends so much as not tu tell me of it till thay hard the danger wos ovar. I am hartyly glad you ar so well com hom. i pray god erge you so pra take hede of bein to ventaros, and Deare brother let mee entret you not tu be so ventaros as tu let pore Mon [Ralph's eldest boy] com hom. I am so frad of that child that i du wis him heare with all my hart. brother i du thanke you for the care you have takin of my tronk, and am resolvede it shall fare as yours dus. With many thanks for this and all other favors . . . . I heare the Kinge is comin up tu London and i am very glad att itt for i shall hop tu see my father ther, for i hope tu bee in London some part of this winter, though wher tu bee i cannot it till. My brother and sister Pollmar presents their sarvis to you and the rest of the company.'

Poor Cary, with her fond hopes of meeting her father, little thought what sorrow was in store for her, and how within a fortnight he was to lose his life at Edgehill. No letters exist from her at the time; she was possibly in London, where Ralph was, and had thus no occasion to write to him.

The winter brought fresh troubles, as the war spread further. She writes to Ralph on December 13 : ' The parlement has frittened ous from Hill, and sinc has frittened our carreg that wos comin to ous back agane, and ther it is in danger of plondarin, fore wee hear that it was pot to a vot in the house of comons wher thar my brother Pallmar's [Palmer] house shud be plondared or no. If it twos so dear brother, du your bist to barswad thim from it, for i am shur i shall have the gretist los for my brother has the fortun to send som of his away ; i shall not bee excused for six hondared pound if they shud plondar. We heare tis Sir Roger Borgin [Sir Roger Burgoyne] that moved it. If it was, i hop that you can posswad him from it, your solgers lye at Alsbery. My brother's man was taken there and 2 and fifty pound taken from him and hee imprisoned. Pray if you can save Sir Rogger Borgin's fury.'

In the midst of these dangers and troubles it is strange to come upon a letter full of flowery compliments, almost entirely ignoring the distracted state of the times. Mr. Walter Rolt addresses his epistle ' To the faire hands of the most vertuous Lady Mrs. Cary Gardiner these humbly present,' and it is tied with red silk. ' Lady, had I not the honour to be acquainted wth yor incomparable vertues, I should not adventure to offer my indigested letters to such an exact view as yo^rs whose witt and iudgment so infinitely transcend the low phrase in wch my penn discourseth. It is the noblenes of yor disposition Lady invites mee to this p^rsumption and assures mee you will grant as many pardons as I comit errors, wch indeede are infinite. M^res Bennett hath beene ill since your departure, but much comforted by the frequent visitts of my neighbour Mr. ffishe who (wth great courtship) will helpe to furnish her for her ioyrny to London, and I hope to have the honr to waite on her. At this instant (being occasiond by buisines) he is come into my house and desires his service may be p^rsented to you all, but especially to his Princesse (Alack a weladay Phillida flouts mee) : Lady you see to what a boldnes yor favours have encouraged mee. It is a liberty that hath hertofore found acceptance from those that have honourd me wth their familiarity, wch if you please to vouchsafe, I hope to guarde myselfe wth such circumspection that you shall not repent of yor favours done to yor most obliged and humble servant, WAL: ROLT.

'I humbly begg the favour to have my service p^rsented to Sr. Thomas Gardner and his unknowne Lady, yor noble husband, the Princesse, and my much hon^rd neighbour Sr. William Palmer. I write no newes, Lady, I will not trust these tell-tale papers.'

The chances of war were continually throwing power into the hands of either side to help the other. In 1643 Cary's husband was taken prisoner in an affair near Windsor. Sir Ralph was immediately appealed to, and wrote to Sir Philip Stapleton at the head of the party, with whom he had been serving a few months before on a committee of the House. 'Till last nighte I had no certainty of C^n Gardiner's being taken prisoner, neither can I yett bee satisfied whether hee is hurt, or what necessities may fall upon him in this restraint. S^r, the truth is hee married my sister, and I have sent this servant purposely to be satisfied in what condition he now is. If you please to doe me this favour to obtaine him leave to speake with with him and to afford my brother such respect as may be for a gentleman in his distresse, you will infinitely oblige your . . .,' &c.

Two days afterwards, Captain Gardiner himself wrote from Windsor Castle, 'to his most honored sister the Lady Verney these present. Madam, I am now released out of Windsor Castle, yett I shall never forgett the kindnesse wch your Ly^{pp} hath shewd me, and it was part of the happinesse that I fancied to myselfe when I was taken prisoner that I would have seene you before I got out, but I am commanded away by my lord Generall. Otherwise I should have gotten leave to have the freedom of one day and so have waited on you at London, thatt I might have expressed how I am with all my heart and without any compliment your most faithfull servant and loving Brother.'

He adds a note to Ralph who had obtained his release from his parliamentary allies : 'I am now att my liberty, and have approved by the surest signs how much you have been my friend. I hope God that has preserved me hithertoe will yett give me life that I may face to face expresse to you that I am your,' &c.

In July 1645, the young soldier, who had been sent out with a detachment of the king's army from Oxford, was engaged in a skirmish at Ethrop, a village four or five miles from Ailesbury, and killed on the spot.

Mrs. Isham writes : 'On Aug. 29, this day 3 wicke, i sent you worde as your Sis. Cary was a widdoe and the jointer the Dr. did send for as she mite geet somthinge, for never was a woman lefte porer and lost a beter Hus : But thes miseres become upone us all heare or as bad.'

Dr. Denton, sending the first news to Ralph, says : 'Y^r Brother Gardiner hath left a sad disconsolate widdowe great wth child : she hath lost a very kind Husse, who, though he showed it in severall thinges, yett he did it more especially in the differences betweene her and her Noverca [mother-in-law]. all wch he had soe handsomly reconciled that there was growinge great mutuall love and respect betweene all parties. I pray lett us know who hath her jointure and howe we may come by it . . . : he had an Intention to have setled as much uppon her as he could (soe well did he love her) but God hath p^{r}vented it.' A few weeks later he writes : 'When her husband died he left her not a penny in the house, her father and mother when I left her (wch was above 3 weeks since) had not and I am confident will not contribute a penny towards her releife. I had left her penniless ; had I not supplyed her wth a small pittance of £5 which I feare is spent. . . . To adde yett more to her affliction, her Brother Harry Gardiner (who was and would have beene very kind and helpfull to her) is since slaine, whereby the hopes of recovering 60 or £80 arrears for her use (the only supply she could expect to keepe her alive) is almost frustrated. She looks for her time w^thin lesse then a month and I feare will want many necessaries. I doubt not but my wife will helpe her all she can to whome I spake to supply her farther (if she were necessitated) out of her pittance. . . . I wish I had a purse, estate and power answerable to my heart and desires to help all of her own name. How^r those mites I have I will cast in to their advantages, and especially to her, her father's shee-darlinge and soe like him. I heare since I came away that her bed mother and her husband are kinde to and sollicitous for her.'

Ralph writes to her from France : ' Sweetheart, I heare of your misfortune and suffer with you. I feel in a higher degree then either I can or will express. But at God's decree we must not repine. The best go first, and tis a mercy to be taken away from the evil to come. Were I able to advise or serve you in anything I should do it most gladly, but at this distance I know not well how.'

He has therefore written to the Doctor for help. In

October Cary's baby was born, and Henry Verney writes to Ralph:

'My sister was brought to bed of a gurl to all our grifes [because a boy would have made her more important to the Gardiners]. She is well . . . . and intreated mee to desier you to lend her the blacke and yellow bed which standes in the inner rome in the parlour chamber; it is but a meane wan; if you can spare it, let her have it poore sole, I thinke she wants it.' Her condition was indeed pitiable; a widow at eighteen, with a baby born some four months after its father's death. The child proved sickly, with weak eyes, the comfort and the grief of its mother, and in later years became almost blind. The conduct of the Gardiners under the new circumstances changed entirely. When first she married, Cary, as the daughter of the influential Knight Marshal, on intimate terms with the king, and sister of a man highly respected on the parliament side, was a useful and valuable addition to the Gardiner family, who were proud of the connection. As the wife of the gallant young soldier, the eldest son of his house, warmly attached to his engaging little wife, she had been treated with the utmost consideration. Cary is described in all the letters as of a gentle, kindly, affectionate disposition, and in later times is spoken of as exceedingly popular and very good company. Now her father and husband were [dead, and her brother in exile, she was nobody; she had not even a son and heir, and could be of no use in any schemes of aggrandisement. Her place at Cuddesdon, even her board, were grudged her; difficulties were made about her jointure. 'Sir tomas and my Lady' were extremely unkind, and Mrs. Isham and Doll Leeke write with the utmost indignation concerning their conduct. Not long after her husband's death, Dr. Denton writes that Sir Thomas had made complaints of her which he is confident she does not deserve. 'Ill instruments there will be, and she has suffered much from them, but I hope God in his due time will make her innocent carage appear. I am extremely cozened if she be not much her father's daughter. In your absence I shall doe what I can for her, but I should be glad you were here to doe the businesse better. I pray write to her, for she hath need enough of comfort, and I know it would please her.'

The temper of the fierce old Solicitor-General was not improved by being turned out. 'I am sory,' wrote Lady Sussex, 'they have put Sr Gardiner outt of his poste, becas i doubt it may be of some prejudis to your sister.' The forlorn young widow with her baby took refuge at Claydon, where the other sisters were living at all odd times in great anxiety and poverty after the departure of Sir Ralph and his wife and the sequestration of the estate. They were even in some peril from the parties of lawless soldiers of both armies, who were passing to and fro continually, as Claydon lay on the borderland between them, during the time that the king occupied Oxford.

It must indeed have been a sorrowful little household of women and children, with only the protection of the old steward Roades, and as unlike as possible to the cheerful, happy family party, which had gathered at Claydon, under the wing of Sir Edmund and Margaret Verney, in the previous ten years. From time to time Captain Edmund or Major Henry contrived to spend a few days with their sisters, which afforded them some protection; and once Tom takes great credit to himself for having turned aside a detachment of soldiers 'att the surrender of Oxford, for I gave out to all those commanders that took up men for Flanders and other parts, that I marched to Claydon myself, therefore desired them to go another way, which they did. And by that means Claydon was free from that insufferable charge altogether by my means, which I am confident did save his Lordshipp of Claydon more than seven pounde ten shillings,' which sum Ralph had lent him above his allowance, and Tom, *more suo*, was finding excuses not to repay.

After about two years, Cary married a Mr. Stewkeley, a man of property in Hampshire, who seems to have been a kindly amiable husband, very proud of his fair young wife. He appears to have had a large estate and to have lived handsomely. Cary talks of 'our being thirty in family,' and having a large household to manage. They see Morley, Bishop of Winchester, an old friend of Ralph, and other magnates; there are dinings and dancings going on ; existence has altogether become prosaic and comfortable, a great contrast to the wearing anxieties, to the passionate earnestness with which both sides in the struggle were taking life when first she married.

CHAPTER V.

THE RAISING OF THE STANDARD, 1642.

> The shout
> Of battel now began, and rushing sound
> Of onset ended soon each milder thought.—MILTON.

AFTER the attempt on the five members the chance of any reconciliation between the king and his people became every day more hopeless. To watch the negotiations between them, as given in Mr. Gardiner's most interesting volumes, the downward steps towards that Civil War which had now become inevitable, though both parties were struggling to avoid it by every means in their power, as a fearful misfortune, is like following the course of a full and rapid river just above a great fall: it is stayed for a moment behind the shelter of a promontory, or delayed by a turn in the banks or rocks in the stream, but the resistless current sweeps on to the fearful plunge, unaffected in reality by any of the puny obstacles which seem to control it; hurrying on at increasing speed, with a power which nothing can arrest.

The letters in the Verney correspondence reflect the growing alarm, as the impossibility of agreement

Charles 1.
from a picture by Vandyck at Claydon House.

between the king and the Parliament becomes daily more apparent.

Lady Sussex, writing to Ralph on January 7, thanks him for his help in her business and then goes on: 'for panton truly i thinke him to bee a very carles deboyse man. . . . Wee have beene at our defosyons [devotions] to-day, and ther was somethinge rede from your Parlyment to have all the tranede bandes in a redines [readiness]. the are all in great fear at Sentobornes, and ever hose [every house] they say have bought armes and gons to defend them. i hope i shall be safe heer, though i have neither. It is ill nues to hear there is a pese betwixt Spane and frince, suer the will com uppon us, and helpe eyrlande. I pray God keepe us from the misyres that other nasyons have sufferde by ware. I am very glade to hear your father is so will agane. i have presented him with some ihely [jelly] and ther is eyght pots for you and your lady, how [who] i beceche you rember me most affecynatly to.'

Jan. 19.—'I pray let not your father goo abrode to sone, though now he bee will, he will be apte to take coulde yet.'

Jan. 29.—'I pray god ther may bee agreement betwixt the kainge and his pepell and that pore eyrlande may have some helpe. i pray god your hoses may agree and then i hope all will goo will.' A few days later she sends 'podinges and appiles; give your father some and a pot of the ihely; the pephains loke ill favordy but the are nice and swete.'

VOL. II.   G

Feb. 23.—'i hear your parlyment disposes of all plases in the coustam hose ; i pray sende me word if it bee so for Mrs Poly i belive woulde feene porshis on [purchase one].'

April 5.—'I am truly sorry to heare your parlyment goes on still in cuch a violent way. I pray god wee do not all cuffer by it.'

A fortnight later : 'my esex rents i am suer will be well pade, for the have good peniworth and forfet ther leses if the pay not ; i doubt bucingamsher rents will not be pade well. . . . I thinke you for your nues ; i have harde non good a great while ; i pray god sende some : i hear my lorde of argile hath discouerede some thinge of an armey that shoulde come out of iorlonde to assist the Kainge against us ; i hope it tis not truth ; i pray you sende me worde whether it bee or not ; you have put done the diurnals wee hear ; I am sory for it, for wee was glade to know what you dide; it tis a great favor for you to right so often havinge daly cuch great affars. . . . i pray sende me worde how thinges goo with your father ; i mene in his plas and otherwise.'

Writing again to Ralph's wife she says :

'Swite Mrs. Varny, this goeing of the Kainges to Yorke gives truble to us all, I pray God sende us pese, and then I hope he will make a spedy returne ; I am hartyly trubled for your good father, for if hee shoulde goe after, sartinly it woulde bee very dangours for him cominge from the hote bathes, I pray God derect him for the best, and let me intret a lyne or to from you as sone as you know what his resolutyons are.'

Since the ordinance passed by Parliament for the command of the militia, in direct opposition to the king, the breach between them had widened still more. Urged by the queen, Charles had gone to the north and endeavoured to gain possession of Hull, which was precious as a seaport, where he might receive support from abroad, and which also contained a magazine of arms. Sir John Hotham, the governor, however, had refused him entrance, and the Parliament had entirely supported him in his resistance, and sent a peremptory order that the arms should be removed.

Lady Sussex writes to Ralph at the beginning of May:

'i am very glade you have so good nues from Eyerlande ; i pray God the may have victory still, and then i hope ther will sone bee ane ende of that warr. God keepe it from us hear ; suer the Kainge will harly have pouer hear to ovourcom ; the parlyment will govern. The Kainge sartinly will bee very highly displesede with your mesege to Sir John Hotham and the sogers att hole [Hull] ; my brother wortly foles [foolish] man hath put him selfe into a fare bisyness ; sartinly great punnisment your parlyment will lay uppon them all ; and I say I thinke the desarve it, for them to oppose the parlyment in cuch a way ; when you right to me i pray sende me worde what you thinke will becom of them ; for i have sent up to loke after my rintes; i doubt this nues of Hull will make them pade slowly in, and i must pay supsityes for all my lordes estate and myne to; j pray God mende the distractyons of thes times.'

A petition in very high-flown language, of which Sir Francis Wortley (brother of Lady Sussex) was the chief mover, had been presented to the king by some Yorkshire gentlemen in the name of the county, begging the king to forbid the removal of arms from Hull. Not long afterwards another much wiser document was prepared, repudiating the first. Rushworth, who had been sent to the north with some papers from the Parliament, was present when it was brought to the king, and gave a copy of it to the House. Sir Ralph's account is as follows :

'The King enquired of the petitioners, whether they would defend his majesties person according to there duties. He also asked their advise how to vindicate his majestie's honour for the affront at Hull, and how to put him in possession of the town.' They answered that ' they will defend his person accordinge to there duties and the lawes of the land '—a very prudent and cautious answer. ' They know not how to advise concerning Hull, but to adhere to the councell of the parliment, who are intrissed in it by two messages.' A committee of the Houses was resident in Yorkshire and reported that ' Twine a papist cried, "Com, com, let the sourd doe it," and that Wortley called, "For the King, for the King," and drew his sourd with 20 others against the comittee.'

For this Sir Francis and other principal men were to have been summoned before the House, but when messengers were sent down to apprehend them, they produced warrants from the king, 'charging them not to remove out of the County of York.' Lady Sussex writes, concerning her brother's offence :

'I am sory to hear my brother wortly hath cariede himsefe so folisly. Ane unfortunat man he is every way—your parlyment suer will lay hevy punishment uppon him. i cannot but have some sense of him as he is my brother, but i may speke it to you, he hade never much of my hart for i thought him ever full of fanity, though belive me he hath many good parts hade he wisdom to have managede them.'

Mrs. Eure writes to Ralph from Malton in Yorkshire in great distress at the unsettled state of the country. 'I know you heare all the newes before we doe, thoe we are soe neare the kinge, for we see not the face of A sole. . .' 'May 5. I hope the parliment will laye no more taxes on the cuntrye for rents are paid noe where. God helpe us. we are liket to have misorobull times I am afraid at my hart. . . I pray set your helping hand to mend it first by prayer, then you know what folows.' Two days later: 'O that the swete parliment woold com—with the olive branch in its mouth, it would refresh and glad all our harts here in the north. Wee are soe maney frighted peopell ; for my part if I here but A dore creeke I take it to be A drom, and am redey to run out of that little valer I have. poore Sir

John Hotham is so afrighted if anything comes but neere him, that when ouer goods com but to Harborow he sent to know what they ware. God he knows as there was nothing but clothes and 2 hogsheds of wine: the poore man is deseved if he thought to have found aneything else.'

'May 21 : I consider thes are ill times for tenants althou my land lies as well as aney, by reson they are within on daies journey as neere to York as London, so as thay may send ther cattell hither. All things growe one by degreese here, what will becom of all I know not. I dought no good. The newes here is that the parliment men intend to come down with twenty thowsant to atend them, but I wish you all to loocke to your selves, for you will have A now [enough] to incounter with you, for the wimin in this cuntrey begin to rise; there hath bin A 100 with the King, and above, to have these greevaunces redrest, and he hath given them soe good content that they saye he is as proper A man as is in ingland. I wish you all to take heed of wimen, for this verey varmin have puld down an inclosure which sum of them ware put in prison for it by the justisis, that had their pipe to goe before them, and ther alle and cakes to make themselves merey when thay had done thare fetes of activity. I right you this newes to let you see what brave spirits is in the north. I wishe all ware well ended, for things stand in soe ill a condition here as we can make noe money of our Colpits. If rents faill and those faill to, we shall be in A hard case.

You will not read my leter for I rit it in such haste
I have ofered to read it myselfe but cannot, soe I will
make an end, and let you have it to trie what you
can doe. Your faithful and loving Ante.'

Sir Edmund's position was a painful one, with
the prospect of being bound in honour to fight for
a cause with which he could not sympathise, while
he was not entirely trusted by either side. No
wonder that Lady Sussex wrote to Ralph : ' Your
father i finde is full of sade thoughts.' In another
letter she writes about Sir Edmund's joining the king
at York : ' he saith littill to me of it, but sath if the
kainge commands he must goo : I dorst not say more
to him becose i woulde not have him thinke you sade
any thinge to me of it: you are truly good and considerate of him ever way: happy is hee that hath
such a childe and i that have cuch a frinde as yourself,
how [who] i proteste i do and shall ever love and
valy above any one [' Methinks the lady doth protest
too much '] . . . you i know have serious thoughts
consideringe your father many ways.' A little later :
' Your father sende me worde the kainge hath given
him leve to stay till he sendes for him : i am very
glade of it for when he gooes i doubt the love of the
parlyment hee will lose quite, which i fear will make
them do him any ill offis the can. I am sory to hear
the lordes are rasinge mony and hors ; truly if the
sende to my lorde wee will parte with non : i hope
the will not for wee are pore, and my lorde of his
estate but tenent for life cannot till how to pay a debt

if we rone into it : your parlymente still goo so hye that i fear wee shall all bee runede by it.' June 20 : 'Your father lyke a good sarvant i belive is much for his master, and so i thinke wee are all ; i wish he may keepe that pouer that is fit for him, but I confes i woulde not have the papests to powerfull ; the most of them i belive woulde be glade to see the prodistants of inglende in as misirable a condisyon as the are in Eyerlande, if it was in ther pouer to make them so. In a fue wekes now i hope wee shall see all that is intendede ; i pray daly wee may have no fitinge ; i hope the Kainge will commande your father to stay wher he is ; i presume it will bee more to his adfantige than to goo. . . . [P.S.] Sir, Since I right this letter i resevede your last, many thinkes for your nues ; truly the Lordes protestasyon my thinkes is a very good on ; to defende the Kainges parson honor and estate and lafull progative, and priviledge of parlyment ; my thinkes every on shoulde subscribe to this. I am loth to ete in puter yet, but truly i have put up most of my plat, and say it tis solde, i hope the will sende to boro no mony of my lorde ; if the doo wee must denye, it tis anofe for us to pay the subsities ; the talke strange thinges of my lorde of Iesex that he will seek the Kainge to London dede or alive ; this is hye my thinke for pepell to talke so, i pray god keepe us in safty and pese, and that wee may be to gather on month this somer att lest.'

The protestation here referred to was one signed by thirty-five peers, who therein expressed their belief that the king had no intention of making war on his Parliament, 'but that all his endeavours tend to the firm and constant settlement of the true Protestant religion; the just privileges of Parliament; the liberty of the subject; the law, peace, and prosperity of this kingdom.' This protestation may be said to mark the beginning of that party of which Clarendon was the moving spirit.

Ralph himself writes in a letter to Lady Barrymore at this time: 'Peace and our liberties are the only things wee aime at; till wee have peace I am sure wee can enjoy noe liberties, and without our liberties I shall not heartily desire peace: both these togeather may make us all happy, but on without the other I must confesse can never satisfie mee.'

But though each party made use of nearly the same terms, the difficulty of agreement between them as to what constituted the 'true Protestant religion,' and 'our liberties,' was the rock on which all their negotiations inevitably split. The king had called on all the lords and commons who would support him, to come to York. The lord keeper had gone there, bringing with him the great seal, and many other peers and gentlemen had followed, while a large number of members of the Lower House showed their distrust of the Parliamentary leaders by absenting themselves from the sittings.

To the great distress of his father, Ralph Verney continued to hold with the Parliament, though the consequent estrangement between them made him utterly miserable, all the more as he evidently began to feel uncertain whether his party was not now going 'too hye,' as Lady Sussex so often repeated. Nothing could be less like the 'light heart' with which both parties in France undertook the wars of the Fronde just then beginning, than the spirit of Englishmen, Cavaliers and Puritans alike.

Lady Sussex writes: *June* 24.—' Both sides promisis so fare that i cannot see what it tis the shoulde fight for. Thes fines and subsities on both sides will be a ruin to this kaindom and us. if thinges should longe holde as they are, we have nede fast and pray as much for this kaindom as for Eirlande. I am very sensable of the many ways of your truble, i wish i could share a part with you. i am very sory to hear your lady is not well, it hath been a general disese, a sore throat with a cold. i have been much out of tune with it, and many in my hose.'

Mrs. Eure writes at the same time from the north: 'Times are soe bad here as we have not made on peney of ower coles, and we have not received on peney from misterton, soe my husband was forst to send for thos rents as were gathered up to keepe life and sole together, which was but on hundred pounds. I have still about halfe my rents behind. . . .'

> 'We do not suffer here alone,
> Though we are beggar'd, so's the King;
> 'Tis sin t'have wealth when he has none,
> Tush! poverty's a Royal thing!'

wrote Brome cheerily, a royalist attorney turned song-writer. Mrs. Eure went on with her lamentations : 'I am in such a great rage with the parliment as nothing will passify me, for thay promised as all should be well, if my Lord Straford's hed ware of, and since then there is nothing beter, but I thinke we shall be undon with taxis, and if wee have no rents neither, it will be a hard cace. This daye the King hath set forth an answer to a boocke as cam forth 26 of Maye. I here as he will set but on more forth, and that shall conclud all ; and so much for riting. We here strange newes from London, which is that maney have oferid to keepe horses for the parliment to fight against there kinge, and that my lord of Holond is generald, which puts me in the most comfort that we shall have peace, for he hath had good fortewen not to fight hitherto [he had, indeed, been suspected of cowardice]. I hope he will prove luckey still. I am sorey as your father comes not down all this while ; I beleeve as he was expected before this time.'

Possibly Sir Edmund still had hopes of an agreement between the king and the Parliament. Lady Sussex writes at the end of June : 'I pray god your parlyment may still continue in the good mynde the was in ; for i harde ther was something sade that showede the was inclynede to an accomadatyon : if that good worke was nowe don i hope we may live to see some good times agane, and our frinde happy and cherfull. . . . i hope your father will not goo into the north if ther bee likelyhode of an accomidasyon : the kainge, i belive, will thinke he may do him better sarvis wher he is [i.e. in Parliament] then to com to him.'

The hopes of an 'accomidasyon' were but ill-founded. The last propositions of the Parliament had been indignantly rejected by Charles, who declared that, should he grant such demands, he 'would no longer be more than the image, but the mere shadow of a king.'

Both sides were now levying troops and collecting money and plate from their followers. Charles attempted to get possession of his fleet in the Downs, which, however, declared for the Parliament with Warwick as their admiral, and a similar attempt on the magazine of arms in Leicestershire failed. This was accepted as a declaration of war by the whole Parliament, lords and commons; they appointed a committee of safety on July 4, and the Civil War virtually began. Though Sir Edmund did not join the king at York until July, he had made preparations beforehand for taking up arms in his cause. On June 19 he wrote to his steward to get his horses into condition in view of a campaign: 'I praye take upp my mare .. and lett her be kept att house. I shall shortly send for my coach mairs. When my mare Lea hath foaled, let the foale bee knockt on the head, and the mare taken to Howse, for I cannot spare her this summer. . . . There will be a press shortly in the country. I praye let there bee care taken to thinck of some able boddyed young man to goe in King's roome for I am loth he should goe.'

He writes again on June 30 : 'When I sent for my Arms I forgott to send for one peece as I thinck, and that was for my Gorgett, it is that which goes about the neck, I pray lett Will Browne looke for it, and faill not to send it to mee to bee heere on Tuesday next by Moyses, praye forgett it not, you must send mee upp by him a paire of Pistolls with firelocks, ther is but one paire of them left at Cleydon. Send mee woard wheather Tom Isham has bought mee another gelding or noe, you shall receave a saddle from Mr. Busby, lett it bee well layed upp, bidd the groome bee carefull of my Horses.'

Ralph had also written for 'a paire of my father's Pistolls of the Best sort ; my father tells mee there is a paire that have White Stocks, and part of the Locks are Blew, and they are very light. Let Moses bring them upp, and bee carefull to keepe them from wett, and let the Moulds, and other implements belonging to them come upp with them.'

On July 5 came the news of the arrival of a ship in the Humber, bringing munitions of war for the king, sent by the queen from Holland. Lady Sussex writes : 'The quine ever is plesede if she have so many favourites with hur ; i doubt we shall all fare the worse for it ; so many heds togather will bee bysie in ther plots aganst us.' Again : 'I pray god rase up some good harts about the kainge to seconde the desiers of his parlyment.' On July 11 it was declared by both Houses that the king had begun the war. He had granted commissions for raising cavalry, and had placed himself at the head of a small force at Beverley. It was resolved in the Commons that an army of 10,000 should at once be raised, and Lord Essex was appointed general.

Sir Edmund had now gone to join the king at York, and with sad anticipation of the bad times to come, wrote letters of direction to his steward : ' I praye have the carbines att home in reddyness for the defence of the Howse if need bee ; and gett powder and Bulletts reddy ; for I feare a time maye come when Roags maye looke for booty in such houses ; therfore bee not unprovided ; but saye noething of it, for that maye invite more to mischeefe that thinck not of it yett.' Again : ' I praye have a care of my howse, that roages break not into it, have stoare of bullett and powder, and gett some boddy to lodg in the howse that maye defend it if need bee. Have my waggon in readiness, if I should att any time send for it ; gett in all such monnys as are owing you with all speede, for wee shall certainly have a great warr. Have a care of harvest, and God send uss well to receave the blessing of and returne thancks for it. I can saye no more—Your loving master.'

Ralph also writes : ' I thinke you have lodged the people in ye hous very well. I pray, bee careful of the Dores in ye Daytime. I thinke 2 men were enough to watch in ye Towne [village] a nights, untell the times grow fuller of dainger.'

Cary Gardiner, writing from the neighbourhood of

Oxford, says: 'Here is nothing but soulgers going up and down. The first that came, under the command of Col: Brown, a cochman, passed very quickly away, and lefte no scores. But Coll: Goodwin's soulgers, and those that came to guard Lord Saye's person has pillaged all the colleges but three already, and this day are about the rest; and say when they have don they will see what pillage the contry has, so, for aught as I see, we are lik to be undone.

'My lady Lee on Thursday came to Oxford to speake with my lord Saye concerning the armes she had sent to the Kinge. If she could she would have made peace with him. But he not being a courtier would not listen to her, so she returned away with a great blame the contry laid upon her; her being a widow made her to be a little pittied, twas that her fearfulness. Pray God send us better times or I shall wish myself at London.'

A short time before Hyde had taken refuge with Lady Lee at Ditchley, fearing to be stopped by the Parliament on his road to join the king at York. The lady's coach with six horses carried him to a village near Coventry, thirty miles, starting in the morning; 'they then took their horses out of all roads at night,' and at length reached York. So that for many reasons Lady Lee was in bad odour with the Parliament.

Lady Sussex writes: 'My lady Monmouth[1] hath

---

[1] Her father-in-law Carey was the first to bring the news of Queen Elizabeth's death to James I., and was created Earl of Monmouth.

bene with me, how [who] is a much trublede woman ; she fiers all will goo as ill as may bee, but i have bettir hopes.' Mrs. Eure is more despairing : ' In my poore jugment this times can bring no good end to them : all that wimen can dou is to praye for beter, for sure it is an ill time with them of all cretuers for thay are exposed to all vilinoeys. God can turne all this in A moment ; it is want of ower prayers that this jugmentes are com uppon a nation.' In another letter : 'I am much troubled to see things goe as they dou ; it will bring us all to rewin ; neither papist, nor puritan, aye nor protestant but will be the loosers by it, I believe, but I trust in God as he will helpe us, for man is unabell of himselfe to doe aneything, and that I doe dailey see. I pray God as that side may prevaile as hath truth on its side.'

On August 9 the king proclaimed Essex and his followers traitors ; the Commons in reply called upon all members to swear that they would live and die with the Earl of Essex, " for the safety of the King's person, the defense of both Houses of Parliament . . . and for the preservation of the true religion, laws, liberties, and peace of the kingdom,' and on the 18th issued a counter-declaration by which all those who assisted the king were pronounced to be traitors. Preparations for war were vigorously carried forward on both sides. The 22nd of August,

He was tutor to Prince Charles (afterwards Charles I.), with whom his son was ' bred up' and sent to travel. He was killed at Marston Moor.

THE RAISING OF THE STANDARD, 1642

1642, was a memorable day in Sir Edmund Verney's career. The king set up the royal standard at Nottingham and confided it to his keeping.

A good deal of outward pomp marked the occasion, though flashing armour and bright sword-scarves covered heavy hearts.

The standard itself needed twenty supporters; it was 'much of the fashion of the City Streamers used at the Lord Mayor's Show,' old Rushworth tells us, and 'on the top of it hung a Flag, the King's Arms quartered, with a Hand pointing to the Crown . . . above this motto, Give Cesar his due'; a motto neither side would have objected to—but *what* was Cæsar's due had yet to be determined in many a hard-fought field. There were several knights, baronets, and 'three Troops of Horse to wait upon the Standard and to bear the same backwards and forwards with about 600 Foot Souldiers. It was conducted to the Field in great State, His Majesty, the Prince [of Wales], Prince Rupert, with divers other Lords and Gentlemen . . . besides a great company of Horse and Foot in all to the number of 2,000.' At the last moment, when the trumpets were to sound and the herald at arms was to make a proclamation of the causes of setting up the standard, the king, with characteristic vacillation, called for the paper, made some hasty erasures, and gave it back to the herald, 'who proclaimed the same to the People though with some difficulty after his Majesty's corrections . . . and the whole Multitude threw up their Hats and cried God save the King.' The standard was carried back into the castle at night, and the same ceremony was gone through in the king's presence on the two following days, 'with sound of drums and Trumpets.'

But in spite of Rushworth's impressive capitals, the People and the Multitude, in a military sense at all events, were conspicuous by their absence. ' Melancholy men,' says Clarendon, ' observed many ill Presages about that time. There was not one Regiment of foot yet drawn thither, so that the Train'd-bands, which the Sheriff had drawn together, were all the strength the King had for his Person, and the Guard of the Standard. There appeared no Conflux of Men in obedience to the Proclamation; the Armes, and Ammunition were not yet come from York, and a General Sadness cover'd the whole Town.'

Finally, to complete the mournful signs of the times, the standard ' was blown down . . . by a very strong and unruly wind, and could not be fixed again in a day or two, till the tempest was allayed.' But Sir Edmund Verney was no fair-weather friend. ' Severely honest in time of peace and undauntedly valiant in time of war,' he had won what every soldier covets—the post of honour and of danger, and he said as he accepted the charge: ' That by the grace of God [his word always] they that would wrest that standard from his hand, must first wrest his soul from his body.'[1] His title of Knight

---
[1] *Lloyd's Memorials.*

Marshal, with its more peaceful duties, is merged in that of 'the Standard-Bearer,' by which he is henceforth distinguished in the family annals.

Doll Leeke who, in attendance on Lady Sydenham, was with a part of the royal army, writes to Ralph to reassure him about his father; 'the enemy are very near us; my unkell will not be amongst them, for the King has given him the Standard, and he must goe no further then that; it will not remove this 3 or 4 dayes, and so long he will be safe.' She had written confidently to Lady Verney from York, a fortnight before: 'The King is in very good condition and increaseth in strength every day; we have nothing but good nuse to send you.' She still hoped apparently that Ralph would go the same way as his father, for she ends by saying: 'I for my part wish for no more men but your husband, and I do so hartily desire him that I dreame of nothing els. I am confident that he will come. I pray tell him so and present my serves to him.' She writes again from the camp to Lady Verney on September 1: 'I have sent you all the nuse; by the diferanc of my relation and that which you have heard allredy you will be confermed in your opinion of our cavilers [cavaliers]. I am confident thay will difer extremely. I cannot urdg you to beleve my report becaus I find it will not plese you . . . in myself I am satisfied of the truth of it or els I wold not have right a word of it, for willingly I desire not to be the reporter of a ly: for my confidenc of our having the better of the parlement I do not remember, but if thay will promis to fight no better it will strenghten my hopes; but I cannot se if we have the better how you will sufer, for sure your father will have power to save your husband, and if the King faill I beleve my unkell will hardly come of with his life or any that are with them; therfor your condision is not so bad as you beleve it, at least I conseve so. I think non in more dainger then myself and our company, for if we lous the day, what will become of us I know not. We do not louk for any faver of the other side. I do not love to think of it and I trust I shall not live to se it. Part of our trouble now is that the wether grous could and it will be ill traviling, and we have those things which should have kept us warme at Yorke; but by that time we have folloed the camp another yeare we shall have more witt.'

Lady Sydenham writes to Lady Verney at the same time in a more anxious strain. She begins: 'My dere hart,' and wonders that Lady Verney has not received a letter she had sent in answer to one which arrived 'by my lorde of Arundell. . . . My hart i ded as much long for your anser of min, becaus that you ded exspres a trobell in yours to me about your hosbands reselushons. My dere hart now i hope that you ar resalefed [resolved] of what he will do, and that i finde is better to won [one], thin to levef [live] betwen hopes and fars what will happen. i kno he has chossen the strongest part, but i cannot thinke the best, but i am confedent he dus beleve tis the best, and for that he chos it. But truly my hart it stagers me that he shold not se clerly all thar wayes, being it tis so aparrant, for how tis for the lebberty of the subget to tacke all from thim which ar not of thar mind, and to puld don thar houses, and impresen thim, and levef [leave] thim to the marsy of the unruly multetude—i cannot fined that this is the lebberty of the subgete. Nor do i find that it is in god's lay [law] to tacke arms aganst thar laful king to depos him, for shuer thay havef [an original way of spelling 'have'] not mad his parrsen knon to all thos that thay havef implyed in this war to spare him and not to kill him. But i trost god will protecket him, and my dere if any of my frinds fall in this quarill i trost thar soles will be happy, for shuer tis laful to fitt for won's laful king. i ded belevef that thay wold resafe the king's mesech as thay havef don whin it was sent, for shuer tis not pese which thay desier; shuer thay trost in that myti hoste. Dere hart you say in your leter that i sholed mistrost your lovef to me becaus that i hafe not resafed your leters; truly my dere it was never grondid uppon such a weeke fondashon as to let such a thing shacke it, for you won my hart by your worth, and till I fined that wanting i cannot let my lovef gro les; for tho you shold not ryet [write] yet i shold be confedent that you lovefed me, for i am shuer till i do sumthing to desarf your desfavor i shall belefe i havef it, and i am confedent that i never shall never do any thing to lesen your good openyon of me, for my dere i do lovef you with my sole. . . . Thar is non that you havef a more abslate power over thin her that is fathfully your tru frind and houmbell sarvant to my last of beinge. Anne S.'

The king's position was really very far from being secure, and he evidently shrank from carrying on the war, though, as usual, he was swayed to and fro by the opinions of those about him. Lady Sussex wrote: 'I hear from mr bakon how [who] i belive hath it from [*sic*] brother that the Kainge is very much inclinede to pese, and prest much he is to goo on in this way of ware by some ill speriets he gives is eare to, which i becech god may bee removede. . . . i belive the Kainge is not resolvede in his one thoughts wher to setall.'

The defeat of the royalists in a skirmish near Coventry strengthened the peace party with the king, and on August 25 he sent Lord Southampton with Culpepper and Uvedale to London with a proposal that a commission should be appointed to treat for peace, and at the same time he reiterated his desire to maintain the Protestant religion and the laws.

Lady Sussex writes to Ralph on Aug. 28: 'i must thinke you for your lettir, and till you i am very glade all is will at cladon, for i hope wee shall have now the blesinge of pese, my lorde sashamton and dosete sent to boro my koch as the went by, and truly i coulde not bee so unsivell to denye itt. i hope i dide not do a mise [amiss] they gooinge about so good a worke. I hear there hath bene a good yonge captin of the kainges side since with Sr Tomis Mutis, and he i belive hath tolde the truth of all; wee shall have noe fitinge, for the kainge hath neither mony nor men. Ther cam in fue or non att all aftir the standarde was set up, it semes the kainge sent and gave much of his monyes to the trane bandes in yorkesher and other places, thinkainge to make them suer to him, and when he woulde have hade them they all fell of, and sade the woulde not fite aganst ther brethrne, and ever daye his army lesones, the fall away from him; this yonge man was att coventry; to or thre and twenty was kailde; on of my lorde Scidmor's [? Scudamore] brothers was shot in the arme so clos to his shoulder that is arme must bee cut of. My lorde doset sent me worde hee woulde wate uppon me within fue dayes, but i presume that was but in a complyment, i hope he doth not intende it; he sade he hade brought that which woulde bringe pese if the parlyment woulde harken to it; suer the may make ther one condisyons now. God's power is above all, wee coulde not have thoght this woulde have bene within this fue dayes, for that side to submite furst; sartinly the good prayrs hath prefalede much; now i beelive ther will bee much bisynes in the parlyment shorly; for god sake com to me as sone as you can and your swite lady, for i fear i shall not now keepe you as i wode doo; i promisede my selfe your compiny on quartir of a year att lest, and i fear i shall not have that happines but a littill time.'

In reply to the king's proposal the Parliament had refused to treat until the royal standard should be taken down, and the charge of treason against their members withdrawn, and a second attempt on Charles's side to come to terms was equally unsuccessful. Each party meanwhile prepared to carry on the war, and various parts of the country in turn declared for one side or the other.

The following letters show how grievously Sir Edmund felt the division between him and Ralph, how had taken the oath of adherence to the parliamentary cause, and was now therefore in avowed opposition to the king. It must indeed have been a trying time to Ralph also. It was no light matter in those days to take the side of the Parliament; the points in dispute were matters of life and death to every individual, male and female, in the kingdom, and the agony of doubt upon questions which are now to us as clear as the day must have been as the dividing asunder of soul and body. On September 5 Lady Sussex writes to him : 'I hear my lorde fakelande and my lorde Spencer went thro' Sentarbones on Satterday; i imagin it was with some propositions from the Kainge. i pray God the may bee such as may be yieldede to, but I beleeve ther will bee a longe trety before the are brought about for pese, i pray God sende it att last. I long to hear how your father takes your protistasyon to the parlyment. i fear he will bee much trublede att farst, but in a littill i hope will make him pase itt over. i finde by your father's letter you sent me done, he is a most sade man. i pray God he may do well, i fear his trubles togather will make an end of him. He was at Kaillingsworth with the Kinge i harde from my lady Monmouth. Mr Tyerman was this last wike at Nottingham, about a good liveinge, but he falede of it; he did not see your father. All thinges there is as we have harde, much complant for mony amongst the sogers. He suppede with my lord keeper [Lyttelton] who lyes in a minister's hose; he told me in discors to him, he wishede he hade never knone the court. That silver my lorde Warwicke sent in when i was at Chelsey, itt seemes was expectede at Nottingam,'—plate which Lord Warwick was evidently concealing to avoid sending to the help of the king.

About September 9 she has had a letter from Sir Edmund. 'It was a very sade on and his worde was this of you; " madam he hath ever lane near my hart and truly he is ther still;" that he hade many afflictyon uppon him, and that you hade usede him unkaindly; this was the effect of itt. The paper you sent of is [his] letter to you i bornt presently; i shall never open my lipes of that nor any thinge else you trust me with; he is passynate, and much trublede i belive that you declarede yourselfe for the parlyment : a littill time will disgest all I am confident. I hartily wish you coulde have bene with me some littill time when he comes furs [first] to london; may bee he woulde have the Kainge thinke hee was a littill displesede with you for goinge that way : if you can be absent from the parlyment i thinke it woulde be very will : i am suer i shoulde thinke it a very great happines to me your companye and your swite ladyes. Now lett me intrete you as a frende that loves you most hartily, not to right passynatly to your father, but ovour com him with kaindnes ; good man I see hee is infinetly malincoly, for many other thinges i belive besides the difference betwixt you. For god sake give nothinge to the parlyment derectly nor inderectly : i hope in the lorde ther will bee pese ; the parlyment will show ther great strenth, which sartinly will case the Kainge to yealde to most of ther demandes . . . wee have great store of sogers now att Sentaborns cam tonight and the say threcore cartis of amanisyon and thinge for that use, and ten great peses drane uppon whiles [wheels], and the Indes of court gentilimen to garde my lordes parson is com too, the say very fine and well horsede. If this soger be passede, i hope wee shall have no more to friton us. . . . My lorde Willmot hath bene a soger ; an experincede man he is, ther fore it tis will to make him safe. Mr. Goringe[1] i hope must bee punishide sondly. God hath blesede all your prosidinges in parlyment wondorfully. . . . I belive the quine will bee hear shorly, Doctor Myorne [the fashionable physician] tolde me he harde soe much. This lettir I becech you sende to your father by the

---

[1] Lord Goring had held Portsmouth for the king and had been compelled to surrender it to the Parliament, by whom he was justly held in detestation for his worthless character.

next opportunity : i have chidden him truly and sade as well as i can to him.' The next day : ' I sente you a criblede paper yester day, but that i desierde i see is not to bee hade, for my lorde of Esexe is gon by.' She has just received a letter from Sir Edmund : ' i see hee findes some more of his frindes goo of from what he expectede. . . . He sath the [the royalists] are stronger then is belivede.' A few days later : ' I see you to much appryhende this unhapye diffirence betwixt your father and selfe : i am very confident a littill time will make all will agane and his affecyon to you ase deare and harty as ever. i pray bee not sade ; that will doo you a great dell of hurt i am suer. If it ples God your father retorne, i hope one discorse or to, will make all will agane betwixt you. If Mrs. Sidnam and the rest of your frindes with him be not harty in doinge all good offeses betwixt you, the are most file unworthy pepell. If you hade falede in any thinge of duty or love to him it hade bene some jost case of exceptyon, but in goinge the way your consince telles you to be right, i hope he hath more goodnes and religone then to continue in displesuer with you for it.'

In her next letter : ' I am truly sory to hear the Kainge is returnede from Nottingam [Charles had retreated westwards before Essex to gain reinforcements]. i fear he will make this a tedious bissynes, and much blode will bee spilte befor ther be ane ende of it . . . I wish my lorde merkwis [Hertford, who held out in Sherborne Castle for the king] was as safe as the other lordes that hath offendede and are taken ; if he have the bitter of it sartinly it will bee much disadfantige to the parlyment side. Sir tomis chike i belive is not att all plesede with his sone rogers beinge strenth [i.e. aide-de-camp] to my lorde Harfort. As i am thus far of my litter i hear the Kainge hath sente an other mesege to your parlyment, i pray God it bee a good one : your father will cuffer many wayes i fear if the Kainge gos on in this way he begines ; sende not my letter to him, i pray, till you mete with a safe messenger.'

After the middle of September there are no letters from Lady Sussex for a month ; Ralph was apparently staying with her. Whether his father wrote to him during all this time does not appear ; there are no letters from him to be found after the beginning of August.

> O tell me, friends, while yet ye hear—
> May it not be, some coming year,
> These ancient paths that here divide
> Shall yet again run side by side,
> And you from there, and I from here,
> All on a sudden reappear ?
> O tell me, friends, while yet ye hear !—CLOUGH.

CHAPTER VI.

SIR EDMUND STRIKES HIS LAST BLOW FOR THE KING.

And they shall be as when a standardbearer fainteth.—Isaiah x. 18.

In the course of the two months that had elapsed from the raising of the standard, 'that low despised condition the King was in' (which Clarendon describes) had considerably improved. In October he had 6,000 foot, 2,000 horse, and a siege train. The great difficulty was about arms. 800 musquets, 500 pair of pistols, and 200 swords did not amount to a very efficient equipment for reconquering a kingdom, although some more arms were borrowed from the train-bands, and some, but 'very mean,' from the armouries of persons of quality; these were eked out with cudgels, pikes, and pole-axes.

We are apt to forget the exceeding rudeness of the weapons with which the contest was carried on by both parties at the outbreak of the Civil War. In the returns of arms, particularly for the northern levies, the long-bow, the cross-bow, and the brown bill are given among the equipments of a man at arms, together with old armour which had been hung up on the walls of churches, manor-houses, and cottages for years. It was not until the stores at Hull, Newcastle, Plymouth, and in the Tower of London were distributed, that matchlocks and pistols were put into the hands of the ordinary soldier. Many large bodies of men fought only with rude lances and pikes even to the end of the war; several thousand Welshmen on the king's side were only armed with staves and Danish clubs.

'The officers had their full desire,' says Clarendon, 'if they were able to procure old backs and breasts and pots, with pistols or carabines, . . . but no pikeman had a corselet and very few musqueteers had swords.' Nothing could have been more cumbrous and inconvenient than the matchlocks, arquebuses, and musquets even when they were obtained; the guns were of immense length, and could only be fired from an iron rest fixed in the ground, several of which have been ploughed up in the fields about Claydon, where fighting had gone on in the years 1643–44. The very bad powder was ignited by a tarred rope which was carried alight by the soldier, who was obliged to march ' shouldring his gun and rest,' and must have been terribly encumbered.

When Charles was besieging Coventry, Colonel Legge sent him two 'apothecaries mortars,' which were eagerly welcomed.

Guns are said to have been first introduced at the battle of Crecy, but the English cross-bow held its own till the beginning of the Civil War, and the last arrow shot in warfare was believed to have been at

the siege of Devizes under Cromwell. Even this was
a dereliction from the ideal of warfare of the middle
ages, which consisted in a hand-to-hand encounter.
An ancient hero like Bayard declared 'that it was
humiliating that a man with a heart in him should be
exposed to destruction by a wretched gun.' Fighting
at push of pike, looking an enemy in the face, was
the only honourable battle. To hack at each other
with brazen swords, which must have killed, if at all,
by the weight, not the sharpness of the blade; to fell
an enemy by sheer strength of arm with a club, as
did Achilles and Hector at a still earlier period,
were hardly yet out of date. ' Would to God,' said
Moultrie, 'that accursed instrument [the arquebuse]
had never been invented. I should not now bear the
marks of it, and many brave and valiant men would
not have been killed by cowards, who would not dare
to look in the face of him whom they stretched on
the ground with their cursed bullets.'

On October 12, 1642, the king advanced from
Shrewsbury, and decided to march upon London, the
road to which lay open, and he had been two days
on the way before Lord Essex, commanding the parliamentary army at Worcester, became aware of his
design. London was only defended by the train
bands, and if Charles had marched directly on the
Houses of Parliament, he might perhaps have ended
the war. But ' unhappy jealousies were quickly discovered' among his commanders. Prince Rupert
would receive no orders from Lord Lindsey, the

general-in-chief, and quarrelled with Lord Falkland, 'a very evil presage.' The utter ignorance on both sides of the most ordinary maxims of war appears by the fact that 'the two armies, though they were but 20 miles asunder, when they first set forth, and both marched the same way, gave not the least disquiet in ten days march to each other; and in truth, as it appeared afterwards, neither army knew where the other was'![1]

Essex's main body encamped at Keinton, much fatigued by marching through a deep clay country. The parliamentary account says that they intended to rest there during the Sabbath day, 'and the rather that our artillery and the forces left with it might come up.' They had 11 regiments of foot, 42 troops of horse, and about 700 dragoons, in all about 10,000 men. 'In the morning . . . we had news brought us that the enemy was two miles from us, upon a high hill called Edgehill; where upon we presently marched forth into a great broad field under that hill, called the vale of the red horse, and made a stand some half a mile from the foot of the hill, and there drew into battalia, where we saw their forces come down the hill; and drew likewise into battel in the bottom, a great broad company, . . . they that say least, say 14,000.'

The king had reached Edgecot near Banbury. The Royalist account given in Rushworth says that on Sunday morning at three o'clock he received in-

[1] *Clarendon*, Book VI.

telligence of the approach of the rebels, upon which he gave orders for the whole army to march to Edgehill, about four miles off. Here they perceived the rebels' army drawn out in the valley below. The hill is very truly an edge, where the high tableland extending towards Banbury breaks off in a precipitous wooded descent, to the flat ground below Keinton. On the very 'edge' itself is a solitary old inn, 'The Sun Rising,' which existed at the time of the battle, with a magnificent view over the great sea of plain and low hills reaching to the Malvern range to the north-west.

Here Charles breakfasted on the morning of the 23rd, attended by Sir Edmund Verney, and here he left the two boy princes, Charles and James, aged twelve and ten, with their tutor, Dr. Harvey, so busy it is said with his speculations concerning the circulation of the blood, that he did not perceive in time that the king's forces were retreating, and his charges were in considerable danger of being taken prisoners.

The king's position on the high ground was extremely strong, but it was impossible for him to delay the action. It was urged that he was for the moment superior in numbers to the enemy, and that his cavalry could act with great advantage in the plain below; moreover, the country round belonged chiefly to the Lords Brooke and Saye and Sele and was bitterly hostile to him; the soldiers had been forty-eight hours almost without food, and the people were so disaffected that the army could obtain 'neither meat for man or horse,' nor information, and the smiths hid themselves so that the troopers' horses could not be shod, 'of which in those stony ways there was great need.' Charles therefore resolved to give battle, and accordingly the troops were marched down the hill; 'but before that was done and the King's artillery came, it was past two in the afternoon.'

The infantry in the centre of the royal army was commanded by Lord Ruthven and Sir Jacob Astley; Lord Lindsey, accompanied by his son Lord Willoughby, commanded the regiment of guards in which was the king's standard, carried by Sir Edmund Verney, while the insubordinate Prince Rupert was at the head of the right wing of horse. Behind, a little to the right, came the king with his pensioners; he rode clad in armour, and wearing over it a black velvet mantle whereon was his star and garter, with a steel cap covered with velvet on his head. He addressed his troops briefly, 'but yet lovingly and loyally toward you our loyal army,' telling them that God and the justice of his cause, together with the love he bore to his whole kingdom, must encourage them; 'Your King bids you be courageous, and Heaven make you victorious.' The prayer breathed by the veteran Sir Jacob Astley, immediately before the advance, was remembered afterwards:—' Oh Lord, thou knowest how busy I must be this day. If I forget thee, do not thou forget me. March on, boys!'

SIR EDMUND STRIKES HIS LAST BLOW 115

A successful charge by Prince Rupert broke through the enemy: both cavalry and infantry gave way before him, except Lord Brooke's purple coats and Denzil Hollis's red coats, and the pursuit lasted for three miles across the open fields. Here, however, it ended ignominiously in the plunder of the baggage-waggons which had been left unguarded.[1]

Meantime the king's troops, unsupported by cavalry, had been unable to stand against the onslaught of Essex, and before Prince Rupert came back from the pursuit the tide of battle had turned; the king's guards were broken, and, had the advantage been followed up, Charles himself would have been in great danger. The struggle round the standard itself was furious 'in the extream.' It was evidently not the one that had required twenty men to set up at Nottingham, for we are told by old Lloyd that Sir Edmund 'adventured with' it among the enemy, in order that 'the souldiers might be engaged to follow him. He was offered his life by a throng of his enemies, upon condition he would deliver the standard; he answered that his life was his own, but the standard was his and their sovereign's, and he would not deliver it while he lived, and he hoped it would be rescued . . . when he was dead; selling it and his life, at the rate of sixteen gentlemen which fell that day by his sword.' The

[1] When the prince reached the king's side on his return, and found all in confusion, he said he 'could at least give a good account of the enemy's horse.' ' Ay by God, and of their carts too !' exclaimed a cavalier.

standard was taken, and round its staff (says the legend) still clung the hand which had grasped it, faithful in death. On one of the fingers was the ring given to Sir Edmund by the king, and containing his miniature. For two hundred years his disconsolate ghost wandered about the old house at Claydon searching for his hand; the ring still exists and the worm-eaten effigy of Sir Edmund's hand—and if any should dispute the truth of the story, are they not to be seen at Claydon to this very day?

But to return to the battlefield. The royal army was hard pressed, the short evening was closing in; the Parliament's forces had suffered a good deal, Essex could not be persuaded to advance up to the higher ground, and the fighting came to an end, neither party having gained any decisive advantage. The roads were crowded with the dead and wounded who had fallen on both sides; five thousand men, indeed, lay dead on the field, the proportion belonging to each party 'being very stiffly debated.' The king certainly lost more persons of distinction. Lord Lindsey was taken up mortally wounded, and died before he could be carried to Warwick, where his son was already a prisoner; Lord Stewart, Sir Edmund Verney, and Lord Aubigny were dead. The battle was, in fact, a drawn one, but it was clear that the parliamentary troopers could not stand against the cavaliers. The victory was claimed by both sides, but Cromwell (says Carlyle) told his cousin Hampden that they would never get on 'with a set of poor tapsters and town apprentice people fighting against men of honour.' To cope with men of honour they must have men of religion. 'Mr. Hampden answered me it was a good notion if it could be executed,' which was the first dawning in the general's mind of the conception of that army of Ironsides which so soon carried all before them.

'A relation of the Battel printed by his Majesty's command' says: 'If we had had light enough to have given one charge more, we had totally routed all their army, whereupon both armies retreated, ours in such order, that we not only brought off our own cannon but 4 of the Rebells. . . . So both armies facing one another all day [Monday] retired at night to their former quarters. . . . For the slain on both sides the number is uncertain; yet it is most certain that we killed five for one.'

On the other hand the 'relation communicated to the Speaker and Commons' gives 'a narration of a blessed victory which God hath given us upon the army of the Cavaliers and of those Evil Persons, who upon Sunday 23 of this Instant engaged his Majesty in a dangerous and bloody Fight against his faithful subjects.' The fiction was still kept up that they were not fighting against the king, but against his evil counsellors. They confess that 'our Battalia at the very first wholly disbanded and ran away without ever striking stroke.' But then comes an account of the good service done by the rear and the right wing of the horse, and that they 'stood all that night upon the place where the enemy before the fight had drawn up into Battalia.'

This official account mentions amongst special mercies of the day that, 'Sir Edmund Verney who carried the King's Standard was slain by a gentleman of the Lord General's Troop of Horse, who did much other good Service that Day, and the Standard taken; which was afterwards by the Lord General himself delivered unto his Secretary, Mr. Chambers, with an intention to send it back the next day unto his Majesty; but the Secretary, after he had carried it long in his hand, suffered it to be taken away by some of our Troopers, and *as yet we cannot learn where it is.*' We are, however, better informed; Mr. Gardiner [1] is able to tell us how Captain Smith, a Catholic officer of the King's Life Guards, disguising himself with an orange scarf which he picked up on the field, slipped through the enemy's ranks, told Essex's secretary that so great a prize was not fitly bestowed in the hands of a penman, and snatched it from him. He made his way back and triumphantly laid the recovered standard at the feet of the king, who rewarded him with hearty thanks and knighted him on the spot.

Sir Edward Sydenham's account, written from 'Ano on the hill,' close by, on Oct. 27, was sent by hand to Ralph. 'For all our great vycktorie I have had the greatest loss by the death of your nobell father that ever anie freind did, which next to my

[1] *Great Civil War*, vol. i. 57.

wyfe and Master was the greatest misfortune that by death could have falen to me : he himselfe killed two with his owne hands, whereof one of them had killed poore Jason, and brocke the poynt of his standard at push of pike before he fell, which was the last acount I could receave of anie of our owne syde of him. The next day the kinge sent a harald to offer mercie to all that would laye downe armes, and to enquire for my Lord of Lynsee, my Lo Wyllowby and him; he brought word that my Lo Lynsee was hurt, your father dead, and my Lo Wyllowby only prysoner; he would nither put on armes or buff cote the day of battell, the reason I know not; the battell was bloody on your syde, for your hoorss rann awaye at the first charge, and our men had the execution of them for three miles ; it began at 3 a clock and ended at syx. The kinge is a man of the least feare and the greatest mercie and resolution that ever I saw, and had he not bin in the fylde, we might have suffered. My Lord of Essex is retired in great disorder to Warwick, for the next morninge he suffired his connon to be taken away within muskett shott of his armie, and never offired to hindir them; it is sayd ther was killed and run away since, eaygtt thowsand of his armie. This day the kinge tooke in bamberie ; our armie dayly increases; god in mercie send us peace, and although your loss be as great as a sonn can loose in a father, yitt god's chyldren must beare with patience what afflycktion soever he shall please to laye upon them. You have a great tryall, god in mercie give you grace to make a santified use of this great afflyction, and to undergoe this great burden with patience. My humbell sarvise to your sad wyfe. God of his infinite mercie cumfort you bothe which shall be the prayers of your freind and sarvant who shall ever be reddie to performe anie sarvise in the power of your Ed : Sidenham. Ther is delivered to me fyftie two cornetts and colors which was taken ; I beleeve ther be manie more.'

Poor Ralph, heartbroken for the loss of his father, wrote to Lady Sussex from Covent Garden: ' Maddam, I never lov'd to bee the messenger of ill newes : therfore I forbore to send you this ; which is the saddest and deepest affliction that ever befell any poore distressed man ; I will not add to your greife by relating my owne deplorable condition, neither can my pen expresse the meseries I am in ; God's will bee donn, and give mee patience, to support mee in this extremity. there is noe absolute certainty of his Death, that I can yet learne, but sure tis too true. I have sent 3 messengers to both armies to bie informed. on Satterday I expect on of them Back, in the meanetime I am forced to make dilligent enquiries after that which (if it proove true) will make mee most unhappy. I know you are fully sensible of my misfortune, therfore I will say noe more, but humbly begg of you for his sake to continue mee in your favour, and receive mee into your protection, for if hee is gon, I have noe freind in this world but your selfe [his grief makes him more than ever long-winded] ; therfore I must once more beeseech your Ladyshipp ever for his sake that served you soe faithfully, and valued and honord you soe farr above all other creatures, that you will bee pleasd to preserve mee in your good oppinion and esteem me as I am Maddam your most faithful, though most sorrowfull most afflicted and most unfortunate servant R. V.

'I will obay you in waiting uppon you, before you goe downe, soe I might see noe other creature but your selfe.'

Lady Sussex writes to him the same day, having heard the news independently:

'The most heavy nues of your worthy good father's death is come to mee, for which i have the sadist hart and depest wondede sole that ever cretuer hade; he beinge i confes to you the greatist comfort of my life; i pray god fitt me for ane other; for i am suer i shall never have more ioy in this. Your lose, i am very sensable is infinat to: i pray god give us both pasynce. My stay will bee hear [at Chelsea] till tusday i thinke; and though it be an unfitt requist att this time, yet let me bege the favour to see you before i goo home, for you are all the ioy i have left mee now; i am in so missirable a condisyon that i cannot expres my thoughts: my eyes are so full that i cannot say no more; but that i am your most sorifull and most afflictiede frinde Elenor Sussex.'

Poor Ralph's extreme grief for the father whom he loved so tenderly was evidently much increased by the thought of the partial estrangement which had come between them for the past three months.

His next letter to Lady Sussex, a few days later, gives an account of his efforts to get information about his father's fate.

'Maddam, Last night I had a servant from my Lord of Essex Army, that tells mee there is noe possibillity of finding my Deare father's Body, for my Lord Generall, my Lord Brooke, my Lord Grey, Sr Jam Luke and twenty others of my acquaintance assured him hee was never taken prisiner, neither were any of them ever possessed of his Body; but that hee was slaine by an ordinary Trooper. Upon this my man went to all the ministers of severall parishes, that buried the dead that were slaine in the battle, and none of them can give him any information of the body. One of them told him my Lord Aubigney was like to have been buried in the feilds, but that on came by chance that knew him and tooke him into a church, and there laid him in the ground without soe much as a sheete about him, and soe divers others of good quallity were buried: the ministers kept Tallies of all that were buried, and they amount to neare 4,000. Maddam you see I am every way unhappy. I beeseech you afford mee your praires and bee pleasd (though I am now perplexed with a multitude of misfortunes) to account mee as I have ever endeavourd to expresse myselfe your Ladishipps most faithfull servant to command.

'On Wednesday I intend to waite uppon you, if

you please to let mee know about what time of the day I may most conveniently doe it.'

Lady Sussex replies the same day:

'My soro is beyonde all that can bee sade; it tis not possibly to bee greter then it tis; but truly it trubles me much that his body was beriede amonst the multitude; i know itt coulde not have addede anythinge to him, only have sattisfiede his frindes to have hade a cristan beriall; but itt semes in ware ther is no differince made. God's will most bee don in all things, i hope he is bleside and happy. Belive me i acount my gretis happines i have left me the aseurance of your frinship, and for ever shall you bee most dear to me. On Wensday in the aftir none i shall bee most happy to see you; if it may bee without your truble; for non is so much your affecynat true frinde as Elenor Sussex.'

A little later, after she had gone to the country, she writes about some mourning for Sir Edmund, 'for the blakes though you are so good to offer them i belive you make use of them yourselves, and then i woulde by no menes have them, for i see nobody hear.'

Sir Edmund's death seems to have produced a great sensation in the neighbourhood of Edgehill. A curious old pamphlet published three months after the battle, relates that 'portentious apparitions of two jarring and contrary armies where the battell was strucken, were seen at Edge Hill, where are still many unburied karkasses, at between twelve and one of the clock in the morning. As was certified by Persons of Qualitie. These infernal souldiers appeared on Christmas night, and again on two Saturdays after, bearing the King's and Parliament's colours. Pell mell to it they went, where the corporeall armies had shed so much blood, the clattering of armes, noyse of Cannons, cries of soldiers, sounds of petronels, and the alarum was struck up, creating great terrour and amazement. The rumour whereof comming to his Majestie at Oxford, he sent Colonel Kirke and 5 other gentlemen of Credit, who all saw the forementioned prodigies, distinctly knowing divers of the apparitions and incorporeall substances by their faces, as that of Sir Edmund Varney [the only one, however, named] and others, that were there slaine.'

'A sign of God's wrath, and a proof of the Divills dispersed in the empty regions of the Ayre,' is all the explanation vouchsafed for the 'prodigy' thus testified to by 'gentlemen of credit.'

Sir Edmund's ghost haunted not only the battlefield where he fell, and the home where he dwelt, but also the spinneys [i.e. plantations] near Claydon; draining and repairs, however, are sadly inimical to spirits, and it is to be feared that he has now altogether passed away from this earth to which he so long clung.

He was succeeded in the office of Knight Marshal by Sir Edward Sydenham, who writes to Ralph to request 'that I maye have your estate bothe of the prysson [the Marshalsea] and goods ther upon such tearmes as you will parte with them to another.'

Apparently he was well satisfied with Ralph's

answer, for Lady Anne Sydenham writing afterwards in his stead, says that 'he houes you all that will ever ly in his power, and more thin i am shuer he shall ever be so happy as to paye for the hobblegashons that he has had to your selef. . . . You woled never havef chised out me to havef heped your favors on, had you not a ben best plesed with doing corteses to thos that coled gevef no retorn.'

In the 'Life of Clarendon' there is a very graphic account of a conversation between him and Sir Edmund: 'Mr. Hyde was wont often to relate a passage in that melancholick Time, when the Standard was set up at Nottingham, with which he was much affected. Sir Edmund Varney Knight Marshal, who was mentioned before as Standard Bearer, with whom he had great Familiarity, who was a Man of great Courage and generally beloved, came one day to him and told him, " He was very glad to see him, in so universal a damp under which the spirits of most men were oppressed, retain still his natural cheerfulness and vivacity ; that he knew that the condition of the King and the power of the Parliament was not better known to any man than to him (Clarendon) ; and therefore he hoped that he was able to administer some comfort to his friends, that might raise their spirits as it supported his own." He answered " that he was in truth beholden to his constitution, which did not incline him to despair ; otherwise that he had no pleasant prospect before him, but thought us ill of affairs as most men did ; that the other was as far from being melancholick as he, and was known to be a man of great courage (as indeed he was of a very cheerful and a generous nature, and confessedly valiant), and that they could not do the King better service, than by making it their business to raise the dejected minds of men, and root out those apprehensions which . . . could do no good, and did really much mischief." Sir Edmund replied smiling, " I will willingly join with you the best I can, but I shall act it very scurvily. My condition," said he, "is much worse than yours, and different, I believe, from any other man's, and will very well justify the melancholick that I confess to you possesses me. You have satisfaction in your conscience that you are in the right; that the King ought not to grant what is required of him; and so you do your duty and your business together. But for my part I do not like the quarrel, and do heartily wish that the King would yield and consent to what they desire; so that my conscience is only concerned in honour and gratitude to follow my master. I have eaten his bread and served him near thirty years, and will not do so base a thing as to forsake him; and choose rather to lose my Life (which I am sure I shall do) to preserve and defend those things, which are against my conscience to preserve and defend. For I will deal freely with you, I have no reverence for the Bishops, for whom this Quarrel subsists." It was not a time to dispute, and his affection to the Church had never been suspected. He was as good as his word, and was killed at the

Sir Edmund Verney, Kt. Marshal.
Standard bearer to Charles, from a bust in Middle Claydon Church.

battle of Edgehill within two months after this discourse. And if those who had the same and greater obligations, had observed the same rules of gratitude and generosity, whatever their other affections had been, that battle had never been fought, nor any of that mischief been brought to pass, that succeeded it.'

Lloyd's testimony to his high and noble character is equally emphatic : '. . . One of the strictness and piety of a Puritan, of the charity of a Papist, of the civility of an Englishman ; whose family the King his Master would say, " was the model he would propose to the Gentlemen," whose carriage was such that he was called " the only courtier that was not complained of." '

Reliquiæ Edmundi Verney,
Vere militis [1] & Banneretti
Qui Deum timendo nisit (nihil ?) timere didicit,
Nihil non Ansus nisi quod omnes
audent ; peccare.
O In gloriam fortitudinem quæ pati tantum potuit !

---

[1] Ultimus Angliæ Bannerettus.

CHAPTER VII.

CONCERNING EDMUND, THE YOUNG CAVALIER.

> Who doom'd to go in company with pain,
> And fear, and bloodshed, miserable train !
> Turns his necessity to glorious gain . . .
> Or if an unexpected call succeed,
> Come when it will, is equal to the need ;
> He who, though thus endued as with a sense
> And faculty for storm and turbulence,
> Is yet a soul whose master bias leans
> To homefelt pleasures and to gentle scenes.
> WORDSWORTH.

IT was not till July '41 that Edmund heard of the death of his mother from his sister-in-law, Lady Verney. He was with the army at York, and replies from thence : 'Tis most true that the losse of our mother is infinite, but I'll not torture you with expressing it more largely.' She had died three months before, but the mourning clothes sent to him by Ralph had not even then arrived.

He complains of the large arrears still due to the army : ' You lawmakers are lawlesse yourselves, and therefore I have armed myself with my best armoure of proof, exceeding much patience.'

By September the army was disbanded, or 'cashiered,' as he phrases it, and he spent some time

CONCERNING EDMUND, THE YOUNG CAVALIER 129

at Claydon with his sisters, whence he writes playful complaints to Ralph of their teasing. 'I never yet saw such double diligence used in the tormenting a poore man. . . . I cannot live long if these thunder-claps continue.' But he is evidently extremely fond of them, writing tenderly of Cary, who has been ill, but he hopes will soon be well, 'for truely I am much troubled to see her ass she is; shee desires to have me much with her.' Pen, an elder sister, writes of him as 'My dearest combeannion the casseir [cashiered] Captaine.' His cousin Doll Leeke was also very fond of him, and writes to Lady Verney: 'I find by my cosen Mun that he is gon; he writs me word that he hath left with you a ring of his hare. Beshrew him for his conseat, it shews so like a legisi that it has put a sadness into me; it is a fault to be superstisous, and therfore if I can I will forget it.'

His pay was still in arrear, and he tells Ralph 'that it must be his main business to provide uss our money, otherwise you will have many of better quality follow the highway law than yet do; I cannot think it robbery to arrest a parliament man, being you have all engaged your words to us.' The household, apparently, is going up to London, and he shows his kindness by asking Ralph to urge his father to allow horses for the maids to ride up there, instead of going by the carrier, 'for the very name of a waggon is soe offensive to them.' He entreats his father to get him a company in the army about to be sent to Ireland, but in the meantime is anxious to secure the ordering of a suit of clothes from his father's tailor, with gold and silver braid, 'chiefly fitt for London.'

In November the rising in Ireland, and the massacres which were taking place in all directions, had filled everyone with horror, and troops were hurried off. Edmund received his commission as captain, and rode in great haste with his father's horses to West Chester, where they were to embark.

'I have now been here this nine days,' he writes, 'sooner by four than the first that came; five of our companions have not yet come up. . . . I am in infinite haste, but I will write more largely by Hinton, by whom I will send [back] my horses next Monday.' Grooms and coachmen of the same name still continue at Claydon, and have gone on from father to son, trusty and trusted, knowing their work well and doing it.

The next letter says, 'Now we are lyke to come to an active service. I heare Kit Roper, with 4 more captaines and theire companyes, are cutte of to 14 men ass they were attempting to relieve Tredan. My collonell's regiment is much desired, and if wee have a fayre winde wee shall be there within 4 or 5 dayes. Here lyes my lord Parsons his sonne, who hath very good intelligence, and his friends write to him they are in a great doubt Dublin will be beseiged before wee can get over, for the rebells, hearing of our neare approach, resolve to attempt ass high ass they can possibly before our arrivall. Never was more bar-

barousness practised amongst the Heathen then they use now amongst men of very good quality. I hope wee shall be a good meanes to repell them, but wee are but an handfull, and I believe you will be forced (notwithstanding the time of yeare) to send 10 times our number suddenly over. All our care here is how we shall get next month's pay. . . . I pray have a mayne care of that both now and hereafter, and then wee will fight lustily for you, but otherwise, noe longer Pype noe longer dance.' The 'scarlet cloake and shamoy doublet with the silver and gold edging' have not arrived; they may be paid for out of the money due to him, and be sent in the ' Lord Leivetenant's carryages.'

A week later the troops were still at West Chester waiting for a fair wind. He writes to Mary : ' The life that I bide on this syde the sea is very troublesome, and is never sweetened by any delight, but only when I am writing to you; yet there is one thing more which would adde much to my happines, and that is . . . your writing to me. . . . I had one tricke which now I'll leve. I was used never to write under 3 or 4 letters at a time, and when I had not time to write soe many then I was silent to all; but now . . because . . I shall be in a place whence newes will be often desired, sometimes one shall have it and sometimes another, and soe I hope to please all, which is a thing I much desire.'

At the request of his colonel he asked Ralph to get a motion made in the House that the arrears should be paid to the soldiers, but added, ' I believe it is a buisnes you care not to meddle with, and for my owne part I will not at all press you to it; he desired me to write to you, and soe I leave you to doe ass you shall think good. I am now pretty well of my hurt in my shoulder. Here is none but lamentable news from Ireland, and I pray God send us suddenly over ass many more to follow us; but the winde is so inconstant that I desire you would please to write to me [here] by the next post.'

At Christmas he writes that the troops are still wind-bound, but in January '42 he has got to Dublin, which was holding out against the rebels, though the whole country was in revolt except some of the fortified towns with English garrisons, and part of Connaught, where Lord Clanricarde maintained order to some extent.

Edmund complains of the treatment of the army by the treasurer, who stopped sixpence in the pound out of their pay, for which he said he had a patent ' under the broad seale.' The matter was now referred to Parliament, and Edmund asks Ralph to help them. ' Had you sent 10,000 men 6 or 8 weekes since I dare say the rebells had beene neare repelled by this, and now, for ought I know, it may last you many a yeare, and the longer you stay, the more heade they will get; but I hope your delayes is out of your goodness to uss, least wee should suddenly want employment againe, and for that I will excuse you.' In February he wrote again of the distress in the army for want of money, 'he is held a rich man that can maintaine himself.' He asks for a tent (which was afterwards bought by Ralph for 7*l*., and sent over to him) and an 'able pacing gelding.' Concerning an engagement at Swords, of which Ralph had been misinformed, he says, 'I was there myselfe. . . . You mention 13 to be lost besydes Sir Lorenzoe Cary, the rebbels to be treble our number, and alsoe intrenchd, whereas we lost but four in all, and were double the enemy; neither had any other intrenchment than a small work, more like a garden ditch than a trench; . . . I believe they lost 100 men. Ireland is full of castles, and truly strong ones, and thither the rebbells fly, not daring to give us a meeting, although treble our number. I will not say but that the want of armes and ammunition may be much the cause of it, but truly I doe believe them to be of a very cowardly nature. . . . I pray lett uss know when you intend to send uss money, or whither ye intend to send any, that according to your resolutions wee may serve you; this is an age when you have most neede of uss, and this time you choose most to abuse us. I'll assure you wee scarce thinke it a forfeite of our honours even att this time to quitt your service, rather than to continue it on these conditions. I admire how you thinke wee live; wee have bellyes to feede and backs to cloath ass well ass you; wee want yet the hardynes to goe naked, neither have wee been bredd, lyke camelions, to live on ayre. There is scarce a captaine in the army but what to his souldyers and his owne necessary expenses he is £40 worse then he is worth; and believe me, Brother, that which is worse then all this is, that the army cannot subsist without it; tis not here ass it was in Yorkshire; here the inhabitants are neither willing nor able to lend, and it is sport to them to see uss undon. Our souldiers have lived upon nothing this month but salt beefe and herrings, which is soe unusual to our men that came last out of England, that of our 2,500 men, I believe we have 500 sicke; then judge what will be the event if money come not speedily. I yet heare nothing of my doublet and cloake, and now is the time when I should have most use of it. One of my sisters has a stuffe sute, laced with black lace, which I made me in the north, and there is a taby sute which I never yet saw, though it hath beene made for me this 2 yeare. I pray let them be sent ass soone ass you can for summer comes on a pace.'

There is a great contrast between the cool way in which he here spoke of leaving the service of the Parliament, and the intense devotion with which he afterwards wrote of fighting for the king, after the raising of the standard at Nottingham.

There was a proposal of paying the soldiers with land in Ireland, at the same time charging them a price for it, and Edmund protested against the unfairness 'of our paying both in money and the hazard of our lives. . . . Wee, the last Monday stormed the castle of Carrigmaine and took it in, where the common souldyer (though the service were most deperate) expressed ass much courage and resolution ass could be expected from brave commanders, and why should not these men receive another kind of reward then theire 8$d.$ per diem ? .... Now sweete brother take not any of my choller for your selling us lands ass meant to you, for I cannot but thinke you too noble to be of that opinion, and soe I rest yours in all service whatsoever.' He has got a couple of 'very good pilladge nagges,' so he no longer requires the gelding.

It must be remembered that there was hardly any commissariat, that the pay of the soldiers and officers was months in arrear, and that the only means of living was by putting the country under requisition. He mentions that his cousin, Dick Turville, and the troops under his command had taken a castle six miles from Dublin, where they found 300$l.$ worth of corn. He was anxious that his father should get him a troop of horse because 'the country is yet full, and tis the horse get all the pilladge.' The war in the Low Countries had set a frightful standard of severity in the armies, and even the kind-hearted Edmund, writing from Trim in June '42, thus describes the taking a castle which had held out a three days' siege: 'We had 20 men slaine and 30 hurt and 3 officers shot: after we put some four score men to the sword, but like valiant knights errant, gave quarter and liberty to all the women.'

In July he had the command of Dathcoffy Castle,

twelve miles from Dublin, and had gained about 50*l*. by pillage, which paid the expenses of a fever in which he was 'given over of the phisitions for a dead man for almost a week.'

Magdalen Bruce, writing to Ralph from Youghal, says that Edmund was behaving very gallantly and gaining much love.

In September he returned to Dublin, and the news reached him that Ralph had openly taken the side of Parliament, now in arms against the king. He was much distressed and wrote sternly, 'Brother, what I feared is proovd too true, which is your being against the king; give me leave to tell you in my opinion tis most unhandsomely done, and it greeves my hearte to thinke that my father allready and I, who soe dearly love and esteeme you, should be bound in consequence (because in duty to our king) to be your enemy. I heare tis a greate greife to my father. I beseech you consider that majesty is sacred; God sayth, 'Touch not myne anointed'; it troubled Davyd that he cutt but the lapp of Saul's garment; I believe yee will all say yee intend not to hurt the king, but can any of yee warrant any one shott to say it shall not endanger his very person? I am soe much troubled to think of your being of the syde you are that I can write no more, only I shall pray for peace with all my hearte, but if God grant not that, yet that He will be pleased to turne your hearte that you may soe expresse your duty to your king that my father may still have cause to rejoice in you.'

The letter arrived in all the trouble of Sir Edmund's death at Edgehill and the general distress of the family. Ralph did not answer it, and Edmund became very uneasy lest his words should have bred discord between them. He wrote several times, he says to Ralph on February 24, '43, but had received no answer. 'I believe you have written too, and that it is only your heats one way and myne the other that have occasioned the miscarryage of our letters. I beseech you let not our unfortunate silence breede the least distrust of each other's affections, although I would willingly loose my right hand that you had gone the other way, yet I will never consent that this dispute shall make a quarrell between us, there be too many to fight with besides ourselves. I pray God grant a suddaine and a firme peace that we may safely meete in person ass well ass in affection. Though I am tooth and nayle for the king's cause, and shall endure soe to the death, whatsoever his fortune be, yet sweete brother let not this my opinion (for it is guyded by my conscience), nor any report which you can heare of me, cause a diffidence of my true love to you.'

Ralph did not reply till April 21, when he wrote : 'Brother, I know not how saifly this letter may come to your hands, therefore I shall only tell you that in October I received your letter dated September 14, which was soe full of sharpnesse, that I rather chose to forbeare answering it (being willing to avoyd all matters of dispute), then returne such a reply (as that language did deserve) to a brother I love soe well. I have now received another from you in another straine by Mr. Rogers, for which I thanke you, and let me intreate you to stick to the resolution you have taken concerning mee, and I shall promise to doe the like to you. I will send you noe newes least it cause this letter to miscarry. . . . Your truly affectionat Brother to serve you R. V.'

The distress occasioned by the tearing asunder of family ties in hundreds of households among those who loved each other tenderly, but whose consciences compelled them to take opposite sides, must, as in Edmund's case, have been greatly aggravated by the long delay in delivering letters. Edmund once says he has received nothing from Ralph for fifteen months, ' although I have written you sixe letters,' and the anxiety of not knowing the state of mind of those whom he loved so well was a great addition to his troubles. The difficulties arising from political animosities were naturally great ; Lady Sussex, on the winning side, complains again and again that her letters to Ralph have been opened and read, and only those sent by hand seem to have been safe. In one case Edmund gives his brother an address at Dublin, saying, ' merchants' letters pass safely, when malignants of either party are opened,' showing that the term was employed indifferently by both sides.

In February 1643 Edmund took part in an engagement at Rathconnell and received a shot upon the collar of his doublet, ' which, however, only made my neck black and blew, without any further hurt; the rebbells have many officers come daily to them from Flanders and ours go by dozens into England, and I believe in a short time we shall none of us be able to stay here'; the soldiers had been paid nothing for months and the country was so wasted round them, that they could get nothing to eat.

In April he says that he has not heard from Ralph for six or seven months; the times in Ireland grow worse and worse: 'except some very speedy course be taken for our reliefe, this kingdome must needes be lost, for the very officers want mony to feede themselves. About three weekes since the enemy gave my lord marquesse of Ormond battell, where,' as he modestly says, 'I allsoe was. God gave us the victory; the rebbells were more than two for one, yet we lost not above ten men, but there lay slayne of the enemy above 200, most of which were commanders and gentlemen of very good quality. Wee tooke Collonell Cullen leivetenant generall of theire army, serjeant major Butler and more captaines prisoners. About 3 dayes hence I shall goe out in another party with my Lord Moore... I shall this day be serjeant major to Collonell Gybson's regiment, of which I have hitherto been captaine.' Lord Ormond had been made Lord Lieutenant in November '42.

The small force of English, gallantly as they behaved, were so greatly outnumbered by the rebels that it was impossible without support from England to continue the war to any advantage; matters went on from bad to worse till in September a cessation of arms was concluded for a year, and Edmund returned to England.

Meantime the family affairs there were very far from prosperous. The following is from a rough copy made by Ralph of a letter to his brother, which miscarried. 'I am now going into the country for a little aire, and please myselfe with hopes to receive a letter from you there. All the money you writ for is paied as you directed: as for that other which is due to you [i.e. from the Alnage] . . . tis now almost a yeare since any part of it was paied, and then but £100. Till it please God to settle these distractions I feare non will bee gott. The last you sent for, and part of what I paid before, was of my owne money. . . . but if you send for more (whilst I have any) you shall not want it.'

On October 24, '43, Edmund writes, still from Dublin: 'Your distractions in England keepe uss soe poore in Ireland, that we scarce know how to put breade into our mouths.' He has had to take up 100*l.* from the merchant in whose house he lies, for which he sends a bill of exchange that he hopes Ralph will accept on the security of his 600*l.* or 700*l.* arrears of pay. 'I thinke there will be good store of our forces shortly in England; I shall be sure to be one, and though I come with ass mortall a dislyke to those you wish too well to, ass any man that shall come over, yet I pray be assured that I have ass much affection towards you ass any freinde you have.'

Unfortunately this letter only came to hand at the time when Ralph, in trouble with the Parliament, was about to take refuge in France. 'I am infinetly sorry poore Ireland hath tasted soe deeply of our distraction,' he writes, 'and that you have been soe greate a shairer in this common calamity. As for your coming over, you know my oppinion, and I have sufferd too much already to trouble you with it any more, therefore I now only thanke you for those expressions of your love and affection, which you have given mee in this letter, and intreate you to beeleeve, that though perhapps in some things wee may differ in judgment and oppinion, yet nothing of that kinde shall ever prevaile with mee to breake that knot of true affection that ought to bee betwixt us, there are too many others to contend with; sweet Brother, let your breath and mine be spent in praiers for Peace, and though it bee denied us in this world, hereafter wee may finde it. God in mercy blesse you, farewell.'

This touching letter did not reach its destination, and on December 5 Edmund, who had arrived at Oxford, wrote again in great distress at having no answer. He fears that Ralph's 'distance' proceeds from the letter written when he heard of the side taken by his brother: 'For my part I have forgot the contents of it, and never desire to know it, since it bredd soe unhappy a difference. Beleeve me 'twas farr from my thought that it would ever take such effect, but the passion of it deriv'd its birth from ass passionate a one on the same occasion from him [his father] who can never be forgotten, or indeede remembered but with a sadd reverance. I am heartily glad to heare your resolution is altered, let the change of that be accompanyd with a new opinion of me. . . . I hope this absence of yours [he must have heard from others of Ralph's approaching departure] will give me some occasion to serve you, and if I doe it not faythfully may all good men forsake me. . . . I shall not subscribe my name to these lines, I am confident you know the hand, and if you knew the heart ass well, much of what I have here written might have been left out. . . . Deare Brother let me begg you to write to me ass often ass you can, if I doe not the lyke let me suffer the greatest punishment that may be, which will be by your thereby occasion'd silence.'

Edmund felt the loss of his father most keenly and frequently alluded to him in his letters. Writing to Ralph about the provisions of the will, he says: 'Though I am left the best of the three [younger sons] yet it is but halfe of that which I have had a long promise of. Would it had pleased God to continue his lyfe that left it, though I had beggd all myne. It is not that, nor anything else, that can lessen my honour to the memory of that most gallant man; let even the thought of being his children keep us all in unity.'

The money which Sir Edmund intended to leave to his younger children had melted partly away in the king's service and in the depreciation of all securities and investments, but Edmund did not realise the consequent difficulties of Ralph's position, and in a letter to him in February '44 he takes rather a high tone respecting his sisters' fortunes : 'I am confident you are of opinion that if my father when he made his will had had the least thought of these times, he would not have left his younger children theire portions in such an office [i.e. the Alnage]— his intentions were they should have it the full, and wass heartily troubled he could make it no more. Sweete Brother mistake me not, I doe not write this that I thought it reasonable all this losse should lyght on you, but that you having by many degreese the greater share, soe in æquity should beare the greatest burden of it ; I and my other two brothers have our swords to live by, though God knowes they yeeld us but poor livelyhoods in these times, yet while I have it and God blesse my lymbs and grant that I am not taken prisoner, I shall endeavour hereafter to keepe lyfe and soule togeather ass well ass I can by it. But for my sisters I must desire you to continue your allowance to them ass long and in ass high a proportion ass you are able, God knowes they are not able to helpe themselves. I am confident it was ever your intention.'

He had previously demanded his own allowance somewhat peremptorily ; he had even forced the steward at Claydon to give him 80*l*. in the mistaken belief that Ralph was answerable for his fortune, and a coolness between the brothers ensued. Mary, naturally indignant for her husband, seems to have shown her feelings by silence, and Edmund writes humbly to her: 'Sweete Sister it iss now about a yeare and halfe since I receiv'd a letter from you: I have written severall since that time; I remember when you would not have receiv'd soe many without making returne; I put it to yourselfe to judge of whither thinke you these fitt times for those whome allyance tyes to soe strict a unity, to live in any distance; but heretofore I thought allyance the lesser tye that had beene betweene uss and that of freindshipp the greater, and can this be dissolv'd at once? and without any expostulation? it held 10 yeare firme, and can any one houres worke destroy soe strong a foundation and wholly ruine it? Lyfe iss at all times most uncertaine, but I am now in a way that I know not how soone mine may be shortned by accident, and would you willingly entertaine this dispute during lyfe? Sweete Sister [he ends pathetically], beleeve it hath lasted long enough, yea too too long, and therefore now let it dy.'

In the meantime a long-delayed letter from him reached Ralph in France, which he said was 'the greatest comfort and contentment' he had had since leaving 'poore England.' Harmony was thus happily restored, and though the money matters were not thoroughly cleared up till a few years later, the affectionate intimacy between the brothers was only interrupted by Edmund's premature and tragic death.

This question of the fortunes of the younger children from the Alnage is constantly coming up in the letters. Cary Gardiner had some settlements on her marriage, and Margaret was provided for by her godmother, Mrs. Eure; but Susanna, Penelope, Mary, and Elizabeth were advised to petition 'the honorable Committee of the King's Revenue' for their annuities and arrears. Their petition was considered by a Committee of Lords and Commons in September 1647, and was referred to the Solicitor-General for his report by an order signed by Lords Salisbury, Saye and Sele, and Wharton, Henry Mildmay and J. Bond. Oliver St. John made a detailed report in which he established Sir Edmund Verney's claim under the Great Seal of England to this charge 'upon the Aulnage ... and duties payable upon all and all manner of Woolen Cloathes and Stuffs of the old and new draperies made to be sould in the Realme of England, Dominion of Wales and the Isle of Weight.' By the kindness of the Duke of Portland, the originals of the Petition and Report which are in his collection of manuscripts are reproduced in the Appendix.

But although the Verney girls had proved their rights, they were very far from getting their money. Year after year their eldest brother helps them to assert their claims; he writes to all kinds of people, and is met on all sides by hints that presents are expected. Dr. Denton writes that 'hungry curs will eat durty puddings.'

In Sir Ralph's calendar are these entries:

May 22, 1648, he is advised to 'suppresse ye petition and insist on St. John's report'; a few days later he hears that they have received 'a fatal doome about the Aulnage, which was though they could not deny the right, yet they were soe much in Debt, they could not spare it.' Lord Saye and Sele, who signed the report of the Committee that received the petition, was to be referred to. In September, Sir Ralph suggests that they should 'try to get the Aulnage by some order in the Lords' House.' Nothing has been done, for in October he begs the Dentons to 'haunt Lord Wharton about the Aulnage.' In November he hears that the clothiers are petitioning Parliament to do away with the Alnage in the interest of their trade; he can only hope that 'they will satisfie the owners of it, as they did the Officers in the court of Wards, the thing being legall.' Later on there are complaints that certain papers concerning the Alnage are lost, and hints that officials concerned in it expect fees! Dr. Denton writes that their neighbours, the Chaloners, offer to help, but 'the Alnage sticks in Chaloner's hands'; then it seems that the matter depends on Sir Henry Mildmay. In September 1649 the matter is still in suspense: 'Dr. thinks unlesse the whole Alnage fall it will be gott at last,' but if all friends fail 'Dr. will give somebody £100 to get it donne.' 'A Fee to some powerfull man were well given to get this money.'

Dr. Denton goes on consulting 'with all persons about the Aulnage, everybody discomforts him, but hee will offer at it still and watch for an opportunity to advance it.' In 1655, thirteen years after their father's death, the girls are still vainly trying to get their portions; their brother Edmund having long passed beyond the reach of the chances and changes of this troublesome world.

CHAPTER VIII.

SIR RALPH'S CHOICE, THE COVENANT OR EXILE.

> Because you have thrown off your prelate-lord
> And with stiff vows renounced his liturgy. . . .
> Dare ye for this adjure the civil sword
> To force our consciences that Christ set free ?—MILTON.[1]

AT the beginning of 1643. Ralph, though he is too troubled to take notes, is attending Parliament and carrying on his correspondence with Lady Sussex. There are also in the early months of the year voluminous epistles from the scapegrace Tom, who had written in November '42 : 'My full resolution is to goe downe to the king's army, about Wednesday next, and there to proffer my service to his Majesty, which I hope will not only be accepted of, but it may, if it shall pleas God to spare mee my life, be a fortune for me for ever. . . . Now I am noeways able to goe unless you will be pleased either to lend mee a hors, or to give mee a hors !' In January '43 he writes from the Fleet to tell his brother how the troops he was with had been besieged in Chichester and forced to surrender upon quarter, ' But were all taken prisoners,

---

[1] 'On the new forcers of conscience under the Long Parliament.'

and plundered of all except the cloths wee had then on our backs, which hath caused mee to be destitute of everything.' Then follows some very grand language about his 'unlawfull imprisonment, and an urgent request that £10 may be paid to Mr. Fage who doth detaine my cloths.' 'For what I have hitherto done, I will maintaine with my life that it is warrantable . . . with this respect that I did allwayes maintaine that true protestant religion which my father bred and brought mee up in ; next the king's prerogative, then the liberty of the subject, and last of all the just privileges of parliament. . . . Thus charitably will I think of you, that it is not your desire to have the book of common prayer taken out of the churches, but perhapps you would have it a little reformed.' Tom is unapproachable when he poses as a philosopher and a divine ; but it is to be feared that his letters were much less diverting to Sir Ralph than they are to us ; he did not apparently send the 10*l.*, for three days after comes an angry protest : 'I scorne to be fed from hand to mouth, as men doe feed young apes to make them plyable to their dispositions. . . . This is the last I protest to God you shall receive from mee, unless I may be supplied with what I formerly sent for.' On the 16th he has found another cause for complaint : 'I was informed by a freind how scornefully I was spoken of, att the horne taverne in fleet street, by three or foure gentlemen that were in mourneing. The words were thees ; that I was a great malignant and had deserved hanging. . . . More over they were pleased to applaud you, in saying that you were both wise and discreet and in much favour in the parliament hous; now one of thees being by made this answer; why you (being in soe great favour) did not seek my releasment from my close imprisonement. Another of his associates did reply, that you took much distaste at a letter which I lately sent to you, therefore you would neither meddle nor make with mee.' He goes on to reproach Ralph furiously for making his brother a 'laughing stock and talk to every unworthy rascall.' On the 27th comes a very terrible threat: 'Deare Brother, it will be a wounder to see mee in print. Yet I feare what with my unjust imprisonment and your uncharitable affections will move mee to it, which if it doth I shall then make my loyall and true harted affections towards my king and country known to God and all good christians.'

Lady Sussex thus comments to Ralph on Tom's behaviour: 'i am truly sory to hear your naty brother gives so much trouble to you . . . i wish he were in the forfront of the next cermish; for god sake bee more wise then to affict your selfe for any thinge of unkaindnes that can com from him; he gave much truble to his good father and so he will do to you i fear; . . . you have don nothinge of ill, but good to them all.'

In April it appears that the ne'er do weel is married, and she writes that she is much troubled that he 'has made himself so miserable. Sartinly itt tis some mene pore woman . . . let him suffer for his foly and goo his one waye.'

Poor Lady Sussex had a trying life at Gorhambury; what with the danger of being attacked and plundered, the difficulty of getting rents, and the annoyances from soldiers quartered in the neighbourhood, the anxieties of the time were great. In October '42 she mentions how 'my lady Monmouth sent hur horses yesterday to fech up hur children, and the ware taken away from hur servant.'

In November she gets a protection for Gorhambury signed by Lord Essex, and she is taking her own measures to defend herself from the lawlessness of Royalist soldiers.

'my fear is most of prince ropperte, for tho say he hath littill mercy when he comes. . . . I am hear in as sade a condisyon as may bee. . . . i have made up some of the dors and pilede them up so with wode that i belive my hose is able to keepe out a good many now ; if wee escape plonderinge i shall account it a great marsy of god ; the are all about us hear in such grivus fears that if they see but a gentillman ridinge they think it tis to robe them.'

In January '43 she writes : ' They till me ther was something rede in the chorch this sonday, that thos that dide not give to the parlyment must be plonderede presently ; i cannot belive it was so ; but your forses have taken away our srife [? sheriff] as the call him ; i pray god derect the harts of the most powerfull to put an ende to the miserable time which must nedes ruen all if they holde.' January 14 : 'i thanke you for my printide nues, but i belive as you dide the lordes never made the speches. . . . Sometimes when ther is any true thinges put in printe, I shoulde bee glade of them ; but not of all the idel thinges they make.' January 20 : 'Great somes i see must be rasede.' (It was at this time that the Commons, distressed for want of money, dismissed the farmers of the customs and appointed new ones, who agreed to lend 20,000*l*.) She desires that her pictures may not be sent, as they are safer with Sir Ralph. 'Now let mee tell you i am infinetly sory that your good brother [Henry] hath misede of the plas ; the unworthynes of pepell in thes times are beyonde all exampell i thinke ; if itt bee more mony that must do itt, i will helpe somethinge to itt. May bee itt was ill taken that they went not to do ther duty att Oxfort ; you are wise and discrite ; yonger brothers that are to make ther fortunes, must sometimes be forst to doo that which is not plesinge to them . . . i hear your parlyment commandes ther shall bee no passege betwixt Oxfort and London, if itt be so i shall bee in great distres for my chaplen, who apoynts to com up the next wike and to have his bokes brought up which is all his welth . . . in honor i most make good the bokes if the shoulde miscary.' January 28 : 'This retierde life with my sade thoughts truly woulde sone make an ende of me, hade i not more from you than the rest of my frindes to plese me ; thes times give us lettill but terror and fears, and we hear ther is littell hopes of an acomidasyon.'

There is a letter dated Saxham, January 29, from Sir Henry Crofts to his sister-in-law, Lady Sussex, in which he describes 'the miseries and distractions of the generall condition of these times and this kingdome. . . . We have been hetherto in this countye more happye then many other partes, . . . but now we have but too much cause to feare our turnes in sufferinge equally with the rest is neare at hand.' In these circumstances his daughter Hester will prove an 'extraordinary troble' and 'greate affliction,' and he begs that Lady Sussex will receive her 'untill this tirrany maye through God's mercy be over past. . . . I hope God will in his mercy direct me to some place of retreate, whereby I maye avoide the haveinge that tendred to me which I am resolved and am bound in conscience never to subscribe unto [i.e. the Covenant].'

Early in February Lady Sussex wrote: 'Wee have great store of sogers at Sentabornes [St. Albans], the last wike one of the tone sent us worde they did intende to com and plonder us that night; but a thinke God it was not so; i sente presently to ther captins, so they have promisede to have a care of us, and to keepe ther sogers from us: S^r tomis Chike sent us another protexsyon, so that I hope wee shall bee safe . . . . i pray God your hose consent for a sasyon of armes.' On February 7, the lords had voted a cessation of arms, and there was in some quarters an earnest desire that the Commons should support them. Lady Sussex continues on the 16th: '... i must expect littill or noe rent this our lady-day ... Bosby was one that pade bestc, and truly the parlyment side hath usede him very hardly; for his religion i thinke; the have kaillede all his kattill uppon the gronde, taken away his hay, so that itt tis likely he most paye ill now.' March 8: 'i am very sory for the nues of my lorde Broke [his death], ther will be much reioysinge on the other side.'

In the previous December an association had been formed for the defence of the Eastern Counties, and Lady Sussex writes about March 15: 'My lorde Gray hath bene at Senttaborns [St. Albans] 'about the assosasyon; I hear very fue gentimen of the contrye cam in to him, but resonable store of the contry pepell cam in; he made a great spech, but I coulde not hear what it was; he put non to the othes [oaths]; but they say he gave them thre wikes time to consider of it, and he menes to site they say in some other tones in this contry; they have ratede this parish as i hear att fore ponde a leven sillings a wike, and to keepe 8 fote sogers. I hear nothinge of them yet; i hope the will expect nothinge from us, becase I presume wee most pay in esex and wher our lande lyes.' (Gorhambury was only rented by her.) A few days later she mentions that a great lady earnestly entreats her to leave that place; 'but truly as I have stade by it hetherto, so i mene and ples God to continue itt out still, for if this war continue i thinke most plases will bee a like.'

Ralph was moving to a new house, and Lady Sussex's next letter is addressed 'for Sr Rafe Verny att his hose in Lincolnes Inn feilds in the midle of the Row wher the Spanish Embassidor lies.' 'My brother tom tells me it tis a prity fine hose, and i am suer you will make itt convenint and hansome. Ther will bee so much dost in settinge thinges up and with workmen, that mythinkes you and your good swite lady shoulde bee content to leve itt; it will bee my infinet joy when some ever you ples to com, and your chamber i can have without truble to anybody. I shall ever take that fridom to youse you as my one childe, without any cerimony. We have great store of sogers now att Sene tabornes, but wee see non of them. I pray God keepe them still from us for thes bee the rudist I have harde of; they saw them tare the common prayer.'

Early in April she again thanks him 'for his nuse, wee being not all hear of one belife i tell them no more then what i thinke fit for them to know . . . i harde from Oxfort latly and much faxsyon [faction] ther is, and some wickede pepell about the kainge doth labore whatt they can that wee may have no pese; and indede it tis thought by some that knows much of the affars ther, that they will bee shorly removede on way or other.'

After Ralph had been to see her she thanks him for his 'kainde fisites,' and hope he has not suffered 'by so ill a chorny [journey] . . . My baly cam out of esexe that day you was hear, but brought not a peny of mony; ther is a great taxes lade uppon the landes, so hee cam to let mee know the tenents woulde not pay itt, but that i most alowe of itt; so i tolde him i woulde, but that itt shoulde goo in the tenents name . . . i hope no plonderers have bene att Cladon . . . My lorde Gray lay att Sene taborns [St. Albans] fridy nighte with some thre thosonde . . . i got my brother Crofts to goo to him with a complyment, so he hath promisede to do us all the cortisy hee can in his care of us hear.' Ralph's hangings and carpets are to be sent up to him. She hears that tenants in Buckinghamshire are refusing to stock their lands, except on the condition that in case the cattle are driven off, the landlord should deduct their loss from the rent.

In April the negotiations for a treaty came to an end and Sir Edward Sydenham writes: 'all hopes of peace is now taken awaye by the parlyments sendinge awaye for your comissioners, so that I am in dispaire of that great blessinge, so much desyered by all honest men, and no question a curse will fale upon the hinderers of it.'

Mrs. Isham, a sister of Ralph's mother, had lent 1,000*l*. to Sir Edmund when the king exacted contributions for the war. She now wrote to Ralph about the interest for the money. He had offered to settle land in any way she pleased, but she will leave all choice to him, of whose honesty, ability, and care she is very confident, but he may take counsel with her brother, Dr. Denton, 'to avoyde suspicion of other and clamour of the world . . .' Formerly the interest had been 8 per cent., but in these bad times she says that would not be possible for him to pay, 'and it would be a sin in me to receve it, though you should freely offer it.' She is fain to entertain soldiers 'twise a day and keepe them company all the while for feare they should not think us courteous.' 'For the passengers that pass aboute ther bisnes, they lay hold on them.'

There had been depredations on the Claydon fish-ponds, for Lady Sussex says, 'to drag your ponde was a wikede part of them to do; but i hope the hade not time to destroy all your good fish.'

On May 14 there is a letter from the incorrigible Tom, by which it appears that Ralph had been trying to arrange for his release from the Fleet upon conditions of his straightway taking ship in charge of the master. 'The Barbados is the place that I only ayme att. But your weak faith doth not any wayes beleeve that my thoughts are reall . . . Oh! Brother how doe you wish my libertye, and tye mee to soe hard conditions. My conscience telleth mee that neither his lordshipp nor the hous of commons never thought to take mee out of one prison to putt mee into another, I meane in giveing mee in charge to a maister of a shipp, had not you putt it into their minds, haveing an itching desire to have mee gone; for feare I should be chargeable to you hereafter ; which is contrary to my disposition.' On June 1 he says he is getting ready for the voyage to the Barbados, but as his wife's mother will not let her go, he means to wait for six months ; and a month later it is but too evident that he has no intention of relieving his relations in England of his presence, as his wife Joyce writes to Ralph begging his help since the Parliament claimed her goods, and her husband had betaken himself to the king's army. Ralph does not hold out much hope of his assistance, remarking gravely, 'had I had any knowledg of your intentions to match with him, both this and that might have been prevented.'

It does not appear that Mistress Joyce would have welcomed this well-meant interference, and Lady Sussex's surmise that she must be some poor, mean woman, seems to have been a piece of gratuitous ill-nature, prompted by her hearty dislike of Tom. Joyce, who writes and spells better than most of the ladies of Ralph's acquaintance, writes to him of her 'passionate affection to your brother my deare husband. I have parted with an estate and my father is ready to do much more for me, so that my husband performs with him the conditions upon marriage with me . . . I am sorry my husband did not folow your counsell being his wisest frind. But I had rather condeme my selfe then my husband, and I would suffer any thing for him, as I am bound in duty . . . my best hopes was to enjoy his desired company.'

Many disasters befell the Parliament during this summer, among which was the death of Hampden on June 24. Lady Sussex writes: 'i am very sory for mr hamdon; I do not know him att all, but i have harde he is a most discrite good man, i becech god he may recover . . . If all bee true that is reportede . . . the parlyment side hath hade much the worst of itt latly . . . the say hear that farfex hath hade a great ovour thro, and waller will never bee able to appere agane.' Again, a little later, 'the death of mr hamden was a most infinet lose beinge so religious and very wise a man.'

The loss of Hull was but just averted by timely measures. Captain Hotham, son of the governor, being suspected of treachery, was arrested by order of Essex and imprisoned in Nottingham Castle, whence he escaped and joined his father in Hull. Here, however, he was re-arrested by the Mayor. Sir John Hotham hearing of his capture endeavoured to escape, but, failing in his attempt, the father and son were both sent prisoners to London. Lady Sussex remarks: 'Sr hothom is a most unworthy man if it bee true that is thought of him; but sartinly he knowes himselfe gilty of some ill bisynes, or eles he woulde not have indevourde to make an escape; i thought his sone hade bene fast in nottingam castill.'

Early in July Lady Sussex bewails Fairfax's defeat at Adwalton Moor: 'I am truly sory for my lorde farfex, a brave man he is; i hope god will keepe him from falinge into the handes of his enimes. ther plots are still discoverde ; the say in thes parts, ther was a pubblicke fast and thinkesgiveinge att oxfor for this blow my lorde farfex hath hade ; but i belive rather itt was bonfiers.' Two days later she says : ' Sr edwarde terell was a little fearfull ; prince robort hade bene hontinge att his parke [Thornton, near Buckingham], he toke him much with his cortisy to him ; he kailde fife buckes, shote them and his doge boy poullede them down, he dide not ride att all. . . . Prince robort made a shorter stay then he intendede, hearinge my lord esex entendede to bee att bucingam, all his compiny went away soddenly and he and them all laye in the filde that night. My lord of esex armey went thoro some of the pasteurs, dide littill hort ; the most was in Blackegrofe, for ther many of them laye uppon the gras and restede themselves ; the toke not above on shipe [sheep] ; in the common filde wher the laye all night ther was many shipe gon.'

In the end of July 1643 Lord Sussex died, and his widow had a great deal of business to get through. ' The are very mery att oxfort i hear,' she says, ' and thinke to ovour com all soddonly ; i hope the will not finde itt so esye a mattir as the thinke.' Doll Leeke also describes the strength and confidence of the king's side. She would have written to Ralph sooner, she says, could she have conveyed a letter to him. ' I cannot chuse but let you know my opinion of your condision, which I think is so ill that it wear want of frindship in me to conceall it. You have bin all this year thought a violent man against the king and the taking of the Oath [another vow of adherence to the parliamentary cause had been taken by the Commons in June] has confermed it; he sayes himself that all that took it wold be glad of his ruen, and it is the opinion of most that are about him. God has blesed him beyond all your expictasions, and he is now in so good a condision that he nead not fear the parliment, tho they have gon all the wais in the world to destroy him; thay have nether wanted men mouney nor tonnes tell now, but you se how thay have prospred. I beleve the maine party of them have will provided for themselfs, and will leve you and many more in the lurch, therfore consider with your self how you may come off and defere it not, it will not be so easey a thing as you may Imagin, and do not think that the lose of your father will be any healp to you, for that has gained you many enemies hear. From ther love to him proseads ther hate to you, becaus you have continued with thos that killed him, this is the speach of many and I confess gos somthing near me to hear it. Besids the lose of your fortune you must not look for any thing from any that are with the king but disrespect, the family that I am in excepted who ever will be your faithfull frinds, tho it may not be in ther power to serve you as thay desire. Whatsoever your consienc has binn heartofore, I now beleve you see your erour, for it is imposible that you can still continue in so much blindnes. God has given you to lardg a proporsion of senc. Loke upon the king from the begining, and think with your self if god's blising had not gon with him, whether it had bin posible he could have binn in such a condision, as he is now in. I know many that wold be glad to make ther peas and give good somes for it (and such parcons as you wold not beleve wold leave you) and will not be accepted of. . . . I heard my lord wainman and some other which I will not name are upon coming away, you wear mentshoned a mongst them, I wish that part of the story wear true.' She recommends him to 'come with a good many for the number may make you all considerable to the king, which any of you alone wold not be. Cosen, if you cannot find in your hart to do this, leve them and retire to some other plac, I meane the parliment, for assure your self thay will leave you and the kingdom in a very short time. Consider your wiffe and chilldren and brothers and sisters, which must all sufer with you. . . . My obligasions are so greate that it wear ingratitude in me not to discharge my consienc, which I now have don. Your brothers are both well; Tom found forty pound in an ould coberd in the subburbs of Bristow befor we got the towne but I think it will not do him much good.'

Bristol was taken by Prince Rupert on July 26. In August came the negotiations of the Parliament with the Scots, which resulted in the 'Solemn League and Covenant' being drawn up between the two nations for their mutual defence and for the establishment of the Presbyterian system and religious uniformity as understood in Scotland. This document was sworn to at Westminster by 112 members of the Commons ; it became ' a sword to divide.' Sir Ralph's refusal to sign the Covenant proved the turning point of his career, his conscience would no longer permit him to continue with the party he had loved and served so well. In the end of August he left London for Gorhambury. His most intimate friend, Sir Roger Burgoyne, signs the Covenant, and while loving Sir Ralph more than ever, and respecting his scruples, he never ceases to hope that he may yet see it right ' to come in.' He keeps him informed of all that is going on. On August 29 he writes between the lines of a letter ostensibly full of public news, topsy-turvy in sympathetic ink, urging him to return, for 'there was an order made this morning, that a committee be appointed for the putting in execution the former order, for the sequestring the estates of those members of the house as shall absent themselves without leave. I pray thinke of it seriously before you come.' On September 5 he says : ' As you left us, so you may finde us, speaking much, doing little. There is little newes stirring and that is so weary before it comes to the Hall that it seldom can mount so high as the House.'

Other friends are trying to stand up for Sir Ralph in his absence and to gain time for him to consider his decision. Mr. W. Bell writes on September 14 :

'You need not feare about absence, I have made Mr. Speaker myselfe acquainted with that and the reason of it, and he doth approve your absence. Sir theire was some att your house to have sequestred your goods, but I spook with ii of the sequestrators, and bid them take notice from me that you were noe delinquent.' Later he writes: 'A motion was made against you to-day for absenting yourselfe, as if you were gone to the king; Mr. Speaker, Mr. Rennolds, and I told them how the case stood with you, where upon the whole House was very well satisfied with it.'

Deeply hurt that his conduct should be so misconstrued, Sir Ralph wrote to Mr. Robert Reynolds:

'S^r,—Your former favours give mee confidence to trouble you with a letter to excuse my not waiting on you as I intended. The truth is, I am yet soe much unsatisfied in that businesse, that though I have greate desire to comply with you, and some other of my freinds, and submit myselfe to your better judgments, yet for ye present I canot doe it, and being unwilling to give the House the least offence (knowing how uselesse a creature I am), I have resolved to take a jorney and for a while to retire to some such place, where I may have leasure enough to informe my judgment in such things wherin I am yet doubtinge. S^r, perhapps this my absence may give occation to some jellous spirits to suggest (as formerly they have donn) that I am gonn to Oxford, I confesse I care not what such men say, a little time will sufficiently discover those malicious untruths and shame there authours. S^r, whatever others thinke, I am confident you will still preserve mee in your good oppinion, and I must beeseech you to beeleeve, what ever reports are raised, or however I may suffer by them, I shall alwaies honour, and pray for the Parliament, and continue

'Your most affectionate freind and humble servant.'

On September 23, Sir Roger tells him that the House has resolved that the Covenant shall be taken 'by all the members of that house, and all the ministers of the Assembly in St. Margaret's Church in Westminster upon Munday next. Old Mr. White to begin the day in confession, Mr. Nie (whome we sent into Scotland) for to succeed him in exortation and advise, Dr. Goodge to conclude as he shall please. It was agreed upon by the House of Commons that the L^{ds} should be acquainted with o^r resolutions to do so, but not according to the usuall maner to be desired for to concurr with the house in it. You may conjecture the reason.'

A later letter describes how this was carried out. Mr. Nye having made his exhortation, 'Mr. Henderson immediately after made a thing betweene a speech and a preach to us in his seate ; after which Mr. Nie reade the Covenant in the pulpit before us all, which was ingrossed in parchment, then afterwards the house of Comons went up into the Chancel for to subscribe theire names to it ; after them the Scotch Commissioners and the Assembly. One thing I must misplace, which is that after the Covenant was read, all that would take it were to hold up their handes. Ther was a greater apparence both of the house of Com̄ons, and also of the Assembly then was expected. The names of those that tooke it are not yet knowne, nor of those that have not. My Ld Grey of Ruthin, and Mr. Bond of o^r House are by the House ordered to be the notaries for to observe all that come into the house which have not taken the Covenant. . . . Next Wednesday all ministers in London and the suburbs are to explaine the Covenant to theire parish by order from the House, and upon Sunday next they are all to take it.'

The plot was thickening, members were compelled to sign the Covenant with short days of grace, and a penalty of sequestration of all their estates if they did not come in; ruin awaited all those who absented themselves. After Newbury affairs were going against the king, and on the Parliament side, men were scarcely allowed to speak or even to write. 'These inquisitive times silence all our pennes.' On September 28 Sir Roger writes:

'S^r,—I attended the house upon Tuisday, ther cam in but three which had not tooke the Covenant the day before, Sr Harry Vane, M^r. Solliciter, S^r J^o. ffranklin. The two first are ready for to take it when the house shall please, the other desires time to consider of it. . . . Sir Walter Erle reports that some of our forces sallowed (sallied) out of Poole and tooke diverse of the king's forces, amongst which Coll [Henry] Varney was one. . . . I shall attend you at the time and place appointed.' With this letter is a scrap of paper on which is written in the same hand: 'Ordered, that . . . Sr Alexan. Denton, Sr George Stonhowse . . cum multis alijs (you are not in) do attend by October 10 the Committee for sequestring the estates of such members as neglect the service of the howse uppon paine of sequestring their estates.'

Again Sir Roger writes : ' Sir W. Lewis tells me that he will take it [i.e. the Covenant]. He wonders at you for holding of so much, I preethee deare heart, this day or too morrow at the farthest come to thine owne.'

Even Susan has heard of the danger threatening members who ventured to differ from the majority, and writes to her brother, addressing the letter to a servant : ' in this last dyurnall there is how that there is fore outt of the sitty appointed to make Inquire after those which are absent from the howse, and if the bee nott to be found then to make Inquire after ther goods, and whome soever shall bring them outt or give Intelygence where they bee, they shall have the selling of them and ther profitt twelf pence in the pound: where of I heare though Sr Allex. Denton and Sir Ralph Varney though the be nott named, yett they say as the know well enough wheare they be, and if they doe nott com, they shall be fetchet very sudenly and putt in prison. There are none counted so great mallignents as they be. In hast yours.' (No signature.)

It is clear that Ralph had now made up his mind not to sign. The new 'prety house' in Lincoln's Inn Fields, his strong parliamentary interests, the ordering of his and his wife's estates, which he did so well and enjoyed doing, the business for his friends whom he loved so tenderly, was all to be abandoned. His uncomplaining heroism is very remarkable; he never alludes to any of the sacrifices he is making; they seem to him quite simple, he must do what he thinks right, and nothing outside has the slightest effect upon his resolution. His trusted friend Sir Roger writes that Sir John this and Sir William that have 'come in,' that 'Sir Norton Snatchpoole,' Mr. James Fiennes, &c., with whom Ralph has been working side by side in the contest for the rights of Parliament, have had a day or two more grace allowed them, that Sir Harry Vane and Mr. Solliciter have given up the contest and signed their names. It does not make the least impression upon him. What is it to him how other men's consciences allow them to act? The question is, What I, Ralph Verney, believe to be the righteous course in the matter, and that, so help me God, I will take.

My friends consider 'that my over scrupulous conscience taketh the oath for a great perilous thing, when it is indeed but a trifle,' said another Englishman, who had dared to stand alone in a former crisis of England's history, 'and many may think this whom I myself esteem for their learning and virtue. . . . But whether they do or not, does not make any difference to me. . . . I never intend to pin my soul to another man's back. . . . I have counted the possible peril on full many a restless night with a heavy heart, but never thought to change.' Sir Ralph had not the buoyant cheerfulness that carried Sir Thomas More so triumphantly through all sorrows ; he was in the deepest depression of spirits, indeed, he had so little of the stuff in him whereof martyrs are made, that it is touching to see a man so cautious, so careful, so fond of the proprieties and even of the punctilios of life, go forth calmly into what to him was indeed the wilderness. Accustomed to being greatly regarded at home, he went out to face penury and insignificance ; and what, to a man who enjoyed doing every item of his own business with his own head and hands, must have been almost worse, he was obliged to leave his affairs to others. The delays and uncertainties of the foreign post, and the unsettled state of the country, made it difficult for him when abroad even to hear of what his agent was doing for him in his absence—but 'the bigots of the iron time' had affixed a penalty of utter ruin on any independence of judgment. The wrench is great ; it is like the dividing asunder of soul and body ; he has only to walk up St. Margaret's, to sign his name in the chancel, but there is never a halt in his resolution. 'For my owne part I am resolved,' he says, 'that innocency shall be my guard, and then whatsoever

I suffer I can beare without repining.' Mr. John Fountaine, a Royalist lawyer, writes to him: 'I was once in hopes since I last parted with thee, that something might have been done to have caused a happy and peaceable meeting, but all those hopes were soone quashed, and I see nothing now but ye devouring sworde to put an end to o^r differences. I understand something of thy intentions. I wish I might be soe happy that . . . I may speake wth thee before thy departure.' Ralph replies, 'My hart, it greeves mee that I canot invent a way to see thee . . . and it afflicts mee much more to think how longe wee shall bee parted. Had I thy company all places would bee pleasant to mee, but wherever I am, I will bee entirely thine ; and if wee never meete on earth, I hope in heaven wee shall. God in mercy end these miserable times, for my part I never expect to enjoy any more, I see my ruine at the very dore ready to swallow mee.'

Henry has been taken by the parliamentary army. Sir Roger writes on October 3 partly about ' Colonel Varney's' imprisonment, partly about some trunks belonging to Ralph's sister Mary, which had been intercepted and examined by the Committee at ' Harford.' 'Sir John Norwich . . . cannot believe that any thing ther did belonge to Mistress Mary Verney, unless it were a little booke Quarles Emblems uppon which her name was writt.'

Poor Ralph, in the midst of his own distresses, writes to the governor of Portsmouth in Henry's behalf, saying that he will supply his brother's wants as soon as possible. 'In the meanetime I know you are soe noble, that he shall have all necessary accommodations fit for a gentleman.' To Henry himself who had written to beg 20*l*., for 'all the goods thay left mee was a come and a nolmenecke,' he says that he has used all the means he could to effect his desires. 'I know restraint is greivous to your nature, yet you were happie to fall into soe good hands.'

From the letter of a certain Thomas Baker, it appears that there was no doubt about getting an exchange for Henry, but the fame of his gallantry made them think an important one necessary. In the following January we hear that 'Harry is newly released his prison, but it cost him £60 ransome,' and he is shortly after serving again.

'Prince Maurice,' writes Sir Roger on October 23, 'is dead at Exeter of the new disease [i.e. influenza], and this reported with so much confidence as it allmost begetts a beleife in me of the truth of it.' However, three days later he observes: 'Since Prince Maurice is alive, you shall never heare from me that he is dead againe unless he be voted so.' That 'Sir H. Ludlow is dead of the new disease' is mentioned in another letter.

During the summer Sir Ralph's household had been constantly on the *qui vive* for soldiers, the trained bands marching from London to the battle of Newbury passed through Bucks, and the account given by one of the sergeants has been published in the 'History of the Honourable Artillery Company.' 'August 30.—We advanced to a village called Clayden, this day the Lord General's Army and our Regiment of the Trained Band together with the auxiliary forces met at Aylesbury; the great guns were fired at every fort about the town as the Lord General passed by. This was the fast day; our Regiment was quartered this night at Sir Ralph Verney's House, a Parliament man, his father, the King's Standard-bearer, was slain at Edgehill.'

After this, Susan Verney and Sir John Leeke write doleful letters describing how his horses and Sir Ralph's were carried off by the troopers; we 'shoed [showed] them noates under your hand, but they would nott looke upon them. Then we asked them for their commishtion but they would shoe none,' says Susan, and her uncle mourns over the loss of his bay gelding and a beloved old horse Ormond, as 'more grevios than my Irish plunders, for now the owld man must trampe on foote.'

We are 'Wearied with being so often wakened at midnight to fly from the King's and Parliament's troops, both equally feared and equally plundering,' wrote another sufferer in these unsettled times.[1]

Meanwhile, in his methodical way, Sir Ralph was making such arrangements as were possible for the comfort of his wife and family. Before the Navigation

---

[1] *A Cavalier's Note Book.* Longmans, 1881.

Acts, the carrying trade was mainly in the hands of the Dutch, so that travellers going from England to France sent their goods by Holland, even if they went themselves by the direct route. All through September and October, Sir Ralph is settling about the transport of his heavy luggage. He has been warned to keep his secret and to caution his servants not to spread any rumour of his intended departure; but many 'bundles' are coming up from Claydon by degrees. He was evidently preparing for a long absence. The 'bundles' go through sad adventures. A certain Dixon was to convey some of them to Rotterdam. Dr. Peter Chamberlain writes from thence to say that Dixon has arrived but without Sir Ralph's goods or his own, 'like a spider he hath turned the sweetness of your favours into poison . . . we have fallen into the hands of Turkes, the seamen we had to deale withall are most exquisite knaves. . . . Noble Sir, wee are here in a strange country all nacked, till your freindshipp & wisdome helpe us out of these troubles.'

The news that some of his baggage had been found must have been very welcome. Peter Chamberlayne writes on October 28: 'I have your things in my custody in the Hague. I know nott yett the parcells, because they are packt up together where I cannot come to number them, and because of the greatness of them, I must be forced to remove them out of that house which I have hired (where they now are) . . . the charges amount to 190 gulders . . . £14 in gold and 16 shillings if ye gold continue at 13 gulders the Peece. . . . I have likewise furnished y^r carefull servant Samuel Lavington with 14 Rixe Dollers for his return.' Other things are despatched to Amsterdam and Rotterdam, and later on Will Roades sends up 'an inventory of 17 bundles of linen, pikturs and stores, whereof 10 of them are sent to London, and the last seaven are to com up this present 17th Novemb. 1643.'

Ten days later Sir Ralph writes to him again: 'I pray looke well if there is any more Linnon, or any other thinge that is worth removing and may bee come at without trouble; and make it upp in Bundles and send it upp as you have donne the rest.'

The luggage sent on before them amounted to fifty-one 'percells,' including some trunks of valuables belonging to relations confided to his good nature. Other property was hidden away in London; but troublesome as these arrangements must have been, they were nothing to the complicated business to be settled at Claydon.

A protection from the king and one from the Parliament had been obtained for Claydon to defend it, if possible, from harm from either army. Sequestration was imminent, and all sorts of legal fictions were resorted to to ward it off. The estate was vested in trustees, and fictitious leases to friends were drawn up to protect Sir Ralph's London house, and his interest in the Alnage. His three brothers and five unmarried sisters, scarcely realising his difficulties, are clamouring for their portions, and many creditors of Sir Edmund's are pressing their claims. Sir Ralph seems to be aggravated even with the good doctor, though the latter knows how entirely he can trust him. 'I hope your letter,' writes Dr. Denton on his own behalf and Mrs. Isham's, ' was only *ad terrorem*, because you founde some rubbs in it at the first, and I presume you wanted neyther for cunninge nor kindnesse to reserve an hole to thrust Jugge (Mrs Isham) and the D^r in before others. I leave it to your good nature both to supply us for the present, and to secure us for the future. . . . My wife and I desire that your servants and horses may be the carriors and protectors of two clogg bags of ours, one is little and light havinge only a suit of clothes of mine in it, the other is of more concernment both for waight, value and use, it being her childbed linnen. Ffudd I presume may helpe protect it as linnen given to y^r sisters (therefore to be directed to them) by your mother. . . .'

There were the five sisters to be provided for, whose names read like the chorus of an old song. There was Sue and Pen and Peg and Molly, and unruly little Betty, who was only ten years old. Except Susan, who was boarded with the Leekes, they were all to remain at Claydon under the care of Mrs. Alcock, with occasional visits from their brothers, and from their uncles and aunts at Hillesden, three miles off, where a large party of the Dentons and Ishams were residing.

They were dependent on their eldest brother not only for protection, but for bare subsistence. Their own money was locked up in the Alnage, which had been the best possible security when their father left it; but now 'tis almost a yeare,' writes Sir Ralph in August, ' since any part of it was paied. . . . I threaten Dick Blower (who ought to pay it) to send my sisters to his house, and tell him either hee or the parish must keep them.'

Susan, the eldest, was now twenty-two. She was in delicate health, and was in London in October for advice. '. . . I am extremely yeallow, my Aunt Leeke did think it might prove the janders.' Dr. Crag tells her that 'itt proseeds all from mallincolly.' 'I did thinke as I should never abinne sick with that!'

To make matters worse, the poor girls were quarrelling amongst themselves. 'I did spake to Pegge,' writes Mrs. Isham, 'as her mayd might sarve both her & Pen, but she will not let it be so by no meanes. . . . I told her now their father and mother was dead, they should be a helper one to the other . . . but all would not doe. If she will be content to take my godchild [Betty] holy to her, all but wasshing of her, then Nan Fudd [the nurse] will have more time to help Pen, & you need not be att any more charges for a mayd for Pen.'

At the same time Pen writes her views on the proposed arrangements at Claydon. She is to pay 8*s.* a week for her diet out of her allowance, which she inclines to think too much. She is also to find clothes for the maid Bess Coleman. It is a curious bit of human nature that these poor girls, fatherless, motherless, and penniless, cannot forbear standing out for the services to which each considers she has a right from the maids. In this letter, however, Pen is very humble, and says: 'I am to intreat a favour, which is if you can lett Nan fud have soe much time as to come [comb] my head, for I doe heare that bess colman cannot doe it, and if I have not won which can come a hed will, I doe not know what to doe by reason that my hed is soe tender, and to smoth sum of my uppar lining, by reason that bess colman cannot doe them, but I hope in time to bring hur to it. My sister Margearett will teake my sister betty to hur, and hur made shall dres hur and heare hur hur booke and teach hur work.'

Ralph and Mary had now three children living. Edmund, who had been made so much of by Lady Denton and Lady Sussex, had grown past the halcyon days of blue satin coats and nursery petting into a fine tall boy of nearly seven; Margaret, who had taken the place of her dead sisters in her parents' hearts, was a year younger. There are many allusions in the letters to her beauty and the sweetness of her character from witnesses less partial than her devoted father and mother; it was settled that Mun and Peg were to go with them abroad. The fate of the little three-year old John was for some time undecided; his nurse, Nan Fudd, and all his maiden aunts were most anxious that he should remain at Claydon; he was a sturdy little fellow, and his presence was very welcome in the desolate house. Pen wrote to Lady Verney on the 16th of October: '. . . I have noe good nuse to send you, but that your boy Jack is grone a sossy child, God be thonked, and I should be very sory if ye letter which my Aunt first intends to writ to you and my brother should take affect, for I should be loth to part with Jack's good company, for he is now very fond of mee, and I have a very great love for ye child. . . . My love to Mun and Pegg.'

The aunts carried the day, and it was four years before Mary saw her 'sossy' boy again.

Lady Sussex undertook to look to the sale of the horses after their departure. Sir Roger Burgoyne was a man of that rare kind who, when his advice is refused, will set about to help his friends in their way, not in his own. He had thought Sir Ralph utterly mistaken in refusing to sign the Covenant, but, when he found his counsel was rejected, he did his best to help him to find a foreign resting-place; he heard of a house at Rouen, and on November 7 Sir Ralph decides 'to take the Chambors and other roomes, and what else shall bee needful.'

Meanwhile matters in Parliament were growing more and more serious. On November 7 Sir Roger writes of 'three members that refused to take the covenant yeisterday, for which they are only suspended from the Howse during the pleasure of the howse, and untill such time as a punishment be agreed uppon by the howse for to be inflicted uppon the refusers of it.' Sir Roger writes again : 'We heare nothing concerning the three gentlemen ... the punishment is not yet brought forth, but the Com^{tee} is now in travaile ; I wish it prove not a monster. Yeisterday Mr. Pierpoint ... sent his request to the howse ... that he desired theire leave for to go beyond sea, in respect that he c^d not for the present take the Covenant, and that he was very unwilling to refuse it, least he should give any occasion of scandall, and that he will in the meane time resigne up all his estate into the parliaments hand for to dispose of as they shall think fitt, only to allowe a proportion for his wife and children ; and this was for to express himselfe very much the parliaments, and farr from neutrality. It was very much debated, but in the end went against him by one voice only.'

Nothing remained for Sir Ralph but to be gone with all speed if he was to retain his personal freedom.

Having apparently wound up his business, private and political, he sits down in utter grief and weariness, and draws up, *more suo*, two melancholy documents, docketed in his usual tidy fashion, as expressing his wishes—'If I miscarry.'

He writes at great length to Sir R. Burgoyne about the disposal of his goods—24 parcells in Mr. Jonas Abeeles custody in Rotterdam, '27 percells more of goods now in Dr. Peter Chamberlaine's custody in the Hague,' and 'the rest of my goods remaining in your house and in severall other places in London or else where'—for the payment of his debts and the benefit of little Jack left at Claydon.

'And as for those 4 assignments of my house in Lincolnes Inn feilds—of Mr. Mosses lease, of Mr. Wayes Lease, and of the Privie seale for money out of the Alnage, I pray cancell them all foure, and never let them bee seene, for they were only to prevent sequestration. And soe was that lease of all Middle Claydon, dated 30 Octob. last for 2 yeares from the first of this Novemb., therefore cancell this also, and let it not bee seene.

'R. V.'

The second document is as follows :

'If I, my Wife, and my 2 eldest children, doe all of us miscarry in this jorney, before I come to France. Let all my money in your custody bee deliverd to my Lady Sussex to bee by her kept, or disposed as shee and you shall thinke fittest, for my sonn John. and as for that also which you have gotten to bee returned for mee into Roan in France, get it backe againe, and deliver it to her likwise for my sonne Johns use, and desire her to keepe that wch I left in her hands for his use also.

'Only let three hundred pounds of that which was returned into France bee deliverd to my Executors towards the payment of my Debts and other uses mentioned in my Will.

'14 Novemb : 1643.
'My Lady Sussex hath my Will.
[Signed in Sir Ralph's hand :]
'Sr Ralph Verney
Lady Mary Verney
Edmund Verney } Children.'
Margaret Verney

This done, he made a rough draft of a letter to Lady Sussex, in which he took a ceremonious leave of her, ' for I am now hastinge to the shipp, wch perhapps may bee my grave.' Alas! there was no need to hurry. There were still many tedious weeks to be got over, spent chiefly, it appears, under Lady Sussex's hospitable roof at Gorhambury, to which loving farewell letters are addressed by different members of the family. 'Nattycock and Nannycock' (the playful names of happy Claydon days for Sir Nathaniel and Anne Lady Hobart) send 10,000 loves. His aunt, Mrs. Isham—a king's woman to the core—who quarrelled with his going from the opposite point of view to Sir Roger Burgoyne's, writes that she cannot hear of some clothes sent to Claydon for the children :

'Now the armies is aboute, and Mr. J. [Isham] and I could wishe you thire too, thinkeing it the rites [righteous] cause, and in time I hope youre mind will change, if it be in the ronge, or else not, and in the mene while my pray[er] shall be as god would gide us to take his side which ever it be, and so a due wisshing you as well as mine one [own] soule.'

There is a little brown scrap of paper at Claydon labelled ' a Pass for Sir Ralph Verney with his Lady, etc., when they retired into France under the names of Smith '—a time-honoured *alias*, which did good service with all refugees, and in later days sheltered Louis Philippe on his flight to England. The pass is addressed ' To all Captaines and others whom it concernes : '

' London. These are to require you to permitt and suffer Mr. Ralph Smith and his wyfe and his man and mayde to passe by water to Lee in Essex and to returne. So they carry nothinge of Danger.

' November ye 30th 1643.
' By warrant of ye Ld Maier,
' Jo : Beadnege.'

The tempestuous wintry weather added indefinitely to the sufferings and hazards of the journey. Two or three weeks seem to have been spent in vain attempts to get across to France. ' My very cloathes were on Board,' writes Sir Ralph, ' and I myself lay privatly in a close corner ready to bee gonn.' The weather is so bad, that their late kind hostess listens anxiously to the wind howling amongst her trees at Gorhambury, and thinks of them tossing about in the Channel. The terrible voyage over at last, Sir Ralph wrote to her on the last day of the year, 1643 (new style), from Rotterdam : 'This letter hath noe other errand then to acquaint your Ladyshipp that from the first of this month till Friday last, wee lay winde bound, in wch time I spent all my little stock of patience, and then seeing noe hopes of better weather, a shipp or two being ready for Holland, I resolved to come heather. Wee had a most tempestuous and violent winde for 12 houres, but through God's greate mercy on Sunday night wee all arrived heere in saifty. I humbly thank your Ladyshipp for your Furre, certainly you did fore see or prophicie my coming into this cold country. My stay heere is very uncertaine.'—Dec. $\frac{21}{31}$, 1643.

He is so one with his wife that he has never even thought it necessary to express her acquiescence in the line he has taken ; she has evidently been heart and soul with him at every point of the painful struggle ; she has fortified, cheered, and sympathised with him in every step of the sacrifices that have fallen upon both ; she has never even remonstrated for the sake of the children, and after the wretched three days to Rotterdam, Mary, just arrived with her two little ones 'in this cold country,' makes no moan, but only sends her humble service in a postscript to Lady Sussex, and ' desires her wearisome journey may excuse her silence.'

Lady Sussex replies on January 9, 1644 : 'I cannot till you how wellcom your letter was to mee, for the windes was so boyoustrous hear that i had you ofton in my thoughts with fear. . . . the other day I harde all your horses was will, your sarvant brought one of your fine mares hether, i cannot yet put him off. I offerde it for £15, but they will not give so much, for hear is but littil money amongst us, though the hole company be still hear you lefte.' In answer to Mary's postscript, she assures her that her affections are to her as to the dearest of her own, and she hopes she may find ' somethinge of plesuer wher you are, the gittir i hope will take you up much, strive for cherfullnes with itt.' One wonders how the poor guitar had fared during the 'tempestuous violent weather.'[1]

Sir R. Burgoyne congratulates him on ' your safe arrivalls where you are, though a plase never intended,' and adds that Ralph's cousin, Col. Fiennes, is condemned to be beheaded, ' but itt is possible he may live as longe as you or I.'

After a fortnight's rest at Rotterdam, Sir Ralph is arranging to move on to Rouen; he sends ' 26 percells of goods for my use there, marked R.V. No. i. to 26,' 'in the shipp caled the Fortune.' He writes to an agent: ' I hope to bee at Roan before they come, but if I should be stayed longer by any misfortune, I must then intreate you to take care to get them set upp in some saife dry place. . . . The goods containe wering apparrell, Linen, Pickturs, and other Houshold stuffe, all of it hath been

---

[1] It had been alluded to as 'a very good one, it was the most beautiful that could be found, for it was of Ebony enlayd with mother pearle,' bought at Paris.

used ; there is noe Marchandice amongst it. I pray use some meanes that the Searcher may not open any thing till I come with the Keyes, a little money perhapps will Blinde his Eyes, or at least make him deferre the opening of them till the Keyes come. . . .'
Custom-house officers have remained unchanged, with all that has come and gone, since Sir Ralph's travelling days.

CHAPTER IX.

THE BURNING OF HILLESDEN HOUSE.

> 'Rapine has yet took nought from me:
> But if it please my God I be
> Brought at the last to th' utmost bit,
> God make me thankful still for it.
> I have been grateful for my store,
> Let me say grace when there's no more.'—HERRICK.

In February 1644, Sir Ralph is settled at Rouen, but not at all reconciled to his lot. 'The difficulties of my last journeys, and the doubts and feares I have for my little family, together with the miseries of my native country,' he writes, 'have made me soe conversant with afflictions, that this World is growne tedious, and life it selfe a Burden to mee. . . . This place is full of variety of newes concerning England; every one reports as hee would have it—out of w^{ch}, I (that desire, and pray for peace) can gather nothing but ye expectation of a generall ruine.' He has had no news of his friends for four months, 'and I have thought it more than 4 yeares,' and at last in despair he sends a messenger to England to deliver his letters by hand, for 'these unhappie times are soe full of curiosity and soe inquisitive after Letters, I canot say what I desire';

THE BURNING OF HILLESDEN HOUSE 187

and he tells Doll Leeke that, having heard nothing 'from your selfe or any other friende neare you, I have sent a servant to see if there bee any such creatures left alive. Therefore let me intreate you (if you are livinge still) to write and write and write againe and never give over writing till one of your letters come with saifety to your affectionate servant.' To Nat. Hobart he writes : 'certainly the distractions of these times have buried as many men alive as dead,' and to his wife, 'sweet Nan,' he pours out his woes at still greater length :

'I doubt you are now in a very ill condition for want of a playfellow [meaning his wife], for these distractions have banished all mirth out of poore England, and I thinke out of the whole world too, for where I have beene there is noe sign of it, but perhapp my being soe seasond with afflictions like the man whose continuall lookeing through a greene glasse madd all things seeme greene to him, soe my perpetuall troubles make all things appear sad and black to mee. God of his mercy send us peace that wee may once more enjoy our good old friendes. In the meanwhile I shall love and pray for you. Sweete do you the like for me.'

Copies of these letters, and of others sent by the same hand to Mrs. Eure, to 'Brother Gardiner,' and 'Sister Gardiner,' to 'Sir Edward and Lady Siddenham,' and to 'Mr. Ffountaine,' a Royalist imprisoned for not paying taxes to the Parliament, were kept by Sir Ralph ; they are all dated March 7, 1644.

The news from England, so ardently desired, was sad and startling enough when it came. Hillesden, which had been a second home to all Dame Margaret Verney's children, had been besieged, taken, and totally destroyed by fire. Nothing now remains of

INTERIOR OF HILLESDEN CHURCH.
(From a sketch by Lady Verney.)

the pleasant home but a few melancholy looking grass mounds, the lines of what was once a 'great fair terrace,' a square piece of water and a fine avenue of large elms on the crest of the hill, ending in a wilderness. The singularly interesting church, of

Sir Thomas Denton, Kt. of Hillesden, *Tho: Denton*
from a picture at Claydon House.

the Decorated Henry VII. period, stands in solitary beauty in the heart of the undulating rich grass country of Buckinghamshire.

The Dentons had played a considerable part in the county. The estate had been granted by Edward VI. to Thomas Denton, an eminent lawyer, Treasurer of the Temple ; he made it his home, and represented Bucks in the Parliament of 1554. A beautiful alabaster monument, with life size recumbent figures of Sir Thomas and his wife Margaret Mordant, still exists, but it was much mutilated in the civil war. Two generations later comes Sir Thomas Denton (Margaret Verney's father) — married to Susan Temple, of Stowe—an important man in the county, M.P. for Bucks in James I.'s first three Parliaments, and then Knight of the Shire, and again in the first of Charles I., when the ominous questions which were beginning to trouble men's minds began to show themselves in their true colours.

Fortunately for himself, old Sir Thomas had died in 1633, just before the breaking out of strife, and was succeeded by his son Alexander, who represented Buckingham in Charles I.'s two first and two last Parliaments ; and, 'adhering to the king, was a very great sufferer for his loyalty.' He married Mary Hampden, a cousin of the great Buckinghamshire squire, who stood up for the liberties of the people, as so many of his class have done throughout the history of England ; Mary was the niece of Sir Alexander Hampden, supposed to have been the guardian of

John during his minority. Her picture, and that of her husband, Sir Alexander Denton, are both at Claydon. His face is that of an amiable, gentlemanly, conscientious, rather weak man, but with an expression of patient courage. He must have been torn in pieces by the vehemence with which the different members of his family espoused the two sides of the quarrel. His eldest son, John, was a colonel in the king's service, and was killed shortly after; his brother William was the Court physician; his sister, Mrs. Isham, was an enthusiastic Royalist; his brother-in-law, Sir Edmund Verney, had just lost his life in the king's service, and young Edmund Verney was still fighting for the cause; while Ralph had taken strongly the Parliament side, and his wife's famous cousin, John Hampden—their foremost man in the House of Commons and in the field—had in June '43 died an agonising death of his wounds at Chalgrove Field; and Alexander Hampden had been tried by court-martial for complicity in a Royalist plot and had lately died in confinement.

Sir Alexander had recently lost both his wife and his mother. In the beginning of '44, besides his own daughters, and his nieces who were constantly coming over from Claydon to visit their cousins, his sisters, Mistress Susan Denton and Mistress Elizabeth Isham and her husband, were living with him. Mrs. Isham had complained some months before of having soldiers quartered upon them, but whether in her own house or at Hillesden does not clearly appear, they were evidently of the Parliament side—'there is one hundred men in our one House, which my thinkes is very harde to be put in one house, and we being allmost 50 in family.' She had been greatly enraged by the incivility of 'Sir Pie,' who seems to have been in command, the injury he has done her 'will never goe out of her mind'; from the soldiers they have received 'no ronge,' they used them courteously, all but Sir Pie—and Sir Pie has called her a malignant!—she is beside herself with indignation, she will make her 'nagge' wear her colours, to show them to all the world, she would make Sir Pie wear her ribbon if she could get at him, but she had only heard of it after his departure!

Sir Robert Pye, a member of Parliament and J.P. for Westminster, a strong Presbyterian, is alluded to in Sir Ralph's notes. Col. Sir Robert Pye, jun., was particularly obnoxious to Royalists as one of the few soldiers who went against the king, and Mrs. Isham considers her nephew responsible for what she calls 'this Shameful bisnes.' But graver troubles were at the door; Sir Alexander threw himself more and more earnestly into the struggle. Hillesden lay in an important position—between Oxford, where the king was in garrison, and Newport Pagnell, which was held by the Parliament troops under Sir Samuel Luke, with a communication by Aylesbury, securing the north road from London. Sir Alexander fortified his house as a *point d'appui*, establishing a chain of pickets of horse and foot as far as Oxford. Early in 1644

Colonel Smith took command of the place, built barns and stabling for cavalry, and dug a trench half a mile in circumference, enclosing the house and church; far too large an extent, as afterwards appeared, for any troops to occupy.

The country in all directions was swept by forage parties from both sides, and one day Colonel Smith, with a body of troopers, carried off a drove of cattle, with money and other valuables, belonging to a tenant of Mr. Hampden. When they reached Hillesden a violent dispute arose as to the partition of the spoil; Major Amnion, 'an uncommon frenzy man,' claimed all the horses and a large share of the booty for his troop. A general mutiny took place, and the major, who had imprisoned several soldiers, was obliged to release them, and give up his claim. This was not the only ill consequence of the expedition. The owner of the cattle arrived at Hillesden to ransom them, probably much annoyed at having been attacked from a house belonging to a relation of his landlord. He was made to pay £80 for his stock; upon which, indignant at his loss, he claimed compensation of £160 from the Parliamentary commanders at Aylesbury, which first showed them the danger of permitting so strong a Royalist garrison to hold Hillesden. A surprise was attempted by a force of 300 horse and foot, but unsuccessfully; upon which Sir S. Luke prepared for a regular attack with 2,000 men, collected from Aylesbury, Northampton, and the associated counties. One half of these marched, under the command of Colonel Cromwell,

THE BURNING OF HILLESDEN HOUSE 193

to Steeple Claydon, where they encamped for the night around a barn, now marked by an inscription. The Royalist garrison had meantime been hard at work at Hillesden. They had summoned all the country people, manufactured a wooden cannon from an elm tree, stoutly hooped with iron, and had obtained five small pieces of ordnance from Oxford, with ammunition, all of which were stored in the church. Nearly 1,000 labourers were employed to complete the trenches and throw up a mound on which to mount the artillery, which would have made the place safe against any sudden attack. But it was too late, and seeing themselves unexpectedly surrounded on all sides, they sent out a flag of truce. Finding, however, that they could obtain no terms short of unconditional surrender, Colonel Smith proposed to defend the works; but the ditch was only knee deep in places, and the assailants overwhelming in numbers: they soon obtained a footing, the defenders were obliged to retire, some into the house, others to the church. A second assault was made, and the church carried—marks of the struggle being still seen in bullet-holes in the old oak door of the church, and marks of shot in the plaster—when Colonel Smith, seeing the hopelessness of any further defence, surrendered on promise of quarter. All the prisoners, and amongst them Sir Alexander and his brother, were marched off to Padbury, a village some three miles off, 'where they passed the night in great discomfort.' The next day they were taken to Newport Pagnell. It is difficult to ascertain the exact truth about the treatment of the garrison, consisting of 263 men; the *King's News* journal accuses Sir S. Luke of great barbarity. The parliamentary reporter admits the death of thirty-one men.

The morning after the surrender, a trooper, striking his musket against the wainscoting of one of the rooms, discovered a large sum of money; further search was made, and more treasure found concealed, particularly under the lead roof. Later in the day came news of the advance of a great body of troops from Oxford, and it was determined to evacuate the place. Sir S. Luke withdrew to Newport, Colonel Cromwell to Buckingham; the house was set fire to and burnt almost to the ground.

A touching letter from Sir Alexander to his steward has been preserved, written at Newport after he had heard of the destruction of his house:

'Blagrove, I woulde have you send mee by Tyler that bag of silver w^h Berney left wth you long since and Seale it upp. Let him bring it to mee. Bid him also take a viewe of ye house y^t was burnt upon Tuesday, y^t I may have some certayne information of w^t destruction is fallen upon mee, and whether it bee possible to rebuild those walls that are standing if y^e distractions of y^e times should settle. I thancke God I am yet in health notw^{t}standing these many misfortunes are fallen upon mee, and my comfort is I knowe myself not guilty of any fault.

'*Newport, March 6th,* 164$\frac{3}{4}$.'

THE BURNING OF HILLESDEN HOUSE

It is a brave, simple, spirited letter; he was not crushed by his losses, and intent only on doing his best to set things right once more.

He was afterwards removed to London, and committed to the Tower on March 15, whence he wrote a few days later to Sir Ralph :

'S^r,—I was gladd to see your servant, allthough in a place I have not till nowe beene used unto the tower of London whither I was comitted uppon Saturday last, beeinge taken at my owne howse by Liuetenant Generall Cromwell with some 4,000 horse and foote with him, I only cominge accidentally thither some 2 dayes before to remove my familye, the kinge havinge placed a garrison there. . . .'

He writes again :

'Those officers that commanded that place were taken and some 150 men, and some 19 killed on both sydes, the howse pilladged, all my cattell and wine taken away, my house the next day burnt downe to the grounde and but one house left standinge in that end of the toune. Captayne Tho. Verney taken prisoner that came only to see his sisters, and all my own servants are as yett detayned. It endamaged me at the least £16,000. . . . My children and neeces not fayrly used yett noe imodest action, and the resydue of my family are yett at Sir Ralph Verney's howse.' Pen Verney, who with Ralph's other sisters was in the house, wrote : 'When it pleased God to lay that great affliction on my uncle, I was more consarned for him, but I did stand so great a los in my own particular that it has been a half undoing to me. We were not shamefully used in any way by the souldiers, but they took everything and I was not left scarce the clothes of my back'; and Mrs. Isham described afterwards how 'Hillesden parke pales be every one up and burned or else carried away, and the Denton children like to beg.'

Sir Alexander writes again on the 19th of April: 'I perceve you have received my last, you may see what I suffered in 2 dayes, cannot be but allmost every mans fortune by degrees, if these most unhappe tymes continue but a short tyme. I here the kinge hath sent a warrant to gather upp all those rents about our county latelye sequestred (which are very many, some of the principall I will give you, Twiford, Stowe, Fulbrook, Quainton, Doddershall, with many more) and a clause in it, in case the tennants bringe them not in by this day, they must abide the mercy of the soldiers; this warrant beeinge sent to the House my lord Gen. was desyred to send horse into the county to defend them; which will prove the greatest mischeefe is to me a great question. I feare it may be the cause to draw the whole body of both armies into these parts. Now I thinke this sad story wilbe enough to give you a breakfast without any more kickshawes, and if france cann afford me such an other dish of disasters, send it me that I may compare them, but I will close your stomach with a cawdle of comfort, which is, we are in greate hope by the next you shall hear that propositions of peace wilbe sent unto the kinge. I pray God grant there may be nothinge putt into that pott may spoyle the whole mess, my service to your bedfellowe and I shall ever rest.—Yours truly to serv you,

'ALEXANDER DENTON.'

The sufferings of the Dentons at Hillesden were sad enough, but the account which Sir Roger Burgoyne indignantly gives Sir Ralph of another house taken by the Royalists about the same time, contrasts painfully with the moderation shown by Cromwell's soldiers. 'I must acquaint you,' he writes on March 21, 'with the exactest peice of cruelty that ever I heard or read of: that Hopton Castle in Shropshire, which is Mr. Wallop's Castle, of the house of Commons, being straitly besciged by the enemy, was delivered up by our souldiers upon condition of quarter and safe marching away, but no sooner had the enemy power over them, but they most miserably hacked and hewed them, and afterwards most devillishly thrust them into a pitt and buried them all a live, they were about 27 men.'

Ralph writes to his brother Edmund on the same day: 'Suffer me to tell you how much I am afflicted for the ruine of sweet Hillesden and the distresses that hapened to my aunt and sisters. God knowes what is become of my unhappie brother that was there taken. . . . I know all that side hates him and I feare they will make him feell the weight of their displeasure; from w[ch] misfortune God in mercie keepe you and poore Harry—my deare brother farewell.'

After the burning of Hillesden House, Tom Verney was a prisoner for many weeks, part of the time in St. John's College, Cambridge, whence he writes a furious letter to Roades, in great indignation at his not having sent him an additional sum which he pretends that Ralph had meant that he should receive, lest he should want in prison. It is a curious epistle, beginning, 'Governour,' and complaining of having received no answer to three or four letters—all probably on the same subject! He goes on, 'ffor shame; rous up your drowsye and decaying spiritts that the world may not say we have a foole to our governour. Sir Ralphe is liable to the censure of the world, that he being a wise man should chuse a foole to govern his brothers and sisters.' And in a later letter he says, 'I shall find a freind that will furnish mee with as much as will bring me to Claydon : then I hope to have my peniworths. It shall not be your great language or your fleareing looks that shall any wayes daunt mee.' To Ralph he writes in a more humble strain, entreating for a loan of 20*l*. to make up his ransom, his mother-in-law being ready to lend the rest : 'poverty and imprisonment hath made me almost impudent.' Considering that two former loans were yet unpaid, it could hardly be wondered at if Ralph refused his request, but he does send him a few pounds to clear him of debt, so with the help of Mrs. Tom Verney's friends the captive was soon after set free.

The tragedy at Hillesden was relieved by two romantic love stories 'gilding the dusky edge of war.' One of the officers in the attacking force fell in love with Sir Alexander's sister, while the colonel commanding the defence fell in love with his daughter. The former story came to a rapid *dénouement*, almost before the firing had ceased; the second a few months later, amidst the grim surroundings of the Tower of London. The first was quite a middle-aged romance. Miss Susan Denton, whom the young nieces around her must have considered a confirmed old maid, roused a tender passion in the martial breast of a rough captain of the besieging forces—one Jaconiah, or Jeremiah, Abercombie, whose very name shows that he was a Republican and a Covenanter. No particulars are given; whether he was sorry for the poor ruined ladies, who were turned out in such a miserable plight, and that pity was akin to love, so that he proposed to take her and her burdens upon his own shoulders, while she 'did love him as he did pity her,' there is no means of knowing. The courtship must have been carried on during the two or three hours before the poor distressed little group of women and children walked off across the fields, weeping as they went, to take refuge at Claydon. Captain Jaconiah was not allowed a quiet moment for his love-making; three days later, March 6, John Denton, Sir Alexander's brother, writes: 'My sister Susan, her new husband Capt. Abercromy is quartered at Addington, and I feare to the indanger of bringing that house into the condicione of Hillesden.' In June he is still 'a pone sarvis,' but, says Mrs. Isham— 'My sis: Susans marage is to be accomplished very suddnly if her captine be not killed, it tis him as did fust plunder Hilsdon,' certainly a curious form of introduction to his wife's relations. He was not penniless, and Mrs. Isham wrote again : ' The capt. his land is in Irerland, he is half Skotts, half Irish. I think fue of her frinds lik it, but if she hath not him she will never have any, it is gone so far.'

The end of the Jaconiah episode was as sudden as its birth : in the next year Henry Verney wrote : 'Your ante's husband (Captain Abercrombie) was killed this week by a party from Borestall and buried at Hillesden.' So the covenanting captain was quietly laid among the long series of Church and Royalist Dentons in their beautiful old churchyard.

Sir Alexander never regained his liberty ; he was removed on his own petition to Lord Petre's house, used for prisoners when the Tower was very full. Mrs. Isham sends a pitiful account of him a few months before his death, she being with her husband in the same prison. Some of the prisoners hoped to get leave to go out for a time, but he is not likely to be of the number, ' and then I knoe he will not lett me goe, for he doth say as he should be half dead if myselfe was not with him. I must confese he hath had anofe to a broke any mans hart, but that God hath given him a great dell of pachance, for on the seven of Augst last his sunn John was slaine within

Sir Alex^r Denton, Kt of Hillesden.
from a picture at Claydon House.

a worke att Abtone [Abingdon], as Sr. Will Wallers forces had made... To tell you how it was done I shall want the wordes of wore, but nevor did I heare of a more bravor pice of sarvis done, and if his life had bine spared, the hole Towne had bine his one. They came on so Galiently as there tooke ye Pickes out of the Enemies handes, and then a drak[1] wente of and kiled him in the Plase and 7 Bollets was found in his Brest, and beside himselfe thay was but 7 or 8 kiled, none of note but him, for thay all retreted when thay see him fall for he commanded in chefe. This you must thinke is a grete troble to his father as did love him so well.'

Sir Alexander, writing in March, had mentioned that 'Jack some 6 weekes since was shott throwe the thygh endeavouring to gett [?] my house then in the parliaments possession.' Another account says that Colonel John Denton received no less than thirty wounds—'that good young man whose very enemies lament him.' Sir Ralph wrote to Sir Alexander, full of sympathy in his loss: 'I must ever account it as on of my greatest and particular afflictions to loose the man that you and I did love soe well, but this is our comfort, hee lived and died most gallantly, and questionlesse is now most happy; kings must

---

[1] A drake was a brass field gun used in the civil war, 9 ft. long, weight 143 cwt., carrying a 5 lbs. shot and a charge of 4 or 5 lbs. of powder. See a paper by Colonel Hime, R.A., on Field Artillery of the Great Rebellion. *Proceedings* of R.A. Institution, vol. 6, 1870. Many old pieces of artillery were named from animals, a dragon was a carbine; culverin came from the French *couleuvre*, an adder; a drake and a saker from birds.

pile upp there crownes at the gates of the grave, and lay downe there septers at the feet of Death, then let not us poore subjects thinke (or desire) to bee exempted: length of Daies doth oftner make our sinns the greater then our lives the better, then let not us repine at that good hand of God that (observing his inocency) snacht him from this wicked world to reigne with him for ever, but rather let us waite with patience till our owne change comes.' A few days later he writes: 'To you and mee (being now made conversant with sorrowes and misfortunes), it must needes bee good and joyfull tidings to bee assured a day will come (and non knowes how soone), not only to put a period to all our miseries heere, but to crowne us with future glory, and bring us to our old and best friends, (for new are like the times, full of unconstancie and falsehood), with whom wee shall (without compliment) perpetually remaine to on another as I am to you.'

Sir Alexander's letters from the Tower are full of public affairs and the movements of the armies, showing that he was well supplied with news. The deaths and the troubles of all sorts are so fully told in the letters, that it is tantalising to hear so little of other matters; one would so gladly know how Colonel Smith, who had been taken prisoner with the Dentons, and had been with them confined in the Tower, was able to carry on his courtship of Margaret Denton. Sir Roger Burgoyne calls him 'young Smith that once was of the house of Commons, but now a

THE BURNING OF HILLESDEN HOUSE   203

Collonell,' and it must have been a comfort to poor Sir Alexander in his captivity, that his daughter had found a protector. Mrs. Isham, after telling Sir Ralph of John Denton's death, adds on August 15 : ' One sunne is ded, yet another sune in lawe he hath this munth or 5 wickes for Coronall Smyth is mareyed to his dafter [daughter] Margrete, and I thinke will be a happy mach if these ill times doth not hindre it, but he is still a Prisenor. So you may thinke itt a bolde venter, but if these times hold, I thinke thay will be non men lefte for woman.' Later on Colonel Smith made his escape, and his bride, Mrs. Isham and Susan Verney were imprisoned in September on the charge of aiding and abetting him. Mrs. Isham writes to Sir Ralph : ' When I was in prison, thaye would not lett me have so much as a Pene and Incke, but all of us was innocence Prisnors, and so came out without examing, for none could have a worde against us; your Sis Susan, and my nice neece, was my feelore Prissnors, and for our owne passones [persons] noe hurt, only our purssis payd the feeses ; much in gage we be to youre Bro : Tomas and his wife, for thay did more for us than all our friends beside.'

There had been some question of moving them, but Mrs. Isham does not know where it is to ' more than the Summer Islands,' and the company would be only prisoners and strangers to her ; they can receive and forward letters, but ' the gardes will locke into them.'

Susan also gives him her account of it on October

10: 'I make noe question, butt you have hard y^t I was taken prisoner, for bess tells mee y^t she writ you word of itt. I am now released, butt this day my keeper was wth mee to tell mee y^t the iudg advocate was angry that I was released wthout his knowleg, butt I have promised to appeare before him when he will send for mee. I am confident y^t he will never looke after mee further. I was kept prisoner 8 days, so was the rest of my company, butt never examined, the tooke mee only upon suspision: ther was nothing could be brought against mee: for I was noe more giulty of what I was accused of then you ware: itt was thought that I had a hand in helping of my new coson out of prison, butt indeed I had nott—I hope that I shall never under take to doe any shuch thing wheare by I may bring my selfe into trouble,' she adds with a candid selfishness, transparent in its simplicity!

On January 9th, 1645, Sir Ralph's letters from home tell him that 'there is no news stirring, but that the Archbishop of Canterbury is to be beheaded to-morrow upon Tower Hill, and that Sir Alexander Denton dyed in Peterhouse on New Year's day of a feaver.' He was only forty-eight, but his health at last gave way, just when his friends expected to accomplish his release. Henry writes: 'Our poore and dear freind Sir Allaxsander good man is dead, a dyed one newersday, a is tomorow [Jan. 3] caryed to his owne church,' all the Verneys lament him, even Tom writes that 'our dear friend Sir A. D. is dead.'

Sir Alexander was a great loss to Ralph; he reviews the recent troubles in his family, of which 'the chiefe Pillars are already snatcht away by death'; on January 24 he writes about 'the sadd news of the death of my poore Uncle, who within 8 or 9 months last past, did mee more curtesies and expressed more freindshipp and affection to me, then in all his life before. . . . I have such unkinde (nay I may say unnaturall) letters, from some soe neare mee, that truly, did I not see it under there owne Hands. . . . I could not have credited that such a totall decay of freindshipp and common honesty could possibly have beene amoungst those that profess Christianity.' 'I am not naturally suspitious,' he says another time, 'butt these trying times have discovered so much knavery in soe many men that heretofore apeared examples of piety, that hereafter I shall account too much credulity a fault.'

There had been a rumour that Claydon House was threatened to be burnt, Sir Roger Burgoyne wrote: 'I hope God in his mercy will take that man [that intends it] out of the world before he be guilty of so devilish a sin as to wrong so innocent a man. If God shall please to let that devil loose I must account it as an affliction intended from above for me, no personall affliction being bad enough. . . . I have not heard of any such usage that Sr W. Uvedall hath had to be plundered, but I am sure it is not with the approbation of the parliament. As for souldiers I know not what they may do, for I could never trust them.' The hand of the Parliament was heavy also in other directions; even a poor little sermon did not go unpunished. Sir Roger writes: 'Ther was last Thursday a very bad sermon preached neere Uxbridge by one Mr. Love, a young man, which gave a great deale of offence, but the man is imprisoned for it.' Liberty of opinion was as little allowed by the Parliament as by the king.

On all sides Ralph receives tidings of distress; some lines attributed to Charles I. entirely expressed the feelings of Royalists like Mrs. Isham at this time:

> Plunder and murder are the kingdom's laws,
> Tyranny bears the title of taxation,
> Revenge and robbery are reformation,
> Oppression gains the name of sequestration.

That unfortunate woman is continually in trouble, her husband being in prison for a long time, apparently for being unable to pay the heavy exactions which were now laid upon the land, and she cannot approve of his exchanging with another prisoner, as that would prove him a 'delinqute,' as she says. In the plundering and burning of Hillesden House she lost not only money and clothes, but bonds and other business papers, which increased their money difficulties. She presses Ralph to repay the loan she made to his father, or to give her security on certain lands near Claydon, fearing in case of his death that she should lose it. Money he has none, and he cannot grant her the particular land in question, while she on her side objects to the security he offers on another part of his estate, because it is in a disturbed district. Poor Ralph protests that as all his land is within about ten miles there is not much to choose in that matter, and he thinks her fears for the future security of the loan very unjust. 'I am sorry to find such harsh and straing conclusione drawn from bare conjecture, and those against one that from his very childhood hath been her faithful servant.' The miserable condition of the poor lady may partly excuse her. In one letter she writes : ' Through carlisnes of my husband, and the house being burned, he hath nothing to show for Ratcliff; and so it will be seased on as a chattell and go away from him, and wee to lose all as he had . . . and now that as you have of mine if you should die, would be in the like condishune, for I have only your bond for it, and as times goe no debts could be paid as is upon land, and soe I may goe a beggin without something is paid me yearly. I should a thought you would never refused me lande for money, but I remember your anser was when you refused Claydon becase it should holy be your sons. For our clothes we must sew fig leves together, we lost all by fier, and since I have had but one gown. I could wish as it would last me forty yeres as the childrenes of Iserells did, but, however, now I am come to town, I have not where withal to buye another.'

As her troubles increase her language becomes more and more involved : ' blame me not if I press you to take some course . . . should you misskary, and you are but mortall, and since 'you must die att one time, you may die att any time, but the Lord sende you a good and a Longe Life hear as when ever you goe . . . it will be never the sooner, for my sending to you.'

In another letter she writes to tell Sir Ralph of the losses of Mr. Aris, of Hillesden, a relative of the rector of Claydon : ' Nic Arise's House by axcidance on Ester Even was burned downe to the grounde, and all his goods in it with his money, in halfe an houer, himselfe beinge not att home ; some burnt by chance and others on purpos, as I thinke by winter we shall not have a House to be in. The Lorde mende us and put an ende to these unhapy times or ellse parpare us for to in joye a House not made with handes Eternall in the Heavenes.' After all, good Aunt Isham had not lost interest in this world's affairs, for she dates this letter in a postscript—' ye fust of May but never so dule an one, and so fue chases [chaises] in hide Parke as I heare!'

Eventually her husband regains his liberty, and she writes more cheerfully that they hope to be together again, though without half a guinea between them.

Some 250 years have passed since the stormy days of the Hillesden siege. We hear that in 1648 ' they are building there againe and intend to sett upp a little house where the old one stood.' Hillesden House rose from its ashes and was described in the succeeding century as a 'good old house' with 'a very bold terrace.' This house has in its turn been destroyed, so completely that not a trace of it remains. Mrs. Isham has passed beyond the reach of vexatious creditors and 'souldgers'—the 'chases' in great numbers have returned to Hyde Park—but the Dentons are extinct, and 'sweete Hillesden' Church stands once more alone, in the silence of the green lawns and overarching elm trees.

CHAPTER X.

IN EXILE.

'Call it a travel that thou takest for pleasure.'
'My heart will sigh when I miscall it so,
Which finds it an inforcèd pilgrimage.'—*Richard II.*

'ONLY one member of the House of Commons,' says Mr. Gardiner, 'amongst those who had remained at their posts at Westminster after the first months of the Civil War—Sir Ralph Verney—refused the Covenant at the end of 1643, preferring the miseries of exile to the soiling of his conscience.'[1] The 'miseries' had arrived without a moment's delay; scarcely had the poor exiles recovered from the sufferings of their winter journey, when the terrible calamity which overwhelmed the Denton family came to sadden them; the troubles of their other friends, the confusion of public affairs, and Sir Ralph's own doubts as to the right course to be pursued, all contributed to darken what his best friend called 'your most uncomfortable and unhappy absence.'

Sir Ralph had offended his Royalist relations by refusing to side with the king in his prosperous days,

[1] Gardiner's *Great Civil War*, vol. ii. p. 10.

and now he outraged his Parliamentary friends by refusing to go with them a single step beyond what his own conscience approved. George Herbert's 'constant' man can hardly hope to be popular with his own party

>Whose honesty is not
>So loose and easy that a ruffling wind
>Can blow away, or glittering look it blind;
>Who rides his sure and even trot
>While the world now rides by, now lags behind,
>Who when great trials come,
>Nor seeks, nor shuns them; but doth calmly stay,
>Till he the thing, and the example weigh.

Sir Ralph's resolution was assailed from many quarters; cousin Henry Parker takes upon himself to advise and remonstrate.

'In my opinion you steere a course wherein there is almost no hope of indemnity on either side, but certaynty of greate losse and blame from both. If you shall say there is much to be disliked in ether partye, my thinkes that should not seeme strange, or alienate you totally from ether, for in these publicke divisions, where religion and liberty are indangerd all men ought to adhere to that cause which is dictated to them to bee ye better and ye more harmless by ye light of nature and the most forcible indications of reason. No man can say that God has left him no part to act, nor no station to make good; and if some poore mechanick might pleade himselfe to bee wholly unusefull and inconsiderable in these grande cases, yet you are apparently berreft of such excuses. You have an account to make to

God, to y′ Countrye, to y′ Freinds, to y′selfe, and y⁰ charge of that account wilbee high and valuable: and to thinke that you can exonerate all by saying you were dubious, and not satisfied in all particulars is most strange. Tis impossible yᵗ you should bee equilibrious in yᵉ maine or in yᵉ generality of yᵉ controversye, and if ether scale have but one od grayne in it to sway you, you are as much bounde to obey that sway, as He is that has yᵉ strongest propension of judgment.'

Ralph takes the implied reproof very humbly. He replies: 'Since yᵉ perusall of your freindly lines I have had a farr greater desire then ever to satisfie my selfe in those particulars that first induced mee to steere this course, and I shall most willingly use all yᵉ wit I have (joyned with that of others) to facilitate that worke. The truth is when I saw yᵉ covenant pressed with such severity, that your kinnesman meerly for refusall (though in a most modest humble manner) was not only suspended and soe made uncapable to serve his country, but reserved for greater punishment, ... I thought it might be lesse offensive to the House and more convenient for my selfe, to retreate for a while till the fury of that flame were over then to doe that, whereof I soe much doubted, or trouble them to invent punishments (where yᵉ law appointed non), for such an unfortunate creature, for soe I have just cause to stile myself, being I heare yᵉ King hath already sequestred my estate, and yᵉ Parliament dayly threatens to doe that and more. S^r I am very sencible of my owne misfortune and must needes agree with you in this greate truth that what side soever overcomes there is almost noe hope of indemnity. But you well know, rather then make a solemne vow and covenant wherein I am not satisfied I must chuse to suffer, . . . and content my selfe with the testimoney wch my owne conscience will ever afford mee, that whilst there was a probability that I might serve them there I did it faithfully, and further that during the time of my absence, noe one thing to there prejudice hath beene acted by yours etc., R. V.' Henry Verney was quite of Cousin Parker's opinion ; in sporting phrase he urges his brother 'to take the Pitt one way or other . . . these times are likely to hold very long, and beelive it, non will bee in soe sad a condition as those that stand newters.'

The sequestration of Sir Ralph's estate by the king did not entail any loss eventually, since he had transferred it for a term to 'confiding men' and on the deed of trust being produced the sequestration was taken off. But his fears of sequestration by the Parliament were only too well founded.

Doll Leeke had already written to his wife : 'I have heard severall parliment men call your husband a delinquent ; some say he has 3 thousand pound ayeare and that they resolve to have it sudenly ; all the mischefe that they can do him he must expect, which apeares to me a straing cruilty and an ill reward for his good opinion of them.'

The poor family in exile have their share of sickness, and Ralph writes sadly to Doll Leeke of both the children having been ill in bed: 'the Boy hath had a feavour accompanied with a vomiting, and ye Girle very full of ye small Pox, and I myselfe have beene ill and in Phisick, and my wife (in soe many feares and troubles for us all) that I leave you to consider her distresse. But now I thanke my God wee are all in an hopefull way of recovery.' Sir Roger writes of Peg: 'I pray God recovere y^r pretty daughter, I hope it is the greatnesse of your affection to hir, and not the extremity of hir distemper which makes you so solicitous about hir.' Doll Leeke, writing to sympathise with them in their trouble, says: 'I trust God will spare their life; they are miserable times we live in and sartainly those are happiest that goes first . . . my sisters children will be sudenly in a condition to starve, and most of my frinds.' Sir Nathaniel Hobart, 'a stranger in my own country and destitute of friends,' begs for £50; 'Sweet Nan' expects a child, 'an unseasonable blessing,' says the poor man, 'but God's will must bee done.' Susan Verney, who is in delicate health, asks for an extra £10 a year, which Ralph grants, but he says—'would God every one of my own children were sure of £40 a year . . . I should sleep much quieter I assure you . . .' The only pleasant bit of news from Claydon is that 'little Mr. John is in health and walking pretty strongly.'

Sir Ralph writes in February '45 to Sir W.

Hewytt thanking him 'for the constancy of your affections, a rare thing in these days for I beleeve few men can say they have a freind now, whose face they knew a weeke before these troubles.'

In contrast to the high tragic tone of most of the correspondence we have a droll little storm in a teapot in June 1645. Mr. Wakefield, one of the English refugees, is about to take a travelling servant on Sir Ralph's recommendation, when to his horror and delight—like many a man since, he does not quite know which it is—he sees his name in 'the papers from London,' and finds the servant Thomer has been gossiping about him, 'tho' in effect it will prove but an idle busyness, hardly worth a man's taking notice of, yett I can assure you there has been so much talk of me at London,' and so on, and so on. He asks Sir Ralph 'whether it will be safe to nourish such an one and make him, as it were, privy to some of my actions, who for his own ends would not stick at any other occasion to betray me . . . a sickbrained, idle, giddy-headed fellow.' Sir Ralph replies at great length about 'this ugly business,' but characteristically he does not wish to condemn Thomer unheard. There are at least five or six long elaborate letters on this important subject, and finally the printed letter itself is quoted, which is curious enough. 'The Diurnall gives a letter from a Gentleman of quality out of ffrance: "I have now been fifteen days at Paris where our queene of England is with her court at the Louvre, of [at?] the residents Sr Richard Brown we have sermons, the common prayer, the booke of execration against the Parliament and their faction, as they term them, duly and devoutly read by the Bishop of Londonderry, Dr Cousins, who came hither disguised in a miller's habit and others of these worthy instruments of superstition, keeps a constant preachment of railing against the roundheads, just as the capuchins do against the Protestants. The Ladyes of Honour to the queene and the rest of the Royalists are constantly there. The queene goes on Tuesday to St. Germains. Dr Verne, chaplain lately to o^r king is turned Papist and writes against the Protestants. They hate the French Protestants and seldom or never come to church but with the Papists."' The 'Diurnals' themselves have a hard time of it. Sir Roger sends his friend ' The Scout,' but in February '45 he writes, ' The Scout is clapt up heere as I am informed for some unadvised expressions in his pamphlet, he is not this week to be heard of.'

In September 1645, the blow fell that poor Ralph had so much dreaded, and which he had hoped to the last might have been averted. He was voted out of the House of Commons. Sir Roger, deeply grieved, writes to inform him of it:

'In the greatest sadness of my spirits, that which I feared is now com upon me. Curos leves logantur ingentes stupent, no word can express my sorrow but I trust and really do hope that the wisdom of my friend [i.e. Sir Ralph] will receive it with less distraction and trouble then I can send it . . . My friend is voted out etc. the 22nd of this instant; and it was his servants fortune to be at it, who had not been ther long before; his endeavor and care were not wanting in anything he could do, but his absence was the only cause of it, although other things were objected against him, which thanks be to god were proved ontrue. Writs are to be issued for new elections for that place; he is likewise to be sequestred, I would to god I might know his pleasure in all things speedily. Your friend is so openly spok of since that unhappy business and was so curried in the place openly for speaking etc. that I feare he cannot suffer more then my friend will do if he can think of no better way . . . My dearest heart, the L^d of heaven bless and preserve both thee and thine and supply the want of outward comfort to thee by himself.'

Ralph's distress at the news is extreme: he replies to Sir Roger's letter: 'I confess it brought mee tidings of one of the greatest and most inexpressible afflictions that ever yet befell me, for which my soul shall mourn in secret, for I want words to declare my grief. God in mercy give me patience and forgive those that did it, without affording me the favour, nay I might say the justice, of a summons. Deare hart, tell mee what particulars were objected against me, that I may cleare myselfe to thee and one friend more, whome I desire to satisfie, for I protest though I know myselfe guilty of many crimes, yet I am not conscious of any offence committed against them, and were I not well assured of this, my owne Hart would make mee more onhappy then all theire votes can doe.'

He cannot comfort himself at being expelled from his well-beloved House, and writes to one friend and another to inquire more of the reasons. Sir R. Burgoyne refers to 'the sense of your suffering which your letter to Sir John Leeke expresses,' and repeats again that 'it was for no crime in the world but only his long absence; others were laid to his charge of having been in the King's quarters, but a servant of his who was ther present [i.e. himself] did fully satisfy them to the contrary (who, I may say for him thus much that he did leave no means unattempted, nor friend unsolicited to prevent that sad misfortune).' He will not tell him all the particulars as it would only distress them both.

'There are new Burgishes chosen in Buckinghamshire, as one Scott for Aylesbury, and Major Brown of London for Wickhame.' (Lord Fermanagh, in a vicious little note says: 'This Scott was since hanged and quartered.' He was one of the Regicides.) And what makes the whole cut deeper and more cruelly is that it was not an enemy that had done this thing, but 'mine own familiar friend,' the great Patriot party, with whose thoughts and actions Ralph had sympathised so earnestly.

A few weeks later, when Sir John Leeke is ill, Susan writes: 'I am commanded by my unkell to write to you which he cannot do himself, by reason he is this night extremely ill, he decays every day more and more, God Almighty bless him and send him well, if he should miscarry I should have a great loss. He has had discourse with some of your dear friends; one who appears very tender of you and your family; from divers of them he as bein tould that they are amazed that in all this time you should not make your way either to have continued in the House or to keep off your sequestration which is expressed shall fall upon you. Every day you are under the censure of an absolute neglect. It may be you have a more understanding of your bisnes than your friends conceive, but it is thought itt will draw you to a destruction of you and yours, which God of his mercy keep from you. They do generally wish you homewards within a month, or to procure dispensation for your absence, which may keep your estate in some safety; pray mould these into your serious consideration, that the advise of your friends may not be lost.'

All his friends urge him to come home and compound; he would only too gladly do so if consistent with honour and safety, but none could compound without first taking the Covenant. 'I confesse I had much rather suffer at home, soe it might not bee in prison,' he writes, but if 'this single thought [his refusal to sign the Covenant] must needes be hightned to a crime worthy of a total ruine,' he hesitates to leave his harbour of refuge.

Immediately after the fatal vote Mrs. Isham wrote: 'The last wicke I could a sent you the Ill nuse of your being out of the House, for it was my fortine to be att the Dore att the time, a boute my neses [nieces] Denton and all the Rest of the childrine which be licke to bege for it. They holde on the sequestⁿ, and make such busel as you cannot Immagion, and now I feare within a while the Licke [like] will come upone youre land, but if it doth, thare will be noe way but for you to compound for all your Estate, before havoke be made of it; but this way will cost redy money which is more worth then any land. I did axe . . . your frinds and mine which way you had best to take, if you should be sequestred, and this was that as they told me. I should be lofte [loth] to see that befall you, as hath our fammily, but this way is licke to make all of us alike; the Lorde give us all pachinces for a beggen we must all goe if this world holde. Your bond will be taken if you was here, but being absent I know it will never be taken.'

A few days later Henry writes: 'My acquaintance with your friend Sir Roger is not so great as I could wish, yet I am well knowne to him for we meet often at Westminster and other places, where we discourse much of you; I think a loves you dearly. I whish you had been so happy in time to be advised by him for a tells me a did press you by divers letters to return afore the blow was given. That wch is done cannot be recalled, yet, dear friend, let me desire you to take better care for the future, for long absence I doubt will prove an incurable disease; it is the opinion of your best and wisest friends, divers of whom impute your actions to scruple of conscience, or else, beelive it, by the carage of your business they would account you mad.'

In writing to Edmund, Harry expresses himself more tersely; their brother 'has played the bird called the goose,' an opinion which he doubtless expresses in all sorts of society, says Sir Ralph, when the phrase has been kindly brought to his ears.

Ralph, with his heart wholly centred on England, seems to have given but little thought to the country of his banishment; writing was his absorbing occupation, letters from home his greatest solace, he kept a calendar in which he entered an abstract and sometimes a full copy of letters written and received. Sir Thomas Hewett only echoed Ralph's own thoughts when he wrote to him. 'The separation of friends I find to be worse than the sequestration of estates from the continuance of which I daly implore our good God with a piece of our old Letany.'

He seems to have read a good deal during his enforced leisure, to judge by his requests to Dr. Denton for various works and the lists of those that he receives from England from time to time. Inter aliis: Milton's Iconoclastes; The Levellers vindicated; Prynne's Historical Collection of ancient parliaments; an impeachment against Cromwell and Ireton; Ascham; Bishop Andrews 2 Manuals; 'Hooker his 6 and 8 books;' History of Independency; '2 Sclaters.' Dr. Denton heartily recommends Sclater to 'Landlady's reading'; it 'treats or rather indeed mencions AntiXst; .... tell her it is now time to leave her Romantz; to please me it is one of the best bookis I ever read; he is strangely piquante and short and strangely convincinge.' Ralph knew French sufficiently to read and write it, though he had not acquired any fluency in speaking it. Dr. Denton writes to him: 'If y^u would doe a good worke indeed you should translate Canterbury and Chillingworth their books into French, for certainly never any books gave a greater blow to papacy than those two.' 'Laud's Book against Fisher' was one of those which King Charles recommended to his daughter Elizabeth, at their last interview, 'to ground her against Popery,' so this was probably what Dr. Denton referred to as 'Canterbury's' book. Henry Verney also sent Sir Ralph in January '45 'the Bishop's last sermon & prayer; it is I assure you, a true booke & a good one.'

As mistress of the family Mary had at least the comfort of being very busy; they can keep but two maids and one little boy, 'soe we are but 7 in family, and I know not how to do with lesse, because of the children;' the house-keeping does not always go smoothly; Mr. Ogilvy writes from Orleans to apologise not only for the bad service of 'that graceless boy that I was so unhappy to prefer to your Ladyshipp, but also for his impertinent speaches which shall be the cause that he shall hardly find another maister.' One feels how the 'graceless boy' was put upon by the two English maids, and one is not without sympathy for him.

That some of the refugees treated their French servants in the rough and overbearing spirit traditionally attributed to the Englishman abroad, and that the quick-witted Frenchman in return cheated and abused the sons of 'perfide Albion' is evident from some of the letters. Here is one from Sir Henry Puckering Newton, who had set up house at Rouen, to Sir Ralph at Blois: 'I forgott in my last to acquaint you with the parting of my Boy Estienne, Who having of a long time play'd some prankes, made mee at last resolve to pay him his arrearages, Chiefly 3 or 4 dayes before having been very rude to Mrs Cochram and in his words defi'd both her and mee, And telling her if I beate him once I should never doe it twice, wch I understood him was by runing away. And though hee knew he was complain'd of, hee was so sencelesse as for a whole afternoon when my wife and I were abroad with a coach to neglect us and bee debauch'd with another lacquay should have been also following the coach. The next day I bestow'd a little beating of him, and did it heartily, though without passion: Upon wch hee ran to the doore and call'd for his things, and swore hee never would enter again, though a thousand devills drove him, But I over hearing him, sent one that was too strong for him and brought him back, and tooke a little more paines upon him, to shew him hee was mistaken. For I would beate him twice; And to bee beforehand with him, made him unbutton, that so hee might goe his way, as naked as hee came, if hee thought good. This startled him, but heardly wrought peccavi from his high stomach. But I perceiving hee would not stay long and might take some worse opportunity if I permitted it, dispatch'd him going, but with his cloaths, out of the sole respect I have to some at Blois that are his kinred. Every one wonders that one that deserv'd a worser beating so long should take it so unkindly at the last. Hee went from heare by Pont l'Arche (they say) to Paris loaden with balades, in company of one that sings them, and debauch'd him heere. A greater knave never serv'd master, if all bee true is told mee since, of every side. If hee went away without money, it was his owne fault, both for not asking mee pardon, on one side, and for not husbanding what had been given him at times wch would have come to a good sum according to the wage hee gott heere in the house, wch hee requited so unkindly to them that hee never eate bitt of their meate without grumbling, though to my knowledge (and great wonder) hee eate as good as I did and all the same. Nay at Madame Willetts hee would pretende to whole Turkeys for his share, rather than keepe them cold for after the dancing. I could entertaine you some 2 houres longer with much of his story wch never was complain'd of till his back was turn'd. But I am gladd I'm ridd of him so, and so may you bee when you are at the end of his adventures, wch I thought good to tell you in part that you may see the better t'was not without some cause none of his friends would bee caution for him, I being the first master putt him away, Hee ran away from all the rest.'

So much for the foreign lacqueys. English servants were far more reliable, but if they did not consume whole turkeys for supper, they quarrelled with the foreign food, and were as hard to please abroad as their successors of to-day.

'I know noe English maids will ever bee content (or stay a weeke),' wrote Sir Ralph, 'to fare as thes [French] servants faire. . . . Noe English maide will bee content with our diet and way of liveing: for my part since this time twelvemoneth, I have not had one bit of Rost meate to dinner, and now of late, I rost but one night in a weeke for Suppers, which were strainge in an English maide's oppinion.' But though Luce and Besse quarrelled with a diet of 'potages' and 'legumes,' and doubtless thought Sir Ralph's political scruples sadly misplaced, they followed the fallen fortunes of their master's family with exemplary fidelity, and when Ralph writes to Mary in England as to the comparative merits of bringing out an English maid or of getting a French one on the spot, his description of the latter makes one's hair stand on end; 'it is hard to find one here especially of our Religion,' but he has heard of one whom he recommends his wife to take 'with all her faults,' 'her 2 sisters are but Ramping girles,' 'but truly she is a civill wench and playes well of the Lute, she is well cladd and well bredd, but raw to serve, and full of the Itch!' The time devoted to the study of the lute might have been so far more profitably spent in practising with soap and water, but cleanliness in Sir Ralph's eyes ranks very far indeed after godliness, and he goes on discussing the maid's theological opinions. He fears that it may be necessary after all to dispense with Protestant orthodoxy, 'the very minister, and antients here, are served by Papists; but it would trouble us because of Fish dayes; I hope you will get one of our owne religeon either at Rouen or Paris.' When in the autumn of 1646, Mary decides to go to England, Luce goes with her, and Besse remains to look after Sir Ralph and the children; the two maids correspond and their masters enclose their letters. Luce Sheppard is a waiting gentlewoman on intimate terms with her mistress; she is at this time rather disappointing; but after Mary's death she takes very good care of Mrs. Eure's children, and is much trusted and valued. When Lady Verney is about to return to France, she complains that Luce's brother will not allow her to leave England again; knowing that he 'is a very Idle proud fellow' and that he has no comfortable home to offer her, Lady Verney sends a propitiatory offering of 'a pare of gloves trimed, to my maydes brother's wife to make them willing she should stay with me. . . . but to tell the truth methinks the wench is nott soe much troubled to part with me as I am to part with her; which hath taken of the edge of my sorrow to lett her goe.' Sir Ralph replies, very anxious for her comfort on her journey, and entering as he always does into every detail of Mary's anxieties:

'You say chamber maides will have 4 or 5 pounds wages and neither wash, nor starch; that is to say they will doo nothing but dresse you, for I doo not valew theire needle work at a groate a moneth. Tis true if any of us should be sick you would want one to make such Broathes and such like matters, but though Luce could doo it, perhapps you would not findd another that can, nor that can make creames or pyes or dresse meate they are now to find for such matters. My Budd now I have told thee my oppinion take whom you please, and doo in it what you please, for I studdy nothing but your contentment in all that I have writ about it; . . . Now for Luce's wages, it is three pounds English, and I paydd her all at Midsomer 1646, soe that at Christmas next there will bee a yeare and a half wages due to her wch comes to foure pounds ten shillings, unlesse you have payed her some since you went into England. Now for giving of her, if she leave you on a suddaine and unprovided (and espetially if she goe to serve againe) I would give her the lesse, therfore findd that out, and tell her if shee will stay, you will mend her wages. . . . for tis not possible you can come without a maide or woeman to helpe you, though I beeleeve Luce helped you very little at sea. Tis two daies jorney from London to Rye, and one from Deipe to Roüen and being noe more you may borrow or hire a wooman creature for such a purpose.' Eventually Luce settles to go with her mistress to Dieppe, she will take no other service 'but the thoughts of living with her sister like a gentlewoman workes much upon her.'

Besse meanwhile had turned out a perfect treasure, and however cheaply Sir Ralph seems to rate 'a wooman creature,' he freely acknowledges his indebtedness to Besse, for the comfort of the household during her mistress's absence.

'Besse now speakes French enough to buy any thing and uppon this occation I asked her if she had any thoughts of returning home. . . . to which she answered, she had noe thoughts of parting, and that if wee stayed halfe a dozen years abroad, wee might assure ourselves of her; these were her own words. . . . I was glad to have this assurance from her.' As a proof of his regard, he buys Besse a pair of 'trimed gloves' at £1 5s. Mary is troubled to think that Bess's feelings may be hurt if Luce's successor is put over her, after all her faithful service: 'I know not what course in the world to take. . . . I doe not finde being I keepe but toe maydes how I can keepe eyther a fine chambermaide or a gentlewoman for to say truth there is little or noe difference between them, for you and I have a great deale of washing and starching and beside upon those dayes that Bess doth wash there will be a greate deale of ordinary worke to doe as ye getting dinner ready and making cleane ye howse, which none heare that goes so well as Luce will be content to doe, and if I should take a very plaine chambermayde, I feare Bess will not be content to doe the work she now doth to be under a plaine one; and I cannott take Bess next to me because I know she cannott starch and beside I know she can neavor learne to dress me. I am in a great straite.' It is curious that the ladies of rank of the seventeenth century, who are so capable in other matters and so far more conversant with the mysteries of the kitchen, the bakehouse, and the stillroom, than their successors of to-day, are so very helpless about dressing themselves and quite dependent upon a 'gentlewoman in waiting.'

Mary returns to the subject again and again : 'I have not yet mett with a mayde, though I have seene many.' Sir Ralph also is not easy to please :

'Tell me what that maide is in Age and Parts and humour,' he writes, 'for if she bee not young and have some witt, she will bee the longer ere she get the language, and if her humour bee not merry, she will never please soe much as to bee endured in any house.' Mary at last finds a maiden who 'is very goodnatured, and a gentleman's daughter of £400 a yeare .... she is in a gentlewoman's habitt butt she saith she will not refuse to doe any thing.' This admirable young person took 'the measells,' but she seems to have returned at the end of a week prepared once more 'to doe anything.' The sight of a stranger in attendance on her mistress was, however, too much for Luce's feelings.

'Soe att night speaking with Luce aboute my going over,' writes Lady Verney, 'she told me thatt if I would lett her goe for one weeke downe into the country to her brother, to settle her buseness with him, she would goe over with me for a month or toe untell I could find one there fitting to my mind; soe I presently took her att her word, for I am very gladd to have her a month or toe longer upon any termes, because the greatest inconvenience thatt I shall find in a strainger will be in my journey.... soe I will putt of this mayde againe though truly I think tis a very good wench butt she is nott at all hansom which I know would nott please thee.'

Mary takes much pains with her housekeeping, she was famous for making good bread. It is amusing to find that 'sirrup of violets' and 'a firkin of this country butter' are sent as delicacies from Bucks to Normandy; butter and flowers travelling now in the opposite direction. Excellent dried fruits are mentioned from the South of France, 'cerises aigres' [cherries without sugar] and grapes being the best. Mary has a portable oven for roasting apples, 'a cloche,' which she takes home with her, and Ralph advises her to give it ' to Nan Lee or who else you please that loves good apples.' The French wine is commended, but Sir Ralph writes to his wife to send him from Claydon some of the old sack, to give away or to drink at home ; she replies :

'I am in great admiration at your telling me that good canarye sack will be a wellcome present to my acquaintance at blois, for I doe not know any English acquaintance I have there, and certainly you have very much altered the natures of ye french if they are growne to love sack—however I like very well of bringing some over. . . . we may keepe it for our owne use ; for if itt be good sack I beleeve tis a very whollsom wine espetially in that hott country.' Besides her housekeeping Mary had the education of Mun and Peg to occupy her, her music and her embroidery ; she seems to have an elaborate piece of work on hand, for when she goes to England, Ralph writes that if his business in London is like to take her as long to finish as her 'wrought sheete,' he shall not expect her speedy return. At this moment of intolerance in England and before the Revocation of the Edict of Nantes, there was a good deal more religious freedom to be found in France, one reason perhaps, why English families were sending boys abroad for education. Rouen 'is very unfit' for the purpose, wrote Sir Ralph in answer to an inquiry about a boys' school, 'for heere most men speak worse French than the poore people doe English at Northumberland, and there are noe Protestant masters alowed to keepe a schol heere. All things exceeding Deare, but higher in the country. There are divers Universities at Sedan, Saumur, Geneva, and other fine places, and as I am told at noe unreasonable rate and not only protestant scholemasters, but whole colledges of protestants.' They are very good friends with M. Testard, the Protestant pastor at Blois, who takes pupils.

In the summer of 1645 Sir Ralph went to Paris for a time and travelled about the country; a few weeks later he settled his family at Blois, which became their headquarters for the remainder of their exile. In 1646 he and his wife made another little tour. 'I have been out neare two months,' writes Sir Ralph on July 15, ' viewing the Townes uppon this River of Loir, and Rochell, Bordeaux, and severall other parts of this country.' He seems to have planned a longer stay at Nantes, and had ordered provisions to be sent there from Amsterdam; 50 lbs. of sugar, 50 lbs. of raisins of the sun, 50 lbs. currants [it seems as if Mary were preparing for Christmas plum-puddings], and 50 lbs. of rice, ' all these were in bundles and the rice in bags,' they were shipped from Holland in the previous October, but Christmas went by and they had not reached Nantes even by May. A long correspondence ensues in which the ship-master gives in all conscience reasons enough, and to spare, for the disappearance of the 'commodities'; they were shipwrecked, they were shut in by ice [he does not say where], they were disabled by a storm, they feigned to return to another port, they put the provisions into another ship, &c., &c., and they were finally devoured by rats—' two-legged ratts,' writes Ralph, ' advise with some knowing man, I will seeke remedie against the Master in some legall way.' The agent replies that they will get no redress ' to trouble justice on so weake ground,' that the master proves it *was* ' the Ratts,' and ' that tho he had 2 Catts aboard.' So nothing comes of it, but an addition to Ralph's many letters, though he repeats to the last his great desire ' to be quitt with the master,' who has ' first cheated mee of the goods and then layes it to the Ratts ' ; he has all an Englishman's indignation at being defrauded by a foreigner, and is quite willing to spend more than the things are worth to vindicate his rights.

After his return to Blois he says that they would have made a longer tour, but Mary insisted upon their return, they had not a penny left, and ' wifes will chide, and by the king's example, Husbands must obey ! '

The Reformed Churches of the continent watched the struggle in England with keen interest. Mr. Robert Thorner writes from Orleans to Ralph, on his return from a journey to Italy, ' In the Protestant cantons of Switzerland and at Geneva there was a solemne publicke fast on the 10th of this month [June 1646] appointed for the praying for the reconciling of these unhappy differences in greate Brittaine and Ireland.'

Among the smaller worries which Ralph had to endure in France was that of wearing a perriwig, a fashion from which England was still free. The little bills for the wigs themselves, the ribbons, the pomade, and the powder come again and again. Ralph sends minute directions about the length, style, and thickness, and encloses a pattern lock of hair: 'let it be well curled in great rings and not frizzled, and see that he makes it handsomely and fashionably, and with two locks and let them be tyed with black ribbon . . . . let not the wig part behind, charge him to curl it on both sides towards the face.' The cost of this wig was 12 livres. Good hair-powder seems to have been hard to obtain. Sir John Cooke sends 'a small phiole of white Cyprus powder, which I beseech you present to my Lady as an example of the best Montpelier affords, for I saw it made myself. It must be mixed with other powder, else it will bring the headache. There is a powder cheaper, but not so proper for the hair.'

Wealth and poverty are comparative terms, and though hardly knowing where to turn for the necessaries of life, some of its superfluities are still indispensable for self-respect; while Ralph is intent on his 'Pomatums,' Mary's friends amongst the Paris exiles are choosing her 'two fannes' at the Palais Royal, which cost two francs and fifteen sous, and her husband is most anxious that she be furnished with proper 'pinns, oris powder and such matters' from London, 'for they are nought here.' While powder and patches are amongst the ordinary toilette necessaries, tooth-brushes are new and costly luxuries, as late as 1649, an English friend asks Sir Ralph to inquire for him in Paris for the 'little brushes for making cleane of the teeth, most covered with sylver and some few with gold and sylver Twiste, together with some Petits Bouettes [*British* for Boîtes] to put them in.' It is the same at home; English society seems to Ralph's correspondents to be falling to pieces, the only happy people are those whom death releases from the chances and changes of this troublesome world—but as long as life remains the Countess of Warwick must give evening parties, and Anne Lee, who is but little regarded in the new household, must appear at them, and if society demands an evening dress, it may as well be in the latest Paris fashion—hence that young lady's letter to Lady Verney, which reads oddly enough with such a background of anxieties : 'Madam, I hear you ar at pares [Paris], you will be trim in all the new fashones, I will make no new cloues [clothes] till you direct mee, and if you could without any inconvenience by mee any prity coulred stoffe to make mee a peticote, 4 Bredes of saten is enofe ; I never put in more then 5 yard . . . . but I hear thay ware now in Franc coulerd slefes and stomicheres, therefore ther must be somthing alowed for that ; but not by no means if it cannot be without any inconvenience to you, pray let mee know and I will buy mee one heere : I would not have one to cost to much ; 4 or 5 pound and pray let mee know how to send the mony ; and deare Madam bestoe me 30 shelings in anie prety thing for my head, to sote me out a litell.'

She is longing to see Lady Verney again: 'I beseech you let me know as soon as you com to loundon, that I may wait on you, ther has been many shanges sence you went. I have many stories to tell you. . . . I want language to expresse my senc of your sevelity.'

In a letter of Mary's from London in 1647 describing the presents from Paris that her English friends would most value, we learn that 'wooden combs are in greate esteeme heare, butt truly I think they buy them very neare as cheape heare as there'; there is not 'anything that will be soe wellcom as gorgetts, and eyther cutt or painted callicoes to wear under them or whatt is most in fashion; and black or collered cales [calash, a hood] for the head; or little collered peny or toe peny ribonings, and som black patches, or som prety bobbs, butt ye pearle ones are growne very old fashion now.' Kings may be dethroned and Parliaments may totter, but Fashion still rules society with a rod of iron!

Lord Devonshire, sixth earl, had taken refuge in France not long after Sir Ralph went there. In December 1645, he was sent for back to England under pain of the confiscation of all his estates; he writes to tell Sir Ralph, and to hope he will return with him. Ralph replies that he finds 'there is an almost absolute necessity for your return as your case stands. I wish it were in my power to make it otherwise, but since there is no remedy but patience and you must needs go, begon quickly and seem to do it cheerfully, for you are now under the Lash and that of the most severest masters that ever yet were read or heard of, and from first you knew full well 'tis bootless by delays or otherwise to vex them. My Lord, in my opinion you have only one thing now to take a principal care of, which is ye covenant, in which, if you can receive a full and entire satisfaction, 'tis the best, if not I know what ere the hazard be, you will not take it.' He adds that 'his friends,' he finds, 'generally wish him homewards'; he wishes his affairs were in such a state that he might take advantage of Lord Devonshire's friendly offer. The latter, after his arrival in England, was kept as a sort of hostage at Latimer, his place in Bucks.

For a whole year the question of what course Sir Ralph should take, is debated between him and his friends in England. By a resolution, passed in December 1645, in the Parliament it was declared 'the rendering and coming in of persons and shall be understood of such persons onely as shall testifei their affections to the parliament by taking the covenant,' so that, as he says in a letter to Lord Devonshire, his remaining abroad was 'upon the same terms' as heretofore. To Henry he writes: 'You know I never was within the king's quarters nor never contributed, or in any way assisted against them: absence is my onely crime, and you know I have highly suffered for that already and was neaver soe much as somoned to returne soe noe contempt can bee layed to my charge; neither have I refused to pay taxes. Nay more, I sent in horses upon the first volluntary propositions soe that I doe nott know that by any ordinance that I have seene I can be made a delinquent butt yett I stand nott upon my justification. I know that's nott ye way I believe they make a difference in crimes or elce all men's punishments must be alike.'

Sir Roger Burgoyne writes that he has procured an order 'that the com^{tee} shall certifie the cause of their sequestration wth power to examine witnesses uppon oath .... if you could procure us certificates of y^r livinge soe and soe longe in this and that place happily they may be useful to us.'

The sequestration of Claydon appears to have been only absolutely carried out in September '46, though the ordinance was dated '44, in which Sir Ralph had been named a delinquent, and his tenants formally warned that all rents would have to be handed over to the Committee of Sequestration, sitting at Aylesbury. His friends had been able to show that his estate was in the hands of trustees for the payment of 900*l.* a year of debts and annuities, but Roades was compelled to account for all the residue of the rents to the committee. The list of persons mentioned in the Ordinance as liable to be dealt with as delinquents is very comprehensive.

Dr. Denton informs Ralph that the petitions of those who compound have 'this method' running through them all—a declaration that they have assisted the king and therefore that they desire to compound for their delinquency. Without an acknowledgment of delinquency no petition is received. Ralph writes that if the committee will not take off the sequestration he must compound, 'but if they make me petition as others doe that " A. B. humbly sheweth hee hath assisted the king," etc., 'tis a notorious lye, for I never assisted him in my life.' The doctor advises that if he can make some 'steady potent friends,' as Lord Warwick, he believes Ralph may 'gett a dispatch in some reasonable time, but that must be by speciall favour.'

With this end in view it was decided that Lady Verney should come to England, and with the assistance of all the friends they could muster get the sequestration removed. Sir Roger Burgoyne, 15 Jan. 1646, writes to Sir Ralph: 'as for your friends wifes comming over certainly it would not do amiss if shee can bring hir spirit to a soliciting temper and can tell how to use the iuyce of an onion sometimes to soften hard hearts. I spake with Gerrard. I beleeve he will be friend, but I cannot learne that yet any have been meerly sequestred for not taking the C. . . .' Ralph replies: 'As to writing to those named I am very doubtful it may be prejudicial and for the wife's coming I know it is not hard for a wife to dissemble, but there is like to be no need of that for where necessities are so great the juice of an onion will be useless. Some men of good judgements have advised me to sit still awhile, for since the Committee have not meddled with Claydon and there being some hopes they will not 'tis better to be quiet.'

In August '46 Dr. Denton gives his advice to the same effect : ' I am cleere of opinion the best course y^u can take is to send over mischeife wth all the speed y^u can, and to place y^r selfe at Deepe, or Calaies, or some other maritime towne where y^u may receave an account, and returne answers wth speed concerninge y^r owne businesse, not to touch uppon inconveniences of y^r comminge, women were never soe usefull as now, and though y^u should be my agent and sollicitour of all the men I knowe (and therefore much more to be preferred in y^r owne cause) yett I am confident if y^u were here, y^u would doe as our sages doe, instruct y^r wife, and leave her to act it wth committees, their sexe intitles them to many priviledges, and we find the comfort of them more now then ever.'

' The legal question at issue soon made itself clear. The mere absence of a member of Parliament from his duties, even when he had given no assistance to the King, had been declared to be delinquency by an order of the House of Commons, but that order had not been confirmed by the House of Lords. The point to be decided was whether delinquency could be created by anything short of an Ordinance of Parliament. On February 25th, 1647, the Committee of Lords and Commons took the preliminary step to bring this question to an issue by ordering the Bucks Committee to make a certificate of the causes of Sir

Ralph's delinquency.'[1] But before this Mary had reached England; Sir Ralph wrote to Lord Devonshire that 'unlesse innocency proove a crime, I shall not utterly despaire of a returne.'

Ralph escorts his wife to the coast, and writes from Rouen to Henry on November 13, '46: 'Tell your good aunt that Mischeife is coming as soon as wee can finde any tollerable passage from hence to Diepe (by Callais wee durst not goe for the Army is now going into Garrison ... who Rob by 20 or 30 in a company). Of late the weather hath been wonderfull stormie, and the windes exceeding high, soe that wee must attend for a more quiet season: the marchants and shipmasters heere informe mee that in one storme (about six weekes since) ther was 42 shipps cast away uppon the coasts of England, therfore wee have reason to bee very wary.' It is evident that he took all possible care of his beloved 'Mischief,' and was greatly troubled at having to let her make this expedition without him. He wrote special letters of thanks to the two gentlemen to whose charge he confided her, for their care in 'conducting' her on the journey, and the following note, written near midnight a few days after her departure, shows how keenly he felt the separation: 'My deare Hart, though the winde held fare, and the weather good till Satterday at night, soe that I have all the hopes that can bee of thy saife arrivall, yett I confesse a letter from thee now [Tuesday night] to give mee a full assurance

[1] Gardiner's *Great Civil War*, vol. iii. p. 312.

would bee more welcome to mee then ever, especially if it tolde every perticuler how thou hast been since I saw thee . . . 'tis now soe exceeding late that I can only intreate thee to bee carefull of thy selfe, and make hast back againe to mee, for the greife of our fatall separation is not to bee expressed by Thy [unsigned].'

Amongst the scraps of manuscript that have come back from Blois to Claydon, and have so long outlasted the hands that traced their faded characters, are many bits of verse, and songs sung to the guitar. More than one copy has been made of Henry Lawes' exquisite lines ' To his Mistress going to Sea.'[1] They must surely ever after have brought back to Ralph's mind that parting with Mary.

> Fayrewell fayre sainte, may not the seas and winde
> Swell like the Hearts and Eyes you leave beehinde,
> But calm and gentle like the lookes you weare
> Smile in your Face and whisper in your Eare.

---

[1] Out of *Ayres and Dialogues*, published 1653.

Dame Mary Verney,
dau: of John Blacknall Esqre
from a picture by Vandyck at Claydon House.

CHAPTER XI.

MARY LADY VERNEY 'SOLICITING.'

From villany dress'd in a doublet of zeal . . .
From a preacher in buff, and a quarter-staff steeple,
From th' unlimited sovereign power of the people,
From a kingdom that crawls on its knees like a cripple,
    Libera nos, etc.
From a hunger-starved sequestrator's maw. . . .
    Libera nos, etc.
    A Lenten Litany.—CLEVELAND.

DURING the time that Lady Verney was in England looking after her husband's affairs, they kept up a regular and detailed correspondence, and their letters are certainly among the most interesting of the manuscripts preserved at Claydon. The task which she had undertaken was a very difficult one, particularly for a woman, but she applied herself to it with characteristic spirit and tact, and scarcely complained of the sufferings and illnesses she went through, except in so far as they hindered her work. She had to fight against enemies and friends, Lords and Commons, Committees who would not sit, fearful members who would not vote; she had to administer 'French toys' in one direction, a watch in another; and to distribute hard money, according to good advice, to the immaculate members and their wives. She had to stand up for her husband's rights against the men who owed him money and would not or could not pay, and the still more numerous set who had claims upon him. The debts, it must be remembered, were almost all Sir Edmund's, and Sir Ralph had only borrowed in order to pay the interest upon his father's liabilities; yet there is not a line of bitterness and scarcely even any observation of the fact. The revenues of Claydon barely sufficed to pay what was due to Sir Edmund's creditors; but Sir Ralph had taken up the heavy burden without a murmur, and his wife is content to share it with him, although for a time they are reduced to living almost entirely on her fortune.

A set of cypher names had been agreed on between husband and wife before they parted, and they must have had some amusement in settling them together. Lady Sussex, now Lady Warwick, was happily described as 'Old men's wife,' Sir Roger Burgoyne as 'Mr. Good,' Fairfax as 'Brave,' Frank Drake is 'Purchase,' the sequestration and sequestrators are 'Chaine' and 'Chainors,' the covenant is 'Phisick,' money is 'Lead,' property which had shown such an aptitude to fly away appears as 'Feathers,' the Committee of Lords and Commons are 'Freinds Hault et Bas,' the Lords alone 'Hault' and the Commons 'Bas,' the Bucks Committee are 'Hens,' apparently from the name of one of the members; there are also cypher names of places—'Coales' for Newcastle, etc., but in copying the letters the proper names have generally been inserted.

Mary arrived in England the end of November, 1646, and writes to Ralph on the 26th : ' We are at this very instant safely arrived hear in Southwark, but soe extreamly weary that I can scarce hold my penn. . . . We weare in great fear of being stopped at the gardes, but by very great fortune we passed, not being suspishiously acomodated.' She had been kindly treated at Rye by the Cockrams ; he and his wife ' furneshed me with all acomodation both for horses and selfe. I left Sir Edward Herbert and my Lady at Rye . . . they both came to see me, and told me they wear sorry they mett me nott sooner, to have prevented me, as thinking itt a very unfitt time to doe my business. Really they wear both more curtious then evor in theyr lives. . . . I find my change of diett breed a very great allteration in me already, but I hope in God I shall be better when I am settled. I long for nothing more then to hear thou art safe at Bloyse, and wish for noething in this world soe much as to be with thee againe.'

December 3.—' Neyther the ayre nor diett agrees with me, butt I shall make all the hast out of itt that I can, though I feare twill be longe first for I find business of this nature are extreamly tedious, but if it pleas God to give me my helth I will nott neglect one minutes time. I have had soe much company every day since I came, that I have nott stirred forth of dores, onely one day to my sister Alpott's [Susan

Alport] who made an invitation to me, and a very great dinner. . . . Here hath bin Sir Roger, whoe expresseth more afection and love to you then tis posseble for me to wright, and saith if he had knowne you would have come to the sea side, he would have ventured to have seen you. Truly I think he is a very reall frend, which is a thing very diffecult to find in these times. . . . There is one Mr. Pellum, a lawyer of the Bas [the House of Commons] . . . He knows you very well, he is a man of Power and by Aunt Eures interest in him will doe you very much good. I was at his chamber last night, and his opinion is, you are nott chainable [i.e. liable to sequestration] for he saith you were chained onely by an order of the House and not by an ordinance, and he assures me bare order is nott suffitient, having nothing but absence against you, butt others are nott of his opinion. . . . I am att very great charge here, for I pay twelve shilling a week for a chamber for myselfe and another for my mayde twoe pare of staires high, fire, candles, washing, breakfast and diet besides. . . . Coaches are most infenett dear, and there is noe stirring forth without one or a chaire, the towne was neavor so full as tis now. I was forced to take up £50 upon Will Roades and my owne bond; Harry procured the mony; £20 of itt was for him to sattisfy soe much of the £100 as was taken up for peggs [Margaret Elmes] mariage. Indeed he was very Impatient for itt, and though I knew you did nott promise to pay thatt dept untell the other were sattisfied, yett I thought it was better to doe itt then to anger him toe much, for to say truth he is very kind, and soe is the Dr. and follows your busines very hertily. Aunt Eure is very kind and makes very much of me, indeed I could nott have been soe well any where in this towne. . . . Will Roades is now in towne and they [the family] are ready to teare him in pieces, butt I have told him whoesoever suffers, you must be supplyed.'

Ralph replies: ' I see you are at a very greate charge if that make you hast back heather tis well, for I confesse I shall rejoyse at anything that shall bring thee to me againe, though at present money goes very hardly from mee ; but while thou doest stay, loose noe time in thy busines that soe nearely concernes thee and mee and thine, nor spare anything for thy health. . . . I am sorry you did not put of Sue's invitation, for Feasting agrees not with your condition, being not able to returne the like. Avoyd it hereafter, and make some better use of your freinds love, if it bee possible. Make as few visits, and use as few coaches as you can ; for on looseth time, and the other spends money. Rather keepe a good fire, and be merry with your freinds at Home. . . . I am very sorry you have been forced to take upp money already, for though tis hard to get into debt, yet tis much harder to come out of it. It seems Harry had 20 pounds of it [of the £50 which Mary had had to raise] and you but 30 pounds, truly I was noe way obliged to pay that 20 pounds soe soone, therfore J must woonder hee should presse you for it; if you doe not resolve not to give care to any sollicitations of that nature, you will never bee at quiet, nor keepe the love of your freinds; for if Dr. Denton, Mistress Isham, Doll Leeke and some others should presse you to do the same, if you refuse them, theres a quarrell; for why should you not take upp money to pay that which I owe them uppon bond as well as to pay that which I gave another of my owne free will. Take heed, my deare Budd, for this is a most daingerous precedent, therefore conceale it. Once more, Deare Hart, let mee begg of thee to dispatch thy businesses quickly, before your freinds affections coole, that thou mayest speedily returne back to him whose love dayly encreaseth, even beyond thy immagenation or the expression of thy most faithfull Ralph Verney.'

In the next letter Mary writes: 'There cannot be any thing donn [in your business] untell we have a certifycate from the "committee" in the country wherefore you were sequestered; and then they say we must petition the committees in both Houses after we have made all the frendes that posseble we can; and if we can gett off we shall be hapy, elce we shall be referred to Goldsmiths Hall where we must expect nothing but cruelty, and the paing of more lead then I feare we can posseble make. This is the day there of Dr. Denton's hearing; how he will come off as yett I know nott. . . . One Satterday last a great many compounded. My Lord of Dorset paid £5,000, and he presently overed the comittee his whole estate

for £6,000, they paing his depts. . . . All the fear
here now is betweene the Presbeteriens and the Independants; they beginn allready to come to the House
in tumults. Upon Friday there was a thowsand came
downe to the House to demand sixe of their owne
men which were comitted, and they were presently
released. . . . I am most extreamly weary of this
place for hear is noething of frendship left, but all the
falceness that can be imagined. Except Sir R. Burgoyne here hath not been any of that syde, onely
once Frank Drake, whoe is soe fearfull and timerous,
that he dares nott look upon those he hath heretofore
professed freindship toe. The greatest freyndshipp
one can expect from most here is nott to be one's
enymie. One Satterday last I was with ye old men's
wife [Lady Warwick] whoe used me very cyvelly
and enquired very kindly how you did and the children, and alsoe of your estate, butt offered me noething
at all of curtesy, yett I was alone wth her an hower
together and urged her a little to itt for I told her
very many times that itt was frends which did all,
which I doupt was hard to be found and wth out them
nothing could be donne. But for al this she did not
offer to engadge her selfe for her husband nor any
other curtesy. I caried the watch butt brought itt
away againe as nott thinking itt fitt to bestow there.
I think I shall sell itt for the vallue of therty pistolls.
One cheyfe end of my going to her was for y^r
wrightings which you apointe me to take out, but the
trunk is nott in towne she hath sent for itt, but I fear

ye soe long tareing for itt will be a great prejudice to us. Her mayden daughter [Anne Lee] is extreamly kind to me. I gave her the little boxe. . . . I find she [Lady Warwick] hath nott delt very well by her.'

After this Mary does not write for three weeks. She has been for eighteen days in bed with a fever, and much distressed in mind, so that she could not proceed with her husband's business. On January 7, '47, she writes : 'I prayse god I am very much better then I was, and my feavor hath left me, onely itt hath brought me soe low that I am not able to goe twise the lenth of the chamber, and I am soe extreamly opressed with mellencollick that I am almost ready to burst; and, to add to my greater misfortune, my mayde is new fallen sick, soe that I am in soe great a straight thatt I know nott what in the world to doe, for tis a torment to me to have a strainger come neare me, but I trust god will give me patience to beare all these aflictions. Truly D^r [Denton] hath bin and is very carefull of me.' She then goes on to tell how Lady Dacre's man has been asking about the money owed by Ralph, and saying if his land had been made over to Lady Dacre she might have been paid it, and secured the property from sequestration; to which Lady Verney replied that it would not have been much advantage to her as the taxes come to almost as much as the revenue. 'I have nott any creature to send out to enquire for a ship or any thing else, for Hary's man is such a finecall fellow that he thinks much to be sent forth of any ordynary errant. . . . I had butt £25 of that which we took up, for there was noe sattisfiing Hary without £25; truly he was allmost outragious. . . .' In the next letter: 'Harry is very kind, but yet we have had little short disputes about your estate. . . . All my endeavors are to hansomely putt him from the thoughts of liveing with us; for truly he is at a most mighty heith both in his diett and atendance and all things else; I beleeve he foules more linnen in one week than you doe in three. . . . We are very great, therefore keepe very faire with him, butt yett I find that he is all for his owne ends.'

Again and again Mary expresses her gratitude to Dr. Denton. Once she says, 'he is onely a little chargable,' and that she has to try and keep him from going to many lawyers, who are very dear and not much use, 'for tis nott law now but favour.' She hopes the business of the sequestration may not come before the House of Commons, 'because tis very tedious and very difficult to come off from thence. . . .'

'Now for ye old men's wife. I sent your letters to her, and her daughter Ane, whoe is very kind, and I dare say loves us, & truly soe is ye Mother; she came once herselfe to see me since I was sick and hath sent to me very often. Once she sent me a pheasant and 2 bottles of wine; butt, poore woeman, I think she hath made herselfe very poore, & I beleeve hath very little power, for she lives in yᵉ howse like a stranger, & doth not meddle with anything, onely she gives toe partes of three of her estate for her diett; her nue husband hath not made her a peny Joynture; neyther did he ever give her anything butt one ring of diomans, nor ever gave yᵉ Daughter yᵉ worth of sixe pence; neyther hath she donn any thing at all for her; for if she could but have made up her portion foure or five thousand I could by Mr. Lodge's [Henry Verney's] means have helped to a very great fortune—above three thousand a year, cleare estat—a cousin of yours of your owne name; but, however, if I find yᵉ mother's husband may be usefull to us, I will put her to itt though she offer nothing. . . . I neavor wright you noe nues, because I beleeve others doth doe that, and indeed . . . I have nott roome for to tell the crueltees that are donn, and how barbarous a place this is would take up a greatt deale of paper. . . . Your Lady neighbour at Twyford is very angry with us becaus we doe nott keepe one of Sir A[lexander] D[enton's] chilldren; but Mist. Is[ham] answer her very well that we had more need get somebody to keep some of your brothers or sisters. . . . Concerning your removing from the place you are in, I leave itt wholly to thee, for beleeve, my dere hart, soe I have but thy company I care not in what towne itt is or whether I have any other company or nott; for if please god to bring me to thee againe I assure thee itt should be a very strang occasion could evor make me goe from thee againe. I think there could noething come to make me doe itt, for truly, my hart, I find myselfe very unable to beare such a separation. For Mons' Godbeits' house I doe not like it upon noe termes, for tis very Dull and close and Inconvenient. . . . For my part if pleas god to enable us to keepe a coach I shal like the other place as well. . . . I am most impatient to be with thee, for though everybody here is very jolly, yett I nevor hadd soe sadd a time in all my life.' In the next letter she speaks of arrangements for her confinement and says: 'I fear twill be imposseble to dispatch our business here time enoughe to come to thee to lye in, the very thought of which goes to the very soule of me, for to be soe long from thee, and to lye inn without thee, is a greater afliction then I feare I shall be able to beare, but I shall dayly pray for patience. . . . I pay her [Mrs. Eure] £1 a week for diett for my selfe and mayde . . . she would nott name any thing, soe I knew not what to doe; but my brother told me he once mentioned that somme to her, so I bid him offere itt . . . which she took and was very well content. . . . All provisions are most extreamly dear, beef 4^d, veal and mutton 8^d per lb; corn above 8^s the bushel. Fammin is very much feared. . . . I have now receaved your letter dated 10th Jan., which, though itt was butt a kind of an angry chiding letter [he had complained that her letters were too short], yett I forgive thee, because thou didest nott know how sick I was when I writt that little short letter, or noat, as you call it. . . . I have here at my lodging the trunk . . . and a little black boxe. . . . I find they would be troublesom to yᵉ old men's wife; she allsoe this day sent me home the black cloth bedd and chayres, and lett me pay for yᵉ bringing them, which was nott soe hansomly donn.' A little later she tells of more friendly conduct on the part of Lady Warwick: 'Her daughter hath been extreamly sick of a feaver, & is still very ill; I sent my mayd the other day to see her; & old men's wife sent for her into her & expressed very much kindnes to us both, & sent me word if she could doe me any good in our business she be very ready.'

January 28, 1647 : 'Here was neavor greater expectation than is now, nor people between more hopes and feares of a nue warr then at the present, and I beleeve will be soe ontell the comissioners retourne.'

In December Parliament had agreed to pay the Scotch army 400,000*l.* The king was to be delivered up to nine commissioners despatched from Westminster to conduct him to Holmby House. where he was to be kept prisoner. For more than a year past the Independents, strong in the support of the army, had been gaining power. But within the walls of Parliament the Presbyterians were still able to make head against them, sometimes even to carry measures in their despite, and the struggle between the two parties added to the disorganisation of public affairs.

In February Mary was much hindered in her business by the Committee of Sequestration not sitting for three weeks, and without an order from them she could not get the certificate from the Aylesbury Committee.

'Those villaines in the contry might have given me a certifycate, if they had pleased, without putting me to this trouble. . . . There was neavor soe much disorder as is now in this towne, for every one is as much discontented as tis posseble. The Buttchers have begun the way to all the rest, for within this toe dayes they all did rise upon the exise man, and Burnt downe the exise howse, and flung the exise money forth into the middle of the street, and they say hurt some of the exise men. The Houses were in much disorder upon this, but dares not hang any of them; they say they will leave them to the law, which cannott hang them, for the law onely makes itt a riott; but they will not take off the exise, and the butchers have all sworne that they will nott kill one bitt of meat ontell tis taken off. The Houses have sate this 3 dayes about disbanding the armies; some say tis for feare they should turne against them. . . . The committee in the country are very malitious and extreamly Insolent.'

'4th Mar. Most men tell me they beleeve you will come off if we gett a faire certiffycate.' Henry has been asking Ralph to sell him a pension of 20*l*. a year, but Mary wisely remarks that his revenue is not enough to pay all the pensions he has already besides keeping his own family, and that it would be unwise to add to his liabilities before he knew whether the sequestration would be taken off, and whether his debts would make it necessary to sell Claydon. 'Sir Richard Pigott sent a very civell message that he was to goe into the country about a fortnight or three weeks hence, but if there was any thing he could serve me in sooner, he would goe downe one purpose. . . . He is chaireman ther, and they say hath great creditt amongst them. . . . I meane . . . to goe to him before he goes downe. . . . Indeed I am Impatient ontell I am with thee; and soe, my Deare Roge, I am confydent thou beleevest of thine owne.'

On March 11 Mary describes another interview with Lady Warwick:

'Upon tuseday I went to see the old men's wife, it being ye ferst time since my sicknes; she made very much of me; & asked very much after you; but one can neavor find her alone, for her howse is always like a court; before I came away her husband and my lord of holland came in; as soon as my Lo: of Holl: saw me he came to me & asked for you extreamly cyvelly, & told me that al ye sarvis that lay in his power he would be ready to doe us; but her husband sate like a clowne and sayed noething and yet she told him whoe I was: poore sister Nan is most extreamly sick still and hath every day toe docters wth her; they say she is not in sudaine danger; truly I should be very much greived if pleas god should die, for we should loose a very good frend that loves us; her mother desired very much that you would excuse her y^t she had writ noe oftner to you; but she sayes she loves you as well as evor she did; truly I think she hath not time to wright or doe any thing elce; the howse is bravely furneshed wth all her stuff that was you know where: but I beleeve they all thought themselves hapier in the old place; most of ye old sarvants are wth her still.'

Ralph writes in reply: 'I hope Old men's wife will shew herselfe a freind indeed when time serves and need requires, and I beleeve that Noble Lord her Brother in Law [i.e. Lord Holland] will doe you any service hee can, for hee is a gentleman: but for that Vinaigre Faced fellow her husband, I trust wee shall have noe occation to use him, and I should account it a perticular blessing to dispatch my businesse well, without beeing beholding to him, or any such unworthy, & ill-natured creatures.'

On April 8 Mary writes again: 'I have been twice within this week with ye old men's wife; she excuses her selfe much y^t she doth nott wright to you, she sweares she hath nott time; she spake to her husband and he was was att ye Comittee for me; therefore I thinke itt would not doe amiss if you writt her thanks; she is now goeing into ye Country at a place of ye king's called nonesuch; poore nan is very weake still.' 16 May.—' You desire to know how old men's wife playes her part, and in your latter letter you say thatt tis nott her husband bare appearing thatt you shall thank her for ; truly then you must nott thank her for any thing ; for butt his promise to be once att the comittee when itt hapned that they did nott sitt thatt day att all ; I neavor since I came receaved any curtesie from eyther of them ; tis true when I goe to see her she doth aske very kindly after you and after your business ; butt thatt is all.'

There is a loving dispute between the husband and wife about the expected baby's name. Mary writes : 'If itt be a boy I am resollved to have itt of thy owne name, therefore I charge you doe nott contredict itt ; but if itt be a gerle I leave it wholly to thee to chuse. . . . I will be governed by thee in anything but the name if it be a boy, for to tell the truth I must have itt have thy name. And for the suddaine crisning I will obay thee, and gett a minester in the howse that will doe itt the old way, for tis nott the fashion heare to have godfathers or godmothers, butt for the father to bring the child to church and answer for itt. . . . Truly one lives like a heathen in this place ; since I have recovered my helth I have gonn to our parrish church, but could neavor but one time get any roome there for all the money I offered. And eyther I must be at the charge to hire a coach to trye all the churches or else sitt at home ; and when one getts roome one heares a very strange kind of sarvis, and in such a tòne that most people doe noething but laughe at itt.[1] And everybody that receaves must be examined before the elders, whoe they all swere asketh them such questions that would make one blush to relate.'

Ralph replies : ' Now for the name. If it bee a girle and that you have noe conceit because the other died, I desire it may bee Mary ; but if it bee a boy, in earnest you must not deny mee, let it bee Richard or what you please, except my owne name. Really I shall take it ill if you contradict mee in this. If it bee a sonne I trust God will make him a better and a happier man then his father. Now for the Christening. I pray give noe offence to the State ; should it bee donn in the old way perhapps it may bring more trouble uppon you then you can immagen, and all to noe purpose, for soe it bee donn with common ordinarie water, and that these words, " I baptise thee in the name of the Father, and of the Sonne, and of the Holy Ghost," bee used with the water, I know the child is well baptised. All the rest is but matter of forme and cerimoney which differs almost in every

[1] With speech unthought, quick revelation,
With boldness in predestination,
With threats of absolute damnation . . .
   See a new preacher of the town,
   O the town, O the town's new teacher !

With troops expecting him at th' door,
That would hear sermons, and no more ;
With noting tools, and sighs great store,
With Bibles great to turn them o'er,
While he wrests places by the score,
   See a new preacher of the town,
   O the town, O the town's new teacher !
                   CLEVELAND.

country, and though I must needs like one forme better then another, yet wee must not bee soe wedded to any thing of that nature, as to breake the union by a needlesse seperation in such indifferent things of the Church. . . . If you cannot have convenient Roome at Church, finde out some convenient oppertunity either at D^{rs} or elswhere to receive it [i.e. the Communion] in some House ; and doe it quickly, for you know not how soone you may lye in. My Budd, this is a Greate Worke, therfore chuse a time when you have least Businesse, that you may considder it more seariously.'

Mary had troubles enough without those that her brothers-in-law made for her, but they leave her very little peace, and just now she writes again : 'Harry and I have had a hotter dispute then evor we had ; concerning your not answering his letter ; he fell into very high Langguage and sayd you had Injured him very much by delaying him soe. . . . I told him how his letters had miscaried, & that you could not posseble answer . . . sooner, but I had as good have spoken to the post, for he beleevs nothing of itt. . . . He sayed many bitter things, & I was nott much behind hand with him, & in effect I told him I had suffered all this while, but if itt were to be had I would now have wherewithall to subsist. Beleeve me there is nothing puts me in soe great Choller as to heare thee taxed, that I know art soe good & Just to all.'

When Henry received Ralph's answer his behaviour was still worse. His sister-in-law writes: ' I discovered the whole business by another body, & truly I must needs tell you that soe much unworthiness & soe great a cheat I did neavor know any creature more guilty off; the story is to long to relate, butt my Aunt Misterton is soe sencible of his usage of her that I beleeve and feare he must shortly seeke another place to be in. . . . This morning he came and shewed me your letter; to which I sayed noething but that I thought you had donn nothing butt what became a kind and loveing Brother; soe with that he fell into higher Languadge then I can express and sayed he should have expected more kindnes from a Jew . . . and that itt may be there might come times of action againe and then itt might be in his power to be—truly I cannot express the most unworthy language he gave of you.'

A month later we hear, 'harry . . . is out of towne wth his Aunt; you may be sure I will doe my best to keep him in there, butt I very much fear he cannott be long there now. . . . I much wonder he doth not seeke out some Imployment, for sure he cannott think that she or anybody elce will allwayes give him his diett, espetially when they know his humers . . . the Dr keeps good frends with him, butt to my knowledge he hath a worse opinion of him than of any of your Bro: or sisters, and thinks him as falce harted as tis posseble for one to bee.' The week following, after detailing some money transactions in the family, she writes: 'Soe I find tis a cheate from ye beginning to ye end of Harry's side;

& truly I think he studdies noething elce but to doe poore meane things. . . . I know all his kindness to me is butt from the teeth outward.'

Edmund's testimony concerning Henry's character is to the same effect. Once he wrote: 'I am sorry old Harry playes such unbecoming and unhandsome, indeed I may say such horrid tricks'; and another time: 'I cannot but confesse he suffers most in theire opinions that have reason to know him best, which iss a shrewde evidence against him, and I am hartily greiv'd for it. . . . He hath been strangely kinde to me since my comming over, and made me larger proffers then I conceiv'd I could in modesty accept of from one in hiss condition. I feare the nearenesse of hiss fortunes force him into many inconveniencyes and unbecoming wayes, and I doubt he iss too much inclin'd to them in hiss own nature, & too partyall in hiss own cause, & too passionate if things hitt not according to hiss expectation.'

It is evident that Harry was no help to his poor sister-in-law in her business, which progressed most slowly, & others with whom she had to deal were equally bad in their way. In one letter she writes: 'I find Frank Drake to be a very Jack,' and Ralph speaks of Drake's being in a 'frenzie,' which is an 'ill sign' for their business (he was on the committee in Bucks); 'for what kindness can we expect from such a person as is unwilling to do himself a courtesy, lest he should do me a pleasure too.'

By the 1st of April Mary did at length obtain the

certificate of the cause of sequestration: 'It is for noething but absence. . . . They tell me they beleeve itt must be referred to the House before I can come off cleare. . . . It will cost us a great deale of money by the tediousness and delayes that I know we shall find there. Itt cost me now 5/- and 6/- in a morning in coach hier those times that I have gon about itt. I am this day going to Lady Warwick to desire her to speake to her husband to be att the comittee to-morrow, for that is the day that we intend the certificate shall be delivered, & itt may be posseble that we may receave advantage by haveing some freinds there . . . for sometimes a few frends with God's blessing will doe things beyond expectation; & I trust God will direct us for the best. I am sertaine he is able to protect us against all their barbarous usage. . . . Truly I know not whatt I shall doe for money, for 'twill be unposeble to gett enough of Will [Roades] to follow this business. All that I can doe is to gett enough of him to supply my owne perticuler occasions : & yett truly I doe nott spend one penny more then I must needs. . . . I am halfe wild that I have noe letters this weeke. My dearest Roge, farwell. I am thine owne for ever. P.S. Dr Mayerne lives hear in toune; he hath but one daughter which they say is the greatest Mariage in Ingland. . . . Hear is a most desperate booke written against taking the Covenant, which if I can gett I will send you; itt is ordered to be burnt. It will be a little to bigg to send you by the post.'

Ralph must have been well supplied with the family news, for besides his wife's letters he heard constantly from Dr. Denton, with scraps of information about relations and friends, besides endless details of business. On 4th March he writes: 'There is now att Blois Sr Orlando Bridgman, his only sonne a nephewe of his, and one Mr. Fanshawe, all under the tuition of Mr. Cordell. . . . Sir Orlando . . . intends within a twelvemonth to send him [his son] to the Universitie at Sameur or Poictou for 2 years, then to Paris, and soe to the Inns of Court. . . . Though I know not Sir Orl: his sonne, yet I pray make a visitt to him for his Father's sake, and let me know howe he doth, and if it ly in y^r way to doe him a curtesie I pray be kind to him.'

The good doctor had been trying to find out the reasons which were given for various cases of sequestration. On the 24th March he writes to Ralph: 'I writt you word in my last that I wanted H. Cooke his certificate of the cause of his delinquency & sequestration, wch uppon search I find to be just nothinge, for he was sequestered by expresse order of the House without any cause therein expressed, & never any was showed, & yett though his estate be now freed he is outed the House. There is another, Cooke of Gloucester, who was yesterday freed in the House, if I am not misinformed, whose only fault was that he went a woinge to his mistress att Woodstocke before Eghill fight. I heare also that Mr. Catline (against whom some say nothinge is to be alleadged but absence, some say more) . . . is endeavoringe to take off his sequestration. . . . Send me in the next as many arguments as you can for the reason of your travell. If my opinion will goe for anythinge, I will say enough, that it was requisite and very necessary for her health.'

In April, when Mrs. Eure was leaving town, Ralph is very solicitous for his wife and fears she will be lonely: he proposes that she should send for little Jack and his maid, Fudd: 'he will entertaine you and Fud will stay in the House, whilst Luce goes to market. . . . Now I have told you my minde, I leave it wholly to you, doe that which pleaseth you best; and doe not trouble yourselfe for anythinge; what course soever you take (for that little time that you will bee at London) the exterordinary charge will not be considerable, therefore please yourselfe, for contentment I price above any money.'

'The honest Doctor,' as she calls him, is with her at least twice a day and is very anxious about her, as she is exceedingly delicate, but on the 3rd of June, 1647, Mary's child was safely born; the Dr. writes to announce the joyful tidings to Ralph, and she adds in her own hand, 'I have borne you a lusty boy.' He replies, June 20:

'My deare Budd, the longer your letters were the more they were woont to please mee, but I must confesse the three lines you writ me at the end of Dr.'s letter dated 3rd June pleased mee above any that I have yett received from you, because they assured me of thy safe delivery which is a most unspeakable blessing to us both ; God make us thankful for it. If the boye's name is Richard I shall hope he may bee a happy man ; but if it bee otherwise I will not prophecie his ill-fortune, but rather pray to God to make him an honest man, and then he will be happy enough.'

There is great joy in the little house at Blois—but Miss Peg pouts—she had wanted a sister, and holds boys very cheap ! Master Edmund Verney, aged 10, writes to his mother : 'Madame ma bonne mère. Mad^{lle} ma sœur est extrèmement courroucée contre vous par ceque vous avez eue un garçon et non pas une fille. Je prie continuellement pour vous comme mon devoir me le commande. Vous baiserez pour moi Monsieur mon petit frère. Mad^{lle} ma sœur vous baise humblement la main quoique vous l'ayez grandement désobligée.' He asks for her to send good news which will oblige me particularly, 'qui demeurerai éternellement comme je suis, votre plus humble serviteur et fils.'

We learn from Lord Fermanagh's pocket-book, that Mary had her way about the baby's name, he was christened—Ralph—on the 17th of June. Ralph the elder is full of tender anxieties about her ; 'I charge you doe not stirr out too soone, nor leave off too many cloathes at a time though the weather bee hott. When you goe downe about the Inventories I beeleeve twill bee your best way to hier a light coach and foure horses, and then if you stirr very early you may sleepe in the coach, dine at Amershame, and lie at your owne house, and the next day the coach may returne empty. Mornings and evenings are cold, therfore prepare for that. If you goe downe on horsback you must lodg by the way, and if you bee very weary, and that may stay you longer in the country then you intend, which may bee a greate hindrance to my affaires at London ; therfore goe by coach though it bee the Dearer way.' He asks if Lord Roscommon has been to see her, inquires after all his Irish friends of the old days, how Lady Barrymore and 'Cousin Maudlin' fare, and also where Mrs. Freake and her husband are [they owe him money upon bond]. 'Write not too much till you are well able, least it weary you, but I will not abate you a line heerafter, therfore expect it not. I thanke you for your 3 lines, for they did much satisfie mee, but when you are a little stronger, I shall expect to receive a letter every weeke as longe as two or three pamphlets ; but I hope my businesse will receive a good and speedy conclusion, that you may save this labour, and returne quickly to Thine owne.'

Poor Mary made but a slow recovery and was also anxious about the baby, though he was a fine child at his birth. On June 24th she writes : 'Our poore child was soe extreame sick that every body thought itt would have died, butt now I prayse God tis beyond every bodyes expectation strangely recovered. I entend to send itt downe the beginning of ye next weeke ; for my selfe I am soe very weake that ontell yesterday, since I was brought to bed, I have neavor been able to sitt upp an hower at a time ;. I am so tormented with paines in my head, that if I hold it downe but halfe a quarter of an hower, itt puts me into such sweates that I am not able to endure itt. But yet I trust in God if this paine in my head were but gonne, I should recover my strenth a pace, for the D^r makes me eate good brothe. . . . Truly Sir Roger is very kind, and makes the greatest expressions to you that evor I hard in my life.'

Political matters were now in a strange state. On June 2 a troop of horse commanded by Cornet Joyce had suddenly appeared at Holmby House, and in the name of the army had taken possession of the king. The dissension between the Parliament and the army was at its height; the latter was advancing upon London, having demanded the expulsion of eleven members. The greatest alarm prevailed in the town. Mary writes on the 17th of June that the 'parliament men are very humble, and will speake to one now ، . . truly in your wholl life you neavor saw peaple soe sadd and soe dejected as they are all. Every body flyes out of towne; some say we shall have a nue warr and some say noe . . . that which afrights me most is the delayes that these combustions is like to putt upon our busines, and I confesse that fretts me soe that I scarse injoye a quiett hower. . . . [June 24th.]—I hope you will not any longer account itt a misfortune that you were turned out of the House, for I assure you now tis the greatest honner that can be toe any man, to be one of the ferst chosen members turned out by thes old [? new] ones. You cannott posseble Imagion the change without you saw itt.'

When the baby is three weeks old she decides that he shall go to Claydon, and writes to Roades: 'Good Will, upon Tuseday next I intend to send my child to St. Allbanes; the nurse is most extreamly desirous to be att home, soe if you cann posseble I would have you be there one Tuesday night and goe to Tringe on Wednesday. The nurse sayeth her husband hath a very easy-going horse, and she thinks itt will be best for him to carry the child before him upon pillows, becaus she cannott ride between toe panniers and hold the child. When you come there, you will quickly find which will be the best way to carry itt; pray provide for both wayes, and bring a footman to goe by itt. If her husband doth carry the child, she cannott ride behind him, soe you must provide a horse for her; my sister Mary goes downe with them, soe you must bring up a pillion to carry her downe behind you. . . . Pray doe you see that they take a great care of the child, and that they goe very softly, for the weather is very hott; if he carries the child before him itt must be tied about him with a garter, and truly I think itt will be a very good way, for the child will nott endure to be long out of ones armes.'

On July 7 she receives a letter from her husband, dated June 27, full of loving anxiety about her: 'My dear Budd, . . . Now let me charme you once more about your gadding abroad; truly if you stir out . . . halfe a minute before doctor give you leave I shall not forgive you.' He begs her to 'give the child no phisick but such as midwives and old women, with the doctor's approbation, doe prescribe; for assure yourselfe they by experience know better then any phisition how to treate such infants. I will not now dispute with you about his name, but assure your selfe you shall heare of it at large heerafter. . . I presume you have noe better weather at London then wee have heere, which is nothing but raine, & soe cold that I sometimes call for a fire.'

He then tells her, when she goes to Claydon to 'putt upp all the small things (I meane such as will take noe hurt by moathes, rust, or such like) into some Roome by themselves, and bringe the key away with you, for if Will. Roades have the key and that any should aske him for anything there, they would quarrell with him about it; but if you have the key, sure none will be soe impudent as to breake it open.'

On July 1 Mary writes that she is 'still as weak as tis possible for any creature to be.' She tells how she has sent off the baby by the coach to St. Albans, where Roades is to meet him with horses; she is much troubled that Ralph 'should think much of his name, for of all names I desired thine, and I trust the Lord will make him a good man, for he hath wonderfully blessed him hetherto, and restored him from death to life beyond all people's imagination; butt itt will cost me a great deale of money, my lieing Inn, both in phisick & attendance for him and me, but my Deare I assure thee tis no small addition to my Illness and weakeness thatt I cannot see any hopes or likelyhood of a suddaine dispatch of my busenes. Truly the very thoughts of itt continually aflicts me, for were there a possebillety of doeing any buseness yett, everybody adviseth to see how the armye and parliament agree ferst.'

She had hoped to have taken this time for going down to Claydon, ' but the honest D^r will nott by any meanes suffer me to sturr out of towne untell I have taken a course of phisseck ; both he and his wife hath been very earnest with me to come and lie at his howse, but I put itt off as well as I can, for . . . I . . . beleeve . . . twill be much dearer to me. There is many more very earnest with me to be with them, butt I had much rather be by myselfe ; . . . but I entend as soon as . . . I am able . . . to goe to Claydon & soe to Misterton for a little time, & as I come back to bring my boy Jack with me, in hope by that time I may quickly dispatch our busenis & come to thee. . . . If I am able to ride a horsback, I will goe the same way that I sent my child, for if I should hier a coach downe itt would cost me a great deale of money. For Sir R. Burgoyne & D^r. Denton's coming over with me [to France], I know they have a mighty mind to itt, butt I know nott whether theyr wifes will give them leave or nott. I have hard them both very often wish them selfes with you, & Sir Roger did protest to me he . . . . would abate his father 500*l*. a yeare of what was tied upon him, soe he might have enough to live with you where you now are, he and his children ; but I beleeve his wife would say nay.' Ralph writes back in much distress about her health and the pains in her head : he consulted her French doctor, and if they continued 'hee would have you blooded in the foote. . . . You must eate Pottage at Dinner, & but light suppers. This is his advise.'

On July 4 Dr. Denton writes : 'Landlady is churcht & well, but lookes ill enough. . . . The differences betweene army and parliament are yett a riddle to most. . . . I cannot divine what will be the issue ; you may give some ghesse by the bookes I send you. . . . As far as I can looke into a milstone, I guesse that the Independants tooke it ill that they could not sway the House, & now they take this course to purge it of the cheefe Presbeterians, that they may reigne againe ; which when done I believe the army and parliament will quickly shake hands (except a Cavalier party in the army crosse the designe), and happily they may court the kinge by invitinge his returne, settlinge his revenew, etc., and in such things make him a glorious kinge. But if eyther party can prevaile without makinge use of the king's interest, I beleeve they will clipp his power.' Each side feared the other, and Sir Roger writes : 'I durst not write my thoughts, for every word is wrested to the worst sense.' Ralph in his solitude looked out anxiously for news : in one letter he says, 'Send me the Moderate Intelligencer weekly, or any of the king's letters or such small things, for wee have noe newes at all here. . . . I heare Mr. May the poet hath now printed a booke or two concerning my Lord of Essex and the cronicle of these times; certainly they must needes be worth reading, therfore desire Doctor to buy them for mee & pay him for them. I finde hee is resolved to buy mee the booke of ordinances, therfore you must pay him for that also.' For the payment of his debts he proposes to sell some of his wife's land & give a rent charge upon Claydon, but he will do nothing without her consent: 'Unless you conceive this way best for yourself & children, do not give way unto it, as your refusall will bee as welcome to mee as your consent.' Though it is only July, he is anxious she should begin buying what she will require and making preparations for a sudden journey that no time may be lost once the business is done: 'ye winter is coming, nay almost come, and in a little time ye wayes will bee unpassable by reason of souldiers, & further you shall not take another winter journey; therfore get mee some money quickly from Will Roades, & resolve to come quickly to thine owne.'

By the middle of July Mary writes that she is stronger: 'I have been twice abroade and found noe great inconveniency, only this day I have begun a course of steele, and if I can persuade the D^r. to itt I will end itt, for truly I think good broths and a good diett will doe me more good then phissic, though the honest D^r. will nott beleeve itt, his love to us both makes him have soe much care of me, and I tell him hee has toe much aprehention,—for I prayse God I find myselfe much amended wth in this fornight, and I doubt nott by God's helpe, butt I shall enjoy my helth againe if I were but soe happy as to be wth thee againe, & tell then I canott be hapy nor I feare helthful, but there is noe hopes of ending our busenes untell the great busenes betweene the armye and the parlyament be ended.' With regard to his proposal about the debts she says, 'I cannott say I dislike the way you propound, becaus as land goes at present I canott propound a better; butt I must tell you that by that time you have sold my land & that you sell a rent charge of 400*l*. or 500*l*. a yeare out of Claydon, & that you have payed all the anuities which are due yearly to your sisters and others, I cannott see where you will have soe much revenue in present to live on as my owne land was worth, and I confess I should be unwilling to putt myselfe to less than that to live upon, without itt had been to have payed thy owne perticuler depts, & then, beleeve me, I could have suffered anything. For my owne land I confess I should have been very glad to have kept enoughe of itt to have provided well for my toe yonger boyes and my gerll; but if thatt canott bee, thou mayest as freely dispose of that as of myselfe; but in my opinion whattsoever land you part with, you had much better sell outright then for years.' She thinks it 'full enough' to let the creditors have the land at twenty years' purchase and to pay all the interest too: '.... Tis onely because you bid me doe itt, that I trouble you with my silly advise, for I am sure thy owne judgement is much better, and what that leades thee toe will please me.'

Before Mary left town she was treated to some ill-behaviour from brother Tom. Early in the year he was very civil, and, to her surprise, presented her with his portrait. She wrote: 'I have hung itt up in my chamber for the better grace; but I am chidd when I offer to looke on itt; for indeed tis very like him.' Later on matters took a different turn, for Tom, as usual, was in need of money, and had wanted his sister-in-law to set her hand to a note to Roades to pay him 5l. or 10l., which he said would be repaid by his Aunt. Mary was too wise to be thus entrapped, and refused to sign, and moreover mentioned the matter to the Aunt in question, which put Tom into a rage and drew from him a furious letter. She describes the occurrence thus to Ralph: 'Now I must needs tell you that I think you prophesied of your brother Tomes kindness to me, for you told me itt would not last, & to let you see your words prove true I have sent you his letter he writt to me. . . . Y^e other day your Aunt being here she fell a talking of him, and why he was angry with me, soe I told her that this was all ye cause.'

Tom's elegant epistle was as follows: 'Madam, though not with you in person, yet I heare that I was the subject of your discours yesterday. I must confess it is very long since I saw you, and to long for true and cordiall freinds to be asunder. The breach of friendshipp was on your side (first broke) as (upon a true relation of the busyness) it will appeare. You are noe changeling towards mee; your carryage is one and the same. The french clymate hath not a whitt altered you, but rather made you wors; ffor formerly you could keep councell and not discover the secretts of a letter without the consent of the party which sent it. But since you have spued up your inveterate malice against mee, let mee say with the proverb, divill doe thy worst. . . . Had I had your grant I should (if I could not otherwise have paid it) have supplycated with my aunt to have allowed it out of her annuity. I pray God that neither you nor yours may be putt to that shift and want, which I am & have been putt to. If it be soe, without doubt God's word will prove true, the which is—what measure is given the same will be given againe—I wish the same may light on you and yours. Hitherto you have done little good; I know not what good you may doe if you live to Methusalem's yeares. I could be very large in my expressions, but I am very willing to leave of here till a second opportunity proffers itself, which will not be long, till you shall know, and all others that will bestow a peny in the reading of it, that you and your husband are both very unkind to ' (signature cut out).

As to this insolent letter Mary writes to Ralph: ' My hart, when I concider whoe itt comes from and how basely he hath used thee, I doe nott vallue itt, but ye D^r makes himselfe very mery with itt, and calles me noething but " Divell doe thy worst." ' Later she says that the Dr. tells her that ill-words from such a fellow are compliments, and says at breakfast, ' Divell, will you give me some toast?' to make her laugh.

Mary's reply was to send Tom back his portrait ' wch as I heare made him more Blank than all ye letters that I could have sent him.' Ralph compliments her on having stood firm, and says, ' I see you are not to be scolded out of £5. . . . You did very well to return his picture ; it seems he persists in his wildness and rails still. God forgive him and turn his heart ; keep his letter but doe not answer it.' Mary says of Tom, when she returns again to town some months later : ' I sometimes meet him att your Sisters', and he hath ye confydence to talke to me, but I onely make him a curzy !'

The struggle for power between the army and the Parliament resulted in the discomfiture of the latter, and on August 6 the soldiers entered London in triumph. On the 24th the king removed to Hampton Court and carried on negotiations with the army leaders, which at first promised to be successful, but they proved as fruitless as all former attempts had been to come to an understanding with Charles. Becoming anxious for his own safety he took refuge with Colonel Hammond, governor of the Isle of Wight, but Hammond lost no time in letting the Parliament know of his arrival, and the king was as much of a prisoner as ever.

In the beginning of August, Mary at last shakes herself free of Committees and creditors, and gets down to Claydon, where she finds many soldiers, 'God send us well quit of them.' In September she goes to Aunt Eure at Misterton in Leicestershire, and spends about a month there—a restful visit which was most acceptable to her. (Aunt Eure had lately married her third husband, Captain Sherard.) On September 26 she writes from thence: 'I entend to stay ontell the week after Michellmass; indeed my unkle and aunt are extreame civell onto me and will not suffer me to goe away ontell my buseness enforceth me, and truly both providence and discretion makes me willing to spend thatt little Idle time I have in this place, for in a better woman's company I am certain I cannot spend itt, nor with one that loves me better.' The company at Misterton drink Sir Ralph's health two or three times at every meal!

Sir Roger had advised Mary to petition the army about the sequestration, but public affairs continued in so unsettled a state that for many weeks it was useless to expect any private business to be attended to.

Mary writes rather indignantly that Lady Warwick never came to see her in the summer: 'She never soe much as sent to enquier after me . . . though she knew I lay in in London and was then in all the troubles when she was glad to runn out of towne.' Lady Warwick's conduct was probably to be explained by her husband's critical position, for in a former letter Mary wrote: 'Lady Warwick's husband is one of them that the armye demande ; I hear they are much in disorder in that house.'

On October 10 Ralph writes that he 'takes it most kindly' that she has never failed in sending her weekly letter since she was in the country, ' for except your selfe, noe earthly thing can be more pleasing and welcome to mee then your letters. It seemes many of the goods I left in severall places are likly to bee lost; let not that trouble you ; I thanke God we have enough for our present use, and when we want more I trust God will provide them for us.' Concerning her proposal to give the Dr. 20*l.* for her confinement he says : ' Tis much too little ; less then Thirty pounds I shall not give him, and were it not for the strange unhappy troubles of these times, and my owne foressing necessity, I should blush to give him this ; but you must excuse it to him, and assure him I intended it not as a reward, for twill scarce pay for ye shoee leather that hee hath worne out in my service, but desire him to accept it till it pleas God to make me more able. If hee should absolutely refuse money (as I hope hee will not) then you must lay it out in some such plate as you thinke fittest ; I thinke six Trencher plates and a paire of little candlesticks (without sockets) of ten pounds, would doe well, but this I leave to your discreation. Some small thing you must give his Wife, and be sure to give his childe somwhat.' He does not at all approve of her dropping her music. 'But for your Gittarr, if you have forgot any one lesson, nay if you have not gotten many more then you had, truly I shall breake your Fiddle about your pate, therfore looke to your selfe, and follow it hard, and expect noe mercy in this point.'

On October 21 Mary writes of her return to London: 'Yesterday I came very late to town and very weary, for by reason I came all ye way but six miles on horseback . . . and I rid upon a cruell trotting horse to boote: your brother Mun rid before me & brought me as farr as Acton, where I had a coach meet me, and I lay one night by the way at Uxbridge. A coach quite thorough would have cost me a greate deale of money, and I hope after I have a little rested myselfe, twill doe me noe harme. . . . I am now in my old lodging, but I shall leave itt as soone as I can gett another, because this woman whare I now am will let all her house together, which is toe much for my purse to pay, & beside I know nott what to doe wth itt all. I doupt I shall find itt very sadd being alone these long winter nights & if I should diett wth any body but ye honnest D^r. I know his wife would take itt extreamely ill, becaus they have been bothe very earnest with me to come to theyr howse, but truly tis soe close and soe ill a place that I feare I should have very little helth in itt, & beside noebody can drive a coach into ye lane, soe what soevor wether comes I must goe trapesing a foote to ye end of ye lane & all else that comes to me.' Ralph is much concerned for her lodging : if Aunt Sherard comes to London ' I would gladly have you with her this winter ; now days grow short and nights long you will bee too much alone. Were I fully assured you were well and conveniently settled, with good contentment, I should bear your absence with lesse regret.' He hears of many new diseases in London and some say they are infectious—'therfore I pray, nay I charge you (what businesse soever you have) come not neare any that are sick, but pray for all.' ' The Wayes, the Soldiers, and the Sicknesse ' are the standing obstacles to all business and journeys.

In a later letter Mary describes her new lodging, the address of which is, ' York St. next to a chandler's shop, w^{thin} foure doores of ye Goulden Fleece taverne.' She pays the same rent as at her former lodging, 14s. a week ; 'butt here I must find my owne linnen . . . there is butt to roomes of a floore, and I have the dining-room floore, and there is another gentleman wch hath the floore over my head, which I feare will be a greate inconvenience to me . . . butt they are very good people in ye howse, and will not take any lodgers butt those they know extreamely well. . . . Our friends and acquaintance is much changed since we left this kingdom, and yet I thank God here is some as loves us hartily still, and that I dare swear doth the honnest D^r., my Aunt Eure, and Sir R. Burgoyne.' One of the creditors, Mrs. Hyde, has been storming at her for payment. ' She was in great coller thatt I did nott lett her have any money

'... she sayed she did beleeve you were sequestred out of pollecy to cheate ye creditors, & that we lived ourselves. ... I told her if she would undertake to take of ye sequestration I would undertake ... she should be payed every farthing of her money and something toe boote. ... I told her y^t was true, God be thanked, we did live, though twas butt in a poore condition, and that we had fedd by ye plate and stuffe that we had sold at this time, and that consydering what fortune I brought I was reduced to a very low condition, liveing here now wth none butt myselfe and one mayde. ... After much discourse, she sayed she would be content to abate som of her Interest, but nott all ; soe I told her if she and ye rest knew in how ill a condition your estate was she would be glad they had ye princeple.'

Many and long are the wife's letters upon these complicated money matters, and they all wind up with the same loving refrain, repeated in different forms, ' beleeve me I shall nott have one Minute of an howers Contentment, untell thou hast with thee thine owne   MARY VERNEY.'

CHAPTER XII.

MARY LOSES HER CHILDREN AND WINS HER SUIT.

> May I find a woman wise,
> And her wisdom not disguise;
> Hath she wit as well as will,
> Double-armed is she to kill.
>
> May I find a woman true,
> There is beauty's fairest hue,
> There is beauty, love, and wit—
> Happy He can compass it.—BEAUMONT.

THE year 1647 had been one of almost unmixed sadness to the devoted husband and wife, and the month of October found them still divided, with no immediate prospect of reunion. While Mary was doing all the difficult political and financial business in England, which was properly the man's work, Ralph had a heavy task in the care of his children's health and education during their mother's absence, and both gave him no little anxiety. Mary had been much taken up with the care of her new-born baby, 'the lusty boy' she was longing to show her husband, but her heart was full of yearning anxiety about little Mun and Peg at Blois. She had written constantly about their training; she is satisfied that Sir Ralph does not let them learn dancing any longer, 'for 2 or

3 months in the yeare is enough to learne that. I like your motion very well of teaching Mun to sing and play on the gittarr, for tis a great deale of pitty he should loose his time now he is soe younge and capable of breeding; we had better spare itt on him heerafter then now. Every body heer hath often told me they much wonder that we make them nott learne all exercises, but I have allwayes tolld them that you have as great a desire they should lerne as anybody can have, if you had money. Truly I see noebody heere that barres themselfes of anything. Mun must learn to play the gittarr and singe.' She would like 'the gerle' to learn the lute, but perhaps she is rather too young as yet. 'I am sorry to heare she holds her head soe, butt I hope it will nott now be very long before I am with thee, and then I hope to break her of itt. . . . I trust God will give wherewithall to give them breeding.'

Ralph writes carefully and minutely about the clothes that he and the children require, and poor Mary, ill and distracted with anxieties, sends him out things that do not fit. 'Now let me tell you,' he writes, 'ye silke stockinges are good, though much to bigg, but that's noe matter, but the Thred ones have made amends, for they are soe little that they will not come over my Toes; my Foote is bigger then yours, but for your comfort these will neither serve me nor you. As for Mun's gray stockings they are about a handful too short and almost an inch too Little, soe I have layed them upp for your sonn John, and you must buy Mun more. . . . Besse is as well fitted, for Luce sent her 2 paire of Shooes that will come as soon uppon her head as upon her Heeles ; soe we laugh at you Both.' Mary, in return, sends him directions about the housekeeping : ' You must needs buy some suger both fine and course, and some spice, and a few reasons and currants' ; she does not think the children require any more clothes, ' but I think it will be necessary to give faireings to those that you gave unto last yeare.' There is a great annual fair at Blois, and Ralph, as she suggests, buys presents for various neighbours, but when he has done so, he finds he has no money left for the sugars fine and coarse, the raisins and the currants! The groceries are on his mind when he writes to his wife for some more theological works. ' I pray send me the harmony of confession of faith of all Churches and let me know the price of new currants and raisins. If you can, help me to Dr. Vane's book entitled ' the Lost Sheep is Found.'

Mary's summer visit to Claydon had been a very sad one ; to so careful a mistress the state in which she found the place after four years' absence was indeed heart-breaking—she writes to Ralph that ' the house is most lamentably furnished, all the linnen is quite worne out, . . . the feather bedds that were waled up are much eaten with Ratts . . .,' the fire irons, ' spitts and other odd thinges are so extreamly eaten with Rust thatt they canot be evor of any use againe,' and she will have them sold by weight ; ' the cloath of the Musk-coloured stools is spoyled, and the dining-room chairs in Ragges.' Ralph is anxious lest the 'Moathes' should destroy 'the Turkie Worke cushions,' and 'I pray see that the Armes [probably Sir Edmund's] doe not want cleaning and Oylinge, least they bee spoyled with Rust, for I intend them to Bro: Mun when he gets imployment'; if they are likely to bring any danger on the house they are to be removed from the place where they hang, as he would not risk bringing trouble upon Mun for 'tenn times theire worth'; there are also 'the greate churche cushions' and 'the purple satten ones' to be looked after.

The descendants of the 'Ratts' and 'Moathes' still flourish and abound, and rust and damp are time-honoured enemies at Claydon, but the mind of the modern housekeeper refuses to grasp the horrible confusion that must have been brought upon a household by the quartering of soldiers upon it in the Civil War days. Poor Mary's letters are full of this trouble; there had been constant visits from soldiers during her absence, and when she goes from London to Claydon the country is so full of them that she can scarce get 'a nagg' and has to go round by Berkhampstead. She writes a hurried line on her arrival on August 4 for the return coach to take back, that Ralph may not be without his letter: 'I am so very weary that I am scarce able to stand upon my legges,' and after describing how difficult she found it to avoid the soldiers on the roads near Uxbridge, says: 'I left them a fighting at 4 a'clock this morning, but I trust in god they are apeased by this time.' She gets a little respite during the month of August, but to her despair, when she has got things into order and is just leaving Claydon for Misterton in September, a fresh detachment arrives: 'to-morrow I intend to goe, and I shall leave ye house soe full of soldiers, thatt I feare they will make us very poore as beggers; I protest I know nott which way we shall live if the countrey may allwayes quarter soldiers. . . . I vowe I had much rather live with Bread and water then to be amongst them.'

Mary's time at Claydon was fatiguing and laborious in the extreme; her husband, good as he is to her, and thinking of everything that can concern her comfort, yet has no scruple about overwhelming her with business; she stands about day after day making inventories with Mrs. Alcock, or wading through the endless tangle of their accounts with Will Roades.

Another time she says, 'I have spent the whole day searching amongst your papers for the survay you writt for; have looked in all the drawers in youre further closet . . . & I think I have opened a thousand papers.' The large sheets closely written in her beautiful clear hand attest her industry as a correspondent, and yet Sir Ralph is often unsatisfied; there is always something she has not fully explained to his most methodical mind, and he speaks with some severity 'of all those severall perticulers that I have writ to you off in my former letters, & that you have not yet given any answere too. Had I but one letter to write a Weeke, I would not misse answering the least perticuler, but if you canot answere it presently you commonly forget it, and the reason is, because you will not take a noate of Remembrance.'

She replies very gently : ' My deare, thou doest chide me for nott answering thy letters ; truly I am confydent tis by chance if I miss ansering of every perticuler; for I allwayes lay thy letters before me when I wright ; butt howevor, when thou considerest how much I wright and how ill a scribe I am, thou oughtest nott to be angry with me for forgetting now and then a little.' ' I assure you,' she says another time, ' I neavor fayled one Thurseday of wrighting to you nevor since I came over.'

Everything he requires must be done exactly and immediately ; at one time he asks for ' an excellent medicine that Mrs. Francis was wont to make for the Canker, twas black & boyled in an Egg shell ; I pray take an exact receit both of what and how it is made, and send it mee as soone as possibly you can.' Another time he appeals to Mary's tact and patience to make up a quarrel between Mr. Aris and Will Roades. The relations between the House and the Rectory had been very cordial, but in Sir Ralph's absence there was much friction between the rector and the agent—' an inconveniency,' he says, ' that I have long foreseen ' ; he first writes about it to Mary in August, 1647 : ' If W. R. informe mee rightly old Master [the Rector] doth not use me well, but one tale is good till another is heard, therefore I will not condemn him, but I pray use your best endeavour to make them freinds, or at least to keepe all in quiet till my returne, that I may see where the fault lies; you must mannage this matter very tenderly, for this is a captious age.' Mary replies that his fears are but too well founded: 'I find there is a mortall quarrell between W. R. and old Master; he sayes W. R. was the cause of his imprisonment, and W. R. offers to bring wittness of ye contrary, and doth very much justefye himselfe against all that old Master layes to his charge. I nevor heard them speake together, and before old Master I doe avoyde ye speaking of itt, for,' adds the poor woman wearily, 'I cannot Indure to interest myselfe in quarrells.'

Mary has tried to avoid knowing all the details, especially as she finds that Mrs. Rector is still more implacable than her husband, and 'I doe not think it posseble to reconcile them. . . . . . I did shun the hearing of the busenesse all ye while I was there, onely by chance one day W. R. came in to speak with me, and old Master's wife being there, she fell soe bitterly upon him that itt was downeright railing. I cannot tell how to judge of the busenesse. I beleeve W. R. may be in some faulte, but I am sure he had the advantage of her thatt day, for though she gave him very bitter language yett he caried himselfe very handsomely towards her, but they say twass because I was by that he was so temperate. You must know that your bro: Mun and they are very great; and by that meanes I know when they take ill.' Edmund prefers boarding at the Rectory when the house is empty, and they hope that in time he will make peace, though Mr. Aris is inclined to include Sir Ralph in his indignation against his agent.

The neighbours call, and Mary has no time to return their visits Ralph from Blois, sympathising and advising in all troubles great and small, says he would have her send Will Roades 'to Sir Richard Pigott, or any other you are obliged unto, to excuse your not waiting uppon theire wifes; those little incivilities will not hurt you.' One visit she manages to pay to their neighbour at Addington, a lawyer whom they are consulting upon some of their financial perplexities, who had been one of the witnesses of Sir Edmund's will in 1639: 'I was yesterday at M[r] Busby's a horsback, and was very wery with thatt little journey. He is very kind to us about that business; he hath a very fine place, and is very proude of it; truly I think he showed me every hole in the howse; I am sure I was hartily weary with walking up and downe; he hath bestowed a very great deale of money upon it.' Mr. Busby is the only prosperous person at this time that appears in the correspondence; Ralph greatly desires that he should come and see him, and Mary writes again later: 'I spake very hartely to him to meet you, and told him how extreamly joyed you would be to see him. . . . . butt I doe not find y[t] he hath any great Maw to ye journey; he is ritch and fatt, and I

MARY LOSES HER CHILDREN, ETC. 291

dought will be afrayde of hazarding his person. . . . if ye times doth nott suddenly mend, he will give over his profession and leave this kingdom, butt yet he sayes att ye present he hath very much practice;' every one is going to law either to claim his debts or to protect his property. Mary tries to arrange that he should pay them a friendly visit at Blois, and only be paid fees for the business he does with them, and not for his expenses and absence from England. When she is just starting she offers to wait a week or two for him—the greatest compliment she says she could pay to any man; but this 'ritch, fatt' man is much less able to encounter a winter journey than she is, and it falls through.

Mr. Busby 'cannot poseble goe with me by reason of the sizes [assizes] and some other ocassions of his owne. . . . He told me his wife and chilldren was a great tie unto him to keepe him att home. . . . . . I showed him ye letter of atourney too, and he sayes you had better send one thatt is witnessed by some English Menn, for he sayes that noe Jurie heare will vallue this because they understand nott French.'

Among her multifarious business at Claydon Mary had a wedding to arrange for, in which she took the kindest interest. Her housekeeper, Mrs. Frances Allcock, was married to Mr. William Hoare on August 29, 1647, at Middle Claydon Church. The parish register, carefully kept by the Rev. John Aris, shows the troubled state of the times, as from October 18, 1642, to December 19, 1650, no marriage but this one is recorded. The housekeeper and her husband continued to live in the house; Mary gave her the furniture of her room, and Ralph had his say about the most suitable bed and hangings.

In all her work and fatigues Mary has one source of comfort in the presence of her little John, who never leaves her from the first day of their reunion, and trots about the house after her singing, lightening the dull business of the inventories with his sweet voice and funny sayings. In the first hurried note she writes by the return coach on the night of her arrival, she says to Ralph: 'As far as I can tell by candlelight, thy boy Jack apeares to me to be a brave lusty boy.' By daylight her anxious inspection of him proved less satisfactory; he was nearly seven, and had suffered in body and mind from his mother's three years' absence. She writes to her husband a few days later—August 10 :

'I must give thee some acount of our own babyes heare. For Jack his leggs are most miserable, crooked as evor I saw any child's, and yett thank god he goes very strongly, and is very strayte in his body as any child can bee ; and is a very fine child all but his legges, and truly I think would be much finer if we had him in ordering, for they lett him eate anythinge that he hath a mind toe, and he keepes a very ill diett; he hath an Imperfection in his speech, and of all things he hates his booke, truly tis time you had him with you for he learnes noething heare. You would be much pleased with his Company, for he is a very ready witted child and is very good of company, and is soe fond of the name of his father and mother ; he is allwayes with me from the first hower thatt I came, and tells me that he would very fayne goe into france to his father ; he sings prettely.'

'I long to see poor Jack,' Ralph replies ; 'truly the Crookednesse of his Leggs grieves my very Hart, aske some advise about it at London, but doe not Tamper with him.'

'Jack is a very gallant boy,' writes Mary on September 7, 'butt truly if he stay there a little longer he will be utterly spoyled . . . . . he hath noe fault in him beside his leggs, for though tis mine owne I must needs say he is an extreame witty child.' To her great comfort it is settled that Jack shall go back with her to France ; but there is so much sickness in London that he is to remain at Claydon till she is ready to sail.

She has had her share of anxieties about little Ralph; he got through his adventurous journey to Claydon without mishap, and Mary wrote to Roades about him from London : 'Good Will, I am very glad to heare my Child came soe well home, . . . I wish myselfe hartely there toe. . . . I pray speak to Mrs. Allcock to lett the nurse have a Cradle ; one of the worst will sarve her turne and a hard pillow . . . Your frend M. Verney.'

The baby is not with her, but living at his nurse's, and she constantly sees him. During the month of August he is less well again, and she writes to her husband: 'For my little boy Ralph he hath been very ill since I came which has been a great grief to me, butt now I thank God he is reasonable well againe.' She has to change his wet-nurse, and the only fit woman she can find is 'Raph Rodes' wife, and I feare they are but poore and she lookes like a slatterne but she sayeth if she takes the child she will have a mighty care of itt, and truly she hath toe as fine children of her owne as evor I sawe.' The nurse is to have '4^s a week and toe loads of wood; truly tis as little as we can offer her, being she had nott ye cristening, for nurses are much dearer than ever they were . . . poor child I pray god bless him and make him a hapy Man, for he hath had butt a troublesom begining, yett I prayse god he thrives well, and is a lovely baby.' 'I meane to coate him this week [he is nearly three months old]. I have had much adoe to keep the nurse quiett so long without coates.' Before she leaves Claydon she is quite comfortable about him. 'My little Raphe is a very fine boy, and thrives very well.'

Mary had returned to London in October from Misterton, leaving Jack and Ralph at Claydon. 'I am soe weary,' she writes to her husband on the 21st, 'that tis a payne to me to hold ye penn, but yet I cannot conclude, ontell I have chidd thee that thou dost nevor give me an account how thyselfe and boy and gerle have your helthes, and yett I have intreated itt of you before now: tis a duty I weekly performe to thee, and I assure you I expect ye same from you, for

Dr William Denton. Will:m Denton
Physician to Charles 1. from a picture at Claydon House.

my deare hart there is noething in this world soe nearly concernes me. . . . I can not express to thee how sadd a hart I have to think how long tis since I saw thee and how long twill be before I come to thee,' and again she complains that he tells her everything except what she wants most to know, 'how thy Deare selfe and my children have been.'

The poor mother's instinct did not deceive her; both children were very ailing and little Peg, who was never to learn how to hold up her head in this world, was ill with dysentery and fever. Ralph, knowing how she loved her little daughter, had not the courage to tell her of it; he wrote of her sufferings borne with sweet patience to Dr. Denton, but never mentioned them in his letters to Mary; and while she was writing her tender inquiries the child had died.

On October 3 he wrote to Dr. Denton: 'I am soe full of affliction that I can say no more but pray for us'—and his next letter of the 10th is but a sorrowful fragment: 'Oh Dr. Dr. my poore Peg is happy but I am your most afflicted and unfortunate servant. Tell mee how and when this shall bee made knowne to her mother.' He wrote this all unconscious of another loss at Claydon; the baby had died suddenly, and Dr. Denton had a doubly heavy task in breaking the news to his beloved niece. He writes to Ralph of this second sorrow: 'Your own wofull experiences have prepared you for any disasters that any of Job's comforters can present to you, god hath taken away what he gave, I meane your youngest son by convulsion fitts. My wife mett me by the way to let me know soe much and that she had broken it to her. . . . I found her in her bed lamenting and very inquisitive of me alsoe how her children did, expressinge that you had sent her noe worde of them for a month or longer. I thought it best to make but one busines of both and soe I lett her know how happy her gerle was. You may better imagine then I can expresse how closely she laies it to her heart, but I hope time with God's blessinge will give her more patience. . . . She talks very earnestly of cominge suddenly to you, which I doe not yett much contradict, but I thinke for the perfecting of her health to perswade her to stay till after Christmas, because then the approachinge of the sun will make it more seasonable travellinge.'

It was a cruel kindness to keep the poor mother from knowing the exact state of her children's health, and her sufferings under this double bereavement were terrible. She ends her next letter with a pathetic postscript : 'Since I writt this, I have receaved ye sad nues of toe of our deare children's death, which afliction joyned with being absent from thee is—without god's great marcy to me, a heavier burthen than can be borne by thine owne unhapy M.'

She writes on November 4:

'My dearest hart, I was in soe much afliction for ye losse of my deare children, when the last letters went from hence, that I was nott in a condition to wright or doe anything elce and truly att pressent I am soe weake that I am scarse able to goe upp and downe my chamber butt my trust is in my good God ; for he gave them to me and he took them from me, and I hope, and I trust he will in his good time deliver me out of all my troubles and give my mind some quiett and bring me to thee for untell I am with thee I canott take any content in any thing in this world, for the truth is I would nott to gaine ye greatest richess in this world be soe long againe from thee as I have allready beene, butt as soone as I am able to goe abroade I will follow thy buseness night and day, and if please God I may succeede in such a way as I shall be advised to take, I shall esteeme itt a most onspeakeable blessing.'

The Doctor writes again to Ralph : 'I told you in my last that I had acquainted my Landlady with the death of both her children, which though for the present did much afflict and distract her, soe that she spake idly for two nights and sometimes did not know her frends, yett now I thanke God she is out of her bed againe and looks much better then when she lefte London. . . . She is discreet and I hope will not in a time when she hath most need of it make the least use of it.'

But it was not the wife's courage and cheerfulness that gave way ; Ralph himself, usually so collected and reasonable, seems to have lost his head with trouble, and to have worked himself up to the belief that his death would be the best solution of the family troubles and sorrows ; he writes a confused letter to

Mary, hinting at his approaching departure from Blois: 'Court Hopes undid my Father and Country hopes (for soe I may call these that we now gape after) are like to undoe me, therefore if you finde you cannot get my businesse heard and determined. . . . let mee know it as soone as may bee, for whatever becomes of mee I will endeavour to avoyd being kept thus in suspense. On Friday last was Twelvemoneth you arrived at London and I have been patient in expectation from Weeke to Weeke and Moneth to Moneth and yet noe good comes.' He desires her, (vain command) to hurry the business, that he may have her company again, 'which I desire above all earthly things, but if that cannot bee and that for the good of your selfe, and those few Babes that are left us, wee must still be kept asunder, I tell you true, I have not a Hart to stay heere without you . . . . it hath pleased God to provide for my poore sweet girle and I hope hee will soe direct mee in ye disposing of my Boy that this shall not bee for his disadvantage.' To Dr. Denton he is more explicit in his restless misery:

'D^r· I have often both seariously and sadly considered the uncertainty of these times, and what course were best for mee to take. I confesse I could never yet tell what was fittest to bee donn, but could I possibly have foreseene the necessity of my Wifes continuance in England, and some other things that have befallen mee heere, I thinke I should soone have resolved to have spent this winter in Ittaly, and (unless times mend in England) the next in Turkye, and I doubt not but I could soe order my little Family in this place, and myselfe (by changing my name and concealing my condition) in the Jorney, that the charge should noe way exceed what I am necessitated to spend heere. And in my judgment this must needs have proved very advantageous, both to myselfe and Family, for though I had Falen in the Voyage I doubt not but my good God both can and will bring mee to his Heavenly rest, whether I dye in the midst of Roome, or in the deserts of the Heathens. His mercyes are not bound to any climate, the same Sun shines there that does at London, and I know full well hee will afford his providence to Pilgrims as well as Princes. Certainly had this been soe, you need not have imployed either money or Friends to take off sequestration, my Death had conjur'd downe that Devill, and then my Wife and children might have enjoyed my fortune Freely, for Widdowes and Orphans are rarely made Delinquents. D^r I had not troubled you with this discourse, had you not made a question about my comming Over, which of all wayes (as the case stands with mee) I conceive the worst that can bee taken by your most unfortunate friende and servant.'

When poor Mary heard of this extraordinary scheme she seemed to have reached the climax of her troubles. 'I confess I did believe thou hadest hadd other thoughts of me then to think I could brooke such a proposition. Noe my harte you must nott whilest I live have any such desighn withoute you resolve to take me along with you, and then live in whatt parte of the world you most fancye. Itt is not the being intrusted with your estate can give me the least sattisfaction. . . . If itt be nott possible for me to finish your buseness I will leave itt to God's Blessing and the honest Dr's. care. . . . Truly this very notion of yours hath gone soe neare me that I have scarce had one nights rest since I receaved your letter, I had enough upon me before, and I prayse my God that he hath kept my harte from breaking all this while. . . . it cannot be for my good to be heare without thee, nor for your advantage or our toe dear children's to have our smale famylye devided in fower severall places. . . . To tell you truth I cannott be any longer from you, therefore I am resollved to stand or fall with you and I begg of thee nott to lett this desighn any more enter into your thoughts. . . . I am nott able to say one word more but that at this time there is nott a sadder creature in the world then thine owne Deare M.'

Ralph makes no further allusion to his wild scheme, and his subsequent letters are full, as before, of the practical consideration of freeing his estate and paying his debts.

Another letter from Ralph to his wife brings into prominence the strong religious bent of his mind : ' Haveing spake thus much of my affaires, I should now conclude, but I am soe full of griefe for the Death of my poore children, that I must needes vent some part of it to thee. What shall I say? for every line, every word and sillable about this businesse, encreaseth both thy sorrows and my owne. Therefore I shall endeavour to leave deploring theire losse, for they are most unspeakeable gainers by this Change; and since tis soe, (if we did not love our selves much more then them) wee should rather rejoyce at their happinesse, then by repining at the Will of Heaven, pull new Judgments down uppon our owne heads. Tis true they are taken from us, (and thats theire happinesse); but wee shall goe to them, (and that should bee our comfort). And is it not much the better both for us and them, that wee should rather assend to heaven to partake of theire perpetuall blisse, then they descend to Earth to share with us our misfortunes. But perhapps you will say wee must passe by the Gates of Death, and lodge in (the common Inn of all mankinde) the Grave. Alas, have not all our Fathers, nay and these our beloved children too, Trod in the same pathes, and shall wee feare to follow the stepps of soe many Saints that are gonn before us? Had you but seene with what unparraleld patience poore Pegg bore all her paines, and with what discreation and affection she disposed of her wearing cloathes unto her maide that tended her, and lastly with what admirable cheerfulnesse and courage desiring prayres to bee made for her, shee peaceably resigned her soule into the hands of him that gave it, I am most confident thou wouldst have learned of this our innocent Babe to bee courageous in all thy conflicts, patient in all thy afflictions, and her example would have taught thee to submitt all things to the good pleasure of God, how nearely soever they concerne thy selfe or mee.'

Doll Leeke feels deeply for her cousins' loss and writes to Ralph : ' I could have parted with a lim to have saved hir [Peg's] life. God has given you many troubles, but yet so great a happiness with them in joying the blising of such a wife, that you ought to lesen your greaf to preserve yourself to be a comfurt to hir whos consern in this is very high, for I know she had sett hir hart much upon this chilld.' Doll cannot go to Lady Verney at present on account of a dangerous illness of Lady Gawdy. ' The doctor was with us and showed me your lettell paper, which truly struk me to the hart.'

Ralph is not disposed to receive her condolences very graciously ; he is vexed at the pertinacity with which she has demanded the money due to her : ' it was a smale dept,' as Lady Hobart pleaded in her sister's excuse, but ' twas all she had in ye world.'

He writes to his wife: ' You see Dol: L: now writ mee a very kinde letter, the last I had from her was neare a yeare and a quarter since, and much of another straine, farre from any kindnesse I assure you ; twas about money Will Roades had not payed just when she sent for it. I gave her no answere to that, nor doe I intend to answere this in hast, unlesse you both advise mee to it, and say in what way I had best doe it, for she feedes mee as men doe Apes, with a Bobb, and a Bitt, and soe you may say on any occasion if you thinke fit.'

On Nov. 11 Dr. Denton writes : ' Your wife I thanke God is very well . . . she hath not been abroad since I told her of her daughter, but I expect her this hour to come and eat a goose : for all you condemned me to plum pudding and puddle all yet I believe landlady [his pet name for Mary] will tell you that she hath found good nappy all to be very comfortable and to fatten her. As for your petition I putt it yesterday into a good hand (Sir G. Lenthall), and I have promised him £40 and he will give me an account of it very shortly.' This was a petition to be presented to the House in the name of 'the Lady Verney, wife to Sir Ralph Verney, that the whole business of the sequestration be referred to a committee of Lords and Commons,' and a few weeks later Dr. Denton writes an account of how it was carried.

Dec. 20.—' Deare Raphe, I told you in my last that I would drive on the naile furiously, and I have beene as good as my word, for the very next day I drave it beyond all the Pikes of the house against the advice of most. . . . The truth is there was digitus Dei, eminently in it, for beyond all our projects, designs and contrivances, God cast us into a gentlemans hands in the turninge of a hand that very morninge, nay that very moment, as he was goinge into the House, that very nobly and handsomely carried it through a very harde chapter, in soe much that some laughed and jeered att me, to thinke how I would be cozened, because that very moment there was high and mighty expectations of Scotch and Army papers ready for readinge, and by the opinion of all it was not in the power of the most eminent leadinge man there, to have promoted it singly and nakedly. But thus it was. Mr. J. Ash, who was by order to bringe in reports from Goldsmiths Hall (our petition beinge in Frank Drakes hands), was moved by him and two more of us in his passage through the Hall that he would sit quiett whilst F. D. moved it which he absolutely denied, but beinge made sensible of the busines, and of the equity and quick dispatch it would receave uppon very easy intreaty, very much like a gentleman undertooke the delivery of it, soe before he sate down in the midst of his business he gott it read, and soe it passed with some, but not much regrett, and yet the House was fuller (about 300) then in a longe time before. . . . We have had some of our good frends with us att dinner, our bellies are full and I have noe more to say. . . .'

Mary writes the same day : ' Our petition is granted and I trust as God hath wonderfully pleased us in itt, soe he will continue his marcye still and bless our endeavors thatt wee may suddenly dispatch thy busenes which hath cost me many a sadd and tedious hower. Our frends caried in the house to every creatures greate amazement, for twas a mighty full House and att the very same time they had buseness came in of very high concernment, Mr. Selden and Mr. Pierpoint did much discourage us in itt, and sayd twas not posseble to gett itt don, butt yett Mr. Pierpoint did you very good sarvis in itt, and truly Mr. Trevor hath bin hugely much your frend, and soe hath Mr. Knightly and many others that I canott have time to name. They toe dine with me toe day and some others which ye doctor sent me word he would bring that wee are much obleged toe. I took up £40 and payed itt the same day, you may Imagion for what and truly I was neavor better contented to pay any money in my life then I was to pay that. . . . I beginn to have a huge content within me to think how sudenly I shall be with thee, and yet beleeve me this toe months I have still to stay heare will appeare to me seavon yeares. Everybody tells me that there is noe question but thou wilt be cleared att ye comittee [1] of Lords and Comons. In the afternoone we goe aboute making of nue frends ; . . . they all tell me we need nott feare a deniall ; but itt may be if we doe not make frends, we may be delayed.'

Dec. 23.—Dr. Denton writes : ' Myne uncle to my greate griefe goeth out of the towne on to-morrow and returns not this fortnight, which hath a little disordred us for the present. Not that (as we hope) we shall have neede of him, but we would have beene armed against any arguments or peevishnes. I know

[1] See *Great Civil War*, vol. iii. p. 311. S. R. Gardiner.

he could and would have done his uttmost to have struck it dead. Though it be a clere case yett it is policy to have most Lords there. Warwick is alsoe out of town.'

Mary writes the same day : 'All the Lords that we cann make . . . . are out of towne, and tis nessesary we should have as many Lords at the hearing of our busenes as we can gett. . . . You long since bid me advise with the D^r aboute getting leave to travaile . . . I allsoe spake to Mr. Treavor, but he is of opinion that itt is needless to ask itt, for he sayes they nevor call home any private gentleman, and when your sequestration is taken off they canott sequester you againe for the same cause that they have already cleared you, and beside if you have leave itt must be of the House, for the generall nevor doth any such thing as they tell me, and to move such a thing in the house I fear would but rather putt them in mind to call you home, espetially if there be butt such a crabbed peece there as King Arthur, whoe that day our buseness was hard did you all ye mischeyfe he could, but when he had donn the worst he could he sate him down and told them that sate by him he had sayed all he could, and to confes truth you were a good Ingenious gentleman . . . . This day I have more of the Parlia : men dine with me, this charge I am forced to be att, butt I hope I shall reape the benefitt ['twas well donn,' says Sir Ralph, for 'sometimes those civillities worke much uppon men] . . . Sir R. Burgoyne is come to dine with me toe, he laughs at this long letter, and desires to know whether you evor read my letters thorogh.'

At length, on Jan. 5, 1648, the case came before the committee, and Mary's long and difficult task was accomplished—the sequestration was taken off. She writes the good news to Ralph on 'January ye 6th and twelveday,' 'thy buseness was yesterday donn according to thy hartes desire, and I have this day onely time to tell thee soe ... Lady Warwick hath at last in some measure playd her parte, butt I putt her soundly to itt for I have bin 4 or 5 times with her this week; her husband was there and brought others with him whoos pressence did much good; I went Imediattly from the Comittee to give her thanks last night, where her hus: was gott home before me soe I gave them both thanks together.' Lady Warwick herself writes: ' your good wife solicitede your busynes with all the care that posibly might be,' and Sir Roger sends the following account: ' The good providence of God hath caused the sunn once more to appeare through the darkest of clouds, and hath afforded us one day of refreshment midst the variety of o^r troublesome confusions. ... Yesterday the com^{tee} tooke the business into consideration, wher you had my heart though not my tongue, for that you well know hath little of oratory in it. It pleased God, though not without some difficulty, to put a happy period to that most unhappy business. You had many friends there which I must needs confess did prove themselves so indeed. ... I could not have imagined that so much justice should proceed from some of them, but for this one act they shall have my pardon for all that is parst. . . . In generall you are as cleare as our sunn can make you, and now my life shall be for the future as full of hopes as hitherto of feare. . . . Go on deare heart to add life to your intentions and let them turne into resolutions of casting once more an eye upon yor unhappy country.' Ralph could not as yet return to England, but the removal of the sequestration put him in a fair way of paying his debts by degrees, and Mary prepared joyfully to rejoin him in France. 'I beginn to have a huge content within me to think how sudenly I shall be with thee.' He sends his cordial thanks to Lady Warwick for her husband's good offices at the committee; and so great is the difference between the man who refuses and the man who grants your request, that the fair-minded and judicious Ralph forgets that he accounted it a particular blessing to dispatch his business without the assistance of such an unworthy and ill-natured creature; Lord Warwick is no longer 'that Vinaigre-faced fellow'—but he finds out that 'He hath ever been a very greate lover of justice, and a shelter to persons in distresse.' Frank Drake, who was 'a very Jack,' is again an excellent good fellow; the sun has come out from behind the clouds and the world is not entirely filled—as it was—by ungrateful friends and unnatural relations. Mary seems to have written a number of her gracious and well-expressed letters to thank all who had helped her with the business that hath cost her 'many a troublesom and many a sadd howr.' Mr. John Ashe, in acknowledging one to him, feels that he has 'dunne nothing in the least to ballance soe liberall an expression,' and assures her that no man in the future 'shalbe more ready than himself to doe all Lawfull favoures and civillitys to noble and virtuous Ladys.'

She is winding up the Claydon business.

'Bro : Mun has been given the arms, which he was much pleased with, and took very kindly' ; 'the musk couler stooles have been putt out to dressing,' and a large mirror has had its quicksilver renewed, and the frame regilt.

Ralph had been planning her journey ever since the previous September. 'I expect your summons, the winter is come and ye weather soe cold that unless you wrapp yourselfe extraordinary warme, I shall welcome you with a good Cudgell. I know you will have a care to keepe Jack from cold, and when you land you must not throw off much, for that Towne [Calais] standing uppon ye seaside is subject to bitter weather,' and Mary had been urging him not to leave Blois too soon, as neither the date nor the port of her arrival were settled : 'I know thou wilt have a tedious time of itt to wayt long at Diepe.'

'I owe a great deale and cannot sturr ontell I gett money, and besides itt may be I may wayte att Rie a week for seasonable weather at thatt tim of the yeare which you know is something Blusterous. . . .'

Before she can leave London, there are 200*l*. of debts to be paid, besides her husband's larger creditors, and she has also to take a journey into Suffolk to settle money affairs with the Sydenhams. She sends minute directions to Roades for bringing up her little boy Jack, to join her in London. As he will lie but one night on the way, his maid need not come with him; 'I would have John Andrewes or some lustie fellow, come up a foote by your horse to helpe the child if any ocasion should be, and lett him be sett upon a pillow and wrapped extreamly warme with one of the little cradle ruggs and a mantle aboute him.' She also orders him 'a pare of russett shoose pressently, lined with Bais, the sole within the shooe to keepe him warm.'

Ralph had advised her not to bring any clothes for the children, 'unless you can have a very great peneworth, for they are ordinarily cheaper heere than with you, and we must take the thriftiest way. Truly Muns masters and books cost me above 20 pistolls a yeare now, and he must have cloathes too'; but Mary is resolved that her husband at least shall have some new clothes, and says: 'Prethy send me word whether men weare black cloth still there, and how much will mak you a sute and cloke, for I have a great mind to bring you some over because I know you will rather weare any old rusty thing then bestow a new one upon yourselfe.' Also she wishes to bring gloves for Mun: 'I think you had best take a glove of my boy Mun's and cutt the bigness of itt in paper . . . and I will buy some gloves for him hear.' Ralph was certainly most careful to economise in his own wardrobe. In a former letter he had playfully teased her for not having worn her new clothes : ' Sure you meane to sell them and bring mee a minte of money, or else the vanitie of others hath abated your pride, and theire prodigallity made you miserable. Certainly wee are much of a humour at this time about our cloathes, for did you but see how I am patched upp with old Frippery, you could not but admire it ; but I deferre all my bravery till you come (with a minte of money) and then ile make it fly, doe not doubt it.' He desires her to get little presents for all their friends at Blois, ' men, women and children,' and he proposes to purchase some pewter plates, ' they are very much better and cheaper then they are with you : if you send me a pattern I will match them and buy toe dossen more, for I remember mine were handsome and of a good size.'

In contrast to the Verneys' simple way of living, Mary describes how ' Mr. Pierepont is now gon out of toune : he hath bin hear about a fortnight or 3 weeks and hath spent a thousand pound : he keepes a coach and fower footemen and toe gentlemen beside grooms and porter at his doore and cook and very fine coach and liveries, but the very same man he was at Blois. . . . Mr. Smith is with him still . . . but I beleeve will not travayle with him as he is hard a wooing.' Ralph sends a message to Mr. Pierpoint in February to tell him, ' heere hath beene balls in 14 nights together : if hee please to visit this neglected place . . . the joy of his presence will make the toune forget Lent and give at least as many more.' Ralph evidently cared little for the social gaieties, or for the French people among whom he had to live. When Sir Roger writes to him, 'I breathe not in a French ayre so cannot complement, . . . civility begins to be look't upon as a monster now,' he replies, 'should I live ten thousand yeares among these pratlinge people, I thanke God I have not soe much courtshipp, nor soe little honesty, as to learne this flattering quallity.'

> ' Suis-je en état d'entendre ces mots,
> Ces vains compliments, protocoles des sots,
> Où l'on se gêne, où le bon sens expire,
> Dans le travail de parler sans rien dire ? '

Sir Ralph might have found a readier use of the tongue of 'these pratlinge people' very useful to him, as he and his wife constantly needed an interpreter. Mary writes about their meeting : ' As for your onely oficer Jaques truly I think you had best bring him to Roane with you for being we have none with us thatt can speake the Language he will be very usefull to us and necessary and itt is nott much more time that Mun and Bess will be without him, for I suppose we shall nott stay very long at Roane ; I confess I could wish my deare Boy Mun might come along with you toe, butt I dare nott bid you Bring him, for feare itt may prove a prejudice to him for his book, butt truly I long to see him. . . .' Mary is delighted with a letter of little Mun's to Dr. Denton, which he has taken great pains with and written twice over; the busy physician made time to reply and we hear from Sir Ralph 'that Mun jumped at his letter—he is very proud of itt.' Mr. Chaloner, a friend at Blois, sends him an account of little Mun after he has started to meet Mary: ' He not only thrives in stature but in learning; . . . both his masters follow him very hard, so that at your returne I question not but you will find him a docter.' His lute is getting forward that Ralph took such pains in ' rackomeding.'

Week after week goes by and Mary is still waiting for money and to wind up the business of the Marshalsea, which drives her almost distracted. She writes that ' The times are like to be worse than evor they were, itt was a strang Blessing to us thatt we gott our buseness donn in thatt Nick of time for to Men's aprehensions we have gon through impossebilleties; butt God is strongest when we have least hope.' The exchange is bad, and she is told it will be more to her husband's advantage to carry their money, in gold about her person, but she will not do it without his advice, so great is the danger of being robbed; she has a great deal of miscellaneous luggage, a store of oatmeal, the great looking-glass about which Ralph had sent many careful directions, and in addition she writes to Roades: 'I would very faine have a hansome Mastif Dogg, I pray enquier out one, it must be a very large and quiett Dogg.' She gets her heavy luggage off first and sends her husband the list of it : ' 4 greate Bundles, 2 trunks one Boxe, one looking glass in a case of Deale Bourds, 2 flatt Basketts tied together, and one hamper, in all ten parcells . . . and I am soe weary this day with rising betimes and sending them out of the house that I know nott what to doe with my selfe.' She desires him to bring with him to meet her in Paris her ' Black silke gowne and Kirtle thatt is in my greate trunk in my closet, pray doe nott forgett it.'

Mary had one more social duty to perform. She was 'the cheyfe guest' in January ' att the honnest D^{rs}, att his wife's eldest daughter's wedding, whoe is maried to Mr. Gape the apothicary . . . there is none of D^{rs} kindred there, butt myselfe and Frank Drake [married to Elizabeth Denton] and uncle John Denton.' Mary had nearly ended her long letter; she adds a line that she has found one of Ralph's awaiting her 'att the wedding house,' and that she will make ' all the hast to thee I can possebly.' Two of the guests add merry postscripts to Ralph : ' S^r I will mak so much of youre Lady that I will not leave one bitt of her for you yet I am, y^r faithfull sarvant F. D.' About a fortnight later the apothecary entertains them all, not a little proud to receive the King's physician, and his other distinguished guests. 'Hear is a little hundred of us,' writes Mary, ' a house warming at my Aunt D^{rs} daughter's howse—where thou art wished, but I wish myselfe with thee which wish I trust in God I shall suddainly have.' 'Vallentines day ye 14 feb. 164⅞. Dr. Denton adds a postscript : ' We are all a housewarminge and you must not expect much.'

Mary had sent him much less happy accounts of another *ménage* in the family : ' Your Coussen James Fines and his wife are parted ; and they say the reason is because they canott agree in disputes of Conscience ; and thatt she doth nott think him holy enough ; butt in my opinion there is very little Conscience in parting from their husbands.'

Sir Roger is full of sorrow at Lady Verney's departure ; and writes that he ' might enter into a discourse fitt to be cladd with the most sable expressions ; . . . the libertie I have for the present of waiting upon your second selfe, (though in all other respects I may truely say she is *nulli secunda*) affordes the greatest contentment I can be now capable of, but alas ! shee is to be gon. . . . By this meanes I am deprived of that society which so sweetly resembles yourselfe, but heere must I give myselfe the check ; it is not mine but y^r happiness that I desire, and so shall it be a pleasure to me to be miserable.' Dieppe is the best place for combs ; he begs that Ralph will buy him a couple, ' one of bone, ye other of torteshell,' with many directions as to their kind.

There had been some talk of Mary's taking Mrs. Eure's two little girls under her charge at Blois, but Ralph feared it would increase her sorrow for the loss of little Peg. ' It would renew your greife, and breake my hart, for I confesse noe creature knew how much you loved that poore childe. I ever concealed what passion I had for her, and rather appeared to neglect her, least our over fondnesse should spoyle her, or make the others jellous; but I must needes say, I loved her at least equall too (if not above) any childe I had, and truly she deserved it, for there was never a better, nor more patient Babby borne. Till now I never knew what a greife it was to part with a childe. Enough of this, least in Venting my owne, I encrease thy sorrow.'

Mary writes to him of the presents she is making to relations before leaving England: 'if you have enough of my deare girles haire to make braceletts I know you could nott send a more acceptable thing then every one of your sisters a bracelett.'

Everybody thought it needless to have a pass, but Ralph, in his anxiety for his wife's safety, desired her to get one. She writes that at her request three Parliament men wrote to the Speaker for one, but he was very angry and refused. At the last minute she has to delay her journey, having such a 'miserable fitt of the stone' that she is scarcely able to stand, and Dr. Denton will not let her travel. She is very sorry that Ralph went to Dieppe so soon. 'My boy Jack is now heare and very well I prayse God, and I trust in God I shall bring him safe to thee.' She is much troubled that a coach to Rye would cost 7*l*., she hopes if she has 'helth enough to ride on horseback, and I hope I shall carry my boy Jack sayfe and

Lapp him up warm. . . . My dearest Roge itt joyes my hart to think how soone I shall be wth thee. . . . I am for ever thine owne.' She is making anxious inquiries about the hazards at sea ; she hears that in the Channel 'scarce a friggott passes without being robbed.' ' I leave it to you to choose your owne Way,' says Sir Ralph, ' either by Dover, or Rye, but if you come by Rye, you must look well to your shipping ; perhapps some of the Parliament shipps (for the Winter Guard) may lie uppon that Coast, if it were soe tis best coming in one of them, though it cost you double, or if you could watch a Time when some marchants shipps come to Diepe or Havre de Grace, you might goe lie at Dover or the Downes, and soe come in ye Convoy ; but this is somwhat an uncertaine Way.'

' Mun is very observant to me in all things,' Mary writes, ' but as for Harry, I have a worse opinion of him than I have roome in this paper to express.' He offers to accompany her to France, an offer she has not the least wish to accept, nor Sir Ralph either. ' If he still speake of a jorney you know whither, rather Laugh at him for it, then contradict him in it ; for wee are apt to doe all that is forbidd us.' Mun is far more considerate. Mary writes : ' Your Bro : Munn will carry me to the sea-syde and I beleeve a very smale invitation would make him stepp over to you, but I believe he thinks itt would be a charge to you which keeps him from desiring it.' He eventually reached Paris before her, on his own business.

On March 7 Sir Ralph is in Paris to make sure

of meeting his wife at the earliest possible moment. She writes about the 'very many shipps cast away' by recent bad weather, but that the very thought of being with him 'hath already made me one inch fatter than I was!'

At length, on April 10, 1648, husband and wife were reunited. Dr. Denton writes lamentably to Ralph of the loss of her company; he had intended to go with her to the coast, but his child's sudden illness and his wife's 'whinnelling' (Mary says her jealousy) stopped him; 'she will as soone give him leave to goe to Jerusalem, but you know what tis to be bound to a wife, and though you doe not,' she adds merrily, 'yett he must obey.' He says, 'I have with much regrett (pardon my passion for her, for if she be soe worthy of y^r love, y^u cannot blame me if I thinke her soe of mine) returned y^r Jewell. . . . I wish you both and yours all happinesse that Heaven and Earth can contribute, and that God would . . . . in his owne due time . . . . bringe you all safe home to the inheritance of your ffathers. . . . I am glad she is gone soe well, for after her lyinge in . . . . she looked worse then old Dr Bethun, just like death. . . . I shall want [i.e. miss] her here to helpe sollicite, to rost me apples, and poide me bread and sassages and make pottage, and above all her good company, wch I would envy anybody but y^r selfe.'

As a douceur to Frank Drake he suggests that Ralph should 'give him high and mighty thanks . . . . for his care of your businesse. Y^u might doe well also to send his wife some pretty ffrench toyes, ... fitt things to please and reconcile Babies. . . . Make yourselfe as merry as you list with my gowne, mittens, and girdle [which Mary used in making bread for him]. . . . I will allow you to laugh as long as you will allow me to eat, and I am resolved to spoile the jest and eat lustily at your cost. . . . I have not eat one morsell of good bread since mischief went. . . . Tell her that Pragmaticus is for her owne proper use and not for yours, without a capp and a knee and a kisse for me.'

After all her labour, fatigue, and suffering, it is a comfort to think that Mary was restored to her beloved Ralph. She had done her part like a noble woman, simply, cheerfully, with untiring energy, capability, and patience. Everyone seemed to feel the charm of her bright, clever, loving presence. She was a thorough lady, and it was quite indifferent to her whether she received her guests in her old stuff gown, or in the white and blue satin and pearls of her Vandyke picture; whether waited upon by her one maid and cooked for by the lodging-house keeper, or as in the old days with all the advantages of Sir Edmund's Court background and the large establishment at Claydon. She had succeeded in everything; indeed, she was not a woman to fail, but it had been done at the cost of a delicate body, and a very sensitive mind, and the effects of the strain were, unhappily, destined to shorten her life.

CHAPTER XIII.

'SIR MUN' IS TREACHEROUSLY SLAIN.

Was it for mere fool's play, make believe and mumming,
So we battled it like men, not boylike sulked and whined ?
Each of us heard clang God's ' Come ! ' and each of us was coming,
Soldiers all to forward face, not sneaks to lag behind ?

How of the field's fortune ? That concerned our Leader !
Led, we struck our stroke, not cared for doings left and right.
Each as on his sole head failer or succeeder,
Lay the blame or lit the praise, no care for cowards : fight !
BROWNING.

WE go back to 1644 to take up the story of Edmund, the young Cavalier. In March '44, Sir Alexander Denton wrote to Ralph : ' My nephewe Sir Edmund Verney is knighted, his Collonell was taken prisoner, nowe in the tower, and he [Edmund] escaped narrowlye.' An entry in an old note book tells us that on the 24th of the same month ' Edmund Verney was Lieut^t-Govern^r of Chester.' From this time he constantly figures as ' Sir Mun ' in the family correspondence. Will Roades mentions with great respect that he spoke ' with him whom was usually called Mr. Mun : who is now Sir Edmund.' There are not many letters from him at this time.

Sir Edmund Verney, Kt.
from a picture at Claydon House.

In April, 1645, Chester was besieged by the parliamentary forces; in May, however, the king marched from Oxford with 10,000 men, and raised the siege; it was one of his last advantages and the very crisis of the civil war, for in June he was disastrously defeated at Naseby.

Great doubts were now felt as to the possible continuance of the war, and there is an interesting letter from Edmund to Lord Ormonde, nine days after the news reached Chester: 'I wayted on his Maj^{ty} hoping to have receivd hiss commands, and soe immedyetely to have come for Ireland. My Lord Byron wass pleas'd to importune me to continue with him in Chester, and to move the King to write to your Exc^{lly} that it wass by hiss command, and to desire you would send me over a regiment of the first men that came over, and thiss letter Sr Robert Byron hath to bring with him. I have alwayes found my Lord Byron very noble to me, and therefore could not in gratitude but obey hiss commands, which are yet but temporary, that iss untill he should be more firmly settled in these parts and in a better condition than he now iss. I much doubt if your Exc^{lly} should send me a regiment, it might extreamely prejudice my farr more earnest desires, which are wholly bent to settle in some place where I may be a constant attendant on your Exc^{lly}. You are the loadstone that may draw me all over the world, and I am in paine untill I am with you; and therefore would not willingly take any engagement on me that might engage my longer continuance here then the necessity of my Lord Byron's affayres require. The newes for the present iss very ill on the king's part; there are soe many passing over that are able to informe your Exc^cy at large that I shall not, etc.'

Chester was again invested; it was of importance to Charles to retain possession of the place as a port of communication with Ireland. In September, a way was opened into the town by the repulse of a storming force, and the king, coming from Raglan, rode in with his body guard; the next day, however, the parliamentary troops under General Poyntz, who were in pursuit of Charles, came up and defeated him before the walls, on which is still shown the seat whence he saw the fight. The loss was great: '800 men slain, 1,200 taken prisoners, the King absolutely routed and fled to Wales,' was the first exaggerated report; the blow at all events was a crushing one.

Chester, however, still held out gallantly, and in November, Henry wrote to Ralph: 'I can assure you Sr Mun is well, for in less than this fortnight Doll had a letter from him, a speakes not a word of his beinge married, though most here thinke it. Chester is certainly very much straitened, and if not suddenly relieved doubtless will be lost.'

Provisions must have run short by Christmas, and Henry wrote 'that the garrison was in great want,' but the final surrender did not come till February 3, '46, after a most brave defence. 'Honourable conditions were granted to the garrison,' said Henry, 'except to the native Irish,' the fear of whom did the king's cause incalculable harm, which the remembrance of the horrible deeds that had taken place during the Rebellion of course greatly increased. Chester was to have received the Irish troops, to gain whose assistance the Earl of Glamorgan had been carrying on a treaty on behalf of Charles with the rebels, or Confederate Catholics as they styled themselves.

Henry goes on : ' Sir Mun is well and marcht, as I hear, with the rest.' The war in England had come practically to a close, for the king had surrendered himself into the hands of the Scotch, and by the end of August nothing remained to him but a few fortresses.

Edmund immediately joined the Lord-Lieutenant Ormonde at Dublin, who was trying to combine with the Confederate Catholics. Finding, however, that it was impossible to carry this out, Ormonde resolved to give up Dublin, and the other garrisons which still held out, to the Parliament, rather than let Ireland fall into the hands of foreign powers. Through all this trying and dangerous year Edmund was by Lord Ormonde's side.

On the 26th of February, '47, Dr. Denton wrote to Ralph : ' Ormonde hath surrendered all to the Parliament, and I think they are not ill-pleased with him. Mun is with him, but nobody here hath heard of him a great while. I pray God guide all for the best of public and private interests.'

Lord Ormonde had hardly any choice before him; the success of the extreme party among the Catholics would have been a 'standing menace to the development of national life in England'; [1] the Irish Church was cosmopolitan, and 'fear of giving a foothold in Ireland to foreign armies acting in the name of the Church,' had been the basis of the policy of Elizabeth and James. The re-conquest of Ireland had now become inevitable.

Lady Verney was at this time in England, endeavouring to get the sequestration removed from her husband's estates. She wrote to him at Blois: 'I hear Brother Mun stayes with my Lo: Ormond, and is resollved to runn the same course thatt he doth. He lately writt to Doll Leeke and his sisters and others; certainly he thinks we are in some new fownd land, which may be beyond the reach of Letters. . . . Tis thought he cannott apeare heare by reason they are very bitter against him of this side; neyther could he live here without good allowance, there nott being a possebilletye of his haveing any imployment heare. . . . The Doctor is very much for him and doth beleeve he loves you more hartely then any of the rest doth, which I thinke he may easely doe.' Ralph replies: 'If you happen to see my Lord Rosscommon, present my most humble servise to him; aske for Munn, but doe not expresse to him or any other, that you take any thing un-

---

[1] Gardiner's *Great Civil War*, vol. ii. p. 548.

kindly from Munn, but rather incorrage him in the way hee is in. For my part I expect not to heare from him till hee hath need of mee; many of my freinds have served mee soe already, therfore I expect noe better usage from him nor them.' A reproach that Mun deserved least of all men; but, as Sir Ralph said of himself, his continual troubles made all things seem sad and black to him.

In June, Edmund wrote that he was about to leave Ireland and should probably go to France. ' I could not,' he says, ' write to any freinde I had till the wayes were open by a treaty.' He speaks with enthusiastic devotion of his leader, Lord Ormonde: ' he iss ass noble a gentleman ass ever the world bredd; I have received infinite obligations from hiss Lo^{pp}; wee have the honour, and I beleeve it iss the greatest of our honours, to be neare allyde to him by hiss mother.'[1] He hopes that Ralph will wait upon him if ever chance brings them together. ' I am confident you will readily conclude him the noblest and the gallantest gentleman that ever your eyes beheld. I heare your lands are sequesterd, I am heartily sorry for it. I'll deale truely with you, before I hearde thiss I could not beleeve you would have suffered by them. For my own part I have ever beene a declared enemy to them, and till the King declare them his freindes I shall continue soe,

---

[1] Sir Edmund's aunt married Sir Nicholas Poyntz; Lady Ormonde was daughter of a later Sir John Poyntz (*see* vol. i. p. 24).

whatsoever I suffer by it; but howsoever your opinion and mine may differ in thiss, yet I beseech you let uss remember wee are brethren and love one another heartily.'

The next letter is from Bristol: 'I am come into England upon my Lord of Ormond's artickles, and have been thinking how to get suddainely out of it againe, for I finde my sworde must be my best livelyhoode, but I cannot put my selfe into a posture of travailing till I have contriv'd some way how to put mony into my purse. . . . I find thiss kingdome in a strange condition, and very greate probabilityes of a warr to ensue, and yet neither party going the way that I can either in honour or conscience take part with, for I hold fast to my first principles, and therefore I would make all the hast I could out of the kingdome.' He then goes on to ask if Ralph will buy of him the 50*l.* annuity which he is under the belief his father left him. With complete confidence in his brother's fairness and business capacity he says: 'I know not upon what termes to offer thiss thing unto you. I am not more confident of your understanding the full of it, then I am of your integrity in dealing with me in it. . . . I shall leave myselfe wholly to you, and you shall set your own price. . . . God send a lasting and an hon[ble] peace in thiss distracted kingdome, though the greatest benefitt I can hope to reape by it iss that it will proove soe to my freindes, for I never looke to see it again after thiss time's departure.'

When Edmund reached London, he was distressed to find that Ralph, from whom he had been somewhat sharply demanding his money for the last three years, was really not liable for any of his brothers' and sisters' fortunes, the money being 'locked up' as it were in the tax of the Alnage, and in other securities which were now valueless. He wrote to Ralph to 'ingeniously confesse my former mistakes ; truely brother, I never knew till now other then that you were to be my paymaster' ; the money which he had forced out of Roades, the steward at Claydon, 'was a trespasse' which he would willingly repair, but he has not a penny in his purse. He who had formerly liked so much to go 'handsomely clad,' is now sadly reduced in his wardrobe, and his uncle, Dr. Denton, evidently very fond of him, writes of 'poore shabby Mun. . . . who hath neyther cloathes to his back nor money to buy them, and is neyther able to live in this town, nor able to set foot out of it, except somebody relieve him, and if I cannot or doe not, I doe not know who will here ; by which I see that bare worth and honour will give noe man bread nor enable him to live. . . . He is very hasty to be gone beyond sea to get his living by that that he is a great master of —his sword.'

Ralph had divided his father's clothes some time before between Edmund and Henry, but the latter characteristically had appropriated the best of them ; Mun kindly says, however, 'he was very partyale in his dividing of the cloathes, but I did not take notice of it to him.'[1] Edmund could hardly contrive even to ride down to Claydon, and not having received an answer to his former letter asks again if Ralph would buy the 50*l*. annuity. 'If I could get but 100*l*. down for it, the rest to be paid at your convenience, I could rubbe out one six or eight months in the eye of the world,' after which time he felt sure of employment under Lord Ormonde either in Ireland or in foreign parts, where he ' would have great hopes of a hansome way of subsistence by his sword.' 'I know there have been some misunderstandings between uss, and that you seem'd much concern'd for a letter I should write to you in the beginning of these unhappy times ; I wass never yet soe wary ass to keepe a coppy of any thing I writt [unlike his brother !] neither iss my memory apt to prompt me in what I did soe long agoe, only thiss I can say I might take occasion upon some prœcedent letter of my father's to

---

[1] Sir Edmund's clothes left to 'Mun and Harry.'
    Black figured velvet cloak laced with 4 black laces.
    A cloth of silver doublet with a black and silver lace unto it.
    A sad coloured cloth cloak lined with plush, and breeches all laced with 4 silk and gold laces.
    A satin doublet laced to it (this was his best suit that he made to ride before the King to Parliament).
    A scarlet coat laced round and in every seame with 2 gold and silver laces and black silk and set thick with great gold and silver buttons and loops.
    One fine Greek laced band.
    2 prs. fine Greek lace cuffs.
    2 prs. fine Greek lace boot-hose.
    1 pr. fine Greek purled cuffs.
    1 pr. fine Greek purled boot-hose.
    1 fine leg purle Band.

me to write my mind and opinion freely to you, and if it savoured too much of bitternesse I earnestly desire you would impute it to my want of better rhetoricke.'

When the misunderstanding about Edmund's allowance was cleared up, he was once more on the old terms of affection and intimacy with Mary. He spent some days at Claydon in the 'unspeakable happiness of her company,' and when the baby boy died, he wrote a touching letter : ' God of Heaven blesse those who are left you with a long and happy lyfe, that they may be a continuall comfort to you ; theire relation to me by bloude, yours (not only by allyance, but by a nearer bond, a most deare and passionate affection) gives me that interest in all your children that one of them cannot goe out of the world but I must be sensible that I have lost a branch of myselfe ; your griefes and joyes are to me the lyke. I shall proceede farther and that most truely, which iss in thiss, conditionally you might continually enjoy the latter, I should gladly embrace the former ass my companion for ever, soe much doe I vallue your happinesse, or else there iss noe trueth, reallity, or honesty in your most faythfull and humble servant, Edmund Verney.'

In spite of his poverty and his father's debts, Ralph contrives to help him. ' Your obligations,' replies Edmund, ' have been infinite to me ; freindeshipe and naturall affection have seemed to strive for mastery, both which have playde their parts so effectually that I am bound never to know myselfe by other title then your most affectionate brother, æternally obliged to love and serve you.'

Again and again his gratitude is most heartfelt. 'I must either be worse than an infidell or else these kindnesses must strangely oblige me to you.'

His affectionate words are a great comfort to poor exiled Ralph, 'reviving my sadd and drooping spirits,' then sorely tried by the unnatural behaviour of his other two brothers, who, he declares, have 'cast him off.' Edmund, in reply, expresses his 'hearty sorrow for soe greate an unhappinesse,' and would gladly have put things right betwixt him and Henry, had that been possible. 'For the elder [Tom] hiss wayes and courses have not only made him ass a stranger to hiss own family, but allmost to all gentlemen.'

Edmund spent the autumn between Claydon—that home for the destitute—his aunt Eure's, and other visits, with constant letters to Ralph and his wife, which, he says, ' has been a happinesse denied him in the past five years.' In December he went to Gloucestershire, where, he says, 'his opportunities for letters will be few.' He writes the day before from Stapleford : 'My obligations in thiss place have been soe high that I am obliged to spend most of thiss day in making my acknowledgement of the civilityes received.' The charming young soldier was evidently made much of—'to tell you the trueth I stay from church thiss morning to write, and unlesse the parson be very long winded I shall scarce have time to make an ende of all my letters.'

Lady Verney wrote in January, 1648, that Edmund had come up to London, and in February the accounts between him and Ralph were examined and balanced, as we learn from a letter of Uncle John Denton's, who was legal adviser to the whole family. All that was due to Edmund, and more, was paid him by Ralph, and a receipt sealed for it. ' He presst me,' says the uncle, ' to have made this Accompt more particular . . . which I accompted a difficult matter . . . therefore accordinge to the old sayinge I sett the Hare's heade agaynst the Goose gibletts.'

Lady Verney, who was soon to start on her road to join Ralph in France, hoped that Mun would escort her part of the way, but he was obliged to depart earlier, as there was some mysterious business going on for the king's service, to which he only dared to allude. On February 24 she wrote : ' My brother Mun is this night a going away with the post. . . . I will wright to thee againe, for I have soe much company heare now to take their leaves of Mun thatt I cannott say more.' ' The times are so uncertaine, and every one is in such great expectations, that noe man as yett knows how to dispose of himselfe ; he hath much business to doe before he goes.'

They met at Paris soon after, Edmund turning up at St. Germain, where the Marquis of Ormonde had joined the queen and Prince of Wales, and efforts were being redoubled in the king's favour; the prince was to put himself at the head of that part of the fleet which was loyal, and Ormonde had been invited to return to Ireland by the Confederate Catholics; Edmund was to accompany him.

While the expeditions were preparing he remained in Paris, and a great deal of painful private business fell to his share. Tom had got into one of the worst of his scrapes, signing a bill of exchange belonging to Sir Thomas Elmes, who had lately married his sister Margaret; and Doctor Denton wrote word that 'the fellow is in danger of hanging in Paris and of the pillory in London.' He would not, however, stir from France 'without being bought off by Ralph, who employed a friendly Doctor Kirton to treat with him, while Edmund had to use all his eloquence to persuade the scapegrace to go home. 'I am hugely affrayd he will linger and bee caught by justice,' he wrote to Ralph, after the latter had returned to his children at Blois.

Sir Thomas Elmes had arrived in Paris, having left his young wife behind him, whom he treated exceedingly ill, and Doctor Denton, who had no scruple in alarming his friends, observes, 'I heere Tom Elmes is in Paris, wch I am much troubled at, for I doubt Mun will have him by the eares (and truly if he would crop them and slit his nose I should not be overmuch troubled), and I doubt be the death of him if he give him noe better satisfaction concerning Pegge, and I should be very loathe that he should have his hands in blood, and so I have sent him word.' Edmund, however, was a better diplomatist than his uncle. It was a difficult negotiation, and he was appealed to by both sides. Margaret had a high temper, and seems to have returned her husband's ill words in the same coin, 'but Mun so carried matters' with his quiet firmness and gentle determination, that he secured some sort of consideration for his sister from his very unpleasant brother-in-law, and sent him back to England to meet his wife in tolerable humour. 'I am now charming Pegge all I can concerning her behaviour to her husband,' he writes. 'Sir Edmund managed that business gallantly and handsomely,' remarked old Doctor Kirton, admiringly.

One of Henrietta Maria's maids of honour was Mistress Mary, sister of Sir Thomas Gardiner, who had married Ralph's sister. She had evidently a tenderness for the gallant young soldier, and gives him messages to write to Lady Verney, such as 'Mistress Gardiner much laments her misfortune in not kissing your hands; she sends her service to you and my brother, would have written, butt that it iss Communion day and she receives.' Mary Gardiner herself writes smart little ill-spelt notes, tied up with two bits of floss silk, each carefully sealed. In one she says, 'I must bege so much of the justis of your Natoure to believe it was a very gret misfortune that I did not se you—I did in dever it as much as was posabell; but the Princ his going a way, left us no menes of storing [stirring] any ware, for he did not leve but only the Quenes cohes [coaches].'

The merciless conduct of Parliament to Sir Ralph had made no difference in his opinions; neither he nor his wife 'font leur cour' to Henrietta Maria on any of their visits to Paris, so that 'Mistress Mary' may have had real difficulty in bringing the queen's 'coch' to the Verney's door; while the Gardiners had behaved so unkindly to Ralph's sister when she was left a widow, that Ralph may not have had any great desire for the company of the maid of honour.

The negotiations in favour of the king lingered long, and in July Edmund, still at 'S^{nt} Jermynes,' writes to Lady Verney at Blois of his trouble and sadness since they parted: 'I have wysely, though not pollitickely, placed all my happinesse in attending you—wisely in reguarde it would give me the truest and most vallued content, but impollitickly in reguarde it iss soe dissonant to my fortunes and my wandring profession that I am not allowed soe much ass hopes of enjoying it. My joyes are momentary and come ass it were to swell my afflictions, for Suckling tells uss truely, pryvation iss a missery ass much above bare wretchednesse ass that is short of happinesse. I have experimentally founde it ever since you left Paris, and yet I find a strange pleasure in thiss discontentednesse, because it iss soe evident an argument of the vallue I have for you. . . . I shall never esteeme any person in the worlde above you. . . My service to little Wagge [his little nephew].'

Early in the year 1648 insurrections in the king's favour had taken place in various parts of the country, and in Scotland. When the Duke of Hamilton's party got the upper hand, it was resolved to send an army into England to espouse the royal cause. In June the Kentish Royalists were defeated by Fairfax; a party of them retreated into Colchester, where they held out for some time. On July 5 the Scotch army crossed the Border. Edmund, from being so much with Lord Ormonde, had better intelligence of public events than Ralph, and in his letters to his brother he often passes on the latest news from England: 'Aug. 11th.—The Prince of Wales hath stayde foure shipps on the Downes.' 'Aug. 16th.—Collchester still holds out; the Scots are advanced towards Lancaster, Cromwell iss in Yorkeshyre; greate disputes betweene him and one Harry Cholmely, who has 5,000 horse and foote with him . . . and refuses to be commanded by Cromwell. Noe newes of the Prince of Wales.' '21 Augt. Rouen.—Warwicke [the parliamentary admiral] lyes in the river to stopp all shipps that go in and come out. Thirty marchand men are ready fraught, and sweare they will either breake through him and the Prince of Wales alsoe or sincke in the attempt.' 'Havre, 31 Augt.—Sir Baldwyne Wake iss come into this harbour after my Lord Leivetenant with a frigot from the prince of wales . . . the prince hath lately taken another vessell worth £16,000; he hath some 34 sayle of shipps with him. . . . The newes iss very bad thiss weeke; the Scots are certainely totally routed, and I doe not well see which way Duke Hambleton and those horse he hath with him can well get off . . . there iss about 8,000 and 9,000 Scotts prisoners allready.' He had expected on joining Lord Ormonde at Havre to find 'my lady Marquese, but as she resolves to stay in thiss kingdome [France] till it be knowne what will become of our Irish affayres,' he had gone to kiss her hand at Caen, which took him a week there and back, some fifty miles.

It was very touching that when the sequestration was removed, the first money which Ralph received —little enough for his own necessities—was employed in assisting his brother. 'I am very sensible,' replies Edmund, 'of the charge I put you to, and your noble and free way of parting with the money. I confesse I receive not any thing from you but with a trouble, and that I would rather be out of the world than continue chargeable to you. I hope the way I am now going will eyther mend my condition or end me.' 'Havre, 6 Sept.—The Prince and all hiss fleete are gone for Holland . . . . and my Ld Warwicke with about 17 shipps came into the Downs last night. Though victualling iss reported to be the cause of the Prince hiss drawing into Holland, yet I doubt he wass perswaded not to stand Warwicke, ass being thought too weake, for he hath not above 4 tall shipps, the rest are frigots and small vessels.' 'Wee cannot passe into Ireland now without great danger by reason

of my L^d of Warwicke, and woe be to us if we are taken, but I hope better fortunes are decreede for uss. Wee have a gallant vessell with 36 gunnes and shall be well manned, and if wee are not very much over matched shall fight hard before wee give ourselves up. I believe this totall defeate of the Scotts has put the queene, Prince, and all theire Councell soe much to theire witts' end that they know not which way to turne themselves now. I spake with Sir Baldwyne Wake, who came lately from the Prince, and reports it wass really beleev'd that the Prince should have been marryed to Duke Hambleton's daughter.'
'10 Sept.—There iss noe jealousy of duke hamilton's betraying the army, but lieuet. : generall Bayly who gave up the foote iss much talked of, and duke hamilton's courage somewhat questioned.' Another correspondent says it was reported that the duke, 'after hee rendred him selfe prisoner to the Lord Gray, tolde him that this laste Armie of Scotts was Invited into England by more members of the houses of parlament then was the former; but I conceive hee hath don the king noe pleasure in that speach, for if they came really for the king's sarvice, hee should not Reveale the Authors.' Edmund goes on: 'The Scotts are in trueth but in a sadd condition, but yet I thinke they will not give the buisnesse over, neither doe I thinke the English will for all thiss late ill successe. . . . God send them better fortune, even to the downefall of our present Tyrants, for whyle they reigne England

can never be happy. . . . I am of opinion if wee can by any meanes settle Ireland I shall be in England with men next spring.'

On August 28, '48, Colchester had been captured by Fairfax, and two of the prisoners, Sir Charles Lucas and Sir George Lisle, were shot by sentence of a court-martial. Poor Edmund was horrified at the news, and writes on Sept. 14: 'Fayrefaxe's own party doe soe exclayme against the butchery . . . . that it's thought there iss an end of proceedings in that kind. The Parliament are selling the Scotts common prisoners to the Barbadoes and other plantations, which I conceive to be about 12,000 or 14,000 men, and artickle the merchants for theire not returning. I thinke they meane to transplant the whole nation of the Scotts.' Dr. Kirton writes from Paris: 'The Scotts are sold at London to those whoe have plantations abroad for £5 the score.' Again and again Edmund returns to the tragedy of Colchester: '20 Sept.—I shall adde something now which must render Fayrefaxe's murthering those gallant gentlemen the more odious, and theire own diurnalls confirme my argument, for upon the question what mercy wass, it wass resolv'd by Fayrefaxe hiss own commissioners in hiss name "that it wass to kill or save whome the generall pleas'd, but he had given that frequent testimonye of hiss civillity to such ass fell into hiss power that none neede suspect severity, neverthelesse he would not be obliged to mercy." Now let any person judge whither thiss answer and exposition of mercy did not implicitely promise lyfe to all,[1] but it wass a high tyranny to bring thiss extreame into his power, for ass every gentleman and souldyer iss obliged to a punctuall observance of the trust committed to him by defending to hiss utmost all persons, townes, and forts under hiss command, soe there iss a civill and honourable custome, and soe authenticke that it may not impropperly be called a lawe, amongst souldyers to give noble and honourable conditions to theire enemy though in the greatest straight and necessity. I shall only give two examples, and those from noe meane souldyers, and yet when the besieged could not hold out an houre; the one iss from the last prince of Orange to those in the Basse [? Bois-le-Duc] after he had sprung hiss mine and hiss men upon the rampiers, upon a parley beaten of by drumme, he caus'd hiss men to retreate and gave the besieged theire own conditions, and thiss after sixe or eight monthes siege. The other iss from the Earle of Callander to Sr Edmund Cary, governour of Hartlepoole neare Durham. Caryes souldyers conspired to deliver him up, and sent thiss offer of theires to my lord Callander then before the towne, but my lord abhorring thiss treachery, sent in theire base engagement to the governour by a trumpet of hiss own, and withall hiss name to a blanke sheete of paper, and desired him to write hiss own conditions. These gentlemen of Colchester tooke up armes by the prince of Wales

[1] This is incorrect; for the actual words, see Gardiner's *Great Civil War*, vol. iii. p. 458.

hiss commission, and entered into parley for surrender of the towne assoone ass the Scotts (which were theire expected reliefe) were destroyed, and a councell of warr would have condemn'd them had they surrendred sooner, but ass the rebellion of England iss the most notorious of any that ever wass since the beginning of the world, soe certainely it iss prosecuted and justifyed with the most mercilesse inhumanity and barbarisme, otherwise what a time wass made choyce of to exercyse thiss cruelty, just when they had consented to a treaty, and would make all the kingdome beleive they were wholly bent for peace and amity, theire actions have given theire tongues the lye. . . . We heare theire own party cry downe thiss act ass so Horrid and barbarous, that it is beleev'd they will proceede noe further in thiss bloudy manner. The sufferers have dyed with honour and glory, and the actors live in horrour and infamy.' Clarendon gives the following details : ' Sir Charles Lucas was their first work; who fell dead : upon which Sir George Lisle ran to him, embraced him, and kissed him ; and then stood up and looked those who were to execute him in the face; and thinking they stood at too great a distance, spake to them to come nearer ; to which one said, "I'll warrant you, Sir, we'll hit you." "Friends, I have been nearer you when you have missed me," he answered, smiling. . . . He led his men to battle with such an alacrity that no man was ever better followed . . . . yet, added to this fierceness of courage, he had the softest and most

Sir George Lisle, Kt.
from a picture at Claydon House

gentle nature imaginable.' An interesting portrait of Sir George Lisle, fully carrying out this description of his courage and gentleness, hangs in the library at Claydon.

Edmund writes on the 28th of September: 'My Lord is resolved to go aboard this night and to tugge it out with any wind and to sayle on the French coast till he comes to the lands end, for fear of parliament shipps; thuss you see they make us fear them, though wee will not love them.' It does not appear on what day they sailed, but Edmund arranged with Ralph that letters should be sent through Mr. Buck, my Lady Marquesse's gentleman usher.

He encloses a note to little Edmund, aged 12, saying he knows not 'how little time I may have to write, so I take the liberty to trouble you the oftener while I am here'; signed, 'your uncle and humble servant.'

A letter from Mun, dated Oct. 5, within a week of his landing, does not seem to have reached Ralph for months after. On Nov. 23 he writes to Lady Verney from Thurles: 'I shall constantly prœserve not only a never dying, but a constant growing respect towards you.' To Ralph he writes that he is compelled much against his own desire to draw upon him a bill of exchange for twenty pistolls to be paid to Mr. Cowley, 'my lord german's secretary.' He has received the money at Thurles from 'Mr. Daniell Oneale.'

The execution of the king was in the following

January, but we have no letter from Edmund to express the horror he must have felt at the news. On March 11 Ralph writes that he had not once heard from his brother since the latter took ship, and is much troubled ; while two days later Edmund writes from Waterford how, in the extreme difficulty of communication owing to the obstructions at sea and the distractions in France,[1] 'I have received but one letter from you, ... and that within a month after I landed. ... I have not a greater ambition within me then to have it within my power to serve you, ... but if either a naturall or vyolent death should render me uncapable to performe what I soe fervently covet and desire, then be pleas'd to receive thiss acknowledgement from me whyle I have power to make it of your being the best Brother and best freind living,' &c.

Young as he was, Edmund had seen much service, and had been a trusted commander, yet such was the struggle for place among the Irish officers, that he writes : 'Though the peace [between Ormonde and the Confederate Catholics] here hath been concluded these two months, yet it wass not convenient for me till within these two days to have command, for some reasons too long and not materyall to relate. I doe not doubt but that the affayres of thiss kingdome will succeede much to our own desires, and that wee shall allsoe be able to prosecute his Maj$^{tyes.}$ [Charles II.] service in England thiss summer. God

[1] The war of the Fronde.

send such a perioud to all our distractions as may best conduce to the wellfare of the king and the people.'

In April Sir H. Puckering Newton writes: 'My lady Marquesse is sent for to Ireland. I thinke it will turn the sanctuary for us all.' Things were indeed looking so serious in Ireland for the Parliament, that Cromwell himself prepared to take command of the army, but before he could land there, Jones, who had been attacked by Ormonde in Dublin, came out in force and utterly routed the Royalists. The slaughter was tremendous, and a false report reached England that Edmund had been killed. Dr. Denton writes, Aug. 16: 'It is certain that Mun was slain.' 'On Mun his regiment of foot and on Vaughan his regiment of horse, fell all the slaughter. Mun his regiment were killed all on a heape, not one of them as I can heare but fought it out to the last even against horse and foote,—Mun is for certaine slaine, not wth out much regrett, even to his adverse party. Jones himself strooke his hands on his breast, and said he had rather have had him alive than all the prisoners he had, and he should have been as well used as ever was prisoner. . . . It was 1000 to one but Ormond had beene taken, on whom there lights infinite blame, though not fit for any of Mun his friends to say so, he being at tick tak and continued playing after the alarum. . . . My hart hath beene so sad since the newes of Mun as I thinke hath not beene since Edgehill, but we must not repine, it is God not the Sabeans, that takes all away, let him do what seems best in his eyes.' The letter goes on to say that Jones had had Mun honourably buried. This circumstantial story proved to be entirely false. To have been killed in battle would have been a better fate for the brave young soldier than that which was reserved for him. Cromwell hastened his departure, and was followed by Ireton and the remainder of the army. Lord Ormonde, unable to keep the field, threw all his best troops into Drogheda, under Sir Arthur Aston, a first-rate officer; 'the defences of the place were contemptible . . . and in two days a breach was effected, but Aston ordered trenches to be dug within the wall,' and the assailants were twice repulsed with great loss. 'Cromwell now placed himself at the head of the reserve, . . . it chanced that the officer who defended one of the trenches fell; his men wavered; quarter was offered and accepted; and the enemy . . . entered the town. . . . During five days the streets ran with blood; 1000 unresisting victims were immolated together within the walls of the great church.'[1] This was on September 11 and 12, but on November 4, Ralph wrote: 'I am yet between hope and feare concerninge deare deare Mun,' and it was not till November 8 that Mr. Buck sent him word of the death of 'your Brother and my deare freind, Sir Edmund Varny, who behaved himselfe wth the greatest gallentry that could be—he was slaine at Drahoda three dayes after quarter was given him as he was walkinge wth Crum-

[1] Lingard's *History of England*.

well by way of protection. One Ropier who is brother to the Lord Ropier, caled him aside in a pretence to speake wth him, beinge formerly of acquaintance, and insteade of some frendly office wch Sir Ed : might expect from him, he barberously rann him throw wth a tuck, but I am confident to see this act once highly revenged, the next day after, one L$^{t.}$ Col. Boyle, who had quarter likewise given him, as he was at dinner wth my Lady More, sister to the Earle of Sunderland, in the same Towne, one of Crumwell's souldiers came and whispred him in the eare to tell him he must presently be put to deth, who risinge from the table, the lady aske him whither he was goeinge, he answered, Madam to dye, who noe sooner steped out of the roome but hee was shott to deth. These are cruelties of those traitors, who noe doubt will finde the like mercie when they stand in neede of it.'

Here is the relation from the opposite point of view : Cromwell, writing to Bradshaw, Dublin, September 16, 1649, says, ' It hath pleased God to bless our endeavours at Tredah. After battery, we stormed it. The enemy were about 3000 in the town ; they made a stout resistance, and near 1000 of our men being entered, the enemy forced them out again. But God giving a new courage to our men, they attempted again, and entered. . . . Being entered, we refused them quarter : having the day before summoned the town. I believe we put to the sword the whole number of the defendants. I do not think thirty of the whole number escaped with their lives. Those that did are in safe custody for the Barbadoes. . . . This hath been a marvellous great mercy. . . . the enemy had put into this garrison almost all their prime soldiers under the command of their best officers. . . . There were some 7 or 8 regiments, Ormond's being one, under the command of Sir Edmund Varney. I do not believe . . . that any officer escaped with his life, save only one lieutenant . . . I wish that all honest hearts may give the glory of this to God alone.' In a subsequent letter he adds : ' The following officers and soldiers were slain at the storming of Tredah : Sir Arthur Aston, governor ; Sir Edmund Varney, Lieutenant Colonel,' &c.

To Lenthall the Speaker, Cromwell mentions ' the courage God was pleased to give the defenders, so that our men were forced to retreat quite out of the breach.' Then when they had entered the town after a very hot dispute, divers of the enemy having retreated into the Mill Mount, with the governor, Sir Arthur Ashton, and divers considerable officers, ' our men getting up to them, were ordered by me to put them all to the sword. And indeed, being in the heat of action, I forbade them to spare any that were in arms in the town : and I think that night they put to the sword about 2000 men.'

' The next day the other two Towers were summoned ; in one of which was about 6 or 7 score. . . . When they submitted (! !) their officers were knocked on the head ; and every tenth man of the soldiers killed ; and the rest shipped for the Barbadoes.' These were apparently all English soldiers. 'I am persuaded that this is a righteous judgement of God,' wrote Cromwell fiercely, concerning this wholesale slaughter of men who had submitted, and the selling of hundreds more into slavery. 'The defendants in Tredah consisted of the Lord of Ormond's regiment (Sir Edmund Varney Lieutenant Colonel), of 400'; &c., &c. Considering that Lenthall was a kinsman of the Verneys, this could hardly have been an agreeable communication from 'your most obedient servant, Oliver Cromwell.' 'The officers and soldiers of this garrison were the flower of their army,' Cromwell goes on exultingly. 'It was set upon some of our hearts, that a great thing should be done, not by power or might, but by the spirit of God'; adding, 'it is good that God alone have all the glory.' The spirit of a Jew of old smiting Amalek with the sword of the Lord could hardly have been fiercer and more uncompromising, or more convinced that it was the voice of God that commanded the massacre of men who had laid down their arms and were at his mercy ; in his eyes the life of the individual was of no account at all, compared to the interest of the Commonwealth :

> Though now we must appear bloody and cruel,
> As, by our hands and this our present act
> You see we do, yet see you but our hands,
> And this the bleeding business they have done :
> Our hearts you see not ; they are pitiful
> And pity to the general wrong of Rome—
> As fire drives out fire, so pity, pity.

Among all who suffered none seems to have been more regretted than the brave young soldier, Edmund Verney, aged 32. The favourite of his father, an affectionate brother and friend, who won upon every person with whom he had to do by his upright, chivalrous conduct and his care for all the weakly and wanting, thrown upon himself in those difficult years, tender and true, with a healthy ambition to distinguish himself, and a dauntless courage which rejoiced to find itself in the midst of danger, Edmund was indeed the ideal in the best sense of a young cavalier.

> Loyalty is still the same
> Whether it win or lose the game;
> True as the dial to the sun,
> Although it be not shined upon.
>
> SAML. BUTLER.

CHAPTER XIV.

THE 'MACHES' OF THE FIVE GIRLS.

> Gather ye rosebuds while ye may,
>   Old time is still a flying,
> And this same flower that smiles to-day,
>   To-morrow will be dying. . . .
>
> Then be not coy, but use your time,
>   And while ye may, go marry ;
> For having lost but once your prime
>   You may for ever tarry.—HERRICK.

THE passion of love, as it was understood by the knights of old in their high-flown protestations to their 'ladye loves,' and which in the modern three-volume novel gives the keynote to all intercourse between man and woman, hardly existed at this time with regard to marriage, which was usually a purely commercial proceeding—so much 'portion' against so much income. The love of husbands and wives, of parents to their children, was extremely strong, but the ordinary falling in love of young men and maidens is not thought of much importance.

'I mean to marry my daughter to £2,000 a year,' writes Sir John Bacchus to Sir Ralph, quite openly. A man was a mere appendage to the fortune ; children, as generally considered, were only pawns used to advance the position and the wealth of the parents. In the usual way the bargaining was done by friends and relations, but if there were none of these available, the young lady did it herself, and Mary Villiers writes to a pretendant to her hand: 'The distracted times affrights me from thinking of mariing; . . . wheras you desired mee to make enquiere of you and your estate, I cannot hear of any you have at all; and I would have you know without an estate I will never marry you, nor no man living, and such an estate as my friends like of.'[1]

After Sir Edmund's death Lady Sussex writes to Ralph: 'I am afraid in these bad times you will not mach your sisters as you desire,' but on the whole, as far as money and position went, they did well. It is pathetic to see how he strove to do his best for the five motherless girls, from 9 years old to 21, who were left to his charge. Cary was the only one of the sisters who had been provided for in marriage by her father. In time the others were all pretty well disposed of, but the negotiations for their different marriages, the bargaining about money matters, how much could be wrung out of poor Ralph for the bride; how much the bridegroom could be expected to supply; the dropping of one proposal after another by the friends of either party with little scruple and no excuse but the barest motives of interest, give a

---

[1] A madrigal of the time of Elizabeth says:
  If gold thou hast, fond youth, 'twill speed thy wooing,
  But if the purse be empty, come not to me a sueing.

curious picture of the times. There is, however, one love passage in a letter from the second girl, Penelope, in the year after her father's death, with a pretty tribute to her brother's affection and care.

'Sr Ralph, I am very glade to here that you are pleasde with my not going to see my sister: I shall not willingly do anything bout what I shall acqueunt you with beefore I do it. For that good compeannion, wch I speoke to you of in my last letter, I meane that cossan of mine, you will give him meany thankes for the favours that I have rescefed from him. I could never a had more respect from you, had I bin in the house with you, then I had dealy from him. Hee would meany times com and site with mee, or call me to goo a walking with him to or thre ouers together. I am confident that you cannot chuse bout think that I have lost a very good compeanion of him. Hee is my master and hee doth call mee his chearge. Euer hereafter when I have any occation to speake of him to you, that is all the neame that I will give him. I am confident that he doos love my sister very well [probably Ralph's wife], for he did drinke hur helth to mee every day, and no pleace would serve him att the teabull bout by mee, and did hee not come so sone as wee to sit donne, the pleace was left for him.'

The sisters had at times the inestimable benefit of Tom's exertions on their behalf. In November, '44, Susan writes to Ralph about Mr. Richard Alport:

'My brother Thomas has wished mee to a gentillman wch has a very good fortune for mee, for hee has att the least 500 pound a year ; he is of my one oppinion, otherwais I should nott think of itt. All y^t knows the man gives him good commendations. He is a widoer butt has noe child ; his fortune is in his one hands ; he has seene mee, vows y^t itt is the furst time that ever he thought of marriing sence his wif dyed, & if he faile of mee itt shall be the last. Uncle Leeke is coming to town ab^t it. For my portion he never asked what I had ; he is a prisoner for his soverraing, but the has his liberty to goe abroad upon his word.' In the following February Tom delivers himself of his mind concerning his sister's situation : 'Since I am desired to write I shall (with much brevitye) declare in what a sad condition my sisters in generall are now in, and how (with a little help of yours) they may be much bettered. . . . They living att Claydon are subject to the affrights of rude souldiers in rushing in att all houres both by day & night, & not a man there that dares show himself in their defence. My sisters (god help them) are so sencible of their incivilitye allready that I have heard them say that they could not eat hardly in a week one meale's meat contentedly. . . . Judge you of this their dayly troubles, in case they should returne thither againe. . . . My sister pen . . . was ever willing to confine herself to such a small livelyhood as you were able to allow her. Moreover she hath (with that small annuitye) maintained herself like her father's daughter and your sister. Now shee haveing some occasions to London (not dreameing of marryage) I brought a gentleman to her. . . . After I perceived they liked each other, my brother [Harry] & I gave a meeting to his friends to conclude upon busynessess, which my brother not long since sent you the perticulers of.' Ralph does not seem to have acceded to the demands made on him by the suitor, for Pen writes indignantly : 'In the letter you sent to my brother harry was much joy exprest for my hopes of prefarment, for the which I return you many thanks, but I find that youre outward expressions will afford me but little comfort unless theay are mixed with true and reall affection in ading to my livelyhood £20 a yere. The times I must confess are bad, yet thanks be to God you are not driven to that straite but that you may add to my fortin the above specifide sum. . . . Youre house at Cladon I am & ever have bin willing to live in, whilest I had compinny that I liked, but if my to sisters will steay in towne, it willbee extreme uncouth liveing. Howsoever, notwithstanding the outrages of souldiers I shall be very willing to return to the place agane, in case you ar minded to breake this mach of, which if you doe you must give me a live to think, and likewise you must looke to be censured by the world to be the most unkind and unnatural brother. I shall, till this letter is answered, continue in that good opinion I ever had of you, & I hope you will give me no caus to the contrary. Good brother, if you are the manes to breake this match of, I pray give me £5 towards my expencis in london, which will be sum helpe to your most discontented sister.' After all this the affair came to nothing, and Pen returned to Claydon.

Henry does not fancy the marriage that had been talked of for Susan with Mr. Alport, and will have no hand in it. While he is on the subject of his sisters he puts in a word for one of the others : 'Now their is a third sister of yours wants a gowne to dance at the weddinge of the other to as much as thay'; and in another letter: 'You must not forget Pegg, for she intends to daunce.' In June he writes: 'As for Sue's buisiness it is in my onderstandinge at a greate stand, for I doe not finde or here a will accept of any offer as yet but ready money or no to content his creditors; I confess I beelive Sr John [Leeke] hath often Bradge to divers of it, and chifely to you, to gaine you farthrance in it. For my part I have exprest my mind more freely to my sist^r and him then ever I did to you, and indeavoured in a fayre way more than this 3 mounths to breake it, but my counsell will not bee hard, for I see if hee will accept of her she is resolved to take him wth all faults; I shall whish her as much happyness and content as any one livinge, if it proceede, but I dout strongely the goeinge one of it, for a is unconstant in his demands; in a word I dout if it bee not decided suddenly she will suffer in opinnons.' She is evidently rather difficult to manage in the matter, and in September 1645 Henry declares that he will trouble himself no more about her actions : 'let her write as sharpely as she pleaseth to you, be confident it can do you noe hurt.' Again in October : 'She expects daley your answer in accomplishing her demands & desiers, but mistrusts that I will doe my best to prevent it. . . . I told her playnely, as I allwayes did, my oppinion of the mach ; wh^{ch} was if she had him I consived her absolutely undon ; if she have him, & that my words prove not true, hange mee.' About the same date the young lady herself describes an expedition to Claydon : 'Sis peg and mee gott an opportunity of A coach wch was to goe tworts Clay : so wee haveing a grete desire to see my sisters and leetle Jack, made use of y^t & whent thether to see them, butt we lay butt one night there. They are all very well I prays God, & Jacke y^r boy is ye finest lustist child y^t ever I did see, & God be thanked very free from ye ricketts ; he is nott very tall of his age, butt extrem lovely.'

The negotiations with Mr. Alport are still going on, and it seems that her uncle Leeke, with whom Susan is living, favours the match. In November she writes that her suitor 'dus now accept of this last proposition in y^r last letter, if you mean itt as all us understand itt, wch is this, how that he should receve £200 presently, and £100 in Nov. 1646, ye other £100 in Nov. 1647, and you say y^t you will do y^r best to gitt it for him sooner, wch if you can you will pleasure him much.' The stuff for two gowns which Ralph promised her she wishes to have sent when this 'proposition' is 'sett.' 'Pray brother lett mee beg a payer of very leetle french sisers of you, for now I doe intend to turn workwoman, and a very good hus wif, so y^t y^r next letter may conclud all bisnesis, if nott I think y^t I shall have nothing to be good huswife of.'

On January 7, '46, Susan writes her brother a long and piteous account of the trying circumstances in which she is placed. Mr. Alport, she says, ' is very redy to perform all things in 10 days worning, so where the fault lyeth I know nott, but I suffer extremely in the tediousness of itt, both in my honour and purse, which are both beyond my discretion to avoid. I had rather be buried alive than loose my honour, and I have often writt you word that I am att greater expence than I am able to subsist with, yett I doe not find fault with my allowance, for I know itt is moer then my sisters have, yett itt will not keepe mee in london. . . . I am in debt for my diett. . . . My deare uncle and aunt, out of ther affections to mee, and because that I shall nott goe out of town till this busnes is ended one way or other, dus trust mee for my diett, although I know they doe boreow itt, & pawne for itt. These things troubles mee extremely.'

Ralph on his side writes to Henry: 'That which troubles mee most in this perticuler is that I find by a letter from Sir Jo. Leeke . . . that Mr. Alport conceives himselfe neglected, and I am deeply censured because my answere to the letters . . . were not already come. I am in a very hard condition amoungst them, when I must not only be condemned for my owne faults, but the uncertainty of the winde, the stormes at sea, miscarrage and interception of Letters, and a thousand other hazards, all must bee layed to my charge. This is pure love, is it not?'

Henry observes in answer: 'S^r, it is love that makes her pen write soe sharply, and not malise, yet I could whish her more discreete then to condem so good a freind & Brother, being I know faultles.'

Ralph indeed seems to be doing all that he possibly could afford for his sister. On Feb. 22 he writes to Sir John that he is glad his sister's suitor accepts the offer he made on Jan. 25, 'which was that £100 that now lies ready shall bee paied to Mr. Alport, with £100 more assoone as it can bee made of my goods, & also of the assignement of the Land [as security] for moneys due in November 46 & Nov. 47. . . . I shall use my best endeavours to sell my goods in the country with all the speed that may bee. I wish I could doe it in an hower, but you know at what distance they are.' To his sister he writes that it is the best news he has had for a long time that she is contented with his offer: 'It seemes Mr. Alport desires the marrage may bee in Easter Weeke; & that you know noe obsticle but want of cloathes. I wish there may not, & then I shall not doubt it, for I will write to a freind (in case there is noe other obsticle, and that the marrage is soe suddainly) to helpe you to stuffe for three gownes and the £30, either in money or credit which is as good . . . It seemes that Mr. Alport knowes of noe more then £600 of yours in my hands, and that hee hath now againe promised you to quitt mee of all that I owe towards your Portion. Therfore you must bee sure to have him deliver upp all the Bonds for those moneyes that I owe towards your portion, soe that the overplus of the £600 may goe to the payment of your Uncle Leeke and other creditors. Truly what this over plus comes to I doe not know, but I pray deliver this inclosed to your Uncle John Denton and desire him to informe mee; and then according to your owne desire (when Mr. Alport hath discharged mee of the whole) I shall deduct the money I lent you, & in the next place pay your Uncle Leeke (to whome you are infinitly obleiged), and the remainder you must dispose.'

After all these elaborate arrangements there are further delays. It appears that Mr. Alport, fearing lest Ralph should be declared a delinquent, preferred bonds as security from him, instead of the engagement first proposed. Susan is aggrieved because the money for her clothes is not to be given her till the 'joynter' is sealed. 'Sartinly noe frind or foe y^t I have can mistrust y^t he will nott have mee after y^t he has drawn ye Joynter & bought my ring, & gave itt mee befoer all my frinds, and profest y^t he longs till itt be dunne. . . . I cannott chuse butt be in admiration, that my cloaths should be denyed, nay I did butt desire my brother henry butt to helpe me ether to stuff, or so much mony has would bye mee petticoatt & bodys, because that such bodys y^t I wheare cannott be made under three weeks time. . . Suer itt would have binne much handsumer for mee to have had them before I had married . . . itt may begitt a suspition in his frinds y^t I brought noe cloaths to my backe and y^t he bought me those wch you will give mee. . . . I think itt is dune without y^r knowleg.'

In the same letter there is mention of Margaret's matrimonial prospects: 'My sis. peg is likly to be married has soone has I am, to a pretty gentleman of a very great fortune. Itt may be wee should have binne married both of aday, butt I will nott, because she will have cloaths licke her selfe & I shall nott, therfore itt must nott be.' If Pegg had the best trousseau, Sue had secured by far the kindest husband.

Ralph replies: 'You speake of Pegg's marrage; I wish it hartily, but I doubt tis too good newes to bee true, because till now noe creature ever made the least mention of it to your most affectionate freinde & servant R. V.'

Although the letter had not yet arrived, Henry had already written about the match for Peg; it was his own doing and he was vastly pleased with himself for it.

'S^r in the middest of all our crosses and your misfortunes I have some good newse to send you . . . wch is sist^r Pegg is suddenly to be maryed to

Mr. Elmes of Norhamtonshire. his estate is knowne to the world to bee at the lest to thowsand a yeare, onley portions accepted. A makes her of his oune offer five hundred a yeare good securety Joynter.' She had been originally well provided for by her godmother, Mrs. Eure, but apparently of late the interest of her money had not been forthcoming. Henry goes on : ' I will not say I brought the younge man to her, but I may boldly say had it not bine for mee and my credit she will acknowledge it had never a bine don. . . . For my sister's advancement beinge put to the pinch, & in a manner for lacke of sund securety neare broake of by the Gentleman, I was forst . . . to binde my selfe with the helpe of J. D. to pay him £100, in regard neither intrest nor bonds for the whole £2,000 where well payd or secured. Had I not don this one the place wee treated, it could not a proceeded. . . . Without your present assistance my sister must a starved, in respect noe intrest of late at all was ever payd her. Sir, this was a sudden good fortune in my Judgment unexpectedly happened to us, soe that it was not possible for mee to give you notis of my adventuer. Therefore I shall stand to your cuertesie to acquit mee of my ingagement, but if I am not freede of it by you . . . you will conclude I am undon.'

If Susan's match was long on hand, poor Peg's was rather a case of ' Marry in haste, and repent at leisure.' In less than a month from the date of Henry's last letter he writes again : ' This is the weddinge day & I am instantly goeinge to church with my sister, soe you must expect to here but little newse or buisiness from mee at the present, onley give mee leave to . . . tell you the dispute beetwne Sue & I was not a bout the cloathes, for she did not then know I had them. A fore your letter came to my hands she had her taby gowne and £3 of mee, which was more then you gave mee order for, but . . . I did it to plese her. She is now willinge to bee freinds with mee and well she may, for I take God to witness, I never did her wronge more then to deswade her from this mach, which yet I thinke will scarse take effect. The other to gownes I have by your order delivered her, and when she has my uncle John Denton's consent the money shall be ready.'

This was written on May 7. On July 16 Susan composed a voluminous epistle to her brother in which she treats at large of her own circumstances, and touches on Margaret's. It is melancholy to hear of the latter, a bride of a few weeks : 'poore peg has married a very humersume cros boy has ever I see in my life, & she is very much altered for the worse since she was married ; I doe not much blame her for beinge so altered, because sumetims he maks her cry night & day.'

Henry's account of Mr. Elmes is equally unsatisfactory : 'A proves by fitts very bad & divelish jelous, now and then for an houer strangely fond. I must doe her write, she deserves it not ; want of worth & breedinge makes him doe it. I am often forst to speake bigg words when a acts the part of a Madman, & that stills him for a time.'

They seem to have set up house in London. Dr. Denton says, 'Peggie is now a housekeeper and is settled in Coven Garden.' Mr. Elmes was knighted in 1646.

To return to Susan's affairs. She says, 'The bisnese is ended betweene Mr. Alporte & mee, all butt the serimony in the church, which god willing shall be solemnised next weeke. . . . I hope I shall be happy, because his affections has continewed so long to mee nott withstanding all the oppositions.' She is promised a certain overplus of 172*l*. 10*s*. 0*d*. to pay her debts with, and has acquainted Mr. Alport with their amount, but she is ashamed to tell him that a large sum is due to Sir John Leeke, and that until it is paid, his goods and all that he has are in pawn.

After this the wedding follows pretty quickly, and on the day after she writes : ' I was married very privatly, & this day my frinds heareing of itt came to mee, butt I have beged ther pardon for my abceince whilst I writt to you & my sister. In the meane time he keeps them company. . . . My uncle leeke after he had given mee away, stoll outt of towne.' And then comes an earnest request that Ralph will lett her know what he is doing about her debt to Sir John. She continues : ' I hope that I am extremly happy in him [Mr. Alport] ; I would nott have itt to doe againe for anything in this world.' There is a touching little postscript to the next letter: 'I was never so happy sence my father dyed has I am now, I thank god. This is all that I can say of itt now—he presents his sarvice to you.'

The next letter is a curiously cheerful one to be dated from the Fleet: 'The last time that I writt to you I sent you word that I was in the prison with my husband, which it may be you might wonder att, because I have formerly writt you word that before I would marry he would be outt of this place . . . butt . . . the knight that Mr. Alport is bound for is at this present selling of land to redeeme him, and I am confident we shall be out . . . by Candlemas. Itt is noe prison to mee: I live has well heare has ever I lived any wheare in all my life, & dare compare husbands with her that has the best.' In this and the following letters there are urgent applications for money: 'My uncle leeke is in the countrey, & duse send very often to mee for his mony: he would faine have his goods att home with him, that he might com to towne with outt being bauld att for his mony.' She is afraid he will come upon Mr. Alport for the debt, and that this may be 'a means to begett sume words' between her and her husband. 'I should be very sory to have my debts or any thing els allter our affections. Deare brother consider how unhappy I should bee, that itt should fall outt so.' Then comes a list of those to whom she owes money. 'If you will sattisfie theese I shall be a gentlewoman, if nott I am quitt undune.' Ralph promises to do all he can for her, but there are endless difficulties in the way, some of which concern the loss of a 'noate.' In the next letter she has been put to great shifts for money. Her uncle, Sir John Leeke, had died, and her aunt being without so much as a sixpence in the house to bury him, came to Susan for the 32*l*. so long owing. She, poor thing, declares it ' was affliction upon affliction to mee, because I was not in a condition to help her . . . tell my husband of itt I durst nott ' ; neither could the money be procured from any other friend. At length she applied to her brother Elmes, ' and my earnist Intreaty & passion together prevailed with him too lend her 20*l*. . . . He tells me that he cannott tarry longer for itt, butt whilst I send to you.' Then come further entreaties for the money, lest Mr. Elmes should tell Mr. Alport about it, and ' so itt might make a differaunce betweene . . . mee & my husband besids. Such a thing has this is may make a differaunce betwixt man & wife all ther lif time ; when itt is dune you cannott recall it. . . . My unkle dyed so much in debt has I feare wee shall have the corps seised upon before wee can gitt itt outt of towne. He desired to be buried at Chigwell, & thether I am goeing with him.' After this Ralph contrived some means by which the 32*l*. should be paid.

By October 1 a husband had been found for Pen, a certain cousin John Denton. It was not a grand match, but the gentleman was by no means exacting in the way of settlements ; in fact there is reason to believe that he was the admirer of whom she had written three years before, and everything seemed satisfactory except some drawbacks in the character he had at one time borne. There was no time to consult Ralph, nor did the bridegroom ask his father's leave at first. ' One my word,' says Henry, ' I know not one in England would a made her his wife one the like conditions. . . . One my life it was not out of disrespect or contempt to you, for had she stayd for your approbation, she must have lost him ; this one my fayth I must witness for her. S^r, she was sensible her portion lay in a desperate condition, besides, she grew in yeares & was not to all men's likinge ; these reasons made her soe ready to yeeld to his desires, havinge most of her freinds' consent present. I confess when she sent post for mee I knew not of it, but when she told mee I did not oppose it, but prest him much to tarry till I could informe you of it. One noe condition a would not, lest you should putt a stopp to it If his father & mother at their aryvall whome [i.e. home] like of it, I am in greate hopes a will make a kind and lovinge husband . . . a hath in a manner given over drinking, or else you may assuer your selfe I had ever soe much reall Affection for her as never to a yellded to it.' He then goes on say that he has advanced her 30*l*. for ' gownes & linnen,' which he hopes Ralph will repay him, and not think that he has been ' prodegall . . . for had I a bine to a payd it myselfe, I protest I could not a bine more sparinge less she had gon naked to him.' Then comes an entreaty to the parental elder brother that he will also pay a debt of 10*l*. which Pen has incurred, 'that I may justly sware to her new father when wee goe that she is clad like a gentlewoman, & owes not in the world a penny. I purpose in 3 or 4 dayes to carryer whome to him, then I will returne you an account of our wellcome, god grant it may bee a good one.'

Ralph in the meantime had heard something of the matter and wrote to Dr. Denton: 'Now for Penn, if you could marry her to J. D. 'twould bee a master peece of servise, & obleige us all; I thirst after it, therfore I pray try your best skill. I confesse I doe not see any greate inconvenience to the two younge ones if the deed had been donn without acquainting the father, for I beeleeve the Land is setled, & if they carry themselves wisely & with respect to him, a little time & good nature would procure an act of Oblivion. Keepe this to your selfe, for at this distance I cannot judg well of this matter.'

In the end, however, the question whether to dispense with the father's consent did not arise, and Henry wrote: 'I have broake the Mach to his father and mother, soe that thay both approve of it, and have recived her with greate content & make infinite much of her; my sister is well plesed, soe if the Gentleman continue Amorus I hope the mach will be happy for both; as I write you word afore it was an adventuer, but as it did luck it hath suckceeded well. . . . If her hussband prove good, as I hope a will, I dout not at all the kind usage of his freinds, for thay are perfect good and honnest people.'

A fortnight later the newly-married wife herself writes to apologise for not having waited for her eldest brother's consent, and assuring him that she had 'desird no more money then what did supply my present nesesity, and my weding was without haveing my frinds at it, being very sencibull I put you to a further charge . . . give me live to till you that I have an exselent father & mother-in-law, and I hoope A Good husband.'

There were now only two unmarried sisters. Poor little Betty, aged thirteen, produces a letter to her eldest brother in a laboured copybook hand, and desires him 'not to expect many lins from me, for love consist not in words but in deads, for my hart cannot expres it self in the outward apreanc so far as in woardly it is afected, by reson of my tender years.'

Mary or Mall was five years older, and a year before this time had been considered worthy the notice of her brother Henry. He wrote of her, September 5 : ' As for sister Mary she hath left her ould trickes & like to prove the handyest of them all, wch reioyses mee much.' Again : 'I must enlarge myselfe a little conserninge sister Mary ; she is now growne a womman & desiers much with your consent to be a broade ; she is handy & as I thinke most fitt for it ; it is pitty she should continue much longer where she is, for the sight of the world & being in company would doe her much good ; if you a prove of this my motion let mee here your minde, & I shall doe my best to fullfill her desire, wth credit and for as little charge to you; she is witty & very tractable to please.' She should go to some place 'where she may larne a little breedinge, for indeede she lacks it.' Ralph replies he would gladly have it done had he wherewithal, and asks where Henry proposes to place her; where she is now (Claydon) 'her diet and cloathes costs little, and one maid serves her and the rest . . . I pray consider well whether her remove at present may not bee more for her disadvantage, for if that place where shee is should bee sequestred, she beinge there might get something to keepe her from beggery & starving, where as if she bee removed perhapps they would not be soe kinde.'

Henry replies in his grand style : 'I did forbare to tray my friends till I had your consent in generall. I can tell you, to one greate countes or other. I shall say no nore but breedinge she wants much, which at the ende will prove her ruine.' After this gloomy prognostication he goes on to propose that she and Pen should live for a while 'att a Parke, I have lately taken posetion of it, it is Otlands, my cousen hath plast mee in . . . If you will give Mall leave it will I know content her much and please mee well.'

However, in a subsequent letter it appears that 'Sister Mary did not fancy the lodge, in regard it stood alone and that it was in my Absence malencoly.'

The money troubles of the Alports seem never ending. In December '46 Susan gives the history of a quarrel she had had with Tom's wife, to whom she owed 11*l*. This lady hearing that the Alports had received a certain sum, 'she coms with open mouth to my husband for this mony, & swore to him yf hee did nott pay her that she would have his hart bloud outt, yf ever he sett his futt outt of doores, & called mee all to naught and swore she would kick mee. This was dune in the Fleett, which did inrage my husband so extremly that hee sayed sumthing which she tould my brother of . . . my brother sent my husband a challing. . . . I had noe body to stand my frind to take up this bisnes, butt my unkle Doctor . . . who gott my brother Thomas & diverse of my frinds after itt was known, & chid him soundly, butt all that they could say to him did noe good withoutt the mony. That I could nott pay & my hus would nott, so to avoid bloud my unkle Dr. layed downe the £11'; and the upshot of it all is to beg that Ralph will repay the Doctor.

At this time Ralph's wife had just come to London to try to get the order for sequestration taken off his estates. She wrote her husband minute accounts of the family doings, in which she speaks her mind pretty freely concerning her sisters-in-law and their behaviour. 'Tis a very great blessing to us that thay [the elder sisters] are all maried; for I did neavor in my life see or hear of soe much indiscretion as is amongst them; truly there is not one of them that hath any discretion.' A day or two after her arrival she writes: 'My sister Alpott made an invitation to me & a very great dinner . . . I doupt they are poore, butt she hath a mighty kind husband.' Again: 'Sue hath a very kind husband as tis posseble, but very deboche ; soe y^t I feare if he have any estate itt will come to noething very suddainly . . . Truly to say truth she makes very much the best wife of all your sisters, and studdies nothing butt to please her husband, and if you did butt see him you would wonder how she could be soe fond of him, butt indeed I think he is very kind to her ; butt I feare they will come to be in wantes, for I doe nott see any great hopes of his freedom & the lieing there makes him spend a very great deale of money ; I beleeve he had better have payed the dept att ferst twice over ; for lieing there & haveing nothing to doe hath bredd such a habitt of drinking on hime that he can doe noe thing elce.' . . . 'Poore Pegg hath soe ill a husband that I cannott give you a carracter badd enoughe of him ; & I feare she will make herselfe a very unhapy woeman, for I neyther like the councell y^t is given her nor ye way she takes with him' ; and when Cary and her second husband went to stay with the Elmes, Lady Verney says, 'Tis a hundred to one pegg's husband turns them out of his howse again within a fortnight. . . . Betty went ye other day to see her sister Pen : whoe they say looks misserablely ; & thatt they are much in disorder in that house, & y^t her hus : begins to flye out & be deboist againe. . . . I think when pleas god to enable me to goe downe [to Claydon] I had best eyther take away or locke upp all that is of ye best and take away ye keyes my selfe ; for I find they will all take what they have a mind toe elce ; for nott long agoe I sent to Mrs. Francis to send me up a wrought sheete if there were any doun, because I know your mother when she died left some to work . . . butt she sent me word that there was one nott quite fineshed which your sister Penn took away with her; & upon ye same grounds for ought I know they may take away all that is left.'

In August '47 Lady Verney went down to see to matters at Claydon, and wrote from thence to her husband: 'My sister Sue gave my sister Penn noetice of my coming downe; soe she & her husband & his Brother were here 2 or 3 dayes before I came to meete me, & stayed wth us here as long after I came downe; which hindred me very much & I think they would have stayed longer if I had spake much to them; my sister Pegg & Cary hath sent to see whether I was come because they would come hether toe, butt I have gott my Sister Mary to putt them as civelly as she could off from coming because here is neyther bedds nor sheetes to lay them in . . . & I know theyre husbands would think itt a very strange thing to be soe entertained as they must have bin heare, soe I hope they will have more witt then to come . . . for my owne green furnetur wch you putt downe in ye noate to bring away your sister Penn about toe yeares agoe plundred you of itt, & ye side saddle to itt. I neavor knew any thing of itt untell that morning she went away, & then she told me of itt . . . butt I gave them to understand when she was gon how much I resented ye taking away the sheete & that toe without soe much as asking for itt; butt they all say y^t she swore you gave them to her & she would have them by force, & that I had more then that came toe of hers.' August 18.—' I did a little incivelly putt of your sister Cary and Pegg from coming, because I was very unwilling theyr husbands should see y^e sorryfull doings thatt is in this place; butt for penn's husband he is soe very simple thatt twas noe great matter for him, butt in my opinion he is as fitt a match for her as can be, though she outgoes him much in cuning, for she is deadly craffty. . . . here is a great looking Glass & M$^{rs.}$ Francis & Will Roades swers they have had y^e heviest life to keep itt that can be Imagioned; for your sisters have often threatned if they would nott lett them have itt to bring a troupe of horse to break downe the wales where twas.'

The account which Lady Verney writes at first of Mary and Betty is not much more favourable than that given of the elder sisters, though after a while Mary showed capabilities of something better. Her sister-in-law lost no time in trying to get a husband for her, even before she had herself seen the girl. February 4, '47.—' I beleeve our neighbours att the duke's garden are nott yett come . . . but when they doe come be assured I will doe my best to gaine the man you meane, but I feare much he will nott think ye woeman [Mary] hansom enoughe, for every body sayes she is the plainest of them all, butt she hath a great deale of witt & they say is a very good huswife, but extream clownish; every body heare makes great complaints to me that they both have noe breeding & sey itt is nott fitt they should be kept in that place [i.e. Claydon] any longer; I tell them I beleeve you will be very willing to have them any where elce; where they may be better bredd or more pleased; I beleeve they are now upon a desighne of putting ye eldest of the twoe [Mary] eyther wth my sister pegg or Cary; butt I beleeve she will cost you more in eyther of ye then she doth; they sey she must needes learne to dance for toe monthes; send your opinion in all, truly I think you had better allow her a little more & put her out because she is a woeman both in yeares & groweth; but my opinion is she will quickly retourne againe; for they are but very uncertaine places; but truly I should be most extreamly glad if we could make ye match for her wth that man; for certeinly if she had him she were much the hapiest maried of all ye sisters; for I am sure he is very good & civell; & I doupt none of theyres are soe.'

A little later she says, 'A man brought me word that my sister Mall is come to towne which is the ferst word that ever I hard of any such design; itt seemes they keep theyr matters very privately . . . she is now at D^{rs}. Mis Ise [Mrs. Isham] spake to me that you would bestow forty shilling for toe monthes dancing for her, soe I promised her that, but elce I doe not meddle with them . . . she is much the plainest of them all . . . but reasonable straight

... she may make a very good wife, for they say ... she hath witt enough, but as wild as a buck.' Lady Verney took a severe view of their behaviour. On March 25, '47, she writes again: 'I tell you my opinion I think they are all toe Indescreete to gett a descreet Man ... they say Mall shall goe into the country to live wth her Sister Pegg soe soone as she getts her husband's consent, ... I feare if we goe about to cross her in liveing where she may & hath a mind to she will think we are bound to lett her live with us; for they sey she hath a great deale of witt & craft; she hath neavor been but twice wth me since she came to towne, neyther doe they evor ask my advise for any thing they make or doe concerning her; soe I take noe notice of any thing they doe; butt I find Mis Ice [Mrs. Isham] orders most of her matters ... truly she wants fashion much, but I feare where she is [with Cary Gardiner] she will rather learne rudeness, for they are all very wild.'

Ralph replies: 'I much wonder at Mall's coming upp, but more that she did it without your knowledge. that must not bee suffred, unlesse you meane she shall bee your Master, therfore I pray expresse your dislike therof, & mine too (if you thinke fit), for whilst she is at my allowance, I expect bee made acquainted with all such motions. informe mee at large of all that concernes her.'

In another letter Lady Verney gives more details of the arrangements proposed for the girl: 'Now for Mall going to live with her sister. . . . I find they desire thatt you should give her her allowance for her clothes a part & pay for her diett your selfe, & nott lett her doe itt for feare she should spend itt & leave her diett unpayed for; which hath been the greatest hindrance to make Pegg's husband stick att the receaving; for he is soe base thatt he was afrayde he should nott be sure to be payed for her diett . . . your frend M^r Br[owne] y^t lived att ye Duke's garden was wth me yesterday, soe I told him point blank thatt if he would marry I would help him to a wife; I told him the condition of the woeman & how she had been bredd in the country wch he was much pleased withall; I told him her portion was to be a thowsand pound, & how thatt untell that was raysed she had fifety pound a year allowed her . . . now he seemed to like all very well, butt he sayed he thought his owne fortune was to meane to desarve her, for whatt . . . he had untell his mother's deth he gave me to understand was butt fifeteen hundred pound. . . . I did nott name the woeman to him nor told him whatt relation she was to us; now I confess the man is very desarving, but his fortune is meane & whether she would accept of itt I know nott . . . if his fortune were liked off I could lett hime see her wth out letting him know she is your sister untell I knew whether he liked her or nott; though he told me he should nott like her ye worse for nott being very hansom.' May 27.—'Will Johnson (Roades) tells me . . . he hath ever payed 18 pound a yeare for Mall's diett, now truly twelve pound a yeare is very little for her clothes concydering how every body goes heare; yett I would nott give him order to give her any more untell I know your mind; for I find by one of your letters that you reckon she shall cost you but 30 pound a yeare in all . . . Mis. Jce [Mrs. Isham] sayes that there was an allowance payed for Mall's washing beside her diett & she had the helpe of a mayde beside, which noebody will lett her have for 18 pound a yeare.' June 24.—'Next week Mall goes downe toe wth my child . . . truly I thinke her sisters would be all three gladd to have her if thay were in a condition to take her, for they love her very well.' August 10.—' I hear Mall hath a great mind to ye guilte cabbenett that was your mother's . . . soe I entend to give itt her . . . truly I like her ye best of them all ; she is very playne, butt hath a great deale of witt & is nott att all proude butt very thrifty & willing to do any thing for any body.'

After this we hear that Mary has gone to be with Cary, and Ralph is to allow 30l. for her diet and 15l. for her clothes.

Poor Betty seems to have been generally disapproved of in the family, and probably not without reason. The first notice of her in the correspondence between Lady Verney and her husband is in April '47 : 'your sister betty writt me a letter . . . the effect of itt was that she should be content to stay at Claydon untell such time as we should think fitt to dispose of her somewheare elce that might be more to her advantage for to better her breeding.' April 15.—'. . . I hear betty expected I should have sent for her from Claydon as soon as I came over ; they say she is much ye worst natured & willfullest of them all. . . . they say she is a pestelent wench. . . . I have in one of my former letters advised you to lett her have twelve pound a yeare to find her, for she thinks much of wearing any thing but silk ; soe I doe nott see butt one gowne will cost more then halfe that money . . . I hear she makes her selfe sure to live with us ; butt I gave some of them to understand that she is like to be deceaved in those thoughts ; butt I doe nott find any body willing to take her, for they all say she is very ill natured.'

A little later Lady Verney again recommends that Betty should have a fixed allowance of 12*l*. a year for clothes, ' for all heare keepes theyr daughters in silk ; ye Drs Wife ye other day made nue silk gownes for every one of her daughters & I asure you betty doth not point of wearing any other, & Mis. Ice [Mrs. Isham] & all of them think itt fitt itt should be soe, & truly I cannott Imagion which way you can keep her in silk att that rate.' May 20.— ' Now whatt course to take with Betty I vow I cannott Imagion, for upon noe conditions in the world I will nott have her ; & where to place her I know nott, for she growes up apace & thinks her selfe a woeman allready. I think we had best advise with her frends whatt to doe with her & to place her where they shall thinke fitt, for where soevor we should place her if we make itt an act of our owne we shall be condemned in itt. . . . They say she is so cross & willfull y^t noebody that knowes her is willing to take her, I pray God make my chilldren good & enable us to provide for them, as well for theyr eldest Brother's sake as theyr owne. . . . Concerning Mrs. Francis [Alcock] her mariage . . . I writt her word y^t I did beleeve you would give her your consent for to remayne there still, . . . for itt will nott be fitt by noe meanes for Mall & Betty to live at her husband's howse, for he is butt an ordinary Grasiur & a mean condition man . . . Betty is of a cross proud lazy disposition . . . I heare she poyntes much of being wth me.' In another letter Lady Verney writes of a plan for Betty's living with Pegg. The latter had desired her sister-in-law to speak to Sir Thomas Elmes about the matter, 'which,' says Lady Verney, 'I did ; & told him that Betty desired itt, & that I had rather she should be wth his wife then any body elce, because she was grave and descreete & knew how to governe her better then others, & that he should be payed for her diett. . . . Soe when he found he should nott loose by her he told me she should be very wellcom . . . but I beleeve twenty five pound a yeare will be the least that they will take for her diett; & truly I doe nott see how you can give them less to find her in washing & firing & all.'

Betty, however, when taken away from Claydon and Nan Fudd, the nurse who had brought her up, turned desperately homesick. There is a long, quaint letter from Mall to Lady Verney at Misterton describing her behaviour, and in spite of the ill-temper she showed, one cannot help feeling some sympathy for the poor motherless girl. It is written from Green's Norton, the Elmes' place, where Cary and Mall were staying. Brother Edmund, too, had come over on a few days' visit from Misterton, and had evidently been causing much merriment and making himself much beloved by his younger sister.

'My Deare Sister, Just now my wicked brother Mun is com to us, but wee have all moust scrat out his very eyes out of his balle pate, so that hee must see by the holes, or not att all. Hee thretenes to give mee a Spanish fig, but if hee doth not please me beter then hee hath don sence hee cam hether, I will give him a Spanish pill and macke him giddy, so that hee shall never find the waie to Misterten to torment you any more; but I think as I shall not neede to macke him gidy, for that hee hath binne a grete whille, & I feare doth groe everry day more gider then other. For hee had not binn halfe a nower with us but he was a showing mee his faver as my Cousin gave him, & att that Instant he toock gidy & blushed to see as I laft att him. I am som thing fearefull of that parte, but I live in hoopes as it will never be accomplished. My sister bety cam hether last Monday, but is so

werey of beeing heare, as she had rather live att
Claydon all dayes of her life then to stay heare. Shee
cries & tackes on, & is so sad as you cannot Immagen,
& my sis Gardiner & my selfe . . . hath treyed all
the waies as posobell wee could to perswade her to
stay & trey tell shee comes from lundon againe, but
all we can doo will not worcke of her. So that my
sis gardiner desiered mee to right you wood of it, for
shee would goo to Claydon when I goo to lundon.
And truly I doo think as shee will all moust grive
her selfe to deth when wee are gon ; for I think as
my sister gardiner will goo be foare my sister Elmes.
But I can not excues my sister bety's faly att all, for
if I shuld all the world mite condem mee for it &
very Justly, for it showes a gret dell of Indiscreshon
in her to doo as shee doth. . . . Shee sayes as shee had
rather be wheare I am then with any of my sisters. I
confes as my sister Elmes whent to qwick a waie
to her att the furist, & that is not the waie as shee
must have youst, & so my sister gardiner & I told
her. They are both of a very hasty disposishons, &
so much as they will never a gree together, & my sis
bety is sory as shee did not consider of it bee foare
shee cam, but truly my sister & my brother hath
binn very cind to her, but all will not perswade her
to stay heare, & my brother would have his wife to
send her hom on Mundy nex, but I am confident as
shee will repent of her foly when shee groes beger.
But shee sayes as shee had rather live att Claydon
then heare, or att my auntt D^{rs}., for shee hats that

as bad as this. . . . My brother S^r edmund had all moust tore my letter, & I told him as hee would sarved your letter as hee would doo you if it lay in his power. Wee doo wish him with you, or with his Mis againe, for heare is no liveing with him hee is so rud. Now hee sayes as you sayed as wee shuld be a wery of him beefoare night, & truly I am & so wee are all. I bee scheech you parden mee for trobelling you with my longe episells, but I would not abinn so teges [tedious] but that occashon of my sister betys made mee, but I shuld be am bishous of the licke faver as this leter will receve, which is to kis your hand, & to re maine your moust Afecshoned sis & sarvantt to the utmoust of her power Mary V. . . . My sister bety presents her sarves to you & is very sory if shee hath ofended you in this & yearnestly desiers your pardon for it, & begs of you to let her goo to Claydon againe to live.'

Matters seem to have come to a crisis, for a day or two later Lady Elmes writes herself to Lady Verney that Betty had gone the day before. 'I confes the suddennes of hur being wery of my company seemes sumthing strainge to me consedowring with what kindness I yoused hur. . . . She was soe violent to be gon as that she wresolved to goe home a foote wrathor then to stay heare. For my part I thenck hur past being soe very a baby as to doe this owght of chilldishnes, which made me to take it ill from hur. And a nother thing is that she sayes as I am passhionat & soe is she, which makes hur to thencke as we to showlde nevor a gre to gethor, but this I can saifely sweare, Let my pashon be nevor soe great I nevor shoed any att all to hur . . . Pray send munsy back againe quickly to me.'

It was annoying for Lady Verney to receive these letters, just when she thought Betty was safely disposed of, and in writing to her husband she expressed her disapprobation of the girl very freely. 'I must tell you in how great Choller I am with your sister Betty . . . I spake with her before I did any thing in itt, & she told me thatt she should think her selfe very hapy to goe to live with Pegg. . . . If I pass by Claydon I shall lett her know a peece of my mind.'

It is suspected that Nan Fudd is at the bottom of this misbehaviour, hoping by getting back her former charge to become indispensable.

A little later Lady Verney describes an interview she had with the culprit on her way to town. 'She was nott at all sencible of any thing I could say to her, & yett I told her I did nott know any body that would now take her . . . I as I was advised sayed all this & much more to trye her, butt she was nott att all moved att itt, butt was as soone as she was out of the roome as merry as evor she was in her life.'

Ralph replies: 'For Betty, since she is soe straingly in love with her owne Will, let her rest with Mrs. Francis, where she may have leasure enough to repent her Folly. . . . I pray god she proove not a sister Tom, beeleeve mee shee is too like him.'

In the following spring Betty was again taken in hand. Lady Verney had by this time returned to France, and her eldest brother writes from Blois: 'If itt bee thought for Bettie's advantage to bee sent to a scole, though itt be deare I am content to be putt to that charge. Itt seemes the mistress demands £25 a yeare for Diett teaching & all other things.' He then requests that Betty may be fitted out with clothes and placed at the school. 'I pray advise her & charme her too concerning her cariage there.'

Poor Betty seems not to have approved of this change of abode any more than she had liked the former attempt to improve upon her way of living. Her uncle writes: 'She is a strange perverse girle & soe averse from goinge thither that she doth not sticke to threaten her owne death by her owne hands, though my girles (who have beene there) give all the commendation that can be . . . of that schoole.' A few days later: 'On Friday last with many teares & much regrett Betty went to schoole, but I droled it out & there I left her.' Ralph addresses a serious letter of remonstrance to the girl, and is anxious to know whether Betty will be taught religion at school; but another letter from Dr. Denton says his wife has been to see her, and 'Betty is Betty still.'

After this it is really a comfort to hear in the autumn of a complete reformation. In October her uncle goes to see her, and writes : 'It was a visitt well bestowed, for in my life time I ne'er saw soe great a change in countenance, fashion, humor & disposition (& all for the better) in any body, neyther could I imagine it possible it could have beene wrought soe soone. She now seems to be as contented, as ere before she seemed discontented, (and in earnest it was the most bedlam bare that ere I hampered), and if wife can judge . . . she keeps her cloaths as well & as cleanly as can be.' In December '49 there is a 'glass combe case' sent to Sir Ralph in a parcel from home 'wrought by Betty Verney,' by which he is to see 'shee hath not altogether lost her time.' To improve thus decidedly the girl must have had good stuff in her, and when we find from the old note book that Elizabeth Verney married Charles Adams, a minister in Essex, there seems ground for hoping that on the whole she made a good clergyman's wife.

One is glad to hear that Mr. Alport did at length succeed in getting out of the Fleet, and that in June '48 he was able to take his wife to his own house. She writes to Ralph : 'My long expected happynes to see home is com att last, I have binne in Cheshire this ten days, where I find a pittifull reuened house for want of liveing in, not only so butt plundred besids. I found nothing in it but bare walls. I must bee contented with them till Sir Hugh Calabey's debts are payed, & happy shall I bee yf my husband may continew heere. Itt is but a leetle house, butt very pleasant. I cañott brag y^t I am lickly to tarry heer, I feere this happynes will nott last long, for ther is an execution out against my hus for my lord of Loughborough, & Sir Hugh together. . . . Pray give my treu love & sarvice to my sister, whom I had writen to, butt I have had to much company ever senc I cam downe y^t I have nott time to settle my selfe. I am a sorry housekeeper, I have nothing aboutt mee, nott so much as a cow, nor dare nott meddle with any yett, butt am forced to keepe a tenaunt in my house & by all of him.' Overton Manor, the 'leetle house butt very pleasant,' still exists, though sadly modernised. In Susan's time it was a half-timbered, gabled house, projecting in the upper storey (such as are still seen in Chester), with a pointed stone arch over the moat. Built in a sequestered, sheltered nook, it is thus described by a correspondent who has just visited it in March 1892: 'Overton Manor is about a mile from Malpas Church, down hill the whole way. There is a well-defined, narrow moat, not more than four or five feet wide, which inclosed about an acre of ground, an imposing row of new pig-styes between the moat and the house, and a very modern front door; but at the back, completely hemmed in with new buildings, are two rather pretty gable-ends of the old house.'

It is a pleasure after so many worrying applications from Susan to Ralph for money, to find a little note in his handwriting dated March 10, 1650: 'I writ sist. Alport thanks for offring mee her £600, but

I would not accept it, least in these ill times I should not bee able to pay her constantly.'

She did not long enjoy her home, poor thing. In Feb. '51 she died, as the old note book says 'of her 3ᵈ child'; 'they were all still born.'

Her husband writes of her loss : 'You hoped to have heard of my poor geirle's safe deliverance, butt with a really afflicted soule I am enforced to returne you the most truly sadd account, . . . for itt hath pleased Almighty god in his Judgment (for my great sins) to lay the greatest & most heavy affliction uppon mee, that ever was on-any man.' He then goes on to tell of her being taken ill, mentioning 'the gentlewomen with her, mongst which was Mrs. Poole, a sister to my Lrd of Shrosberry, and Mrs. Dutton, Sir Jo: Reinold's daughter, whom I presume you know. . . . Shee sayd aloud—Now I thank God I am delivered—calling mee to kisse her; the child had life in it & stirred an hower after it was borne. . . . shee to all our apprehensions was safe layd in bed; but within a quarter of an hour shee faynted, & . . . could nott bee revived butt a very little space, & faynt again which she continued about three houres, & then itt pleased god shee dyed, which was about twelve A' clocke on Saturday night 1st Feb. . . . which was the fatalls houer that ever befell mee. . . . God sanctify my sorrowes to mee. . . . Itt was no little addiċon to my trobles to finde that shee could nott bee kept so long unburied untill I might have provided all things fitting for funerall. Shee was buried on Munday about 3 aclock in Malpas church, in my owne vault wher I intend (god willing) & hope shortly to ly myselfe, accompanied with all the gentry in this cuntry thither; wher preached Mr. Holland,[1] a most reverend divine, one who hath bin much conversant with her ever since shee came hither, & administred the sacra^t to us not 10 days before; & truly hee did her all right in her commendacon, which was justly very high & I beleeve almost above any of her sex. I am yett a willing prisoner to my greefe in my disconsolate & now altogether comfortlesse chamber.' The beautiful old church of Malpas, on the top of the steep hill up which the sad funeral procession toiled, is one of the most interesting churches in Cheshire. Here Richard Alport's father was buried in 1624, and his own name and that of several of his children are to be found in the parish register. The record of Susan's burial is lost; during the Civil War the entries are imperfect, and some were copied afterwards from loose sheets into the book. Susan must have had an affectionate disposition, and as one reads her husband's description of his bereavement one hopes that she was not an unworthy daughter of her noble father.

[1] The Hon. and Rev. Trevor Kenyon, Rector of Malpas, who has kindly looked up the history of his predecessor, a strong Royalist, writes: 'A sermon of the Rev. William Holland's is extant reprobating the heresies, schisms, and personated holiness of the ruling party in the plenitude of their power. Mr. Holland married Cecily Walthaw, of Wistanson; he left 100*l.* to the poor of Malpas, which, I fear, is no longer extant.'

Penelope's history was very different. Her husband, John Denton, died in 1663; and though they had had three children, none of them lived to grow up. She married secondly a 'Sir John Osborn of Devonshire,' by whom she had no children. She lived till the year before Sir Ralph's death, when she died in Whitehall at the age of seventy-three, and was buried at Claydon.

Poor Margaret's lot does not seem to have grown happier as time went on. 'Peg's husband hath a trick to stop her letters at the post house,' writes Sue, much aggrieved, when recounting her sister's domestic worries. But her fair-minded brother cannot allow that the fault lies entirely with the husband.

Sir Ralph writes in August '48 : 'Elmes complaines that Pegg & her friendes curse him & threaten him, & how his owne Brother was faine to lie at his Baylie's house, & that Pegg's friends put him to Extraordinary charges with Horses etc.; this Pegg ought not to doe nor suffer ; she should rather court his friends if she desire to regaine his hart.' The discomforts of this unhappy *ménage* increased until a formal separation was talked of, and a letter from Sir Ralph to Edmund, who was trying to act as a mediator, is curious as giving a picture of the proprieties of the time for a woman in so difficult a position. Sir Thomas Elmes will give her but a very small allowance. 'I wish with all my hart,' writes Sir Ralph, 'that they were well reconcyled againe, butt I doubt that cannot be donn suddenly, I pray wright to Pegg efectually aboute it & desire her to advise with the D^r [Denton] in what place she had best live, & above all charge her not to exceed in clothes, espetially in bright coulors [she was only five-and-twenty], nor to keep much company, for itt is nott fitt for a person in her condition eyther to flant it in clothes or appeare often in publique as at playhouses and tavernes, though itt be with her owne & nearest frends. a retired country life were much better for her, butt in this time of warr, I doe nott conceave her owne house the fittest place for her, because she will be liable both to quartering soldiery, & a thousand rude actions which too many of your profession doe falcly call gallantry. If she doe leave her house, I hope he will give her good furniture for her chamber & a bedd for her maide, with some linnen for her bed & bord. . . . I am confident he is soe much a gentleman that he will not refuse her these nessesaries, & more then meere nessesaries I hope she will not desire of him.' Another time, when Dr. Denton has them in his house to try and make peace, he says that their language is not to be matched in Billingsgate.

When in recent years the vault underneath the chancel was opened in which the Verneys were buried, a sort of mummy-shaped coffin was seen standing upright. The name on it was Margaret Elmes, and the carpenter on seeing it observed that he now understood the tradition he had heard as a child, that there was one of the Verneys buried there upright, because she had said 'she had been upright in her life and would be the same in death.' It was a curious means that the poor woman took to vindicate her reputation.

Mary was not 'mached' till 1655, when she married Mr. Robert Lloyd of Cheshire. Her son, Captain Verney Lloyd, has left many descendants. When Mary died in 1684, a tablet was put up to her memory in Chester Cathedral, in one of the barbarous inroads to which the cathedral has been exposed, the tablet was torn down and lost, but the present Sir Harry Verney has put up a new one to replace it, the inscription having fortunately been preserved in an old guidebook.

And so we leave the five sisters, who in their early years were a source of so much trouble and perplexity to their brother. Certainly we cannot feel them to have been worthy of their excellent parents, but considering the disadvantages of their youth it may be said that they did as well as can be expected of frail human nature.

CHAPTER XV.

THE END OF MANY THINGS AND PEOPLE.

> Days, that in spite
> Of darkness, by the light
> Of a clear mind, are day all night.
>
> Life, that dares send
> A challenge to his end,
> And when it comes say, Welcome, friend !
> CRASHAW.

THE meeting between Ralph and his wife on her return to France in April 1648 must have been in some ways a sad one. The mother's grief for the loss of her little girl would spring afresh at the sight of the empty nest where she had left the bright face of her beloved Peg ; and the baby boy for whose safety and welfare she had undergone so much, was dead also.

They stayed for several weeks at Paris on their way south, partly no doubt in order to meet Edmund, who was soon to embark on his last journey to Ireland with Lord Ormonde, and perhaps because of a natural shrinking on Mary's part from coming back to Blois. A few weeks after their return thither she writes of being weary of the place. Ralph went by himself to Tours to seek fresh quarters, but could find nothing suitable, and they had to resign themselves to remaining at Blois. The dulness and stagnation of a French country town where, as Ralph declares, 'no newes is ever heard' and 'nothing ever comes to pass in this woful place,' must have told heavily on one fresh from the interesting society of London—seeing and hearing some of the best men and women of that most stirring time—society in which she herself was so well fitted to join and indeed to shine. When one reads how her uncle-doctor brought 'parliament-men' and lawyers to her little lodging, it is clear how he reckoned on the power of her charm and capacity for business to influence and persuade them. Now she had nothing to do but to look after her little household and her two boys, who were most of the day with their tutor, the French *pasteur*, and to cheer the tedious life of her husband. The English exiles come and go; the young Earl of Strafford is in France, Sir John Osborne (afterwards Duke of Leeds), Mr. Pierrepoint, Mr. Ogilvy; none will stay at Blois who can help it. Mrs. Sherard writes to her: 'I find by the Dr that you are verey mallincaley since you went over last. I pray have a care as you imbrace not that hewmor, for it is both trobulsom & dangerus.' Sir Ralph has countless letters still to write about the never ending complexities of his money matters; Dr. Denton is, as ever, his trusted adviser, though he sometimes declines to take the responsibility of decisions from off his friend's shoulders: 'I will not teach my grandam to shoe goslings; you can send Pen (or any body else) an answer that shall signifie nothinge, when you have a mind to it, as well as ever a D^r. in Angleterre!'

The letters that passed between Ralph and other English exiles are chiefly of a sad complexion: the news from home and the difficulties of maintaining themselves being their principal themes. But in contrast to these is one writer of a most lively turn of mind—Sir Henry Puckering Newton—who sports like a butterfly on the troubled surface of society, apparently as little depressed by the course of events in England as if he were on a pleasure-tour. He takes very lightly the dangers of travelling in France, judging by the following letter written to Ralph from Orleans. He promises a fuller account of himself 'when I come swiming doune againe to Blois as wise as I came hither.' There is no company at present to travel with, and he dares not venture alone with 'the messenger. . . . I have taken time to consider till teusday which way to bee *dépouillé* with most contentement, and then Blois, Paris or Rouen, Devill do thy worst.' France was by no means an abode of peace, and even from dull little Blois Ralph writes: 'If these Troubles should force me to leave this Toune . . . at present I know not whither to goe to a better, yet the changes of Warre being various, peradventure I may be compelled to some sudden remove.'

The progress of public events at home was most disquieting. In July 1648 the Scotch army entered England; on the 29th one of the Verney letters describes the dissensions between the Lords and

Commons: 'The Commons have voted the scotts Enemyes to England; the lords refuse to concurre with them. . . . The citty seeme to adhere to the upper house. It is expected that every day now should produce strange and notable effects. The citty are weary of Skippon, and desire an ordinance for Massey or Browne for theire Major generall.'[1] Aug. 11.—' It's certaine the citty and house of commons are at much distance, and the citty are now listing horse without theire order.'

On August 17 came the defeat of the Scotch—a terrible blow for the Royalists and for the Presbyterians. The latter, however, had so far regained the upper hand that negotiations were renewed with the king, and a correspondent of Ralph's wrote: 'It is thought that this treaty will conclude a peace, the King being not unresonable but inclinable to condesend to all.' But the conferences dragged on for two months without any definite result, till on November 29 Charles was seized by order of the army council, without whose consent negotiations with him were henceforward impossible. In a few days Parliament itself had fallen under control of the troops. Dr. Denton writes on November 23 : ' Here is at present a strange consternation of spiritts amongst all people, for the Army hath interposed about the treatie, and the generall

---

[1] One is reminded of the Cavalier song in *Rokeby*, which has the true ring of the old Royalist feeling :

Will you match the base Skippon and Massey and Browne
With the barons of England that fight for the crown ?

expectation is for worse and more sad times then ever.' December 7.—' Drake is att this present in the hands of the Army with many other members, some say 50, others more, others lesse, which was seised uppon yesterday goinge to the house. What the issue will be God knowes. . . . It is an ill time now to treat about land ; . . . noe man will touch uppon that stringe, for the Army is att the Parliament doores, and secure all the members they can light on that they suppose will vote contrary to their remonstrance, particularly they have seized of your acquaintance Drake, Wenman, Ruddier, Nat ffines, Prinne, Sir G. Gerard, and I know not how many besides.' After some details about business the Doctor continues his account mingled with a little sarcasm : ' The Army doe not to-day as yesterday catch and imprison the members . . . but now they only stand att the doore with 2 roules, and if their names be in such a roule then they may enter, if in the other then they may not. Soe that none enter now but our frends, and you shall see we will doe righteous things at last. Most of the secured members lay in Hell last night, and are now gone to the generall. There is scarce enough left free to make a house.'

The army, under the influence mainly of Cromwell, now took the helm. That great general may have been a truly disinterested, high-minded man, but there can be no doubt that when the reign of the law is over, when a country is only to be governed by the sword, we have reached a lower level, and moreover one which must be provisional and transitory.

The party in power was bitterly hostile to the king. On January 2, '49, the Commons passed an ordinance instituting a High Court of Justice by whom he was to be tried. The Upper House, or what remained of it, made a futile attempt at resistance. Dr. Denton wrote: 'I heare the L^{ds} on Tuesday last voted all null since ye army siezed ye members ... It is not to be told ye confusion we are in, ye L^{ds} have adjourned for a weeke; the Commons now declare the legislative power to be in them only. I pray God send peace on earth & write all o^r names in ye booke of life. Deare Raph I am thine in peace or war.' Jan. 11.—'A[lexander] D[enton]'s creditors ... see there is nothinge but land to be had, & they will rather venture all then take it, soe troublesome & cumbersome a thinge is land growne now, it is soe liable to quarter & taxes, & makes one's estate soe visible & consequently the persons more liable to sequestration, for it is almost a crime to have an estate in these days. ... I doubt before this come to you our Kinge will be defunct, and it is feared the sword will govern instead of the crowne.' Jan. 18.—'The complexion of our confusions growes every day more sad & black then other. Y^e scaffolds are buildinge for the tryall of the Kinge, & ye terme putt of for 20 daies for that very reason. It is almost every man's opinion that nothing will satisfie but his head, & I am clearly of ye same opinion except God miraculously divert or divide, or confound councells. Our divines preach generally against these proceedings & not without great vehemence, & some of them begin to writt against them alsoe. Our cavalier L^{ds} have offered to ingage life & fortune for ye King's performance of whatever he shall grant of their demands. The Scotch have mediated & declared absolutely against it, yett nothinge will doe, they are resolved of their course for ought I can find.'

Even Sir Roger Burgoyne, strong parliamentary enthusiast as he was, writes: ' I could be content to be a monke or hermit, rather than a statesman at the present conjunction of affairs. . . . What will become of us in England God only knowes. The passages of late presage the saddest of times.'

On the 25th Dr. Denton writes again : '. . . It is now the dismallest time here that ever our eyes beheld. Noe mediation by Ministry, Scottland, Cavaliers, L^{ds}, or of any body else for ought I can heare, can disswade from doinge execucon uppon ye kinge. I heare the Queene of Bohemia is cominge over if not landed, her son's mediation hath not yett prevailed any thinge, & I doubt hers will prevaile as little. Y^e confusions & distractions are every where soe greate that I know not where to wish my selfe but in Heaven. It is generally beleeved that the Scotts will once again more unanimously come in againe, but if they doe it is thought there will be a risinge or combustion in every country of ye kingdome at once, soe generally are people's hearts agst these proceedings.'

The execution of the king took place on January the 30th. Ralph received an account of it from Mr Cockram, an English merchant at Rouen. 'I doubt not but ear this you have heard the dolefull news of our King's death, whoe was beheaded laste teusday was seaven night, at two of the clock, afternoone, before Whitehall, the moste barbarous Ackt, & lamentable sight that ever any Christians did beholde. The Numerous guarde of horse and foote of Armed Tygers did binde the hands and stopp the mouths of many Thousand beholders, but could not keepe their eyes from weeping, for none but harts of flinte could forbeare. His maies^tie appeared uppon the scaffold with admirable constancie noe way dismayed, did make a very worthy speach shewing his Innocency of what hee was accused & condemned for; & yett with greate charitie did freely forgive all his enemies in rehearsing the example of St John. And to satisfy the people concerninge his Religion hee theare declared that hee dyed a trew Christian according to the open profession of the Church of England, as it was lefte by the deceased king his father: And soe with sundry expressions of piety & godly exhortations hee submitted to that wofull ende, which makes all honest menn's harts to bleede; And is a beginning of England's greater Miserie than ever hath bin hitherto.'

Westminster School was at this time strongly Royalist, and amongst the boys conspicuous for their devotion to the king were the Uvedales, great nephews of Sir Edmund Verney's old friend,[1] Sir William Uvedale. Unable to find vent for their loyalty the boys held a meeting for prayer on the morning of Charles's execution; one wishes that the king could have known the touching way in which their sympathy was shown him. On that terrible day all work must have been suspended, before its close the king was beyond the need of earthly comfort; but Robert Uvedale's devotion to his memory was to be shown in a striking way before his school-days were over. A dignitary of the church who was a Westminster boy when this century was in its teens, recalls an instance of a very different spirit. The boys were made to attend the service in the Abbey, on January 30, to commemorate ' "the Martyrdom of the Blessed King Charles the First," given up (as upon this day) to the violent outrages of wicked men, to be despitefully used & at the last murdered by them,' and while in the words of the Prayer-book they were further exhorted to 're-flect upon so foul an act with horror & astonishment,' the boy next to him, Trelawney, whose ancestors had stoutly resisted the king in life, was muttering between his teeth—' Bloody tyrant,' in a suppressed passion of indignation. But to return to 1649. Among the Duke of Portland's MSS. is a rough draft of the report to the House of Commons of the Committee that made the arrangements for the king's burial, read on February 8, the very day of the funeral. It seemed as if the revulsion of public

---

[1] See vol. i., pp. 102, 313.

feeling already made it expedient to show more outward respect to the dead king than had been granted to him during the last days of his life, and the additions and corrections made to the original draft point in the same direction. The king's body is to be removed to Windsor ' on a Coach, covered with black, with six horses and two troops of horse for a guarde, & that the servants of the ffamyly last allowed to goe thither with it, keep there untill it bee buryed. That the servants attending him since hee came to Windsor bee allowed mourninge; for the furnishing of themselves wherewith ten pounds a peece to bee allowed them that were in office in cheife, & the Coachman & the postilion £5. That Mr. Harberte, Mildmay, Preston & Duckett have mony payd into theyre hands upon acc^t to bee issued out for the charges of the buryall and mayntayninge of the servants with diett the meane while & for theire horses. That the summe to bee payd into their hands for the present bee 400$^£$, out of which the 20$^£$ a peece for mourninge, and the 5$^£$ a day for mayntenance of the ffamily to bee payd, as allsoe the past charges for embalminge & unloadinge the bodye, & the blacks bought for the scaffold & coffin to bee payde for, and the future charges of furnishing out the Coach & providing torches for the removeall & Buryall bee defrayed as farre as it will goe.

'That the Coach bee covered with black bayes [baize] against munday night if it may bee.

THE END OF MANY THINGS AND PEOPLE   401

'That it bee enquyred where his Coach horses are kept, & order taken to have them in readynesse & the Coachman in mowrninge.

'That the Number to bee allowed with the D. of Richmond exceed not 20, with 3 servants to each nobleman & not above two to others, & desired to give in a list of theyre names & servants on Wednesday morninge next, & to have notice now that the buryall will not bee before fryday next, & the just time, as allsoe the place hee shall know on Wednesday morninge.

'The Resolutions to bee reported to the house on Wednesday morning.'[1]

There are no letters from Sir Roger or Dr. Denton till February 21, when their silence is thus accounted for by the former: 'The newes .... of most publique concernement I am confident is longe since come to yor eares; as the kinge beinge executed by Whitehall yeisterday being 3 weekes since, I had not failed to have given you notice of it the same weeke, but that the D^r would not suffer me to send the letter I had written, there being a generall stoppage of all letters.'

The next day Dr Denton writes: 'We are now in the maddest world that ever we mortalls sawe, and have great reason to feare we doe but now begin to drinke the dreggs of our bitter cupp. But God hath taught us that if we see violent pervertinge of judg-

[1] Nalson Collection of MSS., vol. xv. folio 311.

ment in a citty we should not wonder, and though we heare of wars and rumors of war yett wee should not wonder.'

When it was 'voted a capitall crime for any to speake, preach, or write against the present proceedings,' it would seem as if the Despotism was as fierce as anything recorded in English history.

The king's behaviour when called on to face death had won the respect and sympathy of many.

> He nothing common did, or mean,
> Upon that memorable scene.

Mr. Green says his death 'gave fresh vigour to the royalist cause; and the loyalty which it revived was stirred to enthusiasm by the publication of the "Eikon Basilike" .... which was believed to have been composed by the King himself in his later hours of captivity.' Dr Denton writes: 'If I am not disappointed you shall have the king's booke. It hath beene hitherto at 8s. and 10s. price. ... It hath beene much suppressed, the first printer and impression plundered and presses broken.' Again, March 18: 'The king's booke, with his deportment, indurance, att his tryall and on the scaffold, hath amazed the whole kingdome, to see soe much courage, Xstianity, and meekness in one man. The women generally are in mourninge for him, ye men dare not, only some few.' If this was the case with the population in London, the necessities of the widowed queen described in the following extract must have been great indeed. It is from a letter of Sir H. Puckering

Newton's, written from Paris on April 4: 'I find a Court heere sadd & hugely discomposed, but as much for want of money as for anything else; their poverty must needes bee very much, when to this houre the Qu: & D. of Yorke's footmen & many others are not in mourning. I have kiss'd all their hands, & passed a whole day betweene dukes & civilitees.'

The recent proceedings of the English were not likely to bring them into estimation on the continent. John Foss, a merchant at Nantes, puts into a postscript to Ralph: 'Pray, Sir, writt not in the superscription *anglois*, ffor thatt nation is soe much in hatred, thatt he cannott pass the streets in sauftye.' Dr. Kirton writes from Paris: 'The army and Parliament have sett out a manifest to lett the world know why they have kill'd their king and made themselves a Republicke. It is two sheetes of paper, and to be turned by their order into Latin, French, and Duch. I know not what it may prove in other Tongues, but they whoe reade it in English find it poore stuffe.' Monarchy had in fact been abolished on March 17, but perhaps the party which had compassed the death of the king felt some difficulty in deciding on the next step, for it was not till May 19 that an Act of Parliament was passed declaring 'that the People of England. . . . are hereby constituted, made, established, & confirmed to be a Commonwealth and Free State, & shall henceforth be governed as a Commonwealth & Free State by the supreme authority of this nation. . . . and that without any King or House of Lords.'

The bad news of public affairs in England must have weighed all the more heavily on Ralph, as his wife's health caused him growing anxiety. Some months after her return to France she fell dangerously ill of what Ralph calls 'a kind of apoplexiy or Lethargy,' in which she lost her sight for a time. She recovered from this illness but was in delicate health, and the doctor advised her drinking the waters at Bourbon. In June '49 they spent some weeks there, and had expected to have the company of the sprightly Sir Puckering Newton, who wrote to Ralph that he was anxious to 'returne time enough to tipple with my lady at Bourbon, against when I have resolved for so much water that I promise you to deale in none till then, not thinking it an element to bee us'd that way except phiscially.' In a later letter he adds : 'I am growne very weary of good veale and wine ; my mind runnes much on water, therefore beleeve me, S^r, I sitt in thornes untill I can bee a man of my word both unto you and my lady.' In spite of these protestations, however, he never came, and in his next letter it appears that he had flown over to England.

On August 1 Dr. Denton expresses his satisfaction that Mary is better, and hopes that she need return no more to Bourbon : ' it's possible to have a surfeit of water as well as wine. Sir Richard Winn hath mett with it, not to the life but to the death. . . .'

He 'cannot gett a booke for Landladie's pallett'; the works on controversial divinity that the doctor so zealously recommended may well have been heavy reading after the baths of Bourbon in July. They went to Paris for a time, and then Sir Ralph was anxious to take his wife to the South. 'Shee should order you better,' wrote Dr. Denton, 'then to lett you ramble like Tom a Bedlam ten leagues beyond the wide world's end.'

Avignon, he heard, was visited by 'les trois fléaux de Dieu'—famine, pestilence, and the sword— and the plague was also at Nismes, but he hoped to get to Montpellier. Sir Puckering laughs at him for his roving spirit; he says he has received his last letter, 'but where he is that sent it the Lord knowes; pray God hee bee in an honest place, since he dares not oune it. . . . I perceive you do wander and rove up and doune, one knowes not where to have you. You would faine lay the cause upon my good ladie's water drinking, but 'tis your owne good will to the frontinaick which your Godfather K. James infused into you & you are wild after, makes you run such madd journeys as Montpellier. . . . Pray God you return to Blois when they heare of your tippling they doe not shutt the gates against you—you know they are ticklish men of the guard—but I hope by my sober carriage & example there . . . to work so on you & the people, that you may be both reclamed & admitted again. But (without fooling) I am seriously sorry you goe so farr off, . . . my purse is too light & my cloak bag too heavy to follow you.'

He will have no heart to come to Blois if they are both gone. Mary had been shopping in Paris for Mrs. Sherard, & Ralph writes to her that 'my wife . . . hath ventured to present you with a paire of French trimed gloves, a Fan, a paire of Tweezes & an enamiled Box with patches; I blush at her boldnesse but more at my own Folly, for suffering of her, but you know she weares the Breeches & will doe what she list.'

The correspondence about the sisters' fortunes in the Alnage and about their creditors still continues, and in addition to these anxieties Brother Tom is behaving even worse than usual. In the summer of '48 he turned up in Paris in a state of destitution, having, as he said, been 'taken prisoner as a spye for the Spaniard.' Ralph sent him money, but of course he begged for more: 'only this lett mee tell you, I carry all that I have on my back; I have noe linnen at all to shift mee and noe stockins to weare, nor sword nor cloak. . . . Though I have willfully run into this folly yet I would intreat you not to suffer mee to be lousy; which in earnest I must unless I am timely relieved by you.' To this Ralph replies that until he leaves 'these courses' he cannot expect his condition will improve, but he arranges to give him 3*l*. on his return to England over and above the Michaelmas quarterage, which of course he has anticipated.

THE END OF MANY THINGS AND PEOPLE 407

Tom, however, chooses to remain in France, and the next that was heard of him was his forging Brother Elmes's name to a bill (as mentioned in a former chapter). He is in hiding and in terror of his life, and writes to beg for more money from Ralph to discharge his debt for lodgings, which would free him to escape to England. He complains bitterly of Elmes : 'It is malitiously & most unnaturally done of him to prosecute mee to death : . . . in England it is only a pillory matter. I shall petition the queen of England to take my brother off, if I can but get anyone to draw a petition for mee, for in earnest I have not now the understanding of a child, my afflictions have soe besotted mee ; formerly I never had much, but what capacity I ever had is now quite lost.'

In a later letter he says that his informers mistook Elmes (who seems to have treated him with forbearance) ; 'it is the banquier [who payed the money on the forged bill] that seeks after mee . . . vowes to have his money or my life.' He dares not return by way of Rye : 'I am soe well knowe att Diap and att Calais that when I am out of paris I must make chois of a port where I never yet was for my passage home. . . . I have run into a great error. It is too late to recall what I have done, but it is not too late to repent. . . . My dayly study now is to serve God, and to avoid the banquier apprehending mee.' Ralph clears him of debt and renews his promise of 3*l*. when he should reach England. But in spite of protestations that he would depart instantly, the scapegrace stayed on, accumulating fresh debts, till finally, as he describes to a friend, he is 'forced to lye in bed, being destitute of bootes and stockings.' When at length he returned to England his conduct was not more satisfactory, and Ralph wrote that 'he follows his old tricks still.' For a time he appeared 'clinquant & in wonderful equipage both for cloathes and money,' but it was only due to what he 'threatened' out of his aunt Ursula (and probably from unworthy gains as a spy), & then came the usual *da capo*—prison and pious, penitent letters, of which on this occasion Dr. Denton writes : ' to see now his letters you would thinke him a St. or a preacher at least. He goes far that never turnes. God can doe much. Paul persecuted till he could noe longer kick against the pricks.'

But no miracle of reformation was to change Tom's wretched career. In July the Doctor is unhappy and anxious when their letters miscarry, ' especially seeinge Tom is growne the arrantest informer. . . . Direct future letters to Mr. Gape [the worthy apothecary at whose wedding feast Mary had lately assisted], at the Man in the Moon, King St. Westminster.'

Henry was also the cause of much distress to Ralph, but owing to the breach between them, there are no letters from him during this period to show what he was doing. Dr. Denton, writing of the dangerous state of the country in July '48, says :

THE END OF MANY THINGS AND PEOPLE 409

'Harry, as he was only walkinge in the grounds had a pistoll pointed to his breast, & if he had not by chance known y⁰ captaine that did it & soe space [? spake] right, noe excuse had served his turne but to the pott he had gone, & I doubt it will be his end, for I feare he hath to much blood uppon him.' A few months later he says: 'Harry lives like y⁰ wanderinge jew, but mostly I believe at the widdowe's.' Occasionally he is mentioned as visiting his sisters. In May '49 Dr. Denton writes: 'Harry hath gold in both pocketts, & gave Betty 10s.'; and on another occasion when he was much pleased with her he is 'very fierce to give her a goune,' if his uncle would furnish her with a guitar. But the conclusion of the matter was not very satisfactory, as he ended with 'tryeing to get the money for the gown out of Roads!' And Dr. Denton says that he must 'leave Harry & Will to tugge for the payment.'

This is the last we hear of him for a long time. On September 7 Dr. Denton writes from Oxford: 'Two daies since the souldiers of this garrison discarded their officers & are all turned levellers, & it is thought most of the regiments of the army are of the same mould. . . .' Sir Roger writes on the 13th: 'The Levellers have begun to play some more prankes about Oxford, but it is hoped that they will suddenly be quasht, although some much doubt it; it is pitty that souldiers formerly so unanimous in the cause of God, should now begin to clash one with another, but it is verily thought that there are some knaves amongst them which I hope God will one day discover. They talke much of the Kinge of Scotlande having the better upon the seas, & that Ormonde hath beaten Ld. gen. Crumwell since his coming over, the rather because he hath sent over for fresh supplies . . . but I presume you are too discreet to bestow your beliefe upon any fabulous report.' However incredulous about political news, Sir Roger seems to have no doubt about another story he sends to his friend : 'Great store of crown crabs were taken in Cornwall among their pilchards,' four of them were sent from Plymouth to London ; they were 'as bigg as halfe crownes, have shells like crabbs, feet like ducks, faces like men, & crownes on their heads. theire faces & crownes seem as if they were carved upon their shells.'

Mary was getting gradually worse, but many merry messages still pass between her and the good Doctor, sent and received by Ralph. 'You must needs send landlady over in wonderfull post hast to me, for I hear her old prosecutors the Hydes are makinge enquiry after me, & except she come to out scold them, I must goe to Billingsgate and I doubt I shall not match them nor her there. I thinke I mumpt her there!' The Doctor has at last succeeded in letting their London house for 65*l*. 'for this next yeare to the Countesse of Downe.' He has been so busy about their affairs that he has quite neglected his own. 'My absence hath so routed my business that

I am like a crowe in a mist, or rather like an owl at noon.' He attacks Mary again, who had sent him some commissions to do for her. Oct. 15, '49.—' She is a lyinge slutt . . . for I doe not or will not remember that ever she writt to me for nuttmeggs; how ever, tell her she shall neyther have nuttmeggs nor stockins, nor meat neither by my good will, nor money which is worse, nor anythinge but druggs till she write her longe—longe—longe promised letter.'

Sir Puckering Newton, meaning to bring his wife to Blois, writes to ask what Lady Verney would advise, as an 'old housekeeper in France,' for the ordering of their affairs, and 'what stuffe or what cattle' to bring out. Ralph replies that his wife is very angry at being called old housekeeper, 'had you called her old woeman she would never have forgiven you such an injurie. You know a woeman can never bee old (at least not willingly, nor in her owne oppinion); did you dread her displeasure but halfe soe much as I doe, beeleeve me you would run post heather to make your peace.'

They have a sick friend, Lord Alington, at Tours, whom they greatly desire to have with them to nurse him, but his man writes that though he greatly desires the good air and good company now in Blois, yet 'my Lord makes little use, nor will doe these 15 dayes, of any ayre save that of a good fire [it is the beginning of November]; but what . . . stays my Lord heere, is, that should we runne through all France a more warme convenient chamber; a quietter house; a neatter woeman, & good meate better drest were not to be found by us. The woeman is so excellent in making jellies, hartening brothes & all other things necessary for a person that is sicke, that my L^d could not be better in his owne house at Horse Heath.' Later on Lord Alington begs for the loan of 'the King's booke in English; his Lpp hath it in French, but desireth much to reade it in the King's owne tearmes.' No doubt as to the authenticity of the 'Icon Basilicæ,' appears in the letters.

After weeks of suspense about Edmund, they receive towards the end of November the terrible news of his death and of the massacre at Drogheda.

There are some pathetic letters from Doll Leeke about her own and Mary's sorrow; she says she has now lost every one belonging to her who was engaged in the Civil War. She speaks of Edmund as 'our dear Companion & faithfull friend. I cannot express how unhappy I am, but I will leve you to ges by your self who I know had an intire affection for him.' Sir Ralph writes constantly that his wife is better, and Dr. Denton is planning how 'she should be bled after Xmas, & in March enter into a steele diett,' but she was getting beyond the reach of his affectionate care and his terrible remedies.

On Dec. 13 Sir Ralph wrote to a neighbour, Mr. Hatcher: 'I was such a blockhead that I forgot to tell you that on Satterday next (my wife being ill) a friend will give us a sermon & the Sacrament (after the honest old way at home) & if either yourselfe or son please to communicate with us you shall bee very welcome.' Dr. Denton had written: 'I doubt my poore landlady will have *febrem lentam* wch may in time consume her,' but, although not known till after her death, it was a disease of the lungs that was killing her. The move to Montpellier had been given up, as the small-pox was prevalent there; and although when the spring came on, the journey was again talked of, she was by that time too ill to attempt it. And it seems strange that Ralph should have thought poor Mary fit for it. Apparently he could not take in the possibility of death for her; they had been together, for better for worse, in sickness and in health, in poverty and in riches; there had never been a cloud between them, she had stood by him on all the difficult occasions when there was risk to be run, and dangers and penury to face, and above all, that which is most difficult to bear, the doubt whether a course which you take against the wishes and advice of all your friends, is really the wisest. Whatever might have been her private opinion, she had never faltered for a moment. But the burden had been too heavy for her sweet, loving, delicate nature, and now, at the early age of 34, she sank under it. Dr. Denton, so tenderly attached to his niece, had written continually about her health and his fears for her, but when the blow fell Ralph seemed thunderstruck. He wrote but one line to his uncle, telling him of the fact; he, the long-winded, the prolix explainer in everything, could not find a single word. It is the old, old story of Love's sorrow and Love's self-reproach, and Lowell's lament for his wife might have been written by Ralph about Mary :

> How was I worthy so divine a loss,
>   Deepening my midnights, kindling all my morns?
> Why waste such precious wood to make my cross,
>   Such far-sought roses for my crown of thorns?
>
> And when she came how earned I such a gift?
>   Why spent on me, a poor earth-delving mole,
> The fireside sweetnesses, the heavenward lift,
>   The hourly mercy of a woman's soul?

In Sir Ralph's calendar of letters addressed to Dr. Denton are the following entries :

[1] '$\frac{15}{5}$ May 1650. I writ Dr. word I received his letter, but could write of no businesse, Wife beeing soe ill.'

'$\frac{22}{12}$ May 1650. Oh my   my deare deare.'

'$\frac{29}{19}$ May 1650. Friday the $\frac{20}{10}$ May (at 3 in ye morning) was the Fatall day & Hower. The disease a consumption. . . . I shall not need to relate with what a Religeous and a cheerful joy & courage this now happy & most glorious saint, left this unhappy & most wicked world. . . . I intreate you presently to pay one **Mr. Preswell** (a silke man in Paternoster Row) about forty shillings, which hee said she owed for something taken upp there, though she could never call it to her remembrance. Besides the legacies . . . she appointed Tenn pounds to bee payed to the

---

[1] The double dates mark the difference of ten days between the English and French reckoning.

Dame Mary Verney.
from a bust in Middle Claydon Church.

stock of the Poore of Claydon, and Three pounds to Mr. Joyce the Minister, and Twenty pounds unto yourselfe, which she desired you to accept as a Testimony of her most unfeigned Love & affection, and with this earnest request, that for her sake you would perpetuate your friendshipp, care, & kindnesse both to mee and mine. I pray pay Mr. Joyce & give order to W. R. to pay the Poore & your selfe with the first money. As for Mourninge I shall only desire you presently to take upp your owne, & also such others as you (by the customes now used in England, by persons of my Estate & Condition) thinke fit & necessary to bee given for the Best of Wifes. . . . The greate & sad afflictions now uppon me, make me utterly unable to think how I had best dispose of myselfe & children, therefore besides your prayers for our comfort & direction, bee pleased to send your advise at large to your perplexed, distressed & most afflicted servant.' He also notes 'that M. Cordell has this day sent the Dr. the relation at large of her deportment in her sicknesse & at her death, in 6 sheets of paper.' Two days later comes a deed for Mary to sign, 'also a letter from the Dr. to her.'

There is a painful paper a fortnight after her death, addressed by Ralph to Dr. Denton, examining himself as to what wrong deeds of his can have deserved such fearful punishment: 'having now passed neare 40 yeares of my pilgrimage, & had my share both of publique & private afflictions, & even at this very instant groaning under the weight of the greatest greife that ever yet befell me; 'tis high time to search out what iniquities have separated me & my god; and what sinns have made him take away good things from me.' 'You know I have now beene neare seaven yeares abroad, within wch time (and a little before) my good and carefull parents, 2 parts of 3 of my innocent children, and my best beloved Brother, were taken from me; soe that I had neither Father, Mother, Daughter nor kinde Brother to assist me in this unhappy Exile. And yet I thanke my God I was not quite forsaken, for hee was pleased to raise upp you to bee my true and faithfull friende in England, and in a very plentifull measure to supply all other defects by the vertue and affection of my Wife, who was not only willing to suffer for and with mee heere, but by her most exemplary goodnesse and patience both help'd and taught me to support my otherwise almost insupportable Burden. But alas, what shall I now doe! for she being too good to bee kept any longer from her heavenly rest, & I being too unworthy the continuance of soe greate a Blessing, am now deprived of her, and (as if her crowne had encreased my cares) her reward is become my punishment. What course shall I take to reconcile my selfe unto my Maker, & devert the Dreggs of his Fury from mee? he hath covered mee with ashes, filled mee with Bitternesse & made mee drunken with wormwood, & yet I must needes confesse the Lord is just & righteous, for I have rebelled against all his commandements. . . . Being this day to receive yᵉ Sacrament, (yᵉ better to fit me for it) I lately made a Review of my life, wherein though I found enough to make mine Eyes Run downe with Rivers of Water, yet least the love to myselfe or sinns cause mee to bee partiall unto either, I must beeseech & conjure you (who know more of me & my actions then any creature liveing) . . . to tell mee plainly wherein you have observed me to bee faulty, & espetially whether any man hath or is like to suffer unjustly either by or for mee.'

The 'Review' contains a long and painfully elaborate examination into past money transactions with tenants and others, setting forth the reasons and the rules by which he was guided and his readiness to make restitution if the Doctor thinks he was to blame; 'the pane taken out of Radcliffe Church window' years before, a boyish piece of mischief, and rather a hard bargain about Newman's cow, are all enumerated in his morbid conscientiousness at this time of overwhelming sorrow. Even a poor little unpaid bill of 40s. to a brewer in London weighs on his mind, although, as he says, he sent 'neare 20 times unto him to fetch his money but he came not,' and he is the more sorry as he knows neither his name nor dwelling. His trouble is much increased by the death of his good friend M. Testard the minister, which he announces in a postscript. The Doctor's reply is a long, affectionate letter; he begins by deprecating Ralph's choosing him for a confessor:

'It seems I cozened y^u w^n I turned a scurvy sollicitour, & y^u have cozened me in takinge me to be a Confessor & casuist. I confesse the Apostle's p^{r}cept (viz., confesse y^r sinns one to another) I thinke ought not to be monopolized by the priests only, but everyone is left at libertie to whom to doe it; but wherefor to me, who . . . have swallowed downe soe many & mighty sinns wthout remorse or acknowledgm^t that I cannot but thinke these of yours Peccadilloes. Oh that my soule were guiltie of noe higher! . . . I ev^r had an affection for y^u as a kinsman & a Ver[ney], but especially uppon the hopes that we are heires togeather of salvation, wch to me is above all obligaĉons or relations whatsoever, of wch though I nev^r doubted . . . yet these letters are more evidence & assurance to me of it. . . . Seeinge y^u have given me the freedome of discovery of what I know by y^n, I shall intimate one thinge to y^u as freely now as formerly I have done, even soe longe agoe as when we were Academians, wch is that y^u have beene ever (even by most of those who thought they knew y^u best) thought to take pett upon very small occasions agst many, & then very hardly reconcileable, wch hath beene used as an argum^t to me as inconsistent wth love. . . . I must confesse I tremble to have difference wth those who I conceave to be heirs of life wth me, to thinke that we shall have united harts in Heaven & not soe on earth. I know great differences have beene & will be even amongst the best, but I hope God in his Due time will find out a way to unite & reconcile his owne togeather (though nev^r at a greater distance in the generall in this kingdome then now) as to the publiq cause soe alsoe to y^u & any particulars.' He then names four people with whom he seeks to reconcile Ralph—Aunt Isham, 'Ned ff.,' 'the parson' [Mr. Aris, at Claydon], and his brother Henry. Of the first three, 'If I understand them aright they are as much y^r frends as I am. . . . Harry, though I thinke him unhappy, & not to be compared with them—noe, nor wth him that is nott [Edmund] yett I thinke he is putt to his shifts to live, wch makes him doe more unhandsome thinges then otherwaies he would doe, & his choler transport him many times beyond the naturall bias of his heart . . . yet he is y^r Brother still, in whom I thinke you may have comfort still, & happily by your conversation (were y^u here) might be wonne to a more righteous course. . . . If he doe [write] I shall say noe more then remember that short petition, forgive us o^r trespasses as we forgive them that trespass agst us.' Ralph receives his uncle's correction with perfect sweetness : ' Dr, you are a right peace-maker, & cannot misse of the reward, for you doe not only endeavour to preserve peace where it is, but to restore it where it is lost. . . . I doubt I am too guilty of . . . beeing very hardly reconcileable . . . wherfore I often strive agst it in my praiers, saying, . , . O thou who hast comanded me to overcome evil with good, and to pray for them that despightfully use me ; Bee mercifull to myne enemies, O Lord, as to myselfe. Turne thou my hart towards them & theirs towards mee,' &c.

But Brother Harry's unkindness had evidently cut so deep that he can only say : ' for Harry, whose Tongue & Pen, not only on a sudden, but also after long deliberation, hath beene noe lesse bitter then unjust against me (though I am bound to forgive him as I thanke God I doe), yet under your favour I am noe more obleiged to contineu an old, or enter into a new strict league & friendshipp with him then to trust a man that by all the waies & meanes hee can hath endeavoured to deprive me of my life, or (wch is farre more precious) my good name.' The letter ends with a touching reference to his loss. 'But what! have I writt thus farre of my paper without soe much as mentioning of her that alwaies lived, & lately died in peace, & now is reigning with the prince of peace? Alas, Alas, Deare Dr, tis not that I have forgot (or, indeed, ever can forget), the most irreparable Losse of that incomparable creature, but following your precepts I search & seeke & pray for patience, as for ye only remedy that Heaven, as well as necessity, hath ordained for your most afflicted friend & servant.'

He was quite determined that at all events nothing so precious to him as his wife's body should remain in France, and he immediately had it embalmed; but there were many difficulties in the way of getting it carried to England, and he dared not send it ' uppon uncertaine termes; least . . . . it should bee tossed

and tumbled from Place to Place, and being discovered
. . . . run ye hazard of some affront.' For months
it remained in Ralph's house at Blois, and he wrote
' though it bee locked upp in a Roome by itselfe where
noebody comes, yet you must needes thinke it noe
small affliction to me to have it soe neare mee. You
know when Sarah died Abraham made hast to bury
the dead out of his sight.'

He wrote to Dr. Denton : ' I have been shrewdly
put to it in a way you little dreame off, for by y^e
Lawes of France the king is the heire to all strangers,
& (the wife by custome being intituled to on halfe)
a projecting favorite Begged & obteined this Droict
d' Aubaine (that is, ye succession of all my Wife's
estate in France, she dying heere without naturalized
or French borne issue), ... but by the Blessing
of God uppon a good friend's endeavour, there was a
stopp put upon the graunt before the compleat expedition & sealing. (Oh, oh that it had pleased the
Almighty that his decree to deprive me of my deare,
discreet, & most incomparable Wife, were but as easily
revoakable). What Further charge this cunning
Catchpole may bring uppon me, I cannot yet foresee,
but I have taken what care I can to prevent his plots,
& privately disposed the best of my goods, & sent
my coach & horses about 40 miles off (to a French
freind's house) where I shall (even uppon any Termes)
endeavour to have them sould. What a losse this is,
what an expence this puts me to, what gratifications
of freinds will bee expected and must bee performed,

you cannot easily imagen. Oh that the God of Gods were pleased to make the unspeakable losse of my most vertuous wife as easily reparable and as little damageable.'

The reality of Ralph's grief for the loss of his wife was shown by his life-long widowhood and his undying remembrance of her throughout the succeeding forty-six years. Her sweet and noble character was indeed worthy of his devotion, and the references to her in his letters are as true as they are touching.

'You may put upp a greate escutcheon at Claydon,' he writes, 'if you please, before the Corps comes; faile not of anything that is fit for soe unparalleled a creature; her armes are in the Herald's office & will send mine next week if I can finde them. The escutcheon will cost about 40 or 50 shillings . . . . doe what you thinke best and fittest without consideration of any charge.'

At length a safe-conduct for the coffin was found. Sir Ralph followed the ship in thought with loving anxiety, 'every puffe of winde that tosses it at sea, shakes me at land'—the honest Doctor saw it reverently interred in Middle Claydon Church on November 20, 1650. A few relations and friends were present, and it is apparently with reference to Mary's burial that Sir Roger wrote some weeks later: 'Although the sadness of the occasion struck death allmost into me, yet as it was a service both to the living and the dead, it was performed with as much life & heartiness as could be imagined.' Sir Ralph was left to derive what comfort he could from the intelligence that Dame Ursula Verney (widow of Sir Francis) was deeply offended that she had not been invited to the funeral, it was her way of showing her respect for one whom the older members of the family held in such high esteem.

The state of Ralph's affairs did not admit of his returning home, and he wrote to Dr. Denton: 'My mind runs more after Italy; not to delight myselfe with anything there, for since my deare Wife's death I have bid adieu to all that most men count theire Happinesse. The Arabian deserts are now farre more agreeable to my humour then the most pleasant Grotts and Gardens that Rome it selfe affords. Ah, Dr., Dr., her company made every place a paradice unto me, but she being gonn, unlesse god bee most meraculously mercifull, what good can bee expected by your most afflicted and unfortunate servant.'

In advising his quarrelsome sister Margaret Elmes to be submissive to her husband, Sir Ralph pays a touching tribute to Mary's memory: 'Give me leave to set before your eyes my owne deare wife that's now with God. You know she brought a farr better fortune then my Estate deserved, and for her guifts of Grace and nature I may justly say she was inferior to very few, soe that she might well expect all reasonable observance from mee, yet such was her goodnesse that when I was most Peevish she would be most Patient, and as if she meant to aire my frowardnesse and frequent follies by the constancy of her forbearance, studdied nothing more then a sweet compliance. But perhaps you may thinke I was a better husband then your owne; alas, if that were soe, twas she that made me soe, and I may thanke her silence and discreation for your good oppinion of me, for had she (like soe many other wifes) divulged my faults, or in a proud disdainfull way dispised me for my pettish humours, tis tenn to one I had beene found more liable to censure then any other man.'

* * * * * * * *

To read through many thousands of a man's private letters is to know him as one knows very few of one's own contemporaries, and Ralph Verney is a man who stands this most trying test. 'In all time of his tribulation, in all time of his wealth, in the hour of death,' and in the day of his prosperity, he comes out as a high-minded, large-hearted, unselfish, most conscientious man, ever striving to find out the truth and to abide by it in good report and evil report.

There was not in him the chivalrous charm which made his father Sir Edmund so attractive, the gallant soldier who joins the advanced party on the Scotch border and is in the thick of the battle, wherever he thinks it his duty, to the great terror of his unwarlike son. 'You would not wish me to lose any of that little honour in which I have lived,' he writes in answer to Ralph's remonstrance. When 'the vote of Wicombe' is scored against him by the Court, 'and the great ones' look coldly on him in 1641, as his son Henry observes sulkily from the Hague, he pursues unmoved the even tenor of his way. The cheerful spirit in which he enjoyed life, before his troubles and perplexities grew too heavy for him, made him most popular with the great ladies of the Puritan party—Lady Barrymore, Lady Sussex, Lady Carnarvon—as 'a reddy and compleat man for the pleasures of ladyes,' as Sir John Drake writes. When dressed in his 'Isabella satin sute, ornamented with silver and gold buttons and twist' (still preserved at Claydon), he attended Henrietta Maria's Court as gentleman of the privy chamber, or accompanied Charles on his progresses in 'crimson sattin dublit and cloake lyned with pynked plush,' he was regarded as the very model of a gentleman and a courtier. But he was never so happy as when he could return to his home at Claydon to his 'very loving wife' and the six little girls to whom he was such an affectionate father; to look after the 'plashing of the hedgs,' the making of the hay, the letting of the farms, and the management of the 'geldinges and nagges' which, riding often as he did sixty or seventy miles with the king in the day, or out hunting in Whaddon Chase, were as necessary to his active existence as meat and drink. And, finally, when he found it impossible to reconcile his conflicting duties to the sovereign whom he had served faithfully for thirty years, and the country which he believed Charles to be ruining, he went into battle with not even his buff suit, and threw himself on the pikes of the enemy in despair of life, to plunge into ' a sea of troubles, and by opposing end them.' Sir Edmund, with his passionate affections, his deep religious convictions, and his enjoyment of all the purer pleasures, must have been one of the most attractive men of his time, of the type of Lord Falkland on one side of politics and Colonel Hutchinson on the other.

Sir Ralph is the champion of causes and of men when they are unsuccessful and want friends, and falls off when, like Jeshurun, they 'wax fat and kick.' He is on the side of the Parliament, of Pym and Hampden, Holles, Hyde, and St. John, when there is great danger in taking that line against the king. When his party are in the ascendant and he thinks they are going too far, he turns, though moderately, to the side of Charles. When his old allies become triumphant and he might rise with them to the top of the tree and the conduct of affairs, if he will only take the Covenant in religion and the violent republican view of politics, he prefers to spend his life in poverty and isolation abroad, with his beloved Claydon sequestrated, his wife dying, and to remain in lonely exile afterwards, away from all the friends to whom they were so warmly attached. He returned to England only to be the object of Cromwell's suspicion, and was in durance, though not close prison, in St. James's Tennis Court for seventeen weeks in 1655, because he would not give recognisances to the Protector.

At the Restoration, when he might have pleaded

his sufferings for the cause of the king, he was so distressed and disgusted at the arbitrary measures of Charles II. and his government as soon as they became triumphant, that he is in opposition again. His sister, Lady Osborn, lives at Court, at her lodgings 'up the Banqueting House stayres in Whitehall'; every country gentleman of his standing attends at Whitehall as a matter of course, but his name is hardly ever to be found there and he is under a cloud with the ruling party. He was in the House of Commons again after the Restoration, and was elected, with his cousin Sir Richard Temple, of Stowe, in the Parliament of 1680, 'among the very few Whigs who find their way there,' observes Lord Macaulay.

He was turned out of the magistracy of Buckinghamshire (also with Sir Richard Temple) by James II. in the early part of 1688, just before the beginning of the end. Wary and cautious as he was patient, gentle, and long-sighted, with no hot-headed enthusiasms, no passionate genius to support and lead him on, and with all the experience of the bad days, the obloquy and distress in store for those who opposed the men in power, equally arbitrary on whichever side they might be found; he never flinches, but bears his testimony to what he thinks right, and suffers for it in a quiet, unobtrusive way which is inexpressibly touching in a man who so keenly valued the society of his friends, the enjoyment of his pleasant home, and the position to which he had been born. Counting the cost to the full, and willing to endure the penalty, whatever it might be, he held himself ready for any sacrifice that might be demanded of him by his principles. In unfolding the enormous number of packets of letters, a phrase of Lady Vere Gaudy's turned up towards the end of his life, 'You who are so well with the government can certainly get this done for my son.' It read so strangely that I turned to the date and found it was after the accession of William and Mary. Then for the first time the old man had found a government to which he could give his satisfied allegiance, a king at the head of things whom he could trust, and conduct of affairs on which he could look with hope. But he does not thrust himself forward for any personal recognition of his claims from the crown. He attends the Convention Parliament regularly, and then returns each recess to his home, satisfied to do the work in country and estate where he has so much in his power—with no desire for additional rank or position, independent, with a certain quiet pride in owing no man anything, and doing good to all who come in his way, interested in all the great questions of his day, advancing with his age, truly and deeply religious, yet without a tinge of bigotry or conceit. His little foibles have worn away with the varied experiences and sufferings of his early life, he is 'a very fine gentleman,' as comes out in the letters of one of his many lady friends. 'I cannot hope my son-in-law should have the manners of Sir Ralph Verney,' writes another. Pure-minded amidst the unutterable foulness of the times of Charles II., honourable, affectionate, just, relied upon by all his friends for the intelligent help he never refused with all his caution, and the wise sympathy he gave in all their troubles, content with that with which God had blessed him, he was the very ideal of an old English country gentleman.

APPENDIX

DOCUMENTS CONCERNING SIR EDMUND VERNEY'S CLAIMS ON THE ALNAGE. FROM NALSON'S COLLECTION OF MSS., VOL. XV., IN THE POSSESSION OF THE DUKE OF PORTLAND, PRINTED BY HIS KIND PERMISSION.

TO THE HON^{BLE} COM^{TEE} OF THE KING'S REVENUE.

The humble Peticõn of Susanna Verney, Penelope Verney, Mary Verney and Elizabeth Verney, 4 of the daughters of Sr Edmund Verney kn^t deceased,

Humbly sheweth

That our late Soveraigne Lord king James, by his highnesse seuerall Letters Pattents dat 13 Apr. 11° of his raigne, did grant unto Lodowick Duke of Lenox the seuerall Offices of Aulnager and Collect^r of the Subsidy & Aulnage for the terme of 60 yeares under the yearely rent of 909^{li}: 9^s: 4^d payable into the Excheq^r

That his now Matie by his highnesse Letteres pattentes dat. 25° July 14° of his raigne, for great consideracõns therein expressed, did grant unto ye said Sr Edm: Verney his Execut^{rs} Administrat^{rs} & Assignes, one yearely pencõn of 400^{li} for 21 yeares, to be paid by the hands of the Collect^{rs} Farmo^{rs} and Assignees of the said Farmes, out of the said rent of 994^{li}: 9^s: 4^d and did therein grant, that if it should happen that the said Letteres pattents to the said Duke of Lennox, should be surrendred or the estate therein granted to be otherwise determined, the said yeerely penc̃on of 400^ti should be paid to the said Sr Edm: Verney his Executo^rs Administrat^rs and Assignes, out of the Fees and profittes of the said Aulnage, Subsedy and premisses by the Coll^rs Occupyers and receiv^rs thereof.

That the said Sr Edm: Verney, by Indenture dat j̊ Mar. 14 Carol. did grant, assigne and sett over, the said Letteres pattents & Annuity, to certaine persons (therein named) in trust (amongst other things) that 300^ti per an of the said Annuity of 400^ti per an should be employed towards the maintenance of yor petitioners & raysing them the sũme of One thousand pounds a peece, for and towarde theire porc̃ons wch is all yor petitioners hopes or meanes of subsistence, they having no other meanes but the charity of friends to keepe them from starving.

That the said severall Offices and profitts, are · amongst other of his Maties revenue sequestred whereby yor petitioners are deprived of theire said maintenance and porc̃ons without directions from this hon^ble Com^ttee Although the sequestracion of his Maties revenue or the Office and profites of the Duke of Lenox, doth not make void or impeach the said yearely rent of 400^ti per an. And the said 994^ti 9^s 4^d and more, is still made and paid by the said Farm^rs and Collect^rs And all payments before the sequestrac̃on were allowed upon Accompt taken of the old Officers, by the Auditors appointed by Parliam^t by vertue of the said Letteres pattentes.

May it please the Honble Com^ttee to grant theire Order and Warrant to the Officers, Farmo^rs Coll^rs Receivo^rs of the said Aulnage and Subsidy for the time being to pay from time to time the said Annuity or rent charge of 400^ti per an as it shall become due and payable according to the said Letters pattentes And to take such Order for the payment of such Arrears as are incurred since the Sequestrac̃on in reasonable time as yor wisdomes shall thinke fitt.

And yor Petitioners shall ever **pray** &c.

APPENDIX 433

At ye Comittee of Lords & Comons for his M^{ties} Revenue, sitting at Westminster ye xxjst day of September 1647.

Vpon Consideracōn had of ye Peticōn (annexed) of Susanna Verney, Penelope Verney, Mary Verney, & Elizabeth Verney, daughters of Sr Edmund Verney deceased, Praying that ye yeerly Pention of fowre hundred pounds, & ye Arreares, may be paid, Out of ye Rente reserved to y^o Crowne, vpon ye Collection of ye Subsidie of ye Aulnage, according to Sr Edmund Verneys Assignment of his Patent, bearing date ye xxvth July xiiij^{to} Car.

Ordered & Wee doe desire Olliver Saint John Esqr his Maties Sollicitor Generall to peruse the said Patent & Assignment, & to certifie vnto this Comittee vnder his hand, y^e State of them, with his Opinion thereupon.

SALISBURY

Hen. Mildmay   W. Say and Seale
Denis Bond   Wharton.

Mr Sollicitor generall.   Ind.

Report of Oliver St. John, Solicitor General, on the Petition of Sir Edmund Verney's daughters. 164$\frac{7}{8}$.

May it please yor Lord^{ps}

Accordinge to yor Lord^{ps} Order of the xxjth of September last, Whereby I am required to pervse Sr Edmund Verneys Pattent, Wherevpon a pencion of foure hundred pounds and the Arreares thereof are claymed out of the Rent reserved to the Crowne vpon the Collection of the Subsidie of the Alnadge and likewise Sr Edmund Verneys Assignement thereof, And to certifie the State thereof to yor Lord^{ps} I haue pervsed the same and I find that his Matie that now is by his Letters Pattents vnder the great Seale of England beareinge date 25ᵗʰ of July 14° of his Raigne reciteinge that his said Maᵗⁱᵉ two severall Letters Pattents the one beareinge date 26° decemb̃ 1° of his Raigne and the other xxvj° May 2° of his Raigne granted vnto the said Sʳ Edmund Verney Two severall yearely porcions of two hundred pounds a peice for his life payable out of his Maᵗⁱᵉˢ receipt of the Exchequer, and that by other Letters Pattentes beareinge date 16° Febr 1° of his Raigne his Maᵗⁱᵉ granted vnto the said Sʳ Edmund Verney the Office of Marshall of the household and of the Marshall of the Marshallsey of the household and all fees Jurisdicions &c. therevnto belonginge and that a stipend of xˢ per diem is mencõned to be granted by the said last Letteres Pattents to the vnder Marshall of the household paid by the Cofferer of the household to the Marshall for the time beinge and to be disposd of by him And that the said Sʳ Edmund Verney by his deed dated 13° July last past before the date of the first mencõned Letteres Pattents (as much as in him was) released vnto his said Maᵗⁱᵉ the said Stipend of xˢ per diem and the Arrerage thereof. And did Coveñnt wʰ his Maᵗⁱᵉ his heires and Successors that neither himselfe nor his deputie or Deputies or vndʳ Marshall or any other in his or theire behalf should demand or receive the said stipend of xˢ per diem and thereby likewise granted and Surrendered vnto his Maᵗⁱᵉ the said two seuerall Pencõns of CCˡⁱ a peice to him granted as aforesaid by the said two seuerall Letteres Pattents and that his Maᵗⁱᵉ had accepted and approved thereof And reciteing that his late Maᵗⁱᵉ Kinge James by two seuerall Letteres Pattents vnder the great Seale of England dated 13° April 11° of his Raigne and confirmed by two seuerall Indentures likewise vnder the great S[eale] dated 14° April the same yeare granted the seuerall Offices of Aulnadge and Collectʳ of the Subsidie and Aulnadge of the old and new Draperies &c. and alsoe the seuerall farmes of the Subsidies Aulnage, somes of money, Moetie of Forfeitures and duties payable vpon all and all manner of

Woolen Cloathes and Stuffs of the old and new draperies made to be sould in the Realme of England Dominion of Wales and Isle of Weight vnto Lodowicke then Duke of Lenox his Exec. &c. for 60 yeares vnd^r seuerall yearely Rents amountinge in the whole to 994^{li} 9^s 4^d payable into the Receipt of his Maties Excheq^r att Michās and o^r Lady day, did in Consideracōn of the said Surrend^r release and Coveñnt giue and grant vnto ye said Sr Edmund Verney his Exec. Administrato^{rs} and Assignes One yearely penc̄ōn or Somē of 400^{li} per Ann for the Terme of (21) yeares from the Annuncacōn of the Virgin Mary last past before the date of the said first menc̄ōned Letteres Pattents To be pd by the hand of the Collecto^{rs} Farmers and Assignes for the time beinge of the s^d seuerall Farmes and premisses att the feasts of Michās and o^r Lady day by even porc̄ōns or w^{h}in fortie dayes after. But of the said seuerall yearely Rents or somēs of money reserved vpon the said two Letteres Pattents and Indentures made to the said Duke, And his Matie did likewise thereby grant and declare That if the said Letteres Pattents and Indentures made to the said Duke, should be surrendered or his Estate therein otherwise be determined, The said Penc̄ōn of 400^{li} should be pd out of the proffitts arisinge out of the said Subsidies and Aulnage to be paid by the Collecto^{rs} Occupiers and Receivers thereof, And the said Sr Edmund Verney by One Indenture beareing date 1° Mar. 14° Car. and made betweene him the said Sr Edmund Verney [of] the one part, And Sr Alexander Denton of Hillesden in the Countie of Buck Kn^t Ralph Verney Esqr sonne and heire apparent of the said Sr Edmund Verney, John Denton of Lincolnes Inn Esqr, and Willm Denton of the Citty of Westm^r Doctor of Phisicke of the other parte (recitinge as therein is recited) did as well for rayseinge of Porc̄ōns for his Children therein menc̄ōned as for other Consideracōns Assigne over vnto the said Sr Alexander Denton &c. the said Penc̄ōn of 400^{li} granted to him by the said Letteres Pattents dated 24° July,

14° Car. and all his Right Title Terme of yeares Interest and demand therein, And this was vpon Trust.

[1] For the raysinge of 800ˡⁱ towards the payment of his debts.

[2] For the payeinge of 50ˡⁱ per Anñ to his third sonne Edmund Verney for his mainteynance and by fiftie pounds per Anñ more and the benefitt thereof to rayse a stocke of 800ˡⁱ for him, wᵗʰ which an Anuitie of 100ˡⁱ per Anñ should be purchased for him for his Life and when that is rayesed the fiftie pounds per Anñ for his manteynance to cease. And it is thereby provided That if any person authorized by the said Sʳ Edmund Verney in his Life time shall after his death tender 5ˢ in such manner and make such declaracõn as in the said deed is expressed that then the Trusts and paymᵗˢ lymited to his sonne Edmund should cease.

3 To rayse a thousand pound for the marriage porcõn of Susan eldest daughter of the said Sʳ Edmund Verney, and One thousand pound more for the marriage Porcõn of Penelope one other of his Daughters.

4 To rayse 2000ˡⁱ more to be disposed of to such person or persons as yᵉ said Sʳ Edmund Verney shall by any writeing vnder his hand and seale in the presence of three Credible Witnesses appoint and declare.

5 To rayse a 1000ˡⁱ more for the marriage porcõn of Mary Verney 5ᵗ daughter of the said Sʳ Edmund and 1000ˡⁱ more for the marriage Porcõn of Elizabeth Verney his youngest Daughter and after the seuerall Porcõns are raysed the profitt thereof is to be paid them for their manteynance, In which sᵈ Indentur[e] there is this provisor That the said Sʳ Edmund Verney by any writinge vnder his hand and Seale might revoke alter and make voyd any of the Trusts and Paymᵗˢ aforesᵈ (other then such as should be pᵈ & executed before such revocacion) and after such Revocacõn or in Case noe revocacõn or alteracõn should be made the Surplusage of money received or to be received by the sa[id] Trustees or any of them or their

Exec. &c. should be pd to Sr Edmund Verney or vnto his heire att lawe or vnto such as they should appoint in writinge vnder their hand and Seale.

This I conceive to be the state of the case, wch nevertheless I submit to yor Lord^ps wisdome & further direction.

Ol: St JOHN.

8 Feb. 1647.

 Mr Sollicitor

  his report to ye Com^tee of Revenue.

At the Committee of Lords & Commons for his Maties Revenue sitting at Westminster the xvj^th daie of Februarie 1648.

Ordered; that the State (annexed) of Olliver Saint John Esqr late Sollicitor generall, of the right Susanna Verney, Penelope Verney, Marie Verney, & Elizabeth Verney, Daughters of Sr Edmund Verney deceased, hath in fower Hundred pounds per Anū, with the Arrears, paieable Out of the Rent reserved to the Crowne vpon the Collection of the Subsidie of the Aulnage; be reported to the Commons Howse, And wee desire the Lo^d Grey of Grorby to Report the same accordingly vnto the Howse when He Reports the State of the Aulnage.

INDEX

ABB

ABBOT, Archbishop of Canterbury, i. 71
Abeles, Jonas, ii. 179
Abell, Mary, wife of young Edmund Verney, i. 26, 27
Abell, William, i. 26
Abercrombie, Captain Jaconiah, or Jeremiah, ii. 199, 200
Abingdon, Eleanor Lee, Countess of, i. 248
Abingdon, Abbey of, i. 114; mayor of, i. 221
Adams, Rev. Charles, married Eliz. Verney, ii. 384
Adams, John, architect, i. 16
Addington manor, ii. 199
Albury, Herts, i. 59; ii. 4
Aleppo, i. 69
Algiers, i. 63, 65
Alington, William, 1st Lord, ii. 411, 412
Allcock, Frances, housekeeper at Claydon, ii. 17, 175, 287, 288, 291, 293, 371, 372, 378, 382
Allen, Thomas, i. 121
Alnage, duty on woollen cloths, i. 3; ii. 145, 146, 174, 180, 406; Appendix, vol. ii.
Alport, Richard, of Overton Manor, Cheshire, ii. 351, 354, 355, 356, 357, 358, 362, 363, 364, 368, 370, 384, 387, 388
Alport, Susan, Mrs., ii. 246, 359, 360, 361, 368, 369, 370, 371, 384, 385, 388; *see* Verney, Susan
Alsatia, i. 61
Amnion, Major, ii. 192

BAK

Andrews, John, ii. 310
Andrews, Lord, i. 131
Annandale, Sir John Murray, 1st Earl of, i. 229
Anne Boleyn, i. 48
Anne of Cleves, i. 51, 53
Apothecary (*see* Gape), bill of, i. 167
Apsly, Captain, i. 324
Aris, Rev. John, i. 146, 150, 165; ii. 17, 18, 288, 289, 291, 419
Aris, Mrs., ii. 289
Aris, Nicholas, ii. 208
Arms, i. 312, 314, 315, 325; ii. 110, 111, 201
Arundel, Thomas Howard, Earl of, i. 130, 306, 307; ii. 100
Ash, Mr. John, ii. 304, 308
Ashridge, i. 42, 51
Astley, Sir Jacob, i. 334; ii. 114
Aston, Sir Arthur, ii. 344, 346
Aubigny, Lord, ii. 116, 122
Avenel, Alice, i. 30
Aylesbury, i. 28, 29, 327, 328, 329; ii. 74, 172, 191, 192, 218, 255

BACCHUS, Sir John, ii. 349
Bacon, Sir Nathaniel, i. 254
Bacon, Mr., son of Sir Nath., i. 254; ii. 102
Badnage, Bridget Leeke, Mrs., i. 205, 206; *see* Hals, Bridget
Badnage, Mr., i. 96, 204, 205, 206; ii. 50
Baker, Thomas, ii. 171

BAL

Balfour, Sir William, Lieutenant of the Tower, i. 357
Barbadoes, i. 111, 148, 149, 150, 151; ii. 157, 158, 338, 346, 349
Barry, John, ii. 202, 203
Barrymore, Alice, Countess of, i. 101, 134, 195. 196, 200, 202, 203, 302; ii. 15, 16, 43, 44, 53, 55, 56, 89, 267, 425
Barrymore, David Barry, 1st Earl of, i. 195, 196, 202, 215, 227; ii. 45, 50, 52, 55
Bates, Dr. George, born at Maid's Morton, afterwards Cromwell's chief physician, i. 164
Bayly, Lieut.-Gen. Sir William, ii. 337
Beadnege, John, Lord Mayor, ii. 182
Bedford, William Russell, 4th Earl of, i. 105, 199
Bedford, town of, i. 328
Bell, Mr. William, ii. 160, 163
Beresford, Mary Leeke, Mrs., i. 197
Berney, —, ii. 194
Bethune, Dr., ii. 318
Blacknall, John, i. 113
Blacknall, Mary (see Verney, Dame Mary), i. 113, 115
Blagrove, Sir Alex. Denton's steward, ii. 194
Blakeney, Mary, i. 58; see Verney, Dame Mary, 'ould Lady Verney'
Blower, Richard, ii. 176
Bodley, Sir Thomas, i. 215
Bohemia; see Elizabeth, Queen of Bohemia
Bolton, Mr., i. 174
Bond, Denis, M.P., ii. 437
Bond, John, M.P., ii. 145, 166
Booth, Mr., ii. 44
Boreman, Sir William, i. 14
Borlase, Sir John, ii. 41, 42
Botolph House, i. 30
Boyle, Hon. Robert, i. 204
Boyle, Lieut.-Col., ii. 345
Boyle, Lady Katherine, ii. 203, 204
Bradshaw, John, ii. 345
Braye, Lord and Lady, i. 50, 56, 57

CAL

Braye, Elizabeth, i. 50
Braye, Sir Reginald, i. 50
'Brerewood's Logic,' ii. 9
Bridgman, Sir Orlando, ii. 264
Bristol, John Digby, 1st Earl of, i. 70, 83
Broghill, Roger Boyle, Lord, ii. 45, 48
Brooke, Robert Grevile, Lord, i. 185, 305, 353; ii. 113, 115, 122, 154
Broughton, Elizabeth, i. 48
Brown, Colonel, ii. 95
Brown, Major, M.P., ii. 394
Brown, Sir Richard, ii. 216
Brown, Dr., of Christchurch, i. 260
Brown, Mr., a possible husband for Mary Verney, ii. 372, 375
Bruce, John, Esq., Introductory Note; i. 70; ii. 22
Bruce, Magdalen, Mrs.; see Faulkner
Buck, Mr., Lady Ormonde's Gentleman-Usher, ii. 341, 344
Buckingham, George Villiers, Marquis of, i. 75, 76, 78; Duke of, 88, 90, 91, 92, 93
Buckingham, county and town, i. 11, 26, 28, 39, 46, 48, 55, 74, 84, 88, 327, 328, 339; ii. 230, 427
Bulstrode, Henry, i. 330
Burgoyne, Sir Roger, Bart., M.P., i. 14, 134, 344; ii. 163, 178, 179, 197, 220, 239, 244, 246, 249, 268, 271, 272, 306, 307, 312, 397, 401, 409, 410, 422
Burnet, Gilbert, Bishop of Salisbury, i. 248
Busby, Robert, of Addington, i. 298; ii. 93, 290, 291
Byron, John Byron, Lord, ii. 321, 322
Byron, Sir Robert, ii. 321

CALABY, Sir Hugh, ii. 384, 385
Calendar, James Livingstone, 1st Earl of, ii. 339

INDEX 441

Cantelupe, Thomas de, i. 1, 22 note
Cantelupe, William de, i. 22
Canterbury, Archbishops of; *see* Abbot and Laud
Cardinal, Prince, Ferdinand, son of Philip III. of Spain, Governor of the Netherlands, i. 138
Carew, Awdreye, i. 58
Carew, George, i. 62
Carlyle, Lord, i. 185, 219
Carnarvon, Anne Sophia Herbert, Countess of, i. 102; ii. 425
Carnarvon, Robert Dormer, Earl of, i. 102
Cary, Sir Edmund, ii. 339
Cary, Sir Lorenzo, ii. 133
Cary, Margaret Smith, Mrs., afterwards Lady Herbert, i. 252; ii. 58 note
Catherine of Arragon, i. 11, 33, 45, 47
Catline, Mr., ii. 264
Chaloner, Sir Thomas, Ambassador to Spain, i. 34
Chaloner, Sir Thomas, Chamberlain to Prince Henry, i. 33
Chaloner, Thomas, the regicide, i. 34, 344; ii. 146
Chaloner, Edward, Lieut. R.N., i. 35
Chaloner, Mr., ii. 312
Chamberlaine, Dr. Peter, ii. 173, 180
Charles I. as Prince of Wales, i. 71, 74, 75, 77; in Spain, 78, 81, 82; leaves Spain, 83; becomes king, 85; makes Sir E. Verney his Knight-Marshal, 85, 87; disputes with Parliament, 90, 96, 121, 330, 332; summons peers to York, 335; reverses in the North, 334; surrenders Strafford, 358; received by the City, ii. 32, 33; attempts to arrest the five members, 34-37; goes to Hull, 83; meeting at York, 89; commits the royal standard to Sir Edmund Verney, 97; Edgehill, 114; lines attributed to him, 206; taken to Holmby House, 254; goes to Isle of Wight, 277; seized by order of Army Council, 394; scaffolds building for his trial, 396; his execution, 398, 401; his funeral, 399, 400, 401; mourning for him, 402, 403; 'Eikon Basiliké,' 402, 412
Charles II., i. 14, 249; ii. 97, 113, 335, 336, 339, 342, 410, 427, 429
Chicheley, John, i. 69
Chike, Sir Roger, ii. 108
Chike, Sir Thomas, ii. 108, 153
Cholmly, Henry, ii. 325
Clanricarde, Richard, 4th Earl of, i. 201, 208
Clanricarde, Ulick, 5th Earl of, ii. 132
Clarendon, Hyde, Earl of, i. 117, 147, 300, 330, 340; ii. 89, 109, 110, 112, 125; *see also* Hyde
Claydon, Botolph, i. 28, 29, 30, 37
Claydon, East, i. 26, 27, 28
Claydon House, account of, i. 1-18; measures for defence of, ii. 94; state of, during Civil War, ii. 285; protection for, ii. 174; sequestration of, ii. 212, 213; threatened with fire, 205; a refuge for the destitute, ii. 70, 77, 78, 175, 330, 368, 379
Claydon, Middle, church of, i. 19-26; ii. 17, 18, 19, 422; rector of, *see* Aris
Claydon, Steeple, i. 11, 31-36; ii. 193
Clifford, Lord, i. 301
Clothes, Sir Francis Verney's, i. 66, 68; Sir Edmund's, i. 107, 108; ii. 327, 425; Sir Ralph's, i. 124; Mary's, i. 125; Tom's, i. 145; Mrs. Eure's, i. 288; Mrs. Isham's, ii. 207; Anne Lee's, 235; children's clothes, i. 262; ii. 2, 284, 285, 294, 310; Susan's, 357, 359, 361, Betty's, 377; Peg's, 388
Cockram, Mrs., ii. 233
Cockram, Mr., ii. 245, 398
Coggin, Mr., i. 348
Coke, Sir Edward, M.P., ii. 92, 97

COL

Colchester, siege of, ii. 338, 339
Coleman, Bess, ii. 17, 177
Colet, Dean, i. 43
Commons, House of, description of, i. 337-339; discipline of, i. 340, 341, 343
Conway, Sir Edward, 1st Lord, i. 172
Conway, General, i. 333, 334
Conyers, Sir John, i. 172
Cooke, of Gloucester, M.P., ii. 264
Cooke, Henry, M.P., ii. 264
Cooke, Sir John, ii. 234
Cordell, Mr., ii. 264
Cork, Richard Boyle, the great Earl of, i. 195, 196, 206, 207; ii. 47, 202
Cottington, Francis Cottington, 1st Lord, i. 65, 66, 114
Covenant, the Solemn League and, ii. 162, 163, 164, 166, 263
Cowley, Abraham, the poet, i. 120, 325
Crag, Dr., ii. 176
Cranfield, Vincent, i. 101
Craven, Lord, i. 187, 188
Crewe, Sir Randal, i. 61
Crofts, Sir Henry, ii. 153
Crofts, Lady, i. 245
Crofts, Hester, ii. 153
Crofts, Mrs., i. 245
Cromwell, Oliver, i. 36, 37, 74, 75, 104; ii. 27, 30, 48, 111, 117, 192, 194, 195, 335, 343, 344, 345, 346, 347, 395, 410, 426
Crowther, Rev. John, an Oxford tutor, i. 117, 118, 122, 123, 124, 163, 164, 165; ii. 8
Culpepper, Sir John, i. 110; ii. 28
Culpepper, Colonel Sir Thomas, i. 169, 170, 171, 177; ii. 102

DACRE, Lady, ii. 250
Danvers, Anne, of Cornbury, i. 248
Danvers, Beatrice, i. 39
Darrell, Paule, i. 49
Denham, Lady, of Boarstall, i. 115
Denton, family of, ii. 189, 200; *see also* Hillesden

DEN

Denton, Sir Alexander, i. 74, 165, 291, 344; ii. 167, 189, 191, 194-197, 200-205, 252, 320, 396, 435
Denton, Elizabeth, married to Frank Drake, ii. 314
Denton, George, son of Sir Alexander, ii. 8
Denton, John, a lawyer brother of Sir Alexander, ii. 199, 314, 331, 358, 364, 435
Denton, Colonel John, son of Sir Alexander, ii. 190, 200, 201
Denton, John, husband of Penelope Verney, ii. 351, 364, 365, 366, 387
Denton, Margaret, wife of Sir Edward Verney; *see* Verney, Dame Margaret
Denton, Margaret, sister of Sir Alexander; *see* Pulteney, Eure, Sherard
Denton, Margaret, Lady Smith, daughter of Sir Alexander, ii. 199, 202, 203
Denton, Mary Hampden, Lady, wife of Sir Alexander, ii. 190, 199, 200
Denton, Penelope, Mrs. John, ii. 351, 352, 353, 354, 364, 365, 366, 367, 368, 371, 392
Denton, Susan Temple, Lady, mother of Sir Alexander, i. 74, 103, 233; ii. 5, 190
Denton, Susan, Mrs. Abercrombie, sister of Sir Alexander, ii. 190, 199, 200
Denton, Sir Thomas, father of Sir Alexander, i. 73, 88, 89; ii. 9, 189
Denton, Dr. William, brother of Sir Alexander, i. 74, 117, 122, 294, 309, 313, 321, 323; ii. 75, 77, 157, 175, 190, 238, 240, 247, 248, 250, 251, 264, 265, 268, 271, 272, 274, 277, 280, 295, 297, 298, 302, 303, 305, 312, 314, 316, 318, 323, 327, 332, 343, 362, 366, 389, 392, 397, 404, 405, 406, 408, 410, 421, 422, 423, 435
Denton, Mrs. William, widow of Mr. Bert, ii. 314, 318, 377, 384

INDEX 443

Denton, Anne, daughter of Dr. William Denton, ii. 280, 318
Dering, Sir Edward, ii. 28
Devereux, Sir Walter, i. 31
Devonshire, Countess of, wife of 1st Earl of, i. 252, 253, 262
Devonshire, William Cavendish, 3rd Earl of, ii. 236, 237, 241
D'Ewes, Sir Simon, i. 338, 341
Digby, Lord, i. 70
Digby, Sir Kenelm, i. 101, 121, 220
Digby, Venetia, Lady, i. 220
Dillon, Hon. James, i. 102, 134, 215; visits to Claydon, 216, 217; friendship with Doll Leeke, i. 216, 217, 218, 222, 235; Irish land schemes, i. 229; marriage with Strafford's sister, i. 231, 234, 236, 237; becomes Earl of Roscommon, 239; dies at Paris, 239; mentioned, ii. 3, 8, 10, 267, 324
Dillon, Lord, i. 234
Dixon, a servant, ii. 173
Doddershall, ii. 196
Dormer, Sir Fleetwood, i. 161
Dorset, Edward Sackvile, 4th Earl of, ii. 103, 248
Downe, Countess of, ii. 410
Drake, Francis, M.P., i. 298, 318, 344; ii. 244, 249, 262, 304, 308, 314, 395
Drake, Sir John, ii. 425
Drogheda, siege of, ii. 344-347
Duckett, Mr., servant to Charles I., ii. 400
Dudley's conspiracy, i. 54
Dungarvan, Lewis Boyle, Lord, i. 201; ii. 44, 45, 47
Dunluce, Randal Macdonnell, Viscount, i. 315
Dutton, Mrs., Sir John Reynolds's daughter, ii. 386
Dutton, Sir Ralph, i. 193
Dyeale, Lord, i. 308, 309

EARLE, Sir Walter, M.P., ii. 166
Edgehill, battle of, ii. 71, 113-124, 264, 343
Education of children, i. 69, 70,

117, 118, 119, 156, 157, 158, 159, 164, 181; ii. 5, 21, 177, 231, 283, 284, 292, 310, 373, 383
Edward IV., i. 38, 39
Edwards, Thomas, ii. 26
'Eikon Basiliké,' ii. 402, 412
Eliot, Sir John, i. 331; ii. 22, 90, 92, 94, 95
Elizabeth, Queen of Bohemia, i. 54, 58, 186, 187, 189, 397
Elizabeth, Queen, i. 54, 60, 64, 80, 241; 'Queen E.'s rodd' in Ireland, ii. 46, 324
Elizabeth of York, i. 33, 44, 45, 47
Elmes, Margaret, Lady, daughter of Sir Edward Verney, ii. 246, 332, 359, 360, 361, 362, 373, 380, 381, 382, 387, 389, 423
Elmes, Sir Thomas, ii. 332, 360, 361, 362, 364, 370, 371, 372, 378, 379, 380, 387, 407
Epitaphs, ii. 7
Essex, Elizabeth Paulet, Countess of, i. 131, 132
Essex, Earl of, i. 90, 132, 265, 353; ii. 64, 88, 94, 96, 107, 111, 112, 115, 119, 151, 273
Eure, Honble. Colonel William, i. 281, 283, 286, 287, 288, 289, 291, 292, 293
Eure, Lieut., i. 333
Eure, Lord, i. 281, 289, 291, 295
Eure, Margaret Denton, Hon. Mrs., i. 281-296; ii. 85, 86, 90, 96, 187, 246, 247, 253, 265, 315, 330, 360; see also Pulteney and Sherard
Eure, Margaret and Mary, daughters of Mrs. Eure, i. 291, 295; ii. 226, 315
Evelyn, John, i. 239, 248

FAGE, Mr., ii. 149
Fairfax, Thomas, 3rd Viscount, ii. 244, 335, 338
Falkland, Viscount, i. 120, 345, 354, 357; ii. 27, 104, 112, 426
Fanshawe, Mr., ii. 264
Farrant, ii. 21
Faulkner, Magdalen, i. 200, 209,

FEN

211, 212, 227; ii. 52, 53, 54, 55, 136, 267; *see also* Bruce
Fenton, Lady, ii. 43
Fermanagh, Mary Verney, Baroness, i. 16, 18
Fermanagh, Sir John Verney, Viscount, i. 329; ii. 218, 266
Fielding, Lady Mary, i. 11
Fiennes, James, ii. 168, 315
Fiennes, Hon. Nathaniel, M.P., i. 340, 344, 395
Fiennes, Cecilia, i. 10
Finmere, i. 30
Fitzroy, Lady Charlotte, afterwards Countess of Lichfield, i. 249
Fleet Prison, ii. 148, 363, 369, 370, 384
Flood, Lieut., i. 173
Fortescue, Sir Faithful, i. 237
Fortescue, M.P., of Salden, i. 97
Foss, John, a merchant of Nantes, ii. 403
Fountain, John, ii. 170, 187
Francis, —, Sergeant-at-Arms, ii. 34, 35
Franklin, Sir John, ii. 166
Freake, Mr. and Mrs., ii. 267
Fudd, Nan, the nurse at Claydon, ii. 175, 176, 177, 265, 379, 382
Funerals, Lord Bray's, i. 57; 2nd Sir Edward Verney's, i. 59; Earl of Sussex's, i. 268; Dame Margaret Verney's, ii. 14, 20; sermon for 'ould Lady Verney's,' ii. 4; Susan Alport's, ii. 386, 387; Dame Mary Verney's, ii. 422, 423
Futter, Captain, i. 152

G APE, Mr. W., apothecary, ii. 314, 408
Gape, Mrs., née Bert, Dr. Denton's stepdaughter, ii. 314
Gardiner, Cary, Lady, i. 344; ii. 58; married, 59-61; ii. 94, 187, 350, 370, 371, 372, 373, 374, 376, 379
Gardiner, Lady, mother-in-law to Cary, ii. 62, 68, 72, 75, 77
Gardiner, Sir Thomas, Recorder

HAM

of London, i. 343; ii. 59, 60, 62, 64, 76, 77
Gardiner, Captain Sir Thomas, i. 344; ii. 59, 61, 63, 187, 333
Gardiner, Mary, Maid of Honour to Henrietta Maria, ii. 68, 333, 334
Gaudy, Lady Vere, i. 14, 106; ii. 302, 428
Gerard, Sir George, ii. 395
Gerard, M.P., ii. 239
Gibbons, Orlando, ii. 21
Giffards, lease Claydon, i. 19; monuments of Roger and his wife, i. 22; of Alexander Anne, i. 22; of Urian and Lettice, i. 24
Giffard, Captain John, i. 64, 65
Giffard, Sir George, i. 50, 64
Gilpin, Rev., Rector of Albury, ii. 4
Glamorgan, Edward Somerset, Earl of, ii. 323
Glyn, Mr., i. 350
Godbeit, Monsieur, ii. 253
Goodge, Rev. Dr., ii. 165
Goodwin, Colonel, ii. 95
Goring, Lord, i. 70, 172, 190
Goring, Mr., i. 317; ii. 106
Graham, Sir R., i. 75
Grandison, Lord, i. 131
Gray, Lord, ii. 154, 156, 337
Greenwich Park, i. 15
Grey, Lord Arthur, i. 195
Grey, Lord, of Ruthin, ii. 166
Grimston, Sir Harbottle, i. 254, 331, 344
Guildford, Lady Frances, daughter of Lord Downe, i. 248
Guitar, ii. 184, 242, 284

H ABINGTON'S 'Castara,' ii. 13
Hackney-coaches, i. 109; ii. 246
Hair, i. 99, 159, 160; ii. 233, 234
Hals, Bridget Leeke, Mrs., i. 197, 202, 205; *see* Badnage
Hals, Captain, i. 201, 202
Hamilton, James Hamilton, Duke of, ii. 335, 336, 337

INDEX

Hampden, Sir Alexander, ii. 189, 190
Hampden, John, i. 97, 339, 340, 354; ii. 29, 117, 189, 190, 425
Hampden, Mary, ii. 8; see Denton, Mary
Harberte, Mr., servant to Charles I., ii. 400
Harley, Lady Brilliana, i. 332, 358
Harrison, the historian of Queen Elizabeth's reign, quoted, i. 2
Harvey, Dr., ii. 113
Hastings, Sir Richard, i. 239
Hatcher, Mr., ii. 412
Hazelrigg, Sir Arthur, i. 340
Henderson, Alexander, ii. 165
Henrietta Maria, i. 107, 109, 353, 358; ii. 12, 13, 22, 23, 24, 25, 93, 106, 215, 331, 333, 334, 402, 425
Henry VII., i. 44, 50
Henry, Prince of Wales, i. 33, 70, 71, 104, 300; ii. 18
Henslow, Mrs.; see Uvedale, Anne
Herbert, Sir Edward and Lady, i. 134; ii. 60, 245
Herbert, Mrs.; see Cary
Hermit of Finmere, i. 30
Hertford, William Seymour, Marquis of, ii. 107, 108
Hewitt, Sir Thomas, ii. 221
Hewitt, Sir William, ii. 215
Hillesden Church, ii. 188, 189, 193, 200, 209
Hillesden House, i. 36, 74, 76, 84, 88, 103; ii. 3, 5, 175, 188, 189, 191, 193, 194, 197, 208, 209
Hinton, Sir Edmund's groom, ii. 130
Hoare, Mr. William, 'an ordinary grazier,' married to Mrs. Allcock, ii. 291, 378
Hobart, Anne Leeke, Lady, i. 197; ii. 181, 187, 214, 302
Hobart, Frances, i. 11
Hobart, Sir Henry, i. 197
Hobart, Sir Miles, M.P., i. 54, 95, 97
Hobart, Sir Nathaniel, i. 13, 106, 187, 197, 199, 200; ii. 11, 181, 187, 214

Holinshed, i. 2.
Holland, Henry Rich, Earl, i. 310, 311, 320, 321, 322; ii. 256, 257
Holland, Rev. William, Rector of Malpas, ii. 386, 387
Hollis, Denzil, M.P., ii. 34, 35, 37, 115, 352, 353, 426
Homwood, Captain, i. 324
Hotham, Sir John, ii. 22, 33, 86
Housekeeping at Claydon, i. 10; value of linen, i. 10, 153, 253; ii. 17, 18; preserving, &c., i. 12, 13; coffee, tea, and chocolate introduced, i. 13; meat, i. 8; ii. 225; vegetables, i. 8; wine, ii. 230, 231, 405; furniture, i. 5, 6, 15, 16, 255, 256, 285, 300, 371; needlework, i. 10, 11, 253; ii. 227, 231, 356, 371, 384; in London lodgings, ii. 246, 253; at Blois, ii. 230; groceries and stores, ii. 232, 285, 411; good French cooking for an invalid, 412
Howard, Sir William, i. 79
Hunt, Colonel, i. 144
Hutchinson, Colonel, i. 100; ii. 426
Hyde, Mrs., ii. 281, 410
Hyde, i. 102, 117, 344, 354; ii. 27, 29, 30, 95, 426; see Clarendon, Earl of
Hynde, Sir Francis, i. 24

INCHIQUIN, Murrough O'Brien, 1st Earl of, ii. 48
Inchiquin, Lady, ii. 42
Influenza, 'the new disease,' ii. 171
Isham, Elizabeth Denton, Mrs., i. 167, 292; ii. 156, 175, 176, 190, 196, 200, 203, 206, 208, 248, 252, 373, 374, 376, 377, 419
Isham, Thomas, of Pitchley, i. 298; ii. 93, 190, 200, 206, 208
Iwardby, Margaret, i. 47.

JAMES I., i. 81, 85, 86, 93, 221
James, Duke of York, ii. 113, 427

Jansen, Cornelius, i. 99, 221, 227, 242, 313; see Notes on the Illustrations, vol. i.
Jepson, Mr. and Mrs., ii. 42, 44, 49
Jermyn, Harry, i. 245, 355; ii. 12
Jones, Colonel Michael, ii. 343, 344
Joyce, George, Cornet, ii. 268
Joyce, Mr., a minister, ii. 415
Juxon, William, Bishop of London, i. 109

KILNALMECHY, Lady, ii. 42, 45, 47; Lord, 49
Kimbolton, Lord, i. 356
King's Evil, ii. 12
King's Langley, i. 49
Kingston, Sir Anthony, i. 54
Kirton, Dr., ii. 332, 333, 338, 403
Knightley, Mr., ii. 305

LACE-MAKING in Bucks, i. 11
Lady-helps, i. 11; see Faulkner and Sheppard
Lane, Thomas, M.P., i. 329
Laud, William, Archbishop of Canterbury, i. 109, 127; ii. 204, 222
Lavington, Samuel, Sir Ralph's servant, ii. 174
Lawes, Henry, poet and musician, ii. 244
Lee, Anne, daughter of Sir Harry Lee and Lady Sussex, i. 252; ii. 251, 254, 256, 257
Lee, 1st Sir Harry, Kt. of Woodstock, i. 42, 241
Lee, 2nd Sir Harry, 1st Bart., i. 242, 252
Lee, 3rd Sir Harry, 2nd Bart., i. 245, 247, 248, 326
Lee, 4th Sir Harry, 3rd Bart., i. 248
Lee, Sir Edward, created Earl of Lichfield, i. 249
Lee, Lady, daughter of Sir John St. John of Lydyard, i. 246;

married to Lord Wilmot, 247; ii. 95
Lee, Lady Elizabeth, daughter of Lord Downe, i. 248; marries Earl of Lindsey, 249
Leeke, Dorothy, i. 101, 113, 197, 235, 292; ii. 99, 129, 160, 187, 213, 214, 248, 302, 322
Leeke, Sir John, i. 58, 197, 201, 203, 235; ii. 42, 44, 48, 50, 51, 56, 172, 175, 324, 352, 355, 356, 358, 364
Legge, Colonel, ii. 110
Leicester, Robert Sidney, Earl of, ii. 41, 49
Lenthall, William, Speaker of House of Commons, i. 344; ii. 346, 347
Lenthall, Sir John, i. 344; ii. 303
Leslie, General Alexander, Earl of Leven, i. 179, 314
Lewis, Sir William, ii. 167
Libb, Mary Blacknall's guardian, i. 115; Mrs., i. 117
Lichfield, Earl of; see Lee, Sir Edward
Lindsey, Elizabeth Lee, Countess of, i. 249
Lindsey, Robert Bertie, 1st Earl of, ii. 112, 119
Lisle, Sir George, ii. 338, 340, 341
Lithgow, William, travels of, i. 67, 68
Lloyd, David, author of 'Lloyd's Worthies,' i. 70; ii. 115, 127
Lloyd, Robert, of Chester, ii. 390; his son, Captain Verney-Lloyd, ii. 390
Lothian, Lord, son of Earl of Ancram, i. 179
Loughborough, Henry Hastings, Lord, ii. 385
Love, Mr., ii. 206
Lucas, Sir Charles, ii. 338, 340
Ludlow, Sir Henry, ii. 171
Luke, Sir James, ii. 122
Luke, Sir Samuel, ii. 191, 192, 194
Lunsford, Colonel, i. 334
Lyttelton, Lord, Lord-Keeper, ii. 89, 105

INDEX 447

MAID-SERVANTS, ii. 10, 177, 225, 226, 228, 229; nurse, 269, 293, 294; *see* Fudd and Sheppard
Malpas Church, ii. 385, 387
Manord, an Irish squire calling himself Sir William, i. 211
Margaret, daughter of Henry VII., i. 45, 46
Marlow, Great, i. 329
Marriage, early, ii. 6, 7, 22; negotiations for, and settlements, i. 113, 115, 116, 117, 243, 251, 274, 276, 277, 280, 284; ii. 349-357; feast, ii. 314
Marshalsea, the prison, i. 40, 138; Appendix to Vol. i.; ii. 313
Martin, i. 352
Mary, daughter of Henry VII., i. 46
Mary, Queen, i. 53, 54, 55, 56, 57, 85
Mary, daughter of Charles I., Princess of Orange, i. 264; ii. 22, 24, 25
Massey, Colonel Edward, ii. 394
Maurice, Prince, ii. 171
Maxwell, Mr., i. 350
Mayerne, Sir Theodore, Court Physician, ii. 23, 106, 263
'May, Mr., the poet,' ii. 273
Meautis, Sir Thomas, i. 254; ii. 103
Meautis, Anne Bacon, Lady, afterwards Lady Grimston, i. 254
Medicine and sickness, i. 12, 167, 250; for gout, 10; cancer, 288; mineral waters, i. 225, 263; ii. 23, 24, 404; ii. 176, 250, 270, 271, 273, 288, 295, 316, 411, 412, 413; *see* Small-pox
Middlesex, Lord, i. 101
Middleton, Sir Thomas, i. 251
Mildmay, Henry, M.P., ii. 145, 437
Mildmay, Mr., servant to Charles I., ii. 400
Militia, list of gentlemen to command the, ii. 39
Misterton, in Leicestershire, i. 276, 292, 293; ii. 278, 291, 330
Misterton, Aunt; *see* Eure
Monmouth, Lady, ii. 95, 105, 151
Moray, "Mr. —— of the Bedchamber," afterwards Sir Richard, i. 200
More, Sir Thomas, i. 4; ii. 169
More, Lady, sister of Earl of Sunderland, ii. 345
Morley, George, Bishop of Winchester, ii. 79
Morocco, Emperor of, i. 63
Moss, Mr., ii. 180
Mountgarett, Lord, and the Butlers, ii. 44, 45, 46, 49
Mourning, i. 268, 293; ii. 15, 16, 128, 400, 402, 403
Munster, i. 196, 208; ii. 41, 48
Murray, P., i. 71
Muskerry, Donough McCarthy, Viscount, brother-in-law to Ormonde, ii. 51
Music, church, ii. 21, 22; *see* Guitar

NALSON'S MSS., 431
Newcastle, William Cavendish, Earl of, afterwards Marquis, i. 322
Newport Pagnell, ii. 193
Newton, Sir Henry Puckering, ii. 223, 343, 393, 403, 404, 405, 411
Northumberland, Algernon Percy, 10th Earl of, i. 172, 264, 332
Norwich, Sir John, ii. 170
Nursery rule, severity of, ii. 6
Nursery spoiling, ii. 292
Nye, Philip, ii. 165

OGILVY, Mr., a Royalist exile, ii. 222, 392
Olivarez, i. 81
O'Neill, Daniel, ii. 341
Orange, William, Prince of, i. 183, 189, 264, 339, 350; ii. 22
Ormonde, James Butler, Marquis of, i. 239; ii. 46, 139, 321-332, 335, 336, 342-347, 391, 410

448   VERNEY FAMILY DURING THE CIVIL WAR

ORM

Ormonde, Marchioness of, daughter of Sir John Poyntz, ii. 44, 336, 343
Osborn, Lady, ii. 387, 427 ; see Verney, Penelope; Denton, Penelope
Osborn, Sir John, ii. 387, 392
Osborne, Sir John, afterwards Duke of Leeds, ii. 392
Overton Manor, Cheshire, ii. 385
Oxford colleges, i. 118, 160, 161 ; ii. 4, 95
Oxford, Aubrey de Vere, 20th and last Earl of, ii. 155

PALMER, Mrs., née Gardiner, ii. 61, 70
Palmes, Francis, i. 322
Palmes, William, of Lindley, Yorkshire, i. 295
Parker, Henry, ii. 211, 213
Parry, Mr., ii. 5, 6
Parsons, William, ii. 42, 130
Peckham, Dorothy, i. 52
Peckham, Henry, i. 54, 55
Pelham, Henry, M.P., ii. 246
Pembroke, Philip Herbert, 4th Earl of, i. 102, 297, 313
Penley, i. 46, 50, 58
Percy, Henry Percy, Lord, i. 355
Pierrepoint, William, M.P., ii. 179, 304, 311, 392
Pigott, Sir Richard, of Doddershall ; ii. 90, 256
Plague, the, in 1636, ii. 10, 11
Pole, Cardinal, i. 44
Pole, Eleanor, i. 44
Pole, Sir Richard, i. 44
Poles, tombs of, i. 49
Poly, Mrs., ii. 82
Poole, Mrs., sister of Lord Shrewsbury, ii. 386
Pope, Lady Elizabeth ; see Lee, Lady Elizabeth
Portland, Duke of, his manuscripts ; Appendix, vol. i. ; ii. 145, 399
Poyntz, Sir Nicolas, i. 24
Poyntz, Sedenham, Major-General, ii. 322
Preston, Mr., servant to Charles I., ii. 400

ROC

Preswell, Mr., a silk mercer, ii. 414
Prynne, William, i. 223, 224, 225, 344, 395
Pulteney, John, of Misterton, Leicestershire, i. 276, 277
Pulteney, Margaret Denton, Mrs., i. 167, 185, 276-280 ; see Eure and Sherard
Pye, Sir Robert, auditor of the receipt of the Exchequer, ii. 191
Pye, Colonel, Sir Robert Pye, Jun., M.P., married to Anne, daughter of Hampden, ii. 191
Pym, John, M.P., i. 331, 340, 345, 347, 348, 351, 353, 354 ; ii. 34, 35, 37, 426

QUAINTON Manor, i. 62, 69, 196
Quainton Seech, i. 37, 47
Quarles, 'Emblems,' ii. 170

RADCLIFFE Church, Bucks, ii. 417
Radcliffe, Sir George, i. 228, 229, 230, 236
Raleigh, Sir Walter, i. 8, 64, 222
Raleigh, Dame Margaret, i. 39
Remonstrance, the Grand, ii. 25, 27, 28, 33, 34
Rents of land, i. 129, 130
Reynolds, Robert, M.P., ii. 164
Richmond, James Stuart, Duke of, ii. 401
Rings, Charles I.'s Memorial, i. 262, 299 ; ii. 9, 18
Ripon, i. 336
Roades, or Rhodes, John, steward at Claydon, i. 298
Roades, William, steward at Claydon, i. 100, 129, 298 ; ii. 18, 198, 238, 246, 247, 263, 269, 270, 273, 275, 287, 283, 290, 302, 309, 313, 320, 327, 372, 375, 403
Robartes, John Robartes, or Roberts, 2nd Lord, afterwards Earl of Radnor, i. 264
Roch, Lord, ii. 49, 54, 55

INDEX   449

ROC

Roch, Mr., ii. 138
Rochester, Wilmot, Earl of, i. 248, 270
Rodes' Ralph R.'s wife, ii. 293
Rolt, Mr. Walter, ii. 71, 72
Roper, Captain Christopher, ii. 130
Ropier, brother to Lord Ropier, ii. 345
Roscommon, 2nd Earl of, i. 215
Roscommon, James Dillon, 3rd Earl of ; see Dillon, James
Roscommon, Wentworth, 4th Earl of, i. 240
Ruddier, ii. 395
Rudyard, Sir Benjamin, i. 125 ; ii. 29
Rupert, Prince, ii. 97, 111, 115, 151, 160, 162
Rushworth, ii. 35, 84, 97
Russell, Lord, i. 131
Russell, Lady Rachel, ii. 12
Ruthven, Lord, ii. 114

SACRAMENTS, the, administration of, Baptism, ii. 259 ; the Communion, ii. 259, 260, 387, 417
St. Albans, i. 254 ; ii. 153, 154
St. Barbe ; see Blakeney, Mary, and Verney, Ursula
St. John, Sir John, i. 245, 247
St. John, Lady, i. 249
St. John, Oliver, Solicitor-General, i. 332, 350 ; ii. 59, 145, 166, 168, 426, 433-436
St. Leger, Lady, ii. 42
Salisbury, William Cecil, 2nd Earl of, i. 62, 185 ; ii. 145, 437
Sandys, Mr., i. 76
Saye and Sele, William Fiennes, Viscount, i. 135, 305, 353 ; ii. 95, 113, 145, 437
Scott, Sir Gilbert, i. 20
Scott, M.P., ii. 218
Scrope, Adrian, i. 330
Scudamore, of Home Lacy, i. 121, note
Scudamore, Lord, ii. 103
Selden, M.P., ii. 304

SUS

Sheppard, Luce, i. 295 ; ii. 225-230, 265
Sherard, Honourable Philip, Captain, i. 294, 295
Sherard, Margaret Denton, Honourable Mrs., i. 14, 294 ; ii. 278, 281, 392, 406 ; see Eure, Pulteney
Skippon, Philip, ii. 394
Small-pox, i. 245, 246, 252, 324 ; ii. 214, 413
Smith, an alias for English refugees, ii. 182
Smith, Sir John, Captain, knighted at Edgehill, ii. 118
Smith, Colonel, afterwards Sir William, ii. 191, 192, 193, 202, 203
Snatchpole, Sir Norton, ii. 168
Soldiers quartered in private houses, ii. 171, 172, 190, 196, 278, 286, 287, 352, 389
Southampton, Thomas Wriothesley, Earl of, ii. 102
Spencer, Henry Spencer, Lord, ii. 104
Stafford, Sir Thomas, i. 190, 204
Standard, the Royal, ii. 95, 97
Standard, smaller one carried at Edgehill, ii. 115, 116, 118, 119
Stanley, Dr., of Winchester School, i. 58
Stapleton, Sir Philip, ii. 73
Stewart, Lord, ii. 116
Stonehouse, Sir George, ii. 167
Strafford, Wentworth, 1st Earl of, i. 221, 223, 228, 232, 234, 235, 236, 238, 329, 334, 338, 344, 345, 347
Strafford, William Wentworth, 2nd Earl of, ii. 392
Strickland, Sir George, daughter of, i. 11
Suckling, Sir John, i. 355 ; ii. 334
Sussex, Elenor Wortley, Countess of, i. 127 ; marries Sir Harry Lee, 242 ; marries Earl of Sussex, 242 ; strong Parliamentary sympathies, 243 ; loses her son, 246 ; her daughter Anne, 250 ; death of her

VOL. II.   G G

SUS

mother, 253; painted by Vandyck, 257; marries Earl of Warwick (see Warwick, Countess of, mentioned), i. 101, 104, 108, 121, 123, 151, 254, 255, 298, 330, 343, 355, 356; ii. 2, 12, 15, 33, 38, 83, 85, 88, 93, 95, 102, 148, 150, 151, 153, 154, 157, 158, 180, 181, 183, 425
Sussex, George Radcliffe, 6th Earl of, i. 228, 242, 243, 264, 265, 268, 350; ii. 15, 157, 160
Sydenham, Sir Edward, Knight-Marshal in succession to Sir Edward Verney, i. 133, 181, 186, 193; ii. 156, 187, 309
Sydenham, Anne, Lady, i. 106, 235; ii. 99, 100, 118, 156, 187
Sydenham, Mrs., ii. 107

TALLIS, Thomas, ii. 21
Temple, Lady, Dame Denton's mother, ii. 5 note
Temple, Sir John, i. 320
Temple, Sir Peter, i. 74, 97
Temple, Sir Richard, ii. 427
Temples, family of, i. 17
Testard, Mr., French pasteur at Blois, ii. 232, 417
Thomer, a French servant, ii. 215
Thomond, Henry O'Brien, 5th Earl of, i. 204
Thornborough, i. 37
Thorner, Robert, ii. 233
Throgmorton, John, i. 55, 56
Toleration denounced, ii. 26
Tradescant, John, Charles I.'s gardener, i. 15 note
Traquair, John Stuart, Earl of, i. 308
Travers, Jack, ii. 47
Trelawney, —, ii. 399
Trevor, Mr., M.P., ii. 304, 306
T. T., i. 342, 343
Turks, i. 63, 66, 226
Turville; see Blakeney
Turville, Richard, ii. 135
Turville, Thomas, i. 133, 173, 181
Twine, 'a Papist,' ii. 105
Tyerman, Mr., ii. 105

VER

URSULA; see Verney, Ursula; Clark & Chicheley, i. 58
Ussher, Archbishop, i. 94, 215, 220, 221
Uvedale, Sir William, i. 102, 131, 132, 233, 313; ii. 205, 398, 399
Uvedale, Anne, Mrs. Henslow, i. 225, 231, 232, 313; ii. 102
Uvedale, Robert, ii. 399

VANDYCK, Sir Anthony, i. 84, 102, 125, 257, 258, 259, 260, 261; ii. 319
Vane, Sir Harry, i. 305, 340, 347, 348; ii. 166, 168
Vaughan, Sir William, ii. 343
Vavasour, Sir Charles, ii. 48, 51
Velasquez, i. 66, 184
Vermuyden, a Dutch engineer, i. 198, 199
Verne, Dr., Chaplain to Charles I., ii. 216
Verneys, Early History of, 1st Sir Ralph Lord Mayor, i. 38, 39, 40, 327; 1st Sir John, his son, i. 40; 2nd Sir Ralph, i. 41, 42, 43, 46; 3rd Sir Ralph, 46, 47, 48; 4th Sir Ralph, i. 49, 50; 1st Sir Edmund, i. 52, 54, 55, 57, 58; 1st Sir Francis, i. 53, 54, 55; Urian, i. 24; Emme, widow of 1st Sir Ralph, i. 39; Margaret Whittingham, wife of 1st Sir John, i. 40, 41, 42; Eleanor Pole, wife of 2nd Sir Ralph, i. 44, 45, 46, 47; Margaret Iwardby, 1st wife of 3rd Sir Ralph, i. 47; Anne Weston, 2nd wife of do., i. 47, 48, 83; Elizabeth Broughton, 3rd wife of do., i. 48; Elizabeth Bray, wife of 4th Sir Ralph, i. 50; Dorothy Peckham, wife of 1st Sir Edmund, i. 52, 53; Mary, wife of Roger Giffard, i. 22
Verney, 2nd Sir Edmund, father of the Standard-bearer, i. 58, 59; ii. 4
Verney, Dame Awdreye (Carew), 2nd wife of 2nd Sir Edmund, i. 58

INDEX

Verney, Dame Mary (Blakeney), 3rd wife of 2nd Sir Edmund, mother of the Standard-bearer, i. 58; formerly married to Geoffrey Turville, i. 58, and to St. Barbe, i. 58; lawsuit with her stepson, i. 61, 62; lives in Drury Lane, i. 69, 73; i. 221; ii. 3, 10; her death, ii. 4

Verney, 2nd Sir Francis, half-brother to the Standard-bearer, i. 58, 59, 60; disputes his father's will, 62; goes to Palestine, 62; fights for the Emperor of Morocco, 63, 64, 65; a noted pirate, 65; dies at Messina, 67, 68; ii. 423

Verney, Dame Ursula (St. Barbe), wife of 2nd Sir Francis, i. 58, 63; marries Mr. Clark, i. 69; marries John Chicheley, i. 69; her death, i. 69; ii. 408, 423

Verney, 3rd Sir Edmund, Knight-Marshal and Standard-bearer, his birth, i. 59; education, 69; Chief Sewer to Prince Henry, 70; in Prince Charles' household, 72; his marriage, 72; Lieut. of Whaddon Chase, 75, 76; in Spain with Charles, 78, 80, 81; returned to Parliament, 84, 85, 89; Knight-Marshal, 85; his religious opinions, 94, 98, 99; his large family, 103; his clothes, 107, 108, ii.; his patent for hackney-coaches, i. 109; the Alnage, 111; ii. 433; arranges his son's marriage, i. 113; his management of Claydon, 128; Sir W. Uvedale's second in a duel, 132; his advice to his sons, 152, 162; his Irish friends, 195; his friendship with the Lees and Lady Sussex, 241; his indignation at a popish marriage, 283; goes to Scotland with the King, 297, 300, 311-326; in Parliament, 329, 336; his wife's death, ii. 1; marries his daughter Cary, 58; his painful position at the outbreak of the Civil War, 87; his arms, 93; appointed Standard-bearer, 99; divided from his son, 104; his gallant death, 115, 116, 118, 119; Ralph's grief, 120, 122; Sir Edmund's character, 98, 127, 424, 426

Verney, Dame Margaret (Denton), wife of the Standard-bearer, her family, i. 72, 73, 74; her early married life, i. 74; ii. 2, 3, 6; her children, i. 103; her husband's frequent absences, 104, 167; sends Tom to America, 136; writes about the Scotch war, 302; failing health, 244, 326; retiring disposition, ii. 12, 13; her death, will, and funeral, i. 10; ii. 1, 2, 14, 16, 17-20

Verney, Sir Ralph, Knight, eldest son of the Standard-bearer, his birth, i. 120; his business capacity, 112, 113; his marriage, 115; studies at Magdalen Hall, 117; his tutor Crowther, 117-122; loses a child, 123; his devotion to his father, 126; unwarlike nature, 133; his friendship with Dillon, 215-240, and with Lady Sussex, 243, 246, 254, 257; his distress at Mrs. Eure's marriage, 281, 282; his father's executor, 299; his anxieties about his father in the Scotch war, 309, 310; returned to Parliament, 329, 336; his notes of the debates, 341; ii. 20-39; his Parliamentary friends, i. 329; letter on his mother's death, ii. 14; executor to his mother, 17; letters to Cary, 63, 69, 75; differs with his father politically, 89, 108; distress at his father's death, 120, 122; blamed by his brother Edmund, 136; his reply, 137, 141; correspondence with Lady Sussex, 150-162; refuses to sign the Covenant, 163, 164, 168, 169; sends his luggage abroad, 173, 174, 179; his children, 7, 8, 9, 177, 178; driven into exile, 179, 182; life in exile, pining for news, 186, 187; his distress at the burning of Hillesden House, 197; letter of condolence on Colonel Denton's death, 202; he offends both parties, 210, 211; dismissed the House of Commons, 216, 217; his books, 221, 222; travels in France, is cheated by a Dutchman, 232, 233; his wigs, 233; his estate sequestrated, 238; sends his wife to England, 241; letters to his wife, 247, 257, 259, 265, 269, 279, 288; anxieties at Blois, 283; Peg's death, 295; counsels of despair, 297, 298; writes on the death of his children, 300; sequestration removed, 307; his wife's return, 318; anxious about his brother Edmund, 342; negotiations about his sisters' marriage portions and their affairs, 350-388; hears of the King's execution, 398, 401, 403; travels for his wife's health, 404, 405; loses his wife, 414; reviews his life, 415, 416, 417; gives directions for Mary's funeral, 422; his description of her, 423; review of Sir Ralph's character, 426-429

Verney, Dame Mary, wife of Sir Ralph, née Blacknall, i. 113; an orphan heiress, 114, 115; her marriage, 115, 116, 117; her early life at Claydon, 122, 125; her children's births, i. 123, 244; ii. 7, 8, 9; Sir Edmund's affection for her, i. 127; Dillon's friendship for her, i. 218, 219, 221. 233; ii. 3, 10; at Covent Garden, i. 330; avoids the Court, ii. 12, 17; correspondence with the Gardiners, 64, 65, 66, 73; with Lady Sussex, 82; with Edmund, 128, 143, 329; her children, 177, 178; shares her husband's exile, 180, 181, 183, 214; her housekeeping in France, 222-234; dress, &c., 234, 236; goes to England on her husband's business, 239-242; birth of her youngest child, 265; her visit to Claydon, 285-294; loses Peg and Ralph, 295; anxiety about her husband, 299; wins her suit, 306; at the apothecary's wedding, 314; her return to France, 316, 317, 318; reunited with Ralph, 319, 324, 391; in Paris, 331; her opinion of her sisters-in-law, 369-383; failing health, 404, 405, 410, 411, 412, 413; her death, 414; Ralph's tribute to her memory, 414, 416, 423; her burial, 420, 422, 423

Verney, Thomas, 2nd son of the Standard-bearer, i. 122; wishes to marry at school, 135; shipped off to America, 135; comes back again, 137; goes to sea, 137; goes to Flanders, 137; serves in France, 139; goes to Sweden, 141; home again, 143; debt and difficulties. 143-146; goes to Barbadoes, 147; a colonial outfit, 152; his description of Barbadoes, 148; second journey to Barbadoes, 153; sells his labourers, 154; returns home, 154, 166, 299, 326; ii. 78; in the Fleet, ii. 148, 149, 150, 157; taken prisoner at Hillesden, 195, 198, 203; he bullies Mary, 275, 277; introduces Mr. Alport to Susan, 351; quarrels with them, 369; signs a bill of Sir T. Elmes, 332; Edmund helps him out, 333; Ralph pays his debts, 406, 407, 408; spoken of as 'the arrantest informer,' 408

Verney, Joyce, wife to Tom Verney, ii. 158, 198, 203, 368

Verney, Sir Edmund, Knight, 3rd

VER

son of the Standard-bearer, a school-boy, i. 156, 157, 158; at Magdalen Hall, 158; his allowance, 158, 159; fee to tutor, 159; complaints about him, 161; debts, 162; appeals to his brother for money, 163; at Hillesden, 165; in Scotland with the Army, 168; in Flanders, 169; pays his Oxford debts, 169; at Utrecht, 171; nursing his cousin at the Hague, 173; asks for books, 174, 175; his chivalrous ideas, 176; in Scotland again, 177; loses his clothes, 178; with his father in the Scotch war, 303, 315; writes of his nephew, ii. 8; hears of his mother's death, 128; sent to Ireland, 130, 136; reproaches his brother for siding with the Parliament, 137, 141; money troubles, 143, 262; Lieut.-Governor of Chester, 320; knighted, 320; with Ormonde in Ireland, 323–325; at Bristol, 326; at Claydon, 289, 309, 328; his kindness to Mary, 280, 317; letter of condolence, 329; in London, 331; at Paris with Ormonde, 331–338, 391; writes of the siege of Colchester, 338, 339; in Ireland again, 341; report of his death at Dublin, 343; killed after the surrender of Drogheda, 344, 345, 346, 347, 348, 412

Verney, Henry, 4th son of the Standard-bearer, i. 122, 169, 170; sent to Paris, 181; taste for sport, 182; a soldier, 183; at Breda, 183, 184; wins a race, 185; with the Queen of Bohemia, 186, 187; takes leave of Prince of Orange, 189; complains of the family politics, 191; returns home with Queen Henrietta Maria; presented to Charles I., 193, 194, 294, 296; ii. 9, 78; taken prisoner, 170, 171; lectures Ralph, 220, 221,

VER

241, 252, 255; worries Mary for money, 246, 260, 261; Edmund's opinion of him, 262, 317, 408; lives 'like a wandering Jew,' 409; Dr. Denton tries to reconcile Ralph with him, 419, 420

Verney, the daughters of the Standard-bearer—
1. Susanna, i. 166, 167; ii. 145, 147, 167, 172, 175, 176, 190, 195, 203, 204, 218, 351, 354, 355, 356, 357, 358; *see* Alport, Susan, Mrs., Appendix to vol. ii.
2. Penelope, i. 10, 167; ii. 129, 145, 175, 176, 177, 178, 195, 351; *see* Denton, Penelope, Mrs. John; *see* Osborn, Lady
3. Margaret, i. 84, 167, 176, 288, 289, 290, 291; ii. 145; *see* Elmes, Margaret, Lady
4. Cary, ii. 58, 145; *see* Gardiner, Cary, Lady
5. Mary, ii. 170, 175, 367, 368, 371, 372, 373, 375, 376, 379, 381; marries Mr. Robert Lloyd, 390
6. Elizabeth, ii. 3, 175, 177, 367, 370, 372, 376, 377, 378, 379, 381, 382, 383, 409; marries Rev. C. Adams, 384

Verney, children of Sir Ralph—
1. Mary, ii. 7
2. An Infant, i. 123, 124; ii. 7, 8
3. Anna-Maria, i. 232, 233; ii. 3, 8, 9
4. Edmund, i. 103, 167, 244; ii. 2, 5, 9, 17, 177, 181, 183, 214, 231, 266, 283, 312, 313, 341, 415
5. Margaret, i. 146; ii. 9, 18, 177, 181, 214, 231, 266, 283, 284, 295, 296, 300, 301, 302, 315, 391, 416
6. John, ii. 9, 177, 178, 180, 265, 271, 292, 293, 294, 310, 316, 415; *see* Fermanagh
7. Ralph, ii. 265, 266, 267, 269, 270, 283, 293, 294, 296, 300, 329, 391, 416

Verney, Ralph, 2nd Earl, i. 16, 17, 18

Verney, the Right Honourable Sir Harry, Bart., Introd. Note, iii.; Preface to 2nd vol.; i. 328, 337, 340; ii. 390
Villiers, George; see Buckingham
Villiers, Mary, ii. 350

WAIMAN, Lord, ii. 162
Wake, Sir Baldwin, ii. 335, 337
Wakefield, Mr., ii. 215
Wall, Dr., i. 160
Wallop, Mr., of Hopton Castle, ii. 197
Wandesford, ii. 41
Wanman, Sir Thomas, i. 288
Warwick, Robert Richard, Earl of, i. 90, 92, 102, 147, 148, 165, 235, 239, 244, 249, 250, 254, 256, 257, 260, 261, 339
Warwick, Countess of, ii. 244, 263, 279, 307, 308, 336, 337; see Sussex, Countess of
Washington, Charles, i. 82, 83
Wayes, Mr., ii. 180
Welsh, Sir Nicholas, ii. 50
Wentworth, Lady Elizabeth, i. 232, 233, 234, 238
Westminster School, ii. 398
Weston, Anne, i. 47, 83
Weston, Richard, i. 47
Weston, Sir Francis, i. 48
Wharton, Thomas, Lord, i. 248; ii. 145, 437
White, Mr., ii. 165
Whitelock, i. 329

Whittingham, Sir Robert, i. 40, 41, 43
Whittingham, Margaret, wife to Sir John Verney, i. 41, 42
Wilkinson, Henry, i. 118, 159
Wilkinson, Dr., i. 161
Willetts, Mrs., ii. 224
William III., ii. 428
Willis, Browne, the Bucks antiquary, i. 8
Willoughby, Lord, ii. 119
Wills, i. 22, 43; Sir Edmund Verney's, i. 298; Sir H. Lee's, 247; Dame Margaret's, ii. 17; Dame Mary's, 414
Wilmot, Lord, i. 201, 247; ii. 106
Winchester School, i. 156, 157, 158
Wiseman, —, i. 115
Wiseman, Mrs., i. 115, 116
Wortley, Sir Edward, i. 253, 271
Wortley, Sir Francis, ii. 83, 84, 85
Wotton, Sir Henry, i. 70
Wray, Sir John, i. 354
Wycombe, i. 329
Wynne, Sir Richard, i. 78; ii. 404

YONE, Margaret, i. 45
York, Cecily, Duchess of, i. 33

ZAPATA, Cardinal, i. 82
Zouch, De la, i. 1

www.ingramcontent.com/pod-product-compliance
Lightning Source LLC
Chambersburg PA
CBHW021825220426
43663CB00005B/128